THE BIRTH OF FEMINISM

THE BIRTH OF FEMINISM

*Woman as Intellect in
Renaissance Italy and England*

SARAH GWYNETH ROSS

HARVARD UNIVERSITY PRESS
Cambridge, Massachusetts
London, England
2009

Library of Congress Cataloging-in-Publication Data

Ross, Sarah Gwyneth, 1975–
The birth of feminism : woman as intellect in renaissance
Italy and England / Sarah Gwyneth Ross.
p. cm.
Includes bibliographical references and index.
ISBN 978-0-674-03454-9 (alk. paper)
1. Feminism—Italy—History. 2. Feminism—England—History.
3. Women and literature—Italy—History. 4. Women and
literature—England—History. I. Title.
HQ1641.R68 2009
305.420942—dc22   2009005164

For My Father

Quodcumque mihi honoris laudisque est, ex te manasse profitebor.

Contents

Note on the Texts

The translations that appear here are mine, unless otherwise noted. I have retained the original spellings, punctuation, and diacriticals of the Latin and Italian texts, except when meaning would have been obscured without alteration. In the interest of readability, however, I have modernized all quotations from the early modern English. My thanks again to Diana Robin and Kenneth Gouwens, classicists and Italianists of surpassing expertise, for redeeming several infelicities in my translations. And a hearty general thanks as well to the many splendid critical editions that I have consulted, which have both steadied and enriched my interaction with early modern women's writings. All errors that remain are of course my own.

Introduction

Amnesia, not the lack of history, is the most serious problem
for feminism today. Let us therefore refresh our memories.

—Karen Offen, *European Feminisms*

MARY Wollstonecraft (1759–1797) did not invent feminism. Nor were
political philosophers of the Radical Enlightenment, let alone nineteenth-
century suffragettes, the first sodalities determined to create a new place
for women in Western society. In the last decades, scholars have come to
recognize that from the fifteenth century onward "pro-woman" arguments took an increasingly central place in European literature. In 1991
Constance Jordan even offered us "Renaissance feminism" as a conceptual category for understanding the defenses of female dignity and capability that poured out of European presses during the Renaissance era.[1]
At the same time, historians and literary critics have expanded our list of
Renaissance women writers. We now know that hundreds of women
across the European landscape were active contributors to culture, and we
suspect that a significant change occurred in the definition of "womanhood" as well, which leaves us wondering how far back we might trace
feminism's pedigree as an idea, if not a coherent political philosophy.[2]

Our treasury of information now overflows, but older interpretive
models are proving intractable, especially the argument that early modern
women writers were considered "exceptional" and transgressive figures,
whom society consigned to the margins.[3] This is the moment to reassess
that claim. Within the last year (as I write), several studies focusing on the
sixteenth century have demonstrated that women writers, far from being
marginalized, in fact played authoritative roles in contemporary "salons"
and "literary circles"—a defining characteristic of which was the collaboration of male and female colleagues.[4] A historiographical sea-change
is taking place, and it is crucial that we return to some fundamental

questions: What made the appearance of women writers possible in the first place? Did they have any collective impact? What are the connections between women writers, "Renaissance feminism" as an argument particular to its own time, and "feminism" in the *longue durée?*

This book offers an answer to each of these questions, by charting the emergence and entrenchment of secular learned women in literary society in Italy and England from 1400 to 1680. An experiment in collective biography and intellectual history, this book aims for the middle distance between macrostudies of the "woman question" and critical editions of individual women writers. I examine the commonalities in the lives, rhetorical strategies, contemporary reception, and feminist contributions of nineteen women writers who were celebrated in their own time, if not always in ours. This selection of a substantive but not overwhelming number of case studies allows for a close interrogation of a wide range of sources: archival, manuscript, and printed. Italianists may recognize some of the letters, dialogues, and treatises, but the wills, family documents, and biographical compendia will be less familiar. Many of the British sources are examined here for the first time—particularly those from the seventeenth century. As these nineteen cases suggest, the field of early modern women intellectuals was deep. But how exactly did this field come into being?

The rise of the educated woman in the Renaissance era is best understood within a model that I am calling "the intellectual family." Sponsored and often educated by their learned fathers, women authors of the fifteenth and sixteenth centuries enjoyed and capitalized upon the cultural legitimacy that patriarchal sanction—or its representation—afforded. By publishing their works within the safety of family networks and deploying familial metaphor when approaching male patrons, women themselves used "the intellectual family" as a rhetorical device for making their novel status as scholars and authors appealing to contemporary culture. They succeeded. By the seventeenth century, there was a strong tradition of Italian and English women humanists. The learned woman was no longer a startling figure, and the father or father-patron became less crucial as a means to secure legitimacy. Accordingly, the contours of the intellectual family shifted: late sixteenth- and seventeenth-century women writers presented themselves and were embraced by contemporary culture as learned wives, mothers, and equal partners in their household salons. Throughout the early modern period, however, the domestic paradigm remained a powerful discursive tool that ambitious women and their male supporters used to build a foundation of authorial credibility for a new figure in the Western social paradigm: the culturally normal learned woman who was not a queen, not a nun, and most certainly not a courtesan.

Illustrious products of the intellectual family, from Christine de Pizan (ca. 1365–1435) to Bathsua Makin (fl. 1673), did not yet argue for women's political equality, but they represented and often advocated women's intellectual equality as they contributed to the central debates of the era, especially the debate on women. The intellectual family was, in this sense, a subversive success: it legitimized the first feminists.

It would be tempting to avoid using the term "feminism," which so often serves as a lightning rod for criticism. Yet immersion in the writings of Renaissance women intellectuals and in contemporary celebrations of them has begotten in me the conviction that feminism does indeed have a history. In other words, while "feminism" has changed over time, its different manifestations nonetheless share a common motive: the desire to improve the condition of women. However tentative and provisional the demands of early modern intellectuals for a redefinition of "womanhood" and normative female endeavor may appear, segregating Renaissance feminists from our wider discussion of modern political feminism does indeed constitute a dangerous form of "amnesia": it deprives feminism of its history.

This study offers a history of Renaissance feminism in Italy and England from the fifteenth through the seventeenth centuries. Because the following chapters traverse so much chronological, geographical, and conceptual terrain, it seems only fair to introduce here the principal contentions and protagonists to be explored in detail hereafter.

Part I: The Household Academy (1400–1580)

Learned fathers educated and sponsored the first secular female intellectuals within the Western tradition.[5] Fifteenth-century humanism, which made the study of classical antiquity the principal intellectual commitment of learned society, redefined the purpose of education itself. In previous centuries, serious instruction in letters constituted the necessary preparation for an ecclesiastical career. Beginning in the fifteenth century, however, education became the bedrock upon which to build a new conception of virtue in general and of "feminine" virtue in particular. Emphasizing not only Christian morality but classical notions of fortitude and accomplishment, the humanist redefinition of virtue left a fruitful ambiguity at the center of its educational program. It went without question that both men and women should be "virtuous" in terms of Christian morality. The merged classical and Christian definition of virtue, however, prompted some humanists to follow a new logic: if men and women should be "virtuous," and if education presented a principal means to that end, then women should be educated. Opinion on this point was divided. Yet one of the most influential of the quattrocento humanists, Leonardo Bruni, upheld the revolutionary logic in his treatise *On Studies and Letters* (ca. 1423–1426).[6] Later proponents of this line of reasoning included other humanist luminaries, such as Juan Luis Vives, Sir Thomas More, and Erasmus. As Pamela Joseph Benson and Constance Jordan have noted, humanist theory along the Italy-England nexus invented the notion of the "Renaissance woman," at least in literary terms.[7]

Humanist fathers began to wed theory to practice. In the middle of the quattrocento, the Florentine chancellor, Bartolomeo Scala, trained his daughter, Alessandra, in all aspects of the *studia humanitatis* and trumpeted the success of his experiment to the Latinate world. Later intellectual celebrities, such as Francesco Barbaro, Pietro Bembo, Sir Thomas More, and Sir Anthony Cooke, not only provided for their daughters' serious instruction in Latin letters but also ensured that these female prodigies of "learned virtue" received the attention of contemporaries. Humanist fathers made the educated woman not only possible but suddenly plausible.

In the wake of Joan Kelly-Gadol's controversial contention that women "did not have a renaissance, at least not during the Renaissance," scholars have wrestled with explaining the increasing presence of women in letters and the arts as the Renaissance era progressed.[8] Early scholarship on the so-called "women humanists" (especially Alessandra Scala, Isotta Nogarola, Cassandra Fedele, and Laura Cereta) as well as on women authors and artists more generally, defined well-educated women of the era as curiosities, either vilified or offered temporary notoriety for going "beyond their sex."[9] Either way, according to this contention, educated women failed to win the enduring respect of their contemporaries.

Recent scholarship has taken a more positive stance with regard to the writings of early modern Italian women in every conceivable genre, from domestic correspondence to poetry, dialogues, and even theology.[10] Within the English context, similarly, historians and literary critics have begun to challenge the model of "chaste, silent, and obedient" prevalent in the prescriptive literature, by shifting the focus of examination to what women themselves said, wrote, and printed.[11] At the level of erudite composition, scholars have begun to take seriously women's contributions to the so-called "debate on women." Within this framework, we understand the learned woman as a member of "the other voice": a group of thinkers, male and female, who presented an audible counterargument to centuries of biblical and Aristotelian antiwoman sentiment and to the patriarchal structure of Western society, a structure legitimized by the texts of these traditions.[12]

In attempting to answer the question of how these women of the "other voice" were able to make their contributions in the first place, scholars have begun to look at the role of the father. Margaret King has tentatively observed, "One small group of men at least sincerely believed in the female capacity for advanced education. They are the fathers of learned women whose actions themselves testified to their high estimation of their daughters' intelligence."[13] Margaret Rosenthal has noted that the woman writer able to avoid opprobrium often had an influential male patron or father who "personally [fostered her] education [or] assist[ed] in her literary projects."[14] Elizabeth Clarke and Susan Felch, similarly, have noted that Sir Anthony Cooke (tutor to Edward VI) educated his daughters alongside his sons.[15] The issue at this stage is to consider the ways in which a woman capitalized on her good fortune in being born to a forward-thinking father as her career proceeded. Is it even conceivable that the learned woman might prosper alone?

Margaret Ezell's work on Elizabeth Brackley and Jane Cavendish, daughters of the Duke of Newcastle, demonstrates that these educated women considered the duke their "literary progenitor" and stresses the role that the "English Maecenas" had in educating them himself and in encouraging their literary endeavors. Yet Ezell does not analyze the father-daughter interaction systematically, as her interest lies more in proving that the "coterie publishing" (that is, manuscript circulation) in which these two women engaged constituted a serious literary endeavor despite its more limited readership. This focus prevents her from considering the possibility that the desire of Brackley and Cavendish to be Newcastle's daughters "in [their] pens" is only one instance of a broader pattern among the European cultural elite.[16]

Ingrid de Smet has approached the problem in a more integrative spirit, arguing that the unifying theme in the lives and careers of Marie de Gournay, Arcangela Tarabotti, and Anna Maria van Schurman was the lack of marriage and children, which enabled them to focus upon their Latin studies—the prerequisite of participation in the republic of letters. De Smet has observed, moreover, that "because they lived in a patriarchal society, their respective fathers played an important role in their learning: if Tarabotti educated herself in spite of her father, Van Schurman was able to develop her intellectual talents to the full thanks to her father, whilst Gournay had found in her *père d'alliance* Montaigne the stimulus needed to continue her own quest for knowledge."[17] De Smet's analysis, however, focuses upon these women's writings in textual terms rather than upon the father-daughter relationship as such.[18]

The claim advanced in this book, then, is that the patriarch was complicit in the creation of "Renaissance feminism."[19] Italy and England constitute the principal contexts of this study, and much of my evidence comes from the libraries and archives of Venice and London. These cities, as important centers of print culture in the early modern period, offered ready access to publishing and had pronounced concentrations of women writers. It was along the Venice-London axis, moreover, that much of the humanist discussion of pedagogical theory, as well as the debate on women, took place.

A crucial notion posited by Italian and English humanists was the redefinition of female "virtue" (meaning chastity) as a composite of erudition and Christian morality, a composite that I am terming "learned virtue." This redefinition of women's virtue, which became a commonplace in writing about women during the fifteenth century, was part of a larger reality in the intellectual word of humanism: beginning in the fifteenth century, male intellectuals were as likely to be men with families as they were to be ecclesiastics.[20] Thus the family itself, including female members, took on far greater importance in the world of ideas. But what makes all of this "feminist?"

Feminism, far from being monological, has been constituted in different ways depending upon era and cultural context.[21] Constance Jordan has posited that the "feminism" of the Renaissance era is best characterized as a sustained "pro-woman" argument that contested the negative portrayal of womankind's natural character and capabilities found in the Bible and in the Aristotelian corpus.[22] Pamela Joseph Benson has refined Jordan's framework, positing that the literary "pro-feminism" of Renaissance Italy and England evinces a dialectic of innovation and containment: authors were fascinated by the possibilities of the "independent woman" but were afraid of the political critique that this new character implied.[23] This study is indebted to both approaches but departs from them in its method and selection of evidence. Whereas male-authored texts (prescriptive, dialogic, and dramatic) provide the evidentiary base for Jordan and Benson's analyses, I focus upon women's writings and the ways in which they interact with contemporary works by men.[24]

The learned women discussed here, as well as their male supporters and encomiasts, redrew the boundaries of the concept of "woman," introducing the new character "woman as intellect." This redefinition possessed wide appeal, because its proponents did not initially employ the syntax of political antagonism; instead, they used the traditional vocabulary of domesticity. The use of this domestic paradigm should not, however, be understood as evidence of female "containment." Rather, it was a subversive strategy for making the unusual seem acceptable and even praiseworthy. Because gender categories are based in discourse, language can also be the means of their disintegration. But deconstruction is best accomplished one step at a time. As Siep Stuurman has demonstrated, the complete equality of the sexes was a concept that, though by no means mainstream, was at least "intellectually available" to thinkers of the Radical Enlightenment.[25] I chart the initial step in that direction: on their culture's own terms, the women of this study substantiated the idea that men and women could be equal in matters of the mind.

Part I focuses upon the extensive documentary record surrounding famous household academies of Italy and England and the learned father-daughter teams within them, including Tomas and Christine de Pizan, Sir Thomas More and Margaret Roper, Pietro Bembo and his daughter Helena, Sir Anthony Cooke and his four daughters, as well as Henry Fitzalan and his two daughters, Jane and her lesser-known sister Mary. The evidentiary base of Part I thus rests upon an influential group within the cultural but not always aristocratic elite. It was these famous innovators who provided the first incontrovertible evidence for the utility and legitimacy of women's education: female paragons of learned virtue.

The initial formulation of the domestic academy is the subject of

Chapter 1. Utilizing as case studies Christine de Pizan (ca. 1365–1431) and
the most famous of the quattrocento women humanists, Isotta Nogarola
(1418–1466), Cassandra Fedele (1465–1558), and Laura Cereta (1469–
1499), this chapter argues that these first female "stars" in the field of
letters understood themselves and were understood by literary culture
as products of household academies. Chapter 1 thus analyzes a well-
known group of women writers—well-known both to their early modern
contemporaries and to modern scholars. As references to other women
intellectuals of this era will attest, however, they are not the only available examples. Rather than turning to them as the "only" examples, I
have chosen to focus upon these individuals because the prodigious
documentation surrounding them allows for examination of both their
biographies and their rhetorical strategies. The defining characteristic
of this initial Italian model is the father-teacher as a force of legitimation for a new character in the Western social paradigm: the virtuous
learned woman.

But how did that "other" Renaissance in sixteenth-century England
treat women writers? As scholars routinely observe, the English Renaissance was at least in part a response to the literary and artistic revolution
that began in Italy in the previous century. The emergence of "household academies" in sixteenth-century England follows this basic pattern:
The idea of creating and publicizing a domestic enclave in which the
studies of women flourished was unquestionably Italian. Yet the religious controversies raging in England during the reigns of Henry VIII,
Edward VI, and Elizabeth I brought a rather different set of priorities to
bear. Chapter 2 follows the household academy as it adapted itself to
the dominant intellectual trend in sixteenth-century England, so-called
"Christian humanism." I begin by comparing the notion of learned
virtue delineated in the manuscript and published correspondence of
the Venetian humanist Pietro Bembo to his daughter and son concerning their education with the similar but more famous letters of Sir
Thomas More. These documents lend themselves to a closer interrogation
of fathers' motivations in educating daughters alongside sons and particularly to culturally dependent definitions of learned virtue. Whereas the
Venetian humanist saw letters as the means to give his children social
prestige (and secondarily a foundation in ethics), the English humanist
viewed education as the means to give his children an ethical foundation (and secondarily social prestige). The other principal case studies

are the large scholarly families of Sir Anthony Cooke and Henry Fitzalan. These English protagonists, like their Italian counterparts, were for
the most part well known to contemporaries and have also received
modern scholarly attention. In particular, the household school of Sir
Thomas More has long been a subject of interest to historians of women
and of Reformation England. And Sir Anthony Cooke's daughters, especially Anne (1528–1610), are also reasonably well known to historians
and literary critics as translators of devotional material and patrons of
reformist divines. Though familiar to her contemporaries, Jane (or Jo-
hanne) Fitzalan (ca. 1537–1576), later Baroness Lumley, has only recently begun to attract the attention of literary critics, and no sustained
scholarship has yet been done on the Latin juvenilia of her sister Mary
(1540–1557), on her brother Henry, or on the family group as a domestic academy analogous to that of More's and Cooke's.

Contemporary reception is an important measure of the household
academy's success in carving a respected place for women intellectuals in
the republic of letters. Chapter 3 evaluates the rich discussion of Italian
and English women humanists in sixteenth- and seventeenth-century
biographical collections and defenses of women—sources noted but not
yet systematically analyzed in the scholarly literature. Whereas scholars
have traditionally argued that contemporaries viewed learned women
as transgressors and resisted (even attacked) their attempts to forge literary careers, these sources celebrate women humanists as active contributors to their families' intellectual honor and as examples for other
women to follow.

Understanding the significance of women humanists' success, however, ultimately depends upon a close reading of their writings and translations. Chapter 4 undertakes this literary examination, arguing that women
writers on both sides of the Alps contributed to "Renaissance feminism."
The autobiographical writings of Christine de Pizan and Laura Cereta, di-
verging from strict spiritual narrative, introduced a new kind of female subjectivity into the Western canon. Laura Cereta's arguments for women's
education were unprecedented in their stridency. Isotta Nogarola's *Dialogue*
was the first to confute the traditional condemnation of Eve. English
women's "feminism" in this era was often implicit rather than explicit,
but examination of dedicatory epistles and other prefatory material (both
in print and in manuscript) reveal a striking, celebratory feminist theme:
the presentation of the female voice as a scholarly interlocutor in the fields

of classical and patristic scholarship. In the unabashed presentation of the authorial "I," Margaret Roper's daughter, Mary Basset, was no less a "Renaissance feminist" than Laura Cereta. In addition, the publications and manuscript letters of Anne and Mildred Cooke evince their direct engagement with the progress of reformist religion. The male-authored letters to the reader that preface the published translations by Margaret Roper and Anne Cooke also establish these learned women as models of learned virtue to be followed by other women.

Interweaving the different strands of "pro-woman" argument explored in this chapter requires a redefinition of our terms. Whereas "Renaissance feminism" has traditionally encompassed only explicit attacks on misogyny and the patriarchal order, I posit that Renaissance feminism had three different types. Two are apparent: "explicit" critique and the vocal celebration of female excellence (especially that of contemporary women humanists), which I term "celebratory" feminism. A quieter form of Renaissance feminism that nonetheless bolstered these argumentative stances was "participatory" feminism. By doing the same scholarly work as men, women intellectuals made a case for the equality of the sexes in matters of the mind, whether or not they overtly criticized the patriarchal order or praised their female peers.

The household academies examined in Part I by no means disappeared after the first famous women they produced.[26] While the weight of analysis does not rest upon numbers, it is a testament to the cognitive durability of these first domestic academies that both contemporaries and later observers situated Isotta Nogarola, for instance, in the company of her paternal aunt, Angela (an author of Latin spiritual poetry); her sister and fellow humanist, Ginevra; and five later generations of Nogarola women, whose works have apparently been lost but whom biographical compendia term "letterate" and "poetesse" (women of letters). Similarly, I am concerned not only with the temporary fame of Cassandra Fedele or Laura Cereta but with the "Cassandras" and "Lauras" cited in the catalogs of famous women that poured out of the Italian presses in the sixteenth and seventeenth centuries.

In England, legacies are more literal. The Englishwomen humanists all married and most had children, yet they still found time for classical studies despite the their familial obligations. Whereas Ingrid de Smet posits that women's advanced education required dissociating themselves from the reproductive economy, the Englishwomen humanists'

ability to balance the demands of the mind with the more traditional demands of the household suggests that this was not always the case.
While Margaret Roper drew the most attention by association with her
famous father, contemporaries also took note of her siblings, biological
and adoptive. Acclaim for her daughter, Mary [Roper Clarke] Basset, in
fact, exceeded her mother's, since Mary was a respected translator of
both Latin and Greek. Anthony Cooke's household—which one contemporary observer and family friend, Walter Haddon, characterized as
a little "Tusculan" academy, but one in which the studies of women
were flourishing—produced four female scholars and champions of reformist religion.[27] The scholarly productivity of Anne and Mildred Cooke
in particular intensified rather than declined after their marriages to
high-ranking officials at the Elizabethan court. Their children capitalized
on the intellectual pedigree not only of father but also of mother.

Part I thus investigates the structure and reception of famous domestic academies as a new cultural template, within which the "studies
of women" flourished. The salient features of the household academy as
a context include the father-daughter dyad as an intellectual paradigm.
Often fathers literally taught their children themselves, in lieu of or in
conjunction with more "formal" tutors, and exerted a positive influence
as well in promoting these educated daughters.

Equally important, however, was women's subsequent use of the
familial paradigm to establish their authorial credibility. Women's manuscript compositions circulated within family networks and, with the
advent of print, were published either by family members or by close
family friends—a process that situated even explicitly feminist texts within
the rhetorical safe zone of domesticity. Rhetorically, women humanists
made excellent use of the "intellectual family": they invoked their virtue
as literate daughters, wives, and mothers and approached potential male
patrons within what I am calling the father-patron/daughter-client relationship. Both north and south of the Alps, divergent cases, literal and
discursive, of learned women as protégées of a father-patron illustrate a
process of Renaissance "self-fashioning" that neither Stephen Greenblatt nor John Martin have considered in their respective treatments.[28]
Greenblatt and the New Historicists offer a useful lens through which to
examine the processes of construction and representation in Renaissance discourse, but neither he nor John Martin have considered self-
fashioning in gendered terms.[29] Ambitious men of the Renaissance were

also obliged to secure patronage.[30] For women, however, cultural engagement depended upon making the best use of "family" networks: initially, the patronage of a father (whether literal or literary) and as time
wore on broader networks of intellectual kinship, including husbands,
friends, and colleagues.

The father-patron/daughter-client topos derived its utility, in part,
through association with the learned daughters of the classical tradition.
Early modern women's writings and writing about women often evince
what I term the "Hortensian hermeneutic," or an instinct to situate
women's writing and speech within a father-daughter dyad. My research parallels the "filiafocality" that classicist Judith Hallett has found
in the ancient Roman context—that is, the "high valuation of individual
Roman daughters by their fathers, the elaboration of the daughter role
in various Roman social institutions, and the Roman emphasis on ties of
blood and marriage through and to men's female children."[31] In particular, Hallett demonstrates that Roman authors represented women of the
elite as "manifest[ing] and perpetuat[ing] the talents and qualities of their
fathers and individual blood kinsmen, especially those traits that secured
such kinsmen public recognition."[32] One of her principal examples is
Hortensia. Another is Tullia, the daughter of Cicero, who called her "the
image of my countenance, speech and mind" *(effigiem oris, sermonis, an-
imi mei)* in a letter to his brother, Quintus. Cicero's *Familiar Letters,* in
which appear both the quotation above and several references to Cicero's
enjoying his daughter's conversation and trusting her "good sense" *(pru-
dentia),* was a clear best seller throughout the Renaissance era.[33] Although
Tullia appears less frequently than Hortensia in biographical compendia,
she nonetheless receives comment from important feminist authors—
and praise even from some who otherwise demonstrate conservative
views on women's education.

The cooperation of contemporaries, often themselves connected to
the learned woman they praised, in promulgating learned women as
paragons of learned virtue demonstrates that the highly educated women
remained "chaste" within the expanding boundaries of the household
academy. To be sure, the women under investigation here are the success stories. Yet we should not dismiss these women as "exceptions," because success stories tell us at least as much about the mentality of an
era as tales of disappointed hope do. Unlike the learned courtesans of
their era, the women here received little or no public criticism from con-

temporaries. Familial association, literal and discursive, shielded them from the deleterious classical equation of female learning with promiscuity. Unlike the learned nuns of their era, these secular female talents enjoyed not only a "publicity" but one legitimized by the putative male supervision that father, father-patron, or husband afforded.

I do not claim that the intellectual family is the only explanatory model for the profusion of women writers in early modern Europe, but I do argue that it is the best model for explaining the rise of secular and celebrated women intellectuals, who forced contemporary society to rethink female capability. Learned courtesans, while sometimes acclaimed, suffered sexual slurs.[34] By virtue of their profession, these women could not be positive examples for other women. On the other side of the sexual spectrum, learned nuns engaged in vast creative enterprises with less social censure. Elissa Weaver has demonstrated that the convents of early modern Italy housed a rich tradition of women's education and interdisciplinary creativity. In her words, the convent "provided a training ground for women writers," within the genre of sacred plays *(sacre rappresentationi)* and even secular comedic and musical forms.[35] Kate Lowe has shown that some Italian nuns were also historians: their convent chronicles reveal a high level of education (sometimes encompassing the composition of Latin orations) and a clear authorial sensibility.[36] Both scholars contend that enclosure forged creative female communities, which sometimes received outside recognition. And ardent contributors to the debate on women also emerged from the convents. One prime example is the Venetian feminist Suor Arcangela Tarabotti (1604–1652).[37] As a group, however, learned nuns did not prompt the reconsideration of gender categories in the way that laywomen did, because nuns lived outside the reproductive economy. Nuns were understood to be female, but as the brides of Christ and not of men, they constituted a special category of women. By contrast, contemporaries had to account both for the accomplishments and for the womanhood of learned laywomen. The path was smoothed first by the filial image, but, with time, the working wife and mother took her place as a figure in literary society.

Part II: The Household Salon (1580–1680)

By the late sixteenth century, there was a new range of possibilities for women intellectuals. While their predecessors benefited from domestic academies headed by learned fathers, these next generations of learned women emerged from a more expansive domestic framework, in which the dominant theme is the collaboration of wives and husbands. Concomitant with this more egalitarian "intellectual family," literary society itself began to revise its former emphasis upon Latin composition as the prerequisite of erudition. Whereas scholars have posited that the phenomenon of female humanism died out at the close of the sixteenth century, this study argues instead that that it merely changed form. Following the broader patterns of Renaissance culture itself, what we witness is the entrenchment of "woman as intellect" across geographic, disciplinary, and socioeconomic boundaries. This was an era in which literary society increasingly favored erudite vernacular composition, interdisciplinarity, and originality over dogged imitation of Cicero. Women intellectuals from a variety of backgrounds and in a wide range of languages and media participated in literary culture. And their feminism became more consistently explicit.

These transformations (once again) began in Italy. Chapter 5 charts the Italian reformulation of the "household academy" as a "household salon," in which women began to dominate the processes of education and cultural production. At the same time, their self-presentation and modes of reception shifted away from the filial paradigm toward a flexible vocabulary of marital collaboration. Some women writers of the seventeenth century even abandoned domestic rhetoric altogether. The figures who best exemplify this transition—biographical and rhetorical— are the Venetian feminists Moderata Fonte (1555–1592) and Lucrezia Marinella (1571–1653). Explicitly feminist women scholars of this era still used the father-patron/daughter-client relationship to good effect. I explore this intriguing evidence of continuity amid change both within and outside Italian context. A look at two well-known feminists in France and the Netherlands, Marie de Gournay (1566–1645) and Anna Maria van Schurman (1607–1678), illustrates with particular clarity the ongoing utility of the father-daughter topos, even as their arguments broke new ground. Emblematic of the fully formed "household salon" is the Andreini family, the star of which was the famous actress, humanist, and academician Isabella (1562–1604). As we will see, Isabella Andreini characterizes a new age of expanded possibilities: she took delight in defying categories.

A similar series of shifts occurred, albeit slightly later, in Britain.

Much as late sixteenth- and seventeenth-century Italy was characterized by both change and continuity when the life patterns and rhetorical strategies of women intellectuals were concerned, so too the older
model of the "household academy" coexisted with the new form of the
"household salon" in seventeenth-century Britain, remaining important
as a context for women's advanced education and as a rhetorical device
to deploy—especially for explicit feminists. Chapter 6 begins with the issue of continuity. The correspondence of William and Elizabeth Petty illuminates one prominent "household academy" in which sons and
daughters learned the classics. And England's first "explicit" feminist,
Bathsua Makin (fl. 1673), solidified her position in literary society in the
filial mode so successfully employed by her humanist predecessors.
Thereafter, we turn to the issues of change and expansion, devoting particular attention to the lives and strategies of Esther Inglis (1571–1624),
Mary Beale (1633–1699), and Mary More (d. ca. 1716). All three writers made use of scribal publication as a venue for stunning literary
achievements; all three were also artists; and all three made excellent
use of their "household salons" as a base for developing and publicizing
their interdisciplinary creativity. Taken together, chapters 5 and 6 contend that the category "woman as intellect" was no longer populated
only by members of the social and cultural elite nor only by women Latinists, but rather by talented women from across the socioeconomic and
disciplinary landscape.

Emboldened by an awareness that they belonged to an illustrious
tradition of learned women and that they were contributors to an established genre of literature—the debate on women—women authors of
the seventeenth century argued not merely for womankind's dignity or
merit but for their equality and even "rights." Chapter 7 analyzes this es-
calation of feminist argument in seventeenth-century women's writing.
While a full articulation of feminist rights discourse would not appear
until the eighteenth century, paradigmatically in Mary Wollstonecraft's
Vindication of the Rights of Women (1793), women writers such as Moderata Fonte, Lucrezia Marinella, Bathsua Makin, and Mary More paved
the way by introducing "equality" and "rights" into the lexicon of the
debate on women.

As a whole, this study explains the rise of educated women as respected figures in literary society and contends that the emergence of
"woman as intellect" made feminism a prominent theme in European

intellectual history—a preliminary step to the advent of feminism as a prominent theme in Western social history. There is an apparent paradox at the heart of this story. The new category "woman as intellect" derived its legitimacy and popularity by association with women's traditional place, the household. Like the expanded humanist notion of virtue, however, the multivalent definitions of "family" and "household" offered women room for strategic manipulation. In the end, the women graduates of household academies and salons, from Christine de Pizan to Mary More, put their pens to use in redrawing the map of female capability and the boundaries of "proper" female behavior. Thanks in part to their male supporters and in part to their own ingenuity, these women had a renaissance not only during the Renaissance but also in the centuries that followed. In the process, they laid the foundations for the intellectual emancipation of womankind.

I

THE HOUSEHOLD ACADEMY,
1400–1580

1

Her Father's Daughter

"YOUR father, who was a great scientist and philosopher, did not believe that women were worth less by knowing science; rather, as you know, he took great pleasure from seeing your inclination to learning."[1] So Christine de Pizan (ca. 1365–1431), a prolific author in the French vernacular and the first woman known to have made her living by writing, reassured herself in the *Book of the City of Ladies* (1405). Christine was the eldest child of Tomas de Pizan (da Pizzano), a physician, professor of astrology at the University of Bologna, and (from 1357/58 to 1364), a medical counselor in Venice, where Christine was born.[2] Tomas moved Christine, her mother, and her two brothers from Venice to Paris when he became the personal physician and astrologer to King Charles V (ca. 1368).[3] Although her corpus of writings demonstrate that she intertwined her own identity with that of her adoptive country, Christine nonetheless underscored her Italian heritage by referring to herself as a "femme ytallienne."[4] Above all, however, she styled herself as "her father's daughter," not merely in crediting Tomas with her excellent education in the liberal arts but in positioning herself as his intellectual heir.

Christine represents a point of origin for all scholars interested in the history of educated women in the West. Historians have observed that she and one of her younger contemporaries, the Veronese humanist Isotta Nogarola, "launched the tradition of the learned woman in the early modern period, setting up the framework within which learned women expressed themselves over the next several centuries."[5] This chapter examines the commonalities in experience and strategy that contextualized these inaugural voices in the feminist tradition and their direct literary descendants (Cassandra Fedele and Laura Cereta), arguing that the household-as-school and the rhetorical invocation of intellectual kinship constituted the rules of literary engagement that educated women of subsequent centuries followed.

Christine de Pizan

According to her own account, Christine de Pizan became Europe's first professional woman author by accident. She turned to writing as a means to support herself, her mother, and her three children after the death of her husband, Etienne du Castel (one of Charles V's secretaries). Frustrated in her attempts to use the Parisian law courts to collect money owed to her, this young widow proved that necessity is indeed the mother of invention. The Christinian corpus is remarkable for both its depth and breadth. She was a poet, writing *Poésies, Epître d'Othéa a Hector* (1401); a moral philosopher, writing *Enseignements moraux, Le livre de prudence, Le dit de Poissy* (1400), *Le chemin de long estude* (1402), *La mutacion de Fortune* (1403), *Débat de II amans* (1401), *Le livre des III Vertus* (1405), and *Epître à la Reine* (ca. 1406); a disputant in the initial volleys of the *querelle des femmes*, writing *L'épître au dieu d'amour* (1399), *Le dit de la rose* (1402), and *Epîtres sur le Roman*, (1402); a political historian, writing *Les faits et bonnes moeurs du sage Roy Charles V* (1404), *Faits d'armes et de chevalerie* (1406), *Lamentation sur les maux de la guerre civile* (1407), and *Le livre de la paix* (ca. 1413); a historian of women, writing *La cité des dames* (1405), *Le dittié sur Jeanne d'Arc* (1429); an autobiographical chronicler, writing *Lavision-Christine* (1402); an author of devotional works, writing *Psaumes de pénitence* (ca. 1409), *Oraisons* (ca. 1413); and a political counselor: *Le livre du corps de policie* (1407).

The voluminous scholarship on Christine has discussed in minute detail almost every conceivable aspect of her life and writings. This study focuses upon a very recent line of inquiry: Christine's authorial self-presentation—how she explained herself to herself and justified her novel status as a female author. This process of self-justification connects her thematically to subsequent women writers, as does her intervention in the *querelle des femmes*, a field of literature toward which early modern women authors directed a substantive proportion of their effort. No certain claim can be made that her Italian contemporaries modeled themselves upon Christine or were even aware of her.[6] Rather than making such a claim, I begin with Christine as the first known example of a laywoman who did not happen to be either a queen or a courtly patroness engaging with literary culture. The elements in biography and strategy common to Christine and the Italian women humanists, despite the disparities in time, context, and text, substantiate the broader utility of "the intellectual family" as an explanatory paradigm.

Christine was not a humanist, strictly speaking, but the father-daughter dynamic upon which she relied constitutes a prevalent theme for the women humanists who most closely parallel her level of achievement. Christine used classical antiquity as a heuristic tool for understanding her own place in history. In the *Book of the City of Ladies* (1405), she crafts not only a literary space that virtuous and accomplished women of all degrees and stations may inhabit but also a historical lineage for herself. Depressed by the notion that so many of her classical and patristic sources (as well as some male contemporaries) hold the view that educating women makes them domestic liabilities, Christine is reminded by Lady Philosophy that this is not the opinion of all men; nor is it the opinion of the wisest.[7] The most important example of a man who held this wise view is her father, Tomas, who thought it a good thing for his daughter to be educated and who took pleasure in her learning.[8] As historical context for her own father-daughter dyad, however, Lady Philosophy/ Christine adduces one ancient and one modern example. The ancient example is Quintus Hortensius, the famous Roman orator, who

> had a daughter, named Hortensia, whom he greatly loved for the subtlety of her wit. He had her study letters and the science of rhetoric, which she mastered so thoroughly that she resembled her father Hortensius not only in wit and lively memory but also in her excellent delivery and order of speech—in fact, he surpassed her in nothing. As for the subject discussed above, concerning the good which comes through women, the benefits realized by this woman and her learning were, among others, exceptionally remarkable. That is, during the time when Rome was governed by three men, this Hortensia began to support the cause of women and to undertake what no man dared to undertake. There was a question whether certain taxes should be levied on women and on their jewelry during a needy period in Rome. This woman's eloquence was so compelling that she was listened to, no less readily than her father would have been, and she won her case.[9]

Moving beyond her source for Hortensia's story—Giovanni Boccaccio's *De mulieribus claris* (*Concerning Famous Women*, 1362)—Christine
cites an example geographically and chronologically closer to home:

> Giovanni Andrea, a solemn law professor in Bologna not quite sixty
> years ago, was not of the opinion that it was bad for women to be edu-
> cated. He had a fair and good daughter, named Novella, who was edu-
> cated in the law to such an advanced degree that when he was occupied
> by some task and not at leisure to present his lectures to his students, he
> would send Novella, his daughter, in his place to lecture to the students
> from his chair. And to prevent her beauty from distracting the concen-
> tration of her audience, she had a little curtain drawn in front of her. In
> this manner she could on occasion supplement and lighten her father's
> occupation. He loved her so much that, to commemorate her name, he
> wrote a book of remarkable lectures on the law which he entitled *Novella
> super Decretalium*, after his daughter's name.[10]

The title "Novella super Decretalium" literally reads "New Material Concerning the Decretals," but Christine makes "Novella" a name, meaning
"new little girl" or even "strange little girl." Christine used this pun to
create a context for herself as a new and strange character: a secular
female author of subroyal standing. Hortensia was already enshrined
in the Boccaccian tradition as a laudable example of a daughter embodying her orator-father's excellence. Novella's Bolognese heritage (Bologna
being the territory in which Christine's family patrimony resided), as
well as her professor-father, presented an even better parallel to her own
biography.[11]

Christine's autobiographical *Lavision-Christine* highlights the central
role that her father played in her education. Late-medieval conduct literature certainly addressed the issue of noblewomen's education, and the
father-daughter theme appeared in one of the most popular texts within
this genre, the *Livre du Chevalier de la Tour Landry* (ca. 1371–1372).[12] The
"curriculum" adduced in this text, however, did not extend beyond vernacular literacy in the service of chastity. The Knight teaches his three
daughters to read so that they can better distinguish good from evil and
especially so that they will be able to perceive attempts upon their honor
cloaked in the blandishments of potential lovers. The Knight is not interested in whether women learn to write but only that they learn to read so
as to more readily avoid sexual sin.[13] Christine's conception of education

was far more complex, based on her particular experience of the household academy. Her *Book of the Three Virtues* (or *Treasury of the City of Ladies*), as Astrik Gabriel once pointed out, represents a "complete course on feminine education," and her principal argument was that because women have the same aptitudes as men, they then have the right to the same education; in this, Christine followed "her own father's advanced ideas."[14]

Christine's complaint to Lady Philosophy in *Lavision* affords a closer look at what those "advanced ideas" of female education involved. Lamenting her widowhood and its attendant emotional and financial struggles, Christine above all regrets the loss of intellectual kinship that she enjoyed in the company of both her father and her husband. "In my solitude," she recounts, "there came back to me some remnants of Latin and discourses of the beauteous sciences, as well as various maxims and civil discourse that in time past I heard in conversation from my beloved father and husband, despite the fact that, in my youthful folly, I had retained very little."[15] Although she wishes that she had been more diligent in her studies when "those two fountains of philosophy" had been her companions, nonetheless she learned enough of the fundamentals from them that later in life she could take up her books again. "Like a child who first learns the alphabet," Christine narrates, "[I began again with] the ancient histories from the beginnings of the world, the history of the Hebrews, the Assyrians, and the ancient kingdoms, proceeding from one to the other all the way to the Romans, the French, the Britons, and several other historians, and then to scientific learning, to the extent that I was able to understand it, given my limited time for study." Christine continues, "Next I took up the books of the poets, my knowledge increasing bit by bit."[16] Proceeding at last from poetry to moral philosophy and rhetoric, Christine finished her training in the liberal arts.[17]

Christine thus informs her readers that her learned father and husband provided the initial preparation in language, history, poetry, and moral philosophy upon which she could improve later at her own initiative. She suggests that part of her early education involved listening to what she heard her father and husband recite. One historian contends that early modern Italian women often became familiar with the "beauteous sciences" to which Christine refers as a result of listening to relatives, and occasionally an erudite preacher, whose intermittent references to Aristotle and later Plato were intended to encourage the highest ethical conduct among their female listeners.[18] Christine's prolific writing, her ability to engage an impressive array of literature, and especially her references to Latin reading, however, attest substantive formal instruction in youth.[19]

Christine was both the daughter and the granddaughter of university-trained men. Her maternal grandfather was a clerk at the University of Bologna and a counselor in Venice, who introduced his son-in-law to networks of patronage that would ultimately favor Tomas's position at the French court.[20] Prior to taking up this post, Tomas had been a professor of astrology at the University of Bologna, which at the time was the preeminent Italian university, in terms of European prestige second only to the University of Paris. It was in Paris that he decisively enhanced his family's intellectual honor. As Charles V's personal physician and astrological counselor, he was closely associated with a monarch known as "the Wise" for his extensive artistic and literary patronage. Charles V's library was among the best of his age, including numerous commissioned works and a large number of translations from Roman and Greek authors.[21] Tomas intended his daughter, no less than his two sons, to receive this literary patrimony and carry forward the family's reputation for learning. Christine's extensive education was not just a desire to shape her moral character but also the means by which she might play her part in the family business of erudition.

Christine's younger brothers might have seemed more obvious choices to continue the family's reputation for learning. Little, however, is known of their pursuits. She refers to them as "wise and prudent men of good life," whom financial distress forced to return to their paternal estates in Bologna.[22] It seems that in their case the death of Charles V, in 1380, followed by the death of their father between 1385 and 1389, irrevocably diminished their position at court.[23] Scholars have speculated that Christine had been educated alongside her brothers. At the least, her writings suggest no rivalry or animosity between herself and her siblings regarding their intellectual inheritance—a theme that educated women began to stress in subsequent eras.

Nor did Christine consider her husband, Etienne du Castel, an impediment to her scholarly pursuits. As we have seen, she considered him a parallel font of philosophy to her father. Indeed, in 1380 (the year of their marriage), Etienne was made a secretary of the royal chancellery, a position that brought with it considerable scholarly prestige. Etienne would have found himself among a coterie of young intellectuals who were in correspondence with the great humanists of the day, notably Coluccio Salutati.[24]

Christine presents her mother as the principal impediment to her progress in learning. On the one hand, Lady Philosophy reminds Christine that an honorable and pious mother is one of life's principal blessings. "How often," the character remarks, "[has your mother] comforted you and brought you from your impatient thoughts to remember your God."[25] In matters of morality, "mother" is exemplary and her influence benign. On the other hand, in matters of the mind, "mother" represents the full force of customary practice against which the author would wage her literary war. Christine notes that "the feminine opinion of [her] mother . . . was the major obstacle to [Christine] being more involved in the sciences," insofar as her mother wanted Christine to keep "busy with spinning and silly girlishness, following the common custom of women."[26]

Motherhood itself, however, was an important aspect of Christine's life and her self-presentation. Her two surviving children—the eldest a daughter (whose name remains unknown) at the prestigious royal convent at Poissy, and the younger a son, Jean du Castel—both appear in *Lavision*. Lady Philosophy reminds the despondent author that she possesses the three most important worldly blessings: virtuous and noble parents, health, and attractive and intelligent children. Concerning the third blessing, Lady Philosophy praises the daughter's "life of contemplation and devotion" and mentions the consolation that Christine derives from the daughter's "sweet and pious letters, wise and full of understanding . . . in which she, though young and innocent, exhorts [Christine] to put aside worldly concern and to despise prosperity." The son embodies his mother's particular concerns, having "mastered [their] most important branches of knowledge—not one other can be found who is more naturally apt than he is in grammar, rhetoric, or poetic diction; nor anyone else with more subtle understanding than he has."[27] Christine suggests here that she had stepped into the role that her father had played, ensuring that both her female and male children had an extensive education. Proud of her children's virtue and their literary accomplishments, she articulates an intellectual family in three generations: her father to herself to her children.

Jean, however, received the greater share of his mother's attention.

Whereas Christine refers to her daughter's good sense and consolatory letters, suggesting that the young woman engaged with the family's literary heritage to a certain extent, Christine makes a point of Jean's development in the liberal arts (grammar, rhetoric, history, poetry, moral philosophy), studies that are emblematic of her own aspirations and successes. Christine also links her son's early career to her own literary fame, observing that his first patron, the English Earl of Salisbury, had become an admirer of Christine's writings before he offered her son a place at his court. "After he had seen some of my works," she relates, "he persuaded me, despite my reluctance, to send my elder son, a rather clever child and good singer at the age of thirteen, back with him to England so that he could be with one of this own sons of the same age."[28]

The learned mother, then, offered her son his first major career opportunity. Soon after this initial success (ca. 1400), however, Salisbury was beheaded for remaining loyal to the deposed King Richard II—an act that Christine described in one of her ballads as a heinous injustice, typical of "the wicked country of England, where the people are ever changeable."[29] She refused to allow her son to continue at Henry IV's court, despite the king's willingness to take Jean into his own circle, as well as Christine herself, whose work he admired.[30] She tried instead to place her son in the household of Louis, the Duc d'Orléans, brother of Charles VI and well known for his patronage of the arts, but "since the modest abilities of this young boy made little impression among the many great proficients of [the duke's] court, I once again became responsible for his maintenance and received nothing from his service."[31]

Christine's attempt to place her son with Louis, albeit unsuccessful, reveals an intriguing representational strategy for a female author. She equates herself with her creative and biological "offspring," thereby promoting her authorial self and her son at the same time. Between 1400 and 1401, Christine recommended Jean to Louis by means of a poem in which she characterizes both her verses and her son as gifts to the duke. Referring to her poem in the initial stanza, she says, "[I offer] this trifle that I nonetheless hold most dear, / And submit it to you in all sincerity, / If you should wish, noble duke, to receive it." Shifting to the subject of her son in the next stanza, Christine makes Jean "a gift to you, and leave to your own discretion / What you choose to make of him, because of the goodwill / To serve you that issues from his trembling heart; / If you should wish, noble duke to receive him."[32] These first stanzas blur the line between her literary and biological fertility, as at once she submits her poem and her son to the duke.

Jean du Castel did obtain a place in the household of Philip the Bold, Duke of Burgundy. It is likely that Christine employed a similar strategy in obtaining this end because, as in the case of Jean's acceptance into the household of the Earl of Salisbury, the nobleman served as patron to the mother as much as to the son. Shortly after Jean took up residence with him, Philip commissioned Christine to write the biography of his brother, the deceased King Charles V.[33] It therefore appears that Philip had already seen her writings and that his familiarity with her work favored her son's later acceptance at court.

This first professional, secular female author was able to pursue an independent literary career and to serve as her son's agent because of the initial training she received within her intellectual family. It was her father's educative influence and his networks of patronage that gave her both the connections and the authorial credibility necessary to innovate. Christine deployed the image of herself as "her father's daughter" throughout her career. Describing her petitions for widow's aid, for instance, Christine notes that she made her requests to certain French princes "not for any merit of [hers], but in the name of the ancient love which brought [her] father [from Venice] to be their servant."[34]

Contemporaries admired Christine's exceptional literary production in all genres, from poetry to theology, even despite her novel arguments dignifying the moral and educative contributions of secular women to historical and contemporary society in her contributions to the *querelle des femmes*, the *City of Ladies* and the *Treasury of the City of Ladies*. Chancellor of the University of Paris and Christine's fellow combatant against the misogynist *Romance of the Rose*, Jean Gerson characterized Christine as an "exemplary woman, a virile woman" *(insignis faemina, virilis faemina)*.[35] The contemporary poet Eustache Deschamps described himself to Christine as "your disciple" *(ta disciple)*, and Martin Le Franc, whose poetry followed the Christinian tradition in championing the female sex, praised Christine as valiant and virtuous in letters and the Latin language. Even her theoretical opponents in the debate at least appreciated her intelligence: Gontier Col addressed her as "Christine, the wise young woman" *(savent damoiselle Christine),* and Pierre Col termed her "a woman of deep understanding" *(femme de hault entendement).*[36]

The authorial credibility that elicited sponsors for her literary and biological progeny as well as widespread admiration depended upon her position as heir to the intellectual family in which she received her training, and upon her skillful use of the familial paradigm in positioning herself as an author. Christine reformulated the family unit as an academic nucleus, reconstituting its principal constituent elements as the household as school, the father as tutor, the daughter as student, the biological mother as the force of customary practice, and the female author as mother.

The case of Christine de Pizan begins to challenge the influential argument that the learned woman was able to function only within her "book-lined cell" as a kind of secular nun.[37] While Christine did not remarry, her close connections with her son and her ability to extend her own patronage networks to him foregrounded her role as a mother. Rather than finding herself trapped in a formula of perpetual virginity, she layered her multiple roles as her father's daughter, her husband's wife, and her son's mother. Her success in employing these multiple representational strategies suggests that even in the early fifteenth century, ambitious women had a range of possibilities for navigating the labyrinth of gender conventions.

Christine considered gender a professional asset, believing that her novel status as a female author made her works appealing to noble patrons and an elite audience. She explains that she offered literary gifts "as novelties" to certain noblemen, who received them gratefully—an outcome which she attributes "not to the dignity of [her] works, but rather to the fact these had been written by a woman—something that had not been done in quite some time."[38] Yet by this we should not understand that she was collected as a curiosity, which is one explanation sometimes adduced for the positive reception of learned Italian women in subsequent eras.[39] It is inconceivable that her principal patron, Philip the Bold, would have commissioned a mere curiosity for the serious political business of memorializing his brother in biography *(Biography of Charles V)* or of writing a treatise on secular government *(Book of Policy).* Novelty may well have been one element in her reception, but skill was the crucial factor—skill, that is, framed by the legitimizing forces of intellectual kinship and her status as a proper family woman.

Modern scholars often use the epithet "unique" when characterizing Christine's remarkable career. While she was the most prolific woman writer of her day, she was by no means the only female intellect of her era to attract attention. The Italian women humanists Maddalena Scrovegni of Padua (1356–1429) and Battista Montefeltro Malatesta of Urbino (1383–1450) received praise for their erudition, but little of what they wrote remains. The legacy of Scrovegni consists in a few of her letters and an encomium by the Veronese humanist Antonio Loschi, who eulogized her as a widow of exemplary conduct. In the literary "Temple of Chastity" that Loschi creates for Scrovegni, she devotes herself to her books in the privacy of her study *(sacellum)*, which Loschi positions in her father's house.[40] The legacy of Battista Montefeltro Malatesta is more extensive. Malatesta was the dedicatee of Bruni's treatise *De studiis et litteris,* but she herself also wrote a Latin oration to the Emperor Sigismund that enlisted his aid in restoring ancestral lands to her husband and son-in-law.[41] Following her example, Battista's granddaughters, Cecilia Gonzaga of Mantua (1425–1451) and Costanza Varano of Pesaro (1426–1447), were accomplished Latinists.[42] Caterina Caldiera (d. 1463) and Ippolita Sforza of Milan (1445–1488) were similarly celebrated for their mastery of the classics.

Scholars have long been aware that these women, apart from Caterina Caldiera, belonged to powerful aristocratic families. We also know that they received their instruction in Latin from their fathers, brothers, or brothers' tutors. Diana Robin observes, however, that none of these women "represented herself as separate from her family or wrote for causes unconnected to its interests." Robin posits that a distinctive characteristic of later generations of women humanists (especially Cassandra Fedele and Laura Cereta) is that they received some portion of their schooling "from a teacher beyond the range of the panoptic gaze of the father" and "were the first female writers in Italy to mobilize their talents to advance their own interests rather than those of their families."[43] While the range of possibilities for women's literary intervention certainly expanded over time, nonetheless the model of "the intellectual family" sustained women intellectuals throughout the early modern period. Rather than understanding the paternal connection and domestic rhetoric as constraints upon learned women, I contend that "family interests" produced reciprocal benefits.

Compared to the Christinian corpus, however, the writing of this first generation of women humanists does constitute a much more limited range of evidence. The more fitting "heirs" to Christinian precedent in terms of creative contribution in the dominant literary genres and the particular field of the debate on women were Venetian women humanists of the later fifteenth century.

Isotta Nogarola

The closest parallel to Christine in these terms is the Veronese humanist Isotta Nogarola (1418–1466). Nogarola forged her remarkable career in the new world of the humanist *res publica litterarum*. In her case, we witness both another individual's response to biographical circumstances and a change in the cultural form of the intellectual family as it adapted itself to larger societal trends. In Christine's day, a generation prior to Nogarola's, humanism was in its earliest phase, and the highest genres of intellectual attainment remained the treatise and the disputation; the most common genres of vernacular literary composition were still the chronicle, ballad, romance, and allegory. With the entrenchment of humanism in the mid-fifteenth century, however, literary activity shifted toward the classical forms of the letterbook, dialogue, oration, and *consolatio* (letter of consolation). The principal models (formerly Boethius, the Church fathers, and Aristotle) became Cicero, Livy, and Plato. The university and court as intellectual contexts, while not displaced, began to take second place to a broader milieu of civic (and civil) conversation, the lineaments of which were more flexible but also more dependent upon individual initiative.

This process of redefining the intellectual community provided space for women to engage. The most influential of the women humanists came from Venice (Cassandra Fedele) and its subject territories, Verona (Isotta Nogarola), and Brescia (Laura Cereta). Although the latter cities possessed their own cultural traditions, they also functioned as part of the Venetian Republic, connected to the metropolis in legal and military terms, as well as by the exchange of letters between humanists in Venice proper and those on the *terraferma* and by the frequent migration of humanists between the major centers of intellectual activity in Venice, Verona, and Padua.[44] Being in Verona presented no obstacle for Isotta Nogarola in contacting patrons and colleagues elsewhere in the republic. At the westernmost edge of the Venetian dominion, Brescia would have seemed a less propitious venue for engaging with literary society, but Laura Cereta's letterbook circulated among scholars in Verona and Venice as early as 1488.[45] Both Nogarola and Cereta, moreover, had personal connections to the city. Nogarola stayed in Venice with her natal family from 1438 to 1440; she also lived in the household of the patrician humanist and politician Ludovico Foscarini from 1461 to 1466. In 1484/85, Cereta married a Venetian merchant, Pietro Serina, who unfortunately died a mere eighteen months after the wedding.

Isotta Nogarola was the first of such women to make numerous contributions to the humanist conversation, and while she did so in Ciceronian Latin rather than vernacular French and in letters and dialogues rather than poetry, allegory, or biography, the context that framed her successful intervention was similar to her predecessor's in the most important respects. Much like Christine de Pizan, Nogarola was born into a family with a well-established tradition for learning, and many of her male progenitors were university trained. Unlike Christine, however, who enjoyed court sponsorship but was not an aristocrat, Nogarola belonged to a family of the hereditary nobility. Nogarola's family also boasted one previous female author of Latin moral verse, her paternal aunt, Angela. By the age of twenty, Nogarola was well regarded as an intellectual within the republic of letters. Her career, cut short by her death from an unspecified illness in 1466, would encompass all the aforementioned major genres of humanist composition.[46] After her death, biographical catalogs of famous women immortalized her name and accomplishments alongside those of her erudite female kin.

Her father having died when she was still young (between 1425 and 1433), Nogarola's mother, Bianca Borromeo, supervised the extensive classical training of her four daughters and three sons. Since Borromeo herself was unlettered, she hired a humanist, Martino Rizzoni, to tutor her daughters.[47] It is likely, however, that Bianca acted in accordance with her late husband's wishes. His sister had been the principal previous contributor to the family's intellectual honor. Moreover, even if the earlier death date for Nogarola's father (1425) is correct, Nogarola would have been seven, by which time her studies would have commenced.

Martino Rizzoni, also a native of Verona, was at an early stage in his career when he became tutor to the Nogarola daughters in 1431. He had just finished his own studies at the famous school of Guarino Guarini da Verona (1374–1460) in nearby Ferrara, and his decision to take up residence with the eminent Nogarola family represented a desirable step in his own professional development. It is likely, however, that more than considerations of convenience influenced Rizzoni's choice of "postgraduate" employment. The notable humanist and Florentine chancellor Leonardo Bruni had recently written his *De studiis et litteris* (ca. 1423–1426). Dedicated to a noblewoman, Battista Montefeltro, Bruni's treatise represents the first work by a male author to argue for the complete humanist education of women—excepting only oratory and military training. Following this important work of pedagogical theory, the successful training of Isotta Nogarola and her sister Ginevra stood to enhance their tutor's reputation: the sisters' erudite Latin letters garnered praise not only for themselves, but also for Rizzoni. Ludovico Cendrata, another student of Guarino, complimented both students and teacher, stating, "As you see, I know well with what erudition both of you have ornamented yourselves so copiously, under that most expert man, Martino, your tutor."[48]

Isotta and Ginevra Nogarola introduced themselves to the literary elite by writing first to circles of kin, family friends, and the scholarly contacts of Rizzoni, who was at that time a member of their household. As Margaret King and Diana Robin have noted, "the figures surrounding Nogarola as she and her sister first attempted to make themselves known to the male intellectuals of their era . . . were related to the young women as figures known to the Nogarola family, especially to mother Bianca, or vouched for by close friends or kin."[49] What must be stressed, however, is that these letters of introduction represent a considered strategy for maintaining feminine propriety while engaging in public conversation. By beginning their epistolary careers within networks of kin, Isotta and Ginevra remained within the context of the extended household, even as they published themselves from it.

Ermolao Barbaro (ca. 1410–1471), nephew of the famous humanist Francesco, was the Nogarola sisters' first correspondent.[50] Jacopo Lavagnola, a family friend, had provided the introduction.[51] Another of their first correspondents was Ognibene da Lonigo, a humanist teacher and a client of their mother during the 1430s. Sometime between 1433 and 1436, he wrote them a letter of commendation on their successful mastery of the liberal arts. He also sent Isotta, Ginevra, and their mother his Latin translation of John Chrysostom's *On Virginity* as a gift.[52]

The early correspondence of Isotta and Ginevra also reached Giorgio Bevilacqua (1406–ca. 1463). A member of another important family within the Veronese nobility, Bevilacqua was a student of Guarino, like Rizzoni. By 1436–1437, when Bevilacqua wrote to the Nogarola sisters, he was studying law at Padua, where he had become a friend of their brother Antonio. Bevilacqua's letters are similar to those of Ognibene da Lonigo; Bevilacqua praised their reading of Cicero, sent them a work by Lactantius as a gift, and requested that they return his copy of Livy.[53] Another letter from him (ca. 1437) indicates that the sisters' progress in their studies had become public knowledge in Bologna. He reports that Bolognese opinion, which had always respected Verona for its famous men, now regarded it even more highly for its learned women because of Isotta and Ginevra. He also sent the girls another book, this time a devotional work on the death of St. Jerome.[54] Bevilacqua chose a literary gift that praised virginity, much as Lavagnola had done. Rather than taking these gifts to mean that these men wished to contain the academic potential of their female correspondents, we should understand them to demonstrate the givers' concern with propriety. Approaching unmarried women required extreme discretion, even in these cases, in which the correspondents were friends of the family.

This early network of Latinate exchange wove itself on family patterns, interlocking circles of "kinship [and] literary friendship."[55] The domestic rhetoric that Isotta Nogarola employed in approaching male correspondents, however, highlights the strategic utility of framing literary exchange as kinship.

Around 1434, Isotta Nogarola wrote to Ermolao Barbaro as if to a father. While Barbaro was a cleric (at the age of twenty-four, he held the position of apostolic protonotary), the way in which Isotta thematizes domestic connections suggests that she meant more by the term "father" than the appropriate signifier for a clergyman. Beginning her letter with a reference to Petronius, a Roman author who mocked intellectual pride in students of little experience or talent, she states, "I fear that I might be accused of the same thing, most reverend father—who, although I have not yet achieved more than a taste of the humanities, nonetheless dare to submit my compositions (or, better put, my trifles) to be examined by specialists and do not hesitate to write even to an expert like yourself." She emphasizes the domestic framework of their potential exchange by stating that she wrote "at [his] insistence, as well as at the urging of [her] brother Antonio and our Lavagnola" and that she would "rather be thought impudent, than fail to satisfy [Barbaro's] directions and their wishes." Humility tropes abound in humanist correspondence. Nogarola typifies a common strategy of women humanists, however, in her closing: "Most excellent father, I would not want you to wait for an oration."[56] References to family members, to family friends, and to Barbaro as a "father" make a "masculine" application for academic recognition into a "feminine" response to the call of domestic duty.

Nogarola employed similar familial metaphors in approaching secular patrons as well. Between 1436 and 1437, she wrote to her uncle, Antonio Borromeo, to display her erudition and to ask him for money. Seeking to dignify this somewhat embarrassing request, she makes Antonio into another father-patron. She expresses her need for an expensive manuscript of Livy, on the grounds that this volume would be crucial to attaining the erudition attributed to the illustrious women of the classical past. "The *Decades* of Livy of Padua—charming and exquisite—are in my hands and available for purchase," she writes, "but in order to buy the manuscript I would have to rob my cashbox of 50 gold pieces; since I cannot afford that much, I run to you and, as a supplicant, beg for your help. For I know that your kindness and charity toward me is such that you will not mind granting my wish in this case—you are my father, you are my patron, in whom all my hope resides."[57]

The filial persona, useful enough in the relatively minor matter of requesting money from her uncle, became crucial in Isotta's letter of introduction to the famous pedagogue Guarino Veronese (October 1436). The stakes of this letter were enormous. Given Guarino's stature in the literary world, establishing contact with him stood to bring Isotta herself international recognition. He had been her tutor's teacher and had already lauded the accomplishments of the Nogarola sisters in a letter to one of his students, Leonello d'Este. Despite these connections, Isotta needed to satisfy the syntax of patronage, based on disparity (writing as humble petitioner to lofty patron), as well as gender conventions, which amplified this already unequal distribution of power. The "daughter to father" mode accommodated both sets of distinctions without relegating the female client to insignificance: "How much utility and honor, father Guarino, will I gain from you, the very light of virtue and goodness, when I perceive myself and my name commended by you, an esteemed man!

'I am happy to be praised by you, father, who have been praised'—a saying that I believe Cicero attributed to Hector, based upon his reading of Naevius."[58]

In closing her letter, Nogarola plays once again upon Guarino's paternal sympathies. "I commit myself," she affirms, "to your boundless dignity, wisdom and authority; so much do I honor you, father, that I esteem you even in the place of my own father and, venerable father, accept you now with my whole heart. And whatever is honorable and praiseworthy in me, I profess that it has come from you."[59] She not only repeats the term "father" three times (the highest degree of rhetorical emphasis) but even states that she gives him pride of place to her long-deceased biological father. It is telling that she does not esteem Guarino, as a potential source of encouragement, higher than her mother. Indeed, Bianca is invisible in Isotta's writings (save one reference Isotta makes to extreme grief at her mother's death in 1461), despite the fact that Bianca had paid for her daughter's education.[60] Intellectual exchange was coded masculine, so Nogarola emphasized the patriline.

Aiming to create a bond of direct intellectual kinship with Guarino, she declares that he had instilled in her "everything that is honorable or praiseworthy," that is, the *studia humanitatis*. Guarino had taught the humanities to Martino Rizzoni, who thereafter had taught them to Nogarola. In this sense, Guarino was her intellectual grandfather. She elided the generations, however, in order to establish Guarino as her own teacher-father and thereby expedite her connection with his wide circle of students and colleagues. Rather than continuing to work through her tutor, she approached the source of knowledge himself, "the very light of virtue and goodness."[61]

Nogarola's approach succeeded. Although Guarino did not respond to her first letter, he did answer an impassioned rebuke that she wrote after waiting six months for his reply. "For what reason, father Guarino, am I thus disregarded by you?" she asked. "Alas, wretched me! Whereas up to this point my mind struggled between hope and fear, now hope is lost and my mind, exhausted by worry—overcome—stands aghast. Thus, in God's name I beg you, if you deem me worthy of your largesse, to intervene in this anxiety of mine and also (if I may be candid) in the matter of my reputation; and I ask that you do not resolve to commit a crime against decency by your actions."[62] Scholars have emphasized the emotional appeal of this letter.[63] It is necessary, however, to stress that, beyond noting her fear and despair, Nogarola impugned Guarino's conduct by calling him "father," then warning him against "paternally" dishonoring her.

Guarino responded to Nogarola's subtle attack on his fatherly honor in a response that literary scholars have carefully examined for its gender assumptions. Guarino exhorted her to eliminate the elements of her personality that pertained to "feminine" emotionalism in favor of those that evinced "masculine" fortitude. Specifically, he advised her to cultivate a "manly soul" and "create a man within the woman." Drawing upon Boccaccio's *Famous Women*, moreover, he urged Nogarola to model herself upon women from antiquity who superseded the weakness attributed to their sex by performing "masculine" feats of courage and accomplishment. He had already articulated his gendered reading of the Nogarola sisters' scholarship in an earlier letter to his student Leonello d'Este, using their accomplishments to spur the young men of his acquaintance to work even harder in their own studies. Paraphrasing Cicero's words to the young men of Rome, he asked Leonello, "Are you young men behaving like women, and that woman like a man?"[64]

What has not been noted, however, is that Guarino defended himself specifically against Nogarola's accusation that he had failed as a father-figure. He exonerates himself on scholarly and especially domestic grounds, asking why (if she loves him as she claims) she did not "give him the benefit of the doubt" and interpret his silence to mean only that he is "caught up with local and foreign affairs, troubles of his own and those of others, friends and family, study and unceasing bureaucratic nonsense" and that he therefore "has no time for writing, since he is instead occupied with teaching, reading, listening to his huge family, governing so many children, raising, educating and instructing them—indeed, he has little time for rest, still less for sleep and barely any for eating."[65] Having defended himself as a good father who is merely overburdened with domestic and academic responsibility, he reassures her that he esteems her work as much as he ever did and encourages her to pursue her studies to the highest level. He also implicitly accepts the fatherly role she assigned him, as he embraces her letters "like little daughters" *(ut filiolas)*.[66]

This long and carefully crafted letter of support, as King and Robin have noted, "would have affirmed Nogarola's humanist ambitions in the eyes of the citizens of the *res publica litterarum*."[67] The widening circle of her correspondents underscores the success of this resolution with Guarino. The first move was made by Guarino's son, Geronimo. Several months after his father wrote to Isotta, Geronimo followed suit, praising both Isotta and Ginevra as models of classical expertise to which he himself felt inferior.[68] Nogarola responded within days, reassuring him that his letter attested surpassing linguistic credentials—credentials worthy, she emphasized at length, of his illustrious father.[69]

Extending her networks next to Venice in 1438, Nogarola wrote Cardinal Giuliano Cesarini (1398–ca. 1444). Cesarini was an important papal agent in combating both Hussites and Turks during the 1420s. From 1431 to 1437, he presided over the Council of Basel (1431–1449), which called for ecclesiastical reform as well as a settlement of the Hussite controversy. Lest he be branded a conciliarist and draw the ire of Pope Eugenius IV, however, Cesarini also journeyed to Ferrara in 1438 to show his obedience at the Council of Ferrara-Florence. It is likely that Nogarola met the illustrious cardinal that year as he passed through Venice, where she and her family had taken up residence.[70] She expresses her gratitude for his public praise of herself and for his having encouraged her to continue their communication, but her principal aim in this letter was to secure the Cesarini's support of her family and in particular of her younger brother: "We humbly ask that you might wish not only to maintain the solicitude, love and support that you have already shown us, but even increase them; and in the first place that, moved by fatherly feeling, you might assume responsibility for my brother Leonardo, whom all rightly deem ready to be dedicated to the divine cult [priesthood.]"[71] To make this request effective, however, she needed to legitimize her own position as her brother's promoter. In closing, therefore, she again employed filial persona: "Farewell; think of me as the daughter of your prudence and goodwill."[72]

Traces of Leonardo in the archival records suggest a quick ascent in academic and ecclesiastical circles. A private family document of 9 March 1453 calls him "lord and teacher of sacred theology, son of the other lord Leonardo de Nogarola, and procurator of Santa Cecilia in Verona."[73] Nogarola's correspondence from 1438–1441 characterized Leonardo as a young adult (probably indicating that he was no more than twenty).[74] By the time of this document, then, Leonardo would likely have been no more than thirty-five. His sister's facilitation of connections with the illustrious cardinal may have benefited him in much the same way as

Christine de Pizan was able to assist in promoting the career of her son. At the least, Nogarola's efforts did not impede her brother.

In 1439, a year after she sought Cardinal Cesarini's help with her brother, Nogarola confronted the only substantive attack on her own career as a public intellectual. An anonymous invective accused her of promiscuity (the common accusation leveled at outspoken and "public" women), as well as incest with her brother. Late twentieth-century scholarship on Nogarola made this text a central piece of evidence supporting the argument that gender prevented women from real participation in humanist scholarship, but more recent research demonstrates that the impact of this single invective has been overemphasized.[75] Her career was in no sense ruined. She wrote the *Dialogue on Adam and Eve*, arguably her most important and influential composition, in 1451.

In order to contextualize the invective itself, moreover, we must bear in mind that, in a fifteenth-century cultural market increasingly flooded with humanists, competition for celebrity and patronage was always fierce. Fame was a zero-sum game, and male intellectuals routinely attacked each other in Latin invectives.[76] The same culture of mutual vituperation obtained in the world of vernacular letters as well. Lauro Martines has shown that male poets denigrated each other in the grossest possible terms, particularly when competing for patronage. The poet Antonio di Cola Bonciani (fl. 1440–1470), for instance, lambasted his more successful rival on the Florentine poetic stage, Antonio di Guido. "O stinking toad," Bonciani wrote, "unique empire of all vices . . . the ruin and corrupter of Florence . . . You could even be a school for Semiramis, sodomizing your shitty sack—porker, dummy, evil mule, you use your mouth much as you do your ass."[77] Similarly, Luigi Pulci and Matteo Franco engaged in a piquant exchange of vitriol as they each attempted to deprive the other of the Lorenzo de' Medici's patronage. Pulci maligned Franco, who was a cleric and chaplain to Lorenzo's family, as "a low swine . . . born of a nasty sow and whore . . . bastard, mule, pervert and rabid snake."[78] Sharon Strocchia contends that the syntax of insult against women was more often sexual (for example, whore) and against men usually economic (for example, thief or cheat) but she also highlights instances that parallel Martines's findings. Men, too, were attacked in sexual terms as "cuckolds" or "buggers."[79] In this sense, the literary attack on Isotta Nogarola should be understood as one instance of a widespread practice: sexual invective constituted the preferred weapon of defamation in literary exchange. Jealous vituperation from rivals, however unpleasant, demonstrated one's entrance on the public stage no less than elegant praise from colleagues and patrons did. Controversy brought publicity, both in the initial attack and in the subsequent laudatory defenses that it evoked from supporters.

Nogarola's male friends also mitigated the effects of the invective. Niccolò Barbo, a humanist from the Venetian patriciate, dismissed the accusations out of hand, emphasizing that Nogarola was a paragon of chastity.[80] Other admirers would continue this trend by stressing her fusion of learning with saintly virtue. Among these friends, the most important was a Venetian nobleman and *podestà* of Verona, Ludovico Foscarini. He and Nogarola had become acquainted in 1451, the year of his governorship at Verona, and it is likely that her famous *Dialogue* was the written form of a staged debate between herself (playing Eve) and Foscarini (playing Adam) that occurred during one of the famous literary gatherings held at his home that year.[81] Nogarola and Foscarini corresponded thereafter, when he took up governorships elsewhere in the Veneto. Although only one of her letters to him remains, there are twenty extant letters of praise to her from Foscarini.[82] His letters suggest that he viewed her as a kind of spiritual mother—a category of female cultural influence that Gabriella Zarri has shown to be pervasive in early modern Italy.[83]

Foscarini took considerable satisfaction in his friendship with Nogarola, a paragon of learned virtue, and also in his association with her remarkable family. Proud of their "amicitia," he lauded her as a tribute to both her civic and natal family. "Your Verona," he exclaimed in a letter of 1453, "rejoices in its marble theaters, churches, mountains, rivers [and] is admired for your famous progenitors, venerated for most magnanimous fathers; the city nurtured your surpassingly wise mother and your sisters, whose incredible beauty astounds everyone, but triumphs in its most singular ornament, you, who will be recognized as incomparable in both old and new forms of virtue." In Foscarini's estimation, Isotta, of all her illustrious family, was "born to be the glory of [their] age." He believed that she would enjoy a fame at least as enduring as that of the famous poet Cornificia of ancient Rome and predicted that Nogarola's example would, in fact, surpass all others in the long history of learned and pious women. "I won't say any more at this point," he concluded, "nor will I adduce any further exempla, since you already constitute the best example for us and for all succeeding generations; nor will anyone ever wonder about all you are, who already and for a long while—without my needing to write about it, but rather for your own virtue and merits—have earned a fame beyond eternal."[84]

Extravagant praise and assurance of eternal fame appear often in humanist encomia. But Foscarini was not far from the mark. The defining characteristic of success in humanist epistolary exchange was recognition from other humanists. Nogarola exchanged letters with the most important literati of her day and received praise from them. Above all, her *Dialogue,* in which she exonerates Eve, was a thoroughly novel appropriation of the Platonic genre. Her innovative reformulation of this literary framework as a forum for questioning gender assumptions would be imitated by men and women of subsequent centuries as they defended the female sex.

Nogarola also left a substantial intellectual legacy closer to home. Four women, who either were born into or married into the Nogarola family after Isotta died, attained some reputation for learning, thereby augmenting the family's heritage of female erudition begun by Angela and expanded dramatically by Isotta and Ginevra. Laura Nogarola (mentioned in 1471) was considered a "letterata," poet, and author; Caterina Nogarola Pellegrina (mentioned in 1550) was a poet; Lucia (b. 1580) and Isotta Nogarola (later Pindemonte, b. ca. 1690) were also considered "letterate."[85]

Isotta Nogarola also survived in the naming practices of her family. She had been the first of her line with that name, and it is a testament to familial pride concerning her achievements that the male Nogarolas of the principal agnatic line commemorated her, at intervals, by reviving her name. Her brother Lodovico began the trend, calling one of his daughters Isotta and another Ginevra. Four generations later, Giulio Cesare Nogarola named his daughter Isotta, and Alvise Nogarola, Giulio Cesare's great-great-grandson, followed suit. Finally, Alessandro Nogarola, Alvise's son, named his daughter and only child Isotta Pupila.[86]

Cassandra Fedele

The "heir" of Isotta Nogarola, in terms of public acclaim for erudition, was Cassandra Fedele (1465–1558). It is best, however, to begin with one of the principal differences between the two women humanists. While

Nogarola's family was prominent in the Veronese nobility, Fedele's family belonged to the middling ranks of urban Venice. Working for patricians, rather than being themselves patrician, the male members of the Fedele family included a physician, bishop, lawyer, and banker.[87] Several scholars have speculated that Fedele's father taught her Greek and Latin and promoted her career as a public orator in the hopes of garnering greater social prestige for his family.[88] In this sense, Fedele's career suggests the speed with which arguments for and examples of the learned woman began to influence the next level down in the social order.[89]

Much like Christine de Pizan and Isotta Nogarola, however, Fedele came from a large family that included a conjugal couple and multiple siblings, both sisters and brothers. She does not refer to her mother, Barbara Leoni, in her letters, and this may imply that Barbara had died while Cassandra was still young. Cassandra had three sisters and a brother, but unlike the Nogarola family, her siblings do not appear to have engaged in any literary pursuits.

Angelo Fedele tutored his daughter in Latin and Greek, and when she turned twelve, he arranged for her to study with the Servite monk and classicist Gasparino Borro. With Borro, Fedele was able to advance in her studies of Greek, as well as philosophy, the sciences and dialectics. At sixteen, her studies completed, she returned home to begin her epistolary and oratorical career.

Writing first to a series of female patrons, Fedele utilized the sparest form of political rhetoric in approaching them. She was their "humble servant" only. This suggests that she felt a certain degree of safety when communicating with women—even powerful women sovereigns, such as the queen of Aragon. These queens and courtly patronesses, themselves learned women, responded to her in uniformly cordial ways, grateful to have received the attention of an illustrious learned woman, correspondence with whom highlighted their own importance to Renaissance culture.

The event that solidified Fedele's position in learned society, however, was the public oration that she delivered at the University of Padua in January 1487. Striking as this instance of a woman intellectual speaking in public may appear, there was at least one important precedent: Isotta Nogarola, who delivered two orations to the Veronese citizenry in 1453, which inaugurated Ermolao Barbaro's tenure as bishop of Verona.[90] Fedele's oration was commissioned by the rectors of the university for the graduation of her cousin, Bertuccio Lamberti (the canon of Concordia), on his earning honors in the liberal arts.

Fedele began by confronting the peculiarity of what she termed an "unlettered little woman" lecturing a collection of university men. She would have been afraid to speak to such an august body, she states, had not "the ties of friendship and blood" that bound her to Bertuccio necessitated the acceptance (albeit unwilling) of this burden.[91] She thus redirected her listeners' attention from the novelty of a young woman speaking in Latin to the traditional duty to love and honor kin. Lest her oration on the benefits of the liberal arts (the most fitting subject for a graduation ceremony) threaten her audience with its "masculine" rehearsal of numerous ancient authors, she closes by thanking her audience for the honor that they had conveyed on her cousin and herself by their attendance. "I wish to offer you particular thanks," she concluded, "because such a multitude of you has come here today; because you have honored Bertuccio my kinsman and me, his encomiast; and because your have exalted both of us with your most magnificent attendance. For this reason, might I promise, as if on a brother's behalf, our perpetual service to you."[92] The exordium and conclusion both emphasized the hallowed virtues of kinship and service to create a legitimate context for this unusual event.[93]

Fedele also wrote to a number of male intellectuals in the course of her career. The correspondence with some of her celebrated correspondents, for instance, the Florentine humanist Angelo Poliziano, evinces a flexible syntax of friendship. She approached other luminaries, such as Bartolomeo Scala, by employing domestic rhetoric. Her most sustained use of the father-patron/daughter-client topos, however, appears in her correspondence with male humanists unconnected to her primary patronage networks. It seems that she deemed it especially important in these instances to circumvent the potential impropriety of their interchange by making fathers of them. In May of 1487 she wrote to a certain Doctor Ambrosius Miches, apologizing for her long delay in responding to his letters. Reassuring him that her tardy reply did not signify a lack of respect, she stated that her intention was to seek his friendship because of his "maturity and the magnitude of his virtues." Friendship *(amicitia),* in the Ciceronian formulation adopted by the quattrocento humanists, connoted an equal relationship between men but also served as a code word for "patronage."[94] Either way, the terms of "friendship" required significant modification to accommodate a female participant. Fedele turned to the father-daughter theme, imploring Miches to care for her with "fatherly affection," stressing that she loved and respected him as a father, and urging him to "send instructions and assignments" to his "daughter Cassandra." She continued, "My role as daughter will be to follow your orders to the letter. It is a small wonder that you have praised me to the stars, because I know this to have been the effect of paternal responsibility. You are kindling with praise your daughter's passion for the study of literature."[95]

Diana Robin has demonstrated that Fedele often employs a rhetoric of self-deprecation, or "ef-facement," which contrasts with the contemporary male technique of prosopopoeia (mask making in the positive sense)—though Robin cautions that Fedele's humility tropes also contained a good measure of irony.[96] Yet the "dutiful daughter" image, while humble, was not self-deprecatory in either the literal or the ironic register; it was a cohesive, positive persona. The language of filial deference, sanctified on both classical and Christian grounds, satisfied the hierarchical organization of the patriarchal establishment, while at the same time invoking the reciprocal obligation inherent in the ancient concept of domestic *pietas*. The Roman historian Richard Saller, for one, defines the concept as "reciprocal affectionate duty" shared between children, who were expected to display "the virtue not of mere obedience, but of affectionate devotion," and fathers in particular, who were obligated on moral and affective grounds "to care for the interests of their children."[97]

Fedele marshaled the filial simile when correspondents failed to uphold the ideal of reciprocity by being tardy in replying to her letters. One such truant, called Cypriano, provoked an emphatic citation of his obligation to her, a dutiful daughter. "I grieve," she observed, "to have received no news from you. Can you possibly doubt that I love you? Heavens, this is odd! Am I now considered too old? Do I not view myself as a daughter and you as a father, between whom there ought to be reciprocal affection?"[98]

Similarly, after several letters to an Arnulfo Arculani failed to elicit a response, she became concerned that he might misconstrue her persistence in writing to him. She justified her tenacity on three principles: the first two were her "eternal service" to him and what she called the "bond of our friendship." The final reason for her writing was daughterly affection. "For since you are a virtuous and knowledgeable man," she insisted, "I honor you in every way and love you as a father."[99]

Fedele also approached Bartolomeo Scala within the father-patron/daughter-client paradigm. One of the most illustrious humanists of the day and also the chancellor of Florence, Scala was among her most prestigious correspondents. Her letterbook reveals a rich exchange in 1492 with both Bartolomeo and his daughter, Alessandra—another young woman who had recently begun to attract attention throughout Italy for her classical learning. Fedele's introductory letter to Bartolomeo congratulates him on Alessandra's progress in the humanities; the second letter, to Alessandra herself, replies to a question that the young woman had posed in her own introductory letter to Fedele: whether it was better for a woman to devote herself to study or to marry. Fedele's reply equivocates, counseling that Alessandra should direct herself "toward that which nature most compels [her], for Plato affirms that every decision is made with a view toward the ease of the one who must decide."[100] Bartolomeo, however, she commends without qualification for dedicating his virtuous daughter to literary studies and for the eternal fame that he will accrue from her accomplishments.[101]

Bartolomeo did serve as Alessandra's promoter, which suggests that he agreed with Fedele that his daughter's intellectual honor supplemented his own. Another of Fedele's letters to him affirms that she heard news about Alessandra's academic success from Bartolomeo's own letters as well as in conversation with his close friends. She was pleased to learn how much he rejoiced in his daughter's accomplishments and emphasized her own participation in celebrating the triumphs of "our Alessandra." Ingratiating herself further with the illustrious man of letters, Fedele follows her comments in support of his biological daughter by presenting herself as his discursive daughter. "I share your joy," she proceeds, "on account of my boundless affection for you. And my love for you is all the greater, since I myself have been magnified by your praise and, greater still, because I know that I am valued by your family and friends. And so I want you to know that I will never stop loving you like a father."[102]

Fedele's domestic rhetoric incorporated her into Bartolomeo Scala's intellectual family. A letter that she wrote to their mutual friend, the renowned humanist Angelo Poliziano (ca. 1493–1494), thanks him for his praise and requests that he send her regards and those of her whole family "to Marsilio Ficino and Bartolomeo Scala, as most learned civic fathers, and to [her] most distinguished sister, Alessandra."[103] That she calls Alessandra "sister" when writing to a third party attests the degree to which she could rely upon her own status as Bartolomeo's literary daughter.

Around this time (1493), a Modenese humanist and poet, Panfilo Sasso (pseudonym for Sasso da Sassi, ca. 1450–1527), wrote to Fedele within the framework of the father-patron/daughter-client relationship.[104] This rhetorical decision indicates his desire to avoid suspicion concerning his intentions, as well as his concern for her reputation. He was an unmarried and childless man and she, by this point, was twenty-eight years old—well past the customary age of marriage. The quattrocento had no obvious category for a mature woman who was not a wife, a widow, or a nun. The daughter persona constituted a linguistic category helpful at various stages in a woman intellectual's career. When women could not invoke motherhood or widowhood as supplementary personae, the daughter image became even more important—albeit, with advancing age, more incongruous. Hence, Panfilo tested two modes of addressing the woman he wished to praise, calling her a "mother to be honored for her erudition and wisdom" as well as a "most cherished daughter." Also with a view toward propriety, he made a swift transition from emotional to political declarations: "Such is my love for you—or, rather, loyalty—that although the whole world is full of your name, nonetheless among all the learned men I know, I am the greatest and most ardent of your devotees."[105]

Panfilo opted, in the end, for the safest ground: the father-daughter relationship. He enclosed some epigrams written in Fedele's honor by (he said) another man, who had been so inspired by Panfilo's praise of her that he appointed himself as Fedele's "adoptive father." The "other admirer" was Panfilo himself. His abrogation of responsibility for the poems exemplifies another common humanist practice: making one's authorship clear but not explicit. He went on to state that, in lieu of producing brilliant children of his own, he had "adopted" Fedele: "Behold, Cassandra, what glory I will pursue among mortals before I die, since indeed the stars smile so kindly upon me that, while I would have been happier in producing natural children of genius, yet still I derive satisfaction from the voluntary adoption (or appropriation) of other parents' children, as you and Pamphilius—terrestrial stars—are connected."[106]

Panfilo's awkward shifts between the first and third person suggest the difficulty that he experienced in finding a legitimate framework within which he and Fedele might become friends and correspondents. That he ultimately chose the father-daughter model suggests that the familial paradigm was the best means of classifying a new kind of relationship: intellectual exchange between an older man and younger woman.

Fedele remained a daughter in discourse but not in life. In 1499 she married a physician from Vicenza, Gian-Maria Mappelli. She was thirty-four at the time, and it has been suggested that this marriage took place because her career had stalled once she was no longer appealing to Venice as a "child prodigy."[107] No work exists from her twenty married years (Mappelli died in 1520), and she does not seem to have had any children.[108] Yet the decision to marry may also suggest an attempt to shift into another legitimizing framework.

Fedele married within the sector of society that one might term the "lettered" elite, but she retained her patronymic. Sixteenth-century biographers did not realize that she had ever married, and perpetuated the error that she remained a virgin orator.[109] As we will see in subsequent chapters, Italian women intellectuals (especially those who made a point of their classical training) kept their maiden names. This presents a sharp contrast to English women humanists, who were recognized as both their father's daughters and their husband's wives. Within the Italian context, the daughter-orator role was what first attracted notice. Once married, women may also have wished to differentiate their "professional" selves from their "private" selves.

At all events, Fedele seldom made a public point of her marriage or widowhood. One instance in which widowhood did become important was in her epistle to Pope Leo X, dated April 1521, in which she appealed for financial assistance. She sought aid for the relations that depended upon her—by the time of her husband's death, her father, her brother, and one of her sisters had also died.[110] Fedele had corresponded with him before his election to the papacy, and she reminded him that he had once honored her by acting upon her request that he perform a favor for one of her Florentine friends. Having invoked their prior correspondence, as well as her past friendship with his father, Lorenzo il Magnifico, she presented her plea "to Your Sanctity on behalf of one who is neither a relative nor member of your household, but only I myself."[111] She recommended herself as a virtuous widow, eulogizing her husband as "dearer to me than life itself . . . for he excelled to such an extent in good conduct, religion and learning that, deprived of such a husband, I believe that there is no life left for me."[112]

It would in the event be her petition to Pope Paul III of 1547 that garnered her a position as prioress of the orphanage near the church of San Domenico.[113] This last stage of her life was spent in considerable financial difficulty, but she did receive one last invitation by the Venetian senate to give a Latin oration to the visiting queen of Poland. No longer a child prodigy but a nonagenarian, Fedele proved that she still had cultural cachet, at least when the issue was impressing a woman sovereign.

Fedele's will evinces the same pattern of distributing possessions broadly among male and female friends and kin that historians have found common in the testaments of early modern Venetian women.[114] Among her closest friends, to judge by their importance in this document, were Benedetto Baldigara and his wife, Antonia. Baldigara was the notary to whom she dictated her will, but Fedele also made him her principal executor and universal heir. In her words, Baldigara was both her "lawyer" *(avocato)* and "nephew/grandson" *(nepote).* She bequeathed some of her furniture to a cherished female servant, and a small sum of money to five friars of San Domenico, whom she asked to offer expiatory masses for herself and her husband. The residue of her estate, however, she left "to Antonia, wife of the aforementioned Bene[de]tto, whom I make my universal heir."[115] The last specification was the transmission of her literary legacy, which also went to Benedetto's family. She bequeathed to his children "[my] books that [are] here in the priory."[116]

Her will highlights several points of pride and satisfaction, however modest its bequests. As is customary in women's testaments, she situates herself at the outset in relation to her male kin. In her case, she is the daughter of "doctor" Angelo Fedele and widow of Gian-Maria Mappelli, physician; but she also specified her own profession as prioress. Eager to underscore her classical training one last time, she appended a brief affirmation in her own hand, stating that she had read the document and confirmed that Baldigara had recorded her intentions accurately. Even women known to be literate seldom bother to sign their wills, let alone do so by means of appended Latin prose.[117]

Above all, Fedele's testament reveals that she had formed enduring connections within the sector of society characterized by its education: physicians, notaries, and lawyers. One of these, Baldigara, she also represented as extended family. The term *nipote* literally means "nephew" or "niece," "grandson" or "granddaughter," and, more broadly, "descendant." In Fedele's era, however, it was also used to describe relationships that were genetically attenuated but emotionally important—similar to the term "cousin" in early modern English. By the time of her death, she had lost much of her biological intellectual family, but she seems to have created another by choice with Baldigara, his wife, and his children.

Laura Cereta

Like Cassandra Fedele, Laura Cereta (1469–1499) was notable for her collection of Latin letters and orations. Also like Fedele, Cereta was born into a large family of citizen rank within the Venetian territories. She was the eldest of six children (three sons, two other daughters) born to Veronica de Leno and Silvestro Cereto, an attorney and a magistrate in the small urban center of Brescia. Unlike Fedele, however, Cereta married in her midteens (1484/85). Rather than coinciding with (or provoking) a hiatus in intellectual production, moreover, all of Cereta's compositions postdate her wedding. She also thematized her role as wife in her Latin letters to her husband, Pietro Serina (a Venetian merchant) and, after his death less than two years later from a variety of plague, as a widow in references to him throughout her letterbook. Cassandra Fedele and Laura Cereta present analogous cases of recognized women humanists from intellectual families within the Venetian citizenry, but their domestic academies functioned in different ways.

Whereas Angelo Fedele acted as his daughter's first and most important instructor, the pedagogical role of Silvestro Cereto is difficult to assess. Albert Rabil contends that Cereto taught his daughter Latin and Greek and supervised her advanced study of astrology and moral philosophy.[118] Diana Robin, however, minimizes Cereto's educative influence, pointing out that Cereta herself credits a learned nun with teaching her reading, writing, sewing, and basic Latin grammar.[119] Robin also notes that Cereta's single surviving letter to her father makes no reference to his role in her education.[120] However, Cereta does suggest that her father was the active agent in sending her to the convent to be educated.[121] And her fluency with legal terminology, which she used to great rhetorical effect and also applied in its legal sense in her letters to

Silvestro's lawyer-friends—strongly suggests that he had assisted in her study of law.[122]

Cereta's father was unquestionably her first promoter. He fostered her career among the literati of Brescia and sent a copy of her letterbook to a humanist clergyman, Tomaso of Milan.[123] Cereta foregrounds his role as her supporter in asking him to stand as "judge" of her excellence in a letter-writing contest between herself and certain male critics. "You yourself have seen most of the compositions that they have sent," she writes. "Consider, in your capacity as judge, this epistle that took them two days, which you might compare to the one I wrote in the space of an hour as an answer to their boasting."[124]

While Cereta appeals to her father as a mediator in this case, elsewhere she emphasizes her role as his collaborator and surrogate.[125] During the War of Ferrara (1482–1484), she lived with him on Lake Iseo, where he was in charge of helping with fortifications. Later, when he was forced to retire from his magistracy, she acted as his amanuensis, interceding for him with his estranged friends and clients.[126] During this period, she also played "father" herself, sending letters of advice to her two younger brothers and enlisting the prominent humanist Giovanni Olivieri to instruct them.[127]

In fact, domestic themes pervade Cereta's letterbook. Unlike most other humanists, she took the notion of "familiar letters" literally. In addition to the requisite set pieces that display classical scholarship, her epistles contain numerous letters to male and female family members, an unprecedented number of letters to women who were not courtly patronesses, and frank discussions of domestic matters, discussions that are unique in humanist correspondence.[128] Taken as a whole, the letters to her father, mother, brothers, sisters, and husband constitute a sustained publicity campaign for her intellectual family, natal and marital.[129]

From a thematic standpoint, Cereta expressed an ambivalence concerning "mother" similar to that of Christine de Pizan. As Robin has pointed out, there is only one letter addressed to Cereta's mother, and its imagery creates a dynamic of tension—an uncomfortable dialectic between "writing and wounding."[130] In her long autobiographical letter to a female friend and nun, Nazaria Olympica, Cereta represents her mother's presence as an emotional shadow. Describing an incident that followed her father's having called her home from the convent, Cereta relates,

"The moment I crossed the paternal threshold, mother captured me in tight embraces and . . . followed me wherever I went, as if she did not know how to satisfy her joy at my return."[131] Cereta contrasts her mother's well-meaning but restrictive presence with her father's prudent decisiveness: "Father, however, as the active governor of the family and, most importantly, a man of discretion, . . . soon returned me to my female tutor in the liberal arts."[132] To be sure, no humanists put pen to parchment without considering the impression that their words would create. These letters do not, therefore, present unproblematic documentation of her "real" relationships with her parents. What they reveal is a representational strategy very much like the one employed by Christine: "mother" epitomizes traditional femininity; "father" encourages new kinds of female accomplishment.

Cereta's letters also underscore her status as a wife and then a grieving widow. This material hearkens back to Christine's reflections on the loss of her husband and the trials of widowhood. Cereta's letters to her husband suggest that she did not find marriage the blissful experience that Christine described, but Cereta nonetheless devotes much ink to articulating her grief after his sudden death. The cultural capital that Cereta hoped to gain from her widowhood is nowhere better reflected than in her introductory letter to Cassandra Fedele. Deploying an elaborate Virgilian descent into the underworld as a metaphor for her sense of loss, Cereta models herself as the heroic widow.[133]

Part of what makes Cereta's voice so distinctive is her tendency to disregard the modesty topoi favored by other women humanists. On one important occasion, however, even she solicited a male patron by making a discursive father of him. Two letters to Cardinal Ascanio Maria Sforza serve as prologue and epilogue to her letterbook. In both, she represents herself in the usual fashion of the patronage seeker, as a writer of small talent, hoping to find in her glorious patron a champion for her compositions. Cereta did not ordinarily resort to the "father-patron" image favored by Nogarola and Fedele. She adduces it, however, at this pivotal moment (1488), when she is "packaging" her collected works: "I, a suppliant, beg your majesty that you might accept my writings as in every way your 'wards.' For I, to the extent that humble rank allows me, commit myself to your favor—you, my father, my judge and my lord."[134]

Later in this same year, Silvestro Cereto died. Scholars have suggested that his death coincided with Cereta's decision to abandon humanistic endeavor in favor of a quasi-cloistered existence.[135] We should be wary, however, of drawing too many conclusions about Cereta's possible change in attitude toward her career, as she herself died very prematurely, at the age of thirty. Silvestro's support, however, had encouraged her to produce an extensive collection of letters. Under his auspices, she was a participant in the literary culture surrounding her. It should not be forgotten, moreover, that during her lifetime the finished manuscript of her familiar letters circulated among prominent scholars in Brescia, Verona, and Venice and that Cereta's death was mourned by the entirety of her native city.[136]

Women and Humanism

Scholars have often considered the quattrocento women humanists as oddities, momentary transgressors in the male domain of scholarship.[137] Whereas the educated man won governmental and ecclesiastical posts, the educated woman had no purpose beyond a possible ornamental value and an enhanced facility with standing in at moments of crisis for, or in the absence of, the patriarch.[138] As a slight modification of this thesis, it has been suggested that the full mastery of Latin and Greek so prized by humanist theorists actually had no practical value for men, either. With even more doubt about the value of education, we ask, why did Renaissance people teach women Latin?

The theoretical justification with which we began was the humanist notion that direct access to the wisdom of the ancients made anyone wiser and therefore better. Women's humanity was only a subject of real debate among a few scholastic philosophers and polemicists more interested in their ability to prove the seemingly absurd than in making doctrine of the exercise. Women, as humans, would potentially benefit from the *studia humanitatis*, the study of humanity.

Proponents of the *studia humanitatis* also emphasized the ennobling effects of their curriculum. Taking "ennoblement" a step further toward the literal, Pier-Paolo Vergerio construed education as patrimony. In one of the foundational texts of humanist pedagogical theory, *On Noble Customs and Liberal Studies* (ca. 1402), Vergerio praised education as the most lasting gift a father could give his son.[139] The fathers of the quattrocento women intellectuals added daughters to the equation. Tomas de Pizan, Leonardo Nogarola, and Silvestro Cereto all came from families with established intellectual reputations. Contemporaries were not terribly impressed with Angelo Fedele's skills as a humanist, but he certainly knew Latin and aspired to humanist status. For these fathers, as men of learning themselves, advanced instruction was indeed a form of patrimony, an important aspect of their family honor.

But we must also consider the cultural capital that contemporaries attached to the female prodigy. Although the fathers and father figures we have discussed so far could not have known that the fame of their daughters and protégées would endure for centuries, they could nonetheless be reasonably certain that, as Christine de Pizan suggested, a learned woman would attract the attention of contemporaries as "something unseen for quite some time."

Much as Christine situated herself in the tradition of Hortensia, so later biographers viewed subsequent learned women as perpetuations of their fathers' and their family's intellectual honor. In the biographical compendia of the sixteenth century, having a learned daughter—a Hortensia or a Tullia—made the father, by extension, Hortensius or Cicero. This reciprocity of reputation benefited both parties: father and family legitimized the daughter, but for his and their pains, the family could boast of having produced a classicized artifact. Better still, these modern Hortensias and Tullias were even more worthy of admiration than their pagan predecessors, because these modern intellectuals were Christian.

The contribution of quattrocento women humanists and the men who supported them was to create a secular context within which female learnedness flourished. The following chapter examines the appeal of the household academy as a concept for two sixteenth-century humanists, Pietro Bembo and Sir Thomas More, and then charts the emergence of other learned English women who contributed to the culture of "lettered piety" that obtained north of the Alps.

2

Household Academies in Venice and London

IN 1581 Richard Mulcaster, a pedagogical theorist and the first master of the Merchant Taylors' School, exhorted his countrymen to take note of the many learned women in England: "[They are] so excellently well trained, and so rarely qualified, either for the tongues themselves or for the matter in the tongues, as they may be opposed by way of comparison, if not preferred as beyond comparison, even to the best Roman or Greekish paragons, be they never so much praised; to the German or French gentlewomen, by late writers so well liked; to the Italian ladies who dare write themselves, and deserve fame for so doing."[1] By the end of the sixteenth century, there was indeed a substantive heritage of female humanism in England, comparable to that which had taken root in Italy in the fifteenth century. During the sixteenth century, the household academy became a northern phenomenon.

Like their Italian predecessors, English women humanists thrived within household academies headed by learned fathers. Sir Thomas More, Sir Anthony Cooke (tutor to Edward VI), and Henry Fitzalan (Earl of Arundel) all saw to the instruction of their sons and their daughters in the classical languages. Contemporaries understood these women as legitimate intellectuals by virtue of their status as members of household academies. Nicholas Harpsfield, a Catholic zealot, felt certain that anyone who had seen the domestic "school" of Thomas More "would have taken great spiritual and ghostly pleasure [in it] and would have thought himself to have . . . been in Plato's Academy—nay, what say I, Plato's? Not in Plato's, but in some Christian well-ordered academy and university."[2] Walter Haddon, a friend of the Cooke family, praised this household in similar terms as an academy in which women played active intellectal roles.[3] The domestic framework for women's advanced instruction worked as well in the English as in the Italian context. Highly adaptable, it also cut across sectarian boundaries within England.

Predictably, there are differences between household academies in Italy and England, and within England. The first concerns the slightly different definitions of "learned virtue," a humanist fusion of erudition and morality. I examine the nuances of this concept through comparison of two humanists' approaches to female education: the approach of the Venetian Pietro Bembo and that of the English Thomas More. Whereas Bembo's letters concerning the education of his son and daughter stress that Latin learning will bring them reputations for "nobility" (that is, social prestige), those of More present classical training as preparation for scriptural understanding. Italian humanists allowed the definition of "virtue" to waver between classical fortitude and Christian morality; English "Christian" humanists highlighted the moral component. A second difference is that the English household academies were more enduring than the Italian versions insofar as the English female graduates all married and most had children.

While these distinctions are important, what is ultimately the most interesting about humanist intellectual families is their pronounced similarity in diverse contexts. The female humanists of Italy and England who emerged from these contexts are best understood not as exceptions to the "rule" of women's expressive constraint but as success stories. Scholars have long categorized women intellectuals as unique cases and in particular as uncommonly fortunate women in being born to learned fathers who supported their daughters' studies. I challenge this dictum by comparing learned women to each other rather than to all other categories of women. Early modern women should be studied as men are, according to their particular modes of activity and contribution and not as an undifferentiated collectivity. Among what might be termed the "learned" category of men and women, it was more the rule than the exception to find household academies in which the "studies of women" flourished.

Pietro Bembo and Helena Bemba

The Venetian humanist Pietro Bembo (1470–1547) and his longtime mistress, Faustina Morosina della Torre, had two surviving children, both born in Padua after ecclesiastical ambition prompted Bembo to take a vow of celibacy (1522). Bembo was at some pains to place his daughter and son well, as they did not begin life in an optimal position. Letters and virtue, his own obsessions, were the answer from his perspective. Bembo therefore saw to it that both Torquato (b. ca. 1524) and Helena (b. ca 1528) enjoyed a thorough education in Latin. Because he moved from his Paduan household to Rome after 1539, when he was ordained a priest and made a cardinal by Pope Paul III, he oversaw their educational program through his correspondence with them, as well as with their guardians and tutors.[4]

The earliest information about their schooling, however, appears in an autograph testament that Bembo wrote in 1535, the year in which "la Morosina" died. As Bembo was already traveling a good deal, he designated two of his most trusted associates as governors for Helena and Torquato: "I leave as my commissaries, as well as tutors and guardians of my children," he noted, "the reverend Monsignor Gabriele Boldù, canon of Padua, and my particular friend Cola Bruno." He requested that Bruno "not leave [Bembo's] house, but remain there with [the Bembo] children for the rest of his days, just as he [had] already been there for the greater part of his life."[5] Bruno appears to have fulfilled this request, as one of Bembo's letters (1541) to him in Padua responds to information about Helena's progress in the humanities: "Concerning Helena, who is learning grammar, and who writes Latin well, I'm hugely pleased."[6] Part of Helena's education, like that of Laura Cereta's, took place at a local convent. This seems to have been the equivalent of "finishing" school, as mention of her convent education appears in a letter from Bembo to her in December of 1542, the year before she married Piero Gradenigo and moved to Venice. Bembo encourages her to attend to her studies: "Pay attention to learning letters, and don't waste this time that you have. Rather, when you leave the convent, which I hope you will soon have to do, you will want to know that you have made the most of this opportunity."[7]

Bembo also assisted in the education of Helena, urging her to perfect her epistolary skills by writing to him. "I have seen your last letter," he notes, "which your tutor tells me you wrote without his help. This, if it is true, pleases me; and you would please me further by doing likewise once a week." He also encouraged her to keep in practice by writing to her brother "as often as [she] like[d]." He adds, "Don't stop writing on account of having no replies from him, because you never will! Send your letters to Monseigneur Boldù, who will send them on to Torquato via Girolamo Querini in Venice."[8] Bembo did not mean that Torquato disliked his sister but rather that his son was lazy.

From 1540 onward, Bembo's familiar letters include increasingly pressing exhortations to Torquato that he attend more seriously to his studies. Torquato bore the full weight of paternal expectation: he was clearly meant to carry on the family business of humanism. As a teenage boy, however, Torquato's interests inclined more toward sexual escapades than exercises in Latin grammar. In one letter, Bembo begins with a reasonably mild tone: "Leaving aside the issue of your good conduct, since I see no need to address that in this letter, what I have to say is this: if you would adjust your attitude toward making profit in your studies, you would succeed quickly, because you have a good mind and ready intellect—but you won't apply yourself." Warming to his subject, Bembo becomes increasingly aggravated. "I don't know what you're thinking," he scolds. "Don't you see, you blockhead, how much good press men get from their knowledge of letters and mastery of the noble arts? And how they . . . are loved and honored and rewarded by other proficients? And how an ignoramus gets no reward, no honor, no love? . . . Wake up! Wake up!" Mastering letters will not only make Torquato "dear to every king and lord" but will be the only means of winning his father's love: "Don't do what I hate the most, that is, be lazy and slow, or else I'll be slow and lazy in loving you, too, as I've said before."[9]

A few months later, in an altogether different mood, Bembo wrote to his longtime friend and secretary, Cola Bruno, of the pleasure that Bembo derived from seeing the progress that the then thirteen-year-old Helena was making in her studies. He was unquestionably fond of his daughter, but her success in his household academy also served as a goad for his son, "the blockhead" *(sciocco)*. "Concerning Helena," he wrote, "who is learning grammar and writes well in Latin, I'm hugely pleased— and all the more so because her success humiliates that good-for-nothing, Torquato, who should go hide himself."[10]

The issue of Helena's learning, however, for all Bembo's pride, is not raised during his subsequent, unsuccessful attempt to arrange a marriage for her with the Querinis—an influential patrician family in Venice. Isabella Querini and her brother, Girolamo, were among Bembo's closest friends and served as marriage brokers on his behalf. One reason that they were so close is that Bembo had been corresponding with Isabella since at least 1537, when a poetic exchange transpired between them: if two lines of his poetry had rid her of her "fever," Bembo explained, then she was obliged to send him two lines of her poetry so that he, too, might become well.[11] As time wore on, their intellectual friendship deepened. In a letter of 1544, Bembo describes a discussion that Isabella initiated on the subject of whether he should translate his history of Venice from Latin to Italian when he sent it to press. Bembo thanks her, on the one hand, for apprising him of the fact that printing his works in the vernacular would draw in a wider public than Latin could elicit and, on the other hand, for warning him against the infelicities that sloppy translators might introduce and encouraging him to do the translation himself. This is absolutely disingenuous—Bembo had himself been a longtime and ardent champion of the vernacular as a medium for learned composition and a vocal critic of careless translators and printers.[12] Nonetheless, it is proof of his respect for Isabella Querini's erudition that he represents his own cherished arguments as originating from his female colleague.[13]

Thereafter Bembo thanks Querini "for having thought in all this about my greater use and profit, which I myself had not considered—I mean that it had not ever occurred to me that my history should be written in Italian. And now I'm certain that it should be, as you say." He complains of being so occupied with his duties as cardinal and as bishop that he cannot do the translation. "But nonetheless," he continues, "this is not to dismiss your advice. I'm thinking of finding some one of my friends who is up to the task and asking him to do this work in my stead. In this way, I can satisfy both your suggestion and my own need." He treats her as a colleague in taking her advice seriously. He even adds an additional compliment in closing: "Stay well, and continue to delight your friends with your fertile and rare genius." In her capacity as his interlocutor on such weighty matters, moreover, Querini was rhetorically incorporated into Bembo's intellectual family; he loved and honored her specifically "as a sister."[14]

In June of 1542, Isabella Querini and her brother Girolamo began playing as marriage brokers for Helena Bemba. They had suggested Francesco Querini as a good match, an idea to which Bembo responded, "Just as I have never in my life had dearer friends than you two, so I want you to take fully into your charge the dearest thing that I have in this world, which is this little daughter. And don't get the idea that Torquato [that is, his social position] is more on my mind in this matter than she is, since from him I frequently have news that offends me, whereas from Helena I have never had anything other than pleasure and satisfaction and contentment."[15]

Bembo learned soon after that Francesco Querini's father was demanding a ten thousand-ducat dowry in cash. Although a wealthy patrician man, Bembo did not possess that sum at the ready. The way in which he debates disinheriting Torquato to see the match through highlights again Helena's status as first in his affection, if not in his will. "Loving that little daughter as much as I love her," he explains to one of his secretaries, "I would be more than willing to give her two thousand or three thousand ducats more than the asking price. But I can't do more: I don't have cash, as you well know." He thinks it unfortunate that the family is so shortsighted, because if Torquato were to die, Helena would inherit everything: "The house in Padua and my study, with everything that's in it, and all that I have here. And that in itself would be a fine dowry indeed." He adds that he has considered giving everything to Helena anyway, if Torquato fails to give his father the "one pleasure" desired above all. Bembo specifies, "I mean that he make himself learned, to which he seems to me to be very little inclined—then I won't give him a cent more than the benefices I've already given him and I will bequeath everything to my Helena, who pleases me more, in what she can do, than Torquato."[16]

Bembo ultimately decided to seek out a more feasible match. While Helena's facility in Latin does not seem to have been a key factor in the marriage negotiations, Bembo did marry her into a patrician family that was well connected within the literary elite. His correspondence with Helena continued past her marriage, and he wrote often to her husband, the poet Piero Gradenigo, whom he addressed as "my dearest son" *(fili carissime)* and whom he claimed to love "as a father" *(quanto padre).*[17] While Bembo was both a cardinal and Piero's father-in-law, his use of the modifier "quanto" implies that he meant the term in the rhetorical sense so often employed by women humanists of the previous generations and their male correspondents: he intended to emphasize not merely family connection but a bond of literary kinship.

Piero Gradenigo, a writer himself, made a point to inquire about his father-in-law's feelings concerning the recent and unauthorized publication of Bembo's *Rime,* to which Bembo responded, "As regards my poems, published by those printers without my authorization and unedited, there's nothing to be done but to be patient, though it vexes me exceedingly to do so." Piero had also communicated that he had seen an authorized version of the *Rime*, which Piero had himself given to Girolamo Querini to send to Bembo. Bembo expressed keen interest in seeing the new edition of his poems, which Piero said that he had given to Messer Girolamo to send to Bembo, which he had not yet received.[18] In this same letter, Bembo asks Piero to pass along his best regards to two other men of the literary elite, Federico Badoer and Domenico Venier.[19] Although Helena does not seem to have left any compositions herself, this letter attests that she married a man well connected within the "learned" ranks of society. Domenico Venier served as patron to the prominent literati of the day, and among his circle were several women authors— perhaps most notably the courtesan poet Veronica Franco.

Torquato's status as his father's intellectual heir was provisional. He never became a humanist celebrity, but he was the dedicatee of two collections of music published around 1550.[20] These dedications suggest that Torquato enjoyed at least some reputation as a man of culture. Nor did Bembo disinherit him: Torquato remained the principal beneficiary.[21] Torquato's own will (in Latin and Italian, 1570) shows that he had entered the Church. He was at this point the prior of St. Michael's in Brescia. Torquato's heir was probably an illegitimate son, if indeed the "Pietro Bembo" Torquato names as his sole heir was blood kin at all. "My constant and firm opinion," he avers, "is that this Pietro Bembo is my legitimate son, whether he is my son or not, whether the legitimation is good or not, and so he should be 'patron' of all my goods and powers."[22] Both Torquato and his father, then, seem to have been equally unimpressed with canon-law marriage as a venue for producing heirs.

Bembo's letters to his children illustrate that this humanist father invested a great deal of his intellectual honor in their education. It went without question that Torquato must carry on the family business of erudition. Although Bembo did not in fact disinherit Torquato for poor progress in Latin, the father often threatened his son with penury as a form of pedagogical motivation. "You're eighteen now," Bembo wrote in one instance,

> and not only are you still unable to write even one Latin epistle, you can't even write a decent letter in the vernacular. So I remain most displeased with you. If within two years you don't make fine and honorable progress and profit in letters, be certain that you will have no part in my

patrimony—not the house in Padua, nor my study, nor anything that's in the study or in the house, nor anything that I have here, which amounts to a few thousand ducats, and in sum neither a ladle nor a pot. And if I will have lost Helena, and my nephews, the sons of Messer Giovan Matteo Bembo, and the sons of Messer Bernardin Belegno, then I will leave everything I own to some one or other of my friends or servants, who loves and obeys me, rather than to you, who do not obey me and therefore do not love me.[23]

For good measure, he signed this scorching letter "from Rome: Cardinal Bembo, in my own hand and hopping mad," adding as a postscript a final piece of advice: "I remind you again to be careful about getting mixed up with the 'ladies,' who grant their favors easily for money, as I understand that you've begun to do. Besides, all too soon you could get the French disease, which will make your life either short, or forever tormented."[24]

Conversely, Bembo expressed his pleasure in Helena's academic progress. His satisfaction with her literary studies became a matter of public record in the 1560s, when the Venetian editor Francesco Sansovino published Bembo's correspondence. The letters to Helena appear in the fourth volume, "Letters Written by M. Pietro Bembo to Princesses, Court Ladies and other Gentlewomen," alongside those of illustrious learned women, including Brescian-born poet Veronica Gambara (renowned throughout Italy for her erudite compositions) and the famously learned and politically powerful Gonzaga women, Lucrezia Borgia and Vittoria Colonna. Helena was neither a noteworthy author nor powerful patron, but she fits thematically into the collection insofar as Bembo's letters concern her education. These letters also put into sharp relief Bembo's definition of "learned virtue." In the earliest of these (1539), Bembo employs the stern tone that he used more commonly with Torquato. Disturbed by her tutor's report that Helena was inattentive, he wrote:

I have seen most willingly your last letter, in which you write me that you are diligently attending to your literary studies; but if I wanted to know how your work is progressing, I would hear about it from your tutor. In fact, he writes me that you aren't learning anything. Take stock of yourself. Study harder and become as learned as possible, because this is the best way for you to beautify yourself. Concerning your sewing, I'm pleased, but not surprised, since you are in the care of Madonna Laura, who is the most capable mistress of that art in this city, or any other. Above all, I'm pleased that you have learned to say the office and that you're being a good nun, because this could serve you well at such time as you might become abbess . . . Take care that you continue to develop good and holy habits.[25]

Despite his suggestion that Helena might later put her education to good use as a nun, he never encouraged her to choose the cloistered life. On the contrary, while his testament allows for her potential choice to enter a convent, the financial bequest is weighted in favor of her marrying: "I will that to Helena my daughter 5000 gold ducats be given at the time of her marriage. If she does not wish to marry, but rather chooses to become a nun, a thing that I do not advise her to do, I wish that she be given 500 ducats to allow her to take the veil more appropriately."[26] Illegitimate daughters were often packed into the cloister, but Bembo preferred that Helena marry within the upper ranks of Venetian society. This letter exhorts her to "beautify" herself by becoming learned, which suggests that he viewed education as the means to bring her the requisite social cachet to make such a match. Much as he hoped that Torquato would curry political favor for mastery of the "noble arts," Bembo staked his hopes for Helena's social mobility on her progress in humanistic study. Learned virtue was the key to advancement for both illegitimate children.

The next year (1540) Bembo underscored this theme in a letter written to Cola Bruno, in which he urged his factotum to ensure that Helena devoted her time to mastering serious letters rather than the fashionable study of music. She had written requesting her father's permission to begin learning to play the clavichord. Bembo was adamant, however, that she not distract herself with music, which, in his view, suggested a lack of gravity. "Tell her for me," he urged, "that I do not deem it fitting for an honorable woman with intellectual gifts to want to learn how to play. No, I don't by any means like the idea that she should waste time in this sort of thing, just as I have never liked the fact that Antonia, my sister, plays." Aside from demonstrating Bembo's intellectual snobbery, this injunction reflected his fear that attaining proficiency in music would necessitate abandoning all the other and "more laudable studies." He believed that Helena would be better served by devoting herself to letters:

"She will receive much more praise and satisfaction in literary learning than she would do in playing." To this end, he redoubled his order to Bruno that he be "diligent in seeking out some good and modest tutor for Torquato and for Helena."[27] In a letter written soon afterward, Bembo told Bruno to be patient in his search for a tutor for Torquato and congratulated him on finding a worthy teacher for Helena. "Concerning the teacher you haven't been able to find for Torquato," Bembo wrote, "have patience. The goodness and diligence of M. Antonio Fiordibello will be enough for the time being, with your supervision. Concerning the one that you have found for Helena, I'm most pleased."[28]

In a letter of 1541 to Helena, Bembo reinforced her need to focus upon reading and sewing rather than music. "As to the permission that you have requested from me," he stated, "that I should be willing for you to learn to play the monochord, I apprise you of something that, by virtue of your extreme youth you could not know: that playing music is a thing for empty-headed women. And I want you to be the most grave, chaste and modest woman that lives . . . Content yourself with learning letters and sewing, exercises which, if you do them well, will be no small achievement."[29] Bembo's almost obsessive concern regarding Helena's need to make herself appear grave and chaste reflects his desire to bring her social credibility. Another letter in this collection (10 June 1542) demonstrates similar preoccupations. Written to Helena the year before her marriage, while she was staying at a convent in Padua, Bembo urged her to keep out of public view—counseling her against even a seemingly innocuous trip home to his villa. His reason was that his secretary, Bruno, was not there at present. "Although I know that in Lucia's company you would be safe and well cared for anywhere," Bembo explained, "nonetheless I remind you that wicked rumors fly freely and could affect those like you; once suspicions get attached to you, there will be no way to live them down."[30]

Francesco Sansovino published letters that highlighted Bembo's efforts to make Helena a paragon of learned virtue. Concomitantly, Sansovino included some publicity for other laudable women of Bembo's extended household. In so doing, he reinforced the notion that women enhanced the honor of their male kin. Thus the collection includes a brief letter to Bembo's niece Giulia, who, like Helena, stands as something of a misfit alongside so many "prencipesse."[31] The letter itself is thoroughly pedestrian, returning greetings and promising a visit.[32] The letter does, however, foreshadow what would become Sansovino's larger project: publicizing the Bembo women as assets to their intellectual family. Three years after he edited Bembo's correspondence, Sansovino published a separate encomium of Bembo's niece, his "Life of the Illustrious Countess Giulia Bemba della Torre."[33] Although the most important theme for Sansovino was her exemplary piety in life and in the manner of her death, he mentions early on that "in true Religion and in mental virtues she was equal to her husband, and indeed she was gifted with such a happy genius, that much to her praise she learned both Latin and Greek."[34] Giulia Bemba provided further proof that learned virtue was a Bembo family business. Her achievements honored the family, which itself honored Venice. "In the lap of the most noble and magnificent city of Venice," Sansovino begins, "among those families that are famous and indeed illustrious for their nobility, sits the Bembo family." Sansovino noted that the family was celebrated both for civil and military service and for great antiquity.[35]

Sansovino took a leaf out of Bembo's own book, for Bembo himself considered women who possessed learned virtue to contribute to their families' prestige. Accordingly, he attended to his own daughter's schooling and also engaged in substantive correspondence with other learned women throughout his career. Their approach to him and his approach to them exhibit the very same language of domestic discourse that we have seen in the epistolary writings of women humanists.

Metaphoric kinship grafted networks of voluntary association to the biological family tree. One woman who benefited from this type of relationship was Caterina Landa of Piacenza, sister of Agostino Lando and wife of Count Giovanni Fermo. In 1529 Bembo wrote an avuncular letter of consolation to Agostino on the death of their father. If ever he can be a help to Agostino or the Lando family, Bembo explains, he will do so "just as if [he] were [their] uncle." He exhorts Agostino to execute his new role as head of the household with great care, maintaining his father's standards and in particular promoting its reputation for learned virtue, which Agostino and his sister are the first of their line to possess. He urges the young man, "[Maintain] the good name of your household and your own name in particular—and all the more assiduously since you have not only financial wealth but also the ornament of letters, which your father did not have." As for his sister, Bembo exhorts Agostino to be painstaking in finding her a husband "who will be worthy of her, a consolation to her and a credit to [their] family," adding that Agostino should consider his sister "another you yourself."[36]

When discussing Caterina's potential marriage, however, Bembo shifts his rhetorical stance from avuncular to paternal. Certain that Agostino will follow Bembo's injunctions in finding an excellent match for Caterina, he writes to Agostino, "[I will be] rejoicing with you in your well-earned delight, I who consider myself as at least your relative and even as your father, on account of the paternal love that I bear you." His "paternal love" embraces Caterina more emphatically, however: "I have always loved your sister Caterina as a daughter—in the first place, because she is your sister, but also because she has made herself even dearer to me by virtue of the elegant and charming Latin letters that she has sent to me from time to time."[37]

The way to Bembo's heart was indeed through letters. Among his long-term correspondents was the Brescian-born poet Veronica Gambara (ruler of Correggio), who governed as sole lord for thirty-two years after her husband died and was also Bembo's patron and a much-published poet in her own right. Her poems appeared in eighty anthologies between 1505 and 1754. Gambara's compositions in Italian prompted a steady stream of epistolary praise from Bembo during the period 1504 to 1544. Much as the women humanists maintained propriety by invoking kinship ties and using domestic metaphors, Bembo began his correspondence with Gambara with reference to the ties of obligation between their respective fathers. By the end of the correspondence, he characterized their relationship as a dialogue between "brother and sister."

In September 1504, Bembo conveys his regrets for tardiness in responding to one of her letters, in view of the "familial relationship and affection that began two years ago between [her] father the Count and [Bembo], and in view of [her] virtue and the acclaim that surrounds [her]." He goes on to thank Gambara for the great honor she did him in writing to him and assures her that for all that she believes herself indebted to Bembo and his father, all the more is Bembo indebted to her:

> Concerning that which you have said concerning the infinite obligation that you have to my father, who defends your father, and to me, I must say that, the way I see it, you, by virtue of your abundant *humanità* in speaking thus, or perhaps for the love that you might bear me, I know

how much I am obliged to you and to your magnificent and illustrious household; the quality of my father's obligation, I will leave it to him to express—he who has read your letters with the same fervor that I have.

Closing off this long reflection on ties of mutual obligation and reassurance, however, Bembo returns to the theme of Gambara's *humanità*— that is, her status as a writer of considerable elegance and skill. He concludes with an ardent plea that Gambara continue to honor him by sharing her poetry.[38]

This forty-year exchange of affection and literary compositions continued through Gambara's marriage, Bembo's common-law marriage, and the birth of children on both sides. Bembo's tone often bordered on amorous, but the courtly game remained within the bounds of propriety through his punctilious references to her family members. Bembo would send his regards to Gambara's sons in a letter of 1529, referring to them as "the lordships, your sons, who I hear are making themselves valiant young men, worthy of respect."[39]

In 1536 Gambara had sent him a sonnet (as was a common practice between them), which Bembo found "beautiful and charming" and to which he paid reverence by "kiss[ing] many times, thanking it along with [the] most happy genius that produced it, and the beautiful hand that wrote it." It seems that Gambara had expressed some interest in revising this poem (perhaps with a view toward publishing it), to which Bembo responds, "As far as correcting it, Your Ladyship has asked for my suggestions: God forbid that I should even conceive of such a thing. It is so moving and so genteel, that I cannot suggest one change to you that wouldn't make it less dear than otherwise. O most happy you, who always write such perfect poems!" This letter also reveals Gambara's efforts to form connections between her son and Bembo, as Bembo writes, "[Thanks to] your son, Count Girolamo, my Lord, for his greetings, which were most dear and sweet to me." A few years later, the connection appears again in Bembo's comment that he had received one of her letters and one of her poems on the birth of Christ from her son Girolamo during one of Girolamo's visits to Rome.[40]

By the end of their long correspondence, Bembo wrote to Gambara as if to a sister. In 1540 she had expressed thoughts of retiring from literary pursuits. He urged her with fraternal solicitation to continue writing poetry. Referring to her religious poems in particular, Bembo states, "Concerning the sonnet, it seems to me, as I have said to His Reverence, your brother, very beautiful, and moving and solemn. And for this reason I would not wish that you put an end, as you have suggested, to this art—and still less that you should repent of those that you've already written."[41] Underscoring the importance of their emotional and quasi-familial bond, however, Bembo also notes, "If I could be with Your Ladyship as often as I am with His Reverence, your brother, Rome would be dearer to me than she is." He also refers to her as his "most valorous, dearest and sweetest sister."[42] He greets her in the next letter in the same fraternal mode, calling her his "most illustrious and cherished sister" and closing another with the request that she consider him her "brother and servant."[43]

Pietro Bembo's careful attention to his daughter's education, as well as his collegial relationships with women writers, places him in a long tradition of forward-thinking fathers and father-patrons. Beyond serving as yet another example of an enlightened humanist patriarch, however, Bembo in his letters provides a rich documentary record of the attitudes and motivations of learned men who considered their female relatives and colleagues to be significant enhancements to their own intellectual honor. Bembo's will and correspondence offer a closer look at the motivations that may well have driven other Italian fathers to teach their daughters the humanities, and also provide a model of a sixteenth-century Italian household academy that may be compared to those emerging in England at the same time.

The More Family

The first and most famous case of the English household academy was the domestic "school" of Sir Thomas More (ca. 1477–1535), England's foremost humanist and an internationally respected scholar by virtue of his wide epistolary networks and especially his close friendship with Erasmus. Like many of his Italian predecessors, More began his career as a lawyer and moved steadily through the administrative ranks: in 1518 he was appointed a privy councilor of Henry VIII; in 1523 he was elected speaker of the House of Commons; and he was elevated by the king to the office of lord chancellor in 1529. In addition to his legal and political career, however, More's life before his famous break with the king over the question of the royal supremacy was characterized by his dominant role in the development of English humanism.

It is always tempting to present More as an exceptional figure, whether one emphasizes his creation of a new genre of fiction with his *Utopia* (1516), or the compelling narrative of his opposition to the king and subsequent execution (or martyrdom, depending upon one's confessional allegiance). I am arguing, however, that when his pedagogical theories were concerned, More belonged to an Italian humanist tradition. And while he was instrumental in establishing an analogous tradition in England, he was by no means alone.

Like Pietro Bembo, Thomas More aligned himself with the argument first given voice by Leonardo Bruni in the century before: More considered it desirable to instruct gentlewomen in the humanities. More had a slightly different conception of "woman as intellect" than his Italian predecessors and contemporaries did, however: education made "Tullia" an optimal wife for a learned man. Around 1518, when More's famous domestic academy in Chelsea was at its peak, he wrote a long poem to a literary foil called Candidus, "On Choosing a Wife" *(Versus Iambici Dimetri Brachycatalectici ad Candidum, qualis uxor deligenda),* which reveals some of More's theories. More urges the young man to disregard his potential bride's dowry and her physical beauty, both of which are subject to fortune's whim, and seek instead a girl from a good family whose morals are impeccable. Allowing that the ideal woman should be modest, temperate, and sparing in her speech, More would not have her be silent but rather learned. "Let her be either instructed in letters or capable of learning them," he exhorts, explaining that the woman who draws her principles from the best ancient authors is "armed" *(armata)* against the vicissitudes of fortune. The learned wife thus prepared "will neither grow proud in prosperity, nor wail like a wretch in adversity, crestfallen in times of trouble. Rather, she will be always pleasant, never depressed or troubled—a companion for [her husband's] life."[44] A Christian humanist education also makes a woman an ideal mother: "The learned wife will teach your little ones literature even as she nurses them—and one day your grandchildren."[45]

Suggesting that such a wife offers a respite from the affairs of men and can even soothe his cares with her singing and playing, More considers a learned wife's greatest contribution to the household to be her edifying conversation. "You will rejoice," he avers, "to spend days and nights in conversation both pleasant and erudite." Recalling her husband to gravity when he becomes frivolous or cheering him when cares press, the learned wife, with "surpassing eloquence joined to the knowledge of all serious topics," becomes a true partner.[46]

Such an argument in favor not only of women's education but also of female eloquence called for a few pertinent examples of ancient "learned virtue." More first makes a witty reference to Eurydice (wife of Orpheus), speculating that the hero would hardly have made such an effort to retrieve her from Hell if she had been illiterate. In a more sober vein, More points to Ovid's daughter, who "sought to equal her father in poetry." And his final examples are the most familiar figures, Tullia and Cornelia. "We may believe this about Tullia," he announces. "Never was any daughter dearer to her father. And never was any man more learned than he." For her part, Cornelia was "no less a teacher than a parent," because she not only brought the Gracchi into the world but also educated them.[47]

The principal difference in attitudes between Bembo and More concerns their definitions of "virtue." Both were, to a certain extent, products of their cultures. Bembo's letters to his son and, to a lesser degree, to his daughter demonstrate the Italian humanist notion of virtue as a mixture of good conduct and literary achievement, but with a greater emphasis upon Latin virtuosity, which brought cultural cachet. Bembo exhorted his son to master Latin not just to become a good man but to earn the favor of "every king and prince." Thomas More, conversely, demonstrates a view characteristic of English "Christian humanism," which Kenneth Charlton terms "lettered piety."[48] Training in the classical languages and, ideally, in Hebrew as well prepared the individual for understanding scripture and the patristic commentators. Education, in short, served doctrinal precision. While scholars have debunked the old opposition between a "secular" Renaissance in Italy and a "Christian" Renaissance in northern Europe, I nonetheless retain the problematic term "Christian humanist" as the most economical means for indicating a difference in emphasis.[49] Whereas in Italy humanists extolled the benefits of learning for their own sake (or for "moral improvement" loosely defined), this was not the case north of the Alps—especially not during the sixteenth century, when doctrinal controversies never ceased. The objective of study in this context was Christian piety, and by midcentury humanists often presented advanced education as instrumental to the further reformation of religion.

Another difference between the English household academy and its Italian model was structure: in England, "household" included a wider network of people—blood kin, wards, servants, tutors, and colleagues—and marriages often took place within it. In Italy, the father-daughter relationship took rhetorical precedence over all other family ties. In Bembo's case, for instance, the central characters in the correspondence were the father and his children, with occasional references to tutors and overseers. Husband-wife interaction was only hinted at. Conversely, in More's household academy, as well as others in England that appeared subsequently and patterned themselves on its example, a broader conception of "household" obtained. The children-students included not only More's four biological children (Margaret, Elizabeth, Cecily, and John) by his first wife, Jane Colt, but also his wards Margaret Giggs and Giles Heron. The principal resident tutors were William Gonnell and John Clement. Clement became an official family member in 1526, when he married Margaret Giggs. Another marriage that took place among household members was that of Sir Giles Heron to More's daughter Cecily (1525).[50] And Margaret More's marriage to William Roper (1521) was, in a sense, also a result of connections formed within the household academy, as Roper, by his own account, had been More's unofficially adopted son. Another member of More's kinship networks was Richard Hyrde, who would later publish the introduction for Margaret Roper's 1526 translation of Erasmus's *Treatise on the Pater Noster (Praecatio Dominica in septem portiones distributa)*.[51]

The More household was an extensive but tightly knit academy that produced two generations of "learned matrons." The female graduates of More's household became "working mothers" who, unlike their Italian contemporaries, were understood not only as daughter-prodigies but also as optimal wives and mothers. This was a prominent theme in More's poem on choosing a wife and would become central to the representation of his female students by their contemporaries.

Within the first generation, however, Thomas More set the rules for this complex association of learned kin. More expressed the purpose of his "school" most clearly in his letter to his children's principal tutor, William Gonnell, in a letter written circa 1518. Gonnell had given a glowing report of their progress in Latin. More's response concurred with this assessment, as More had already received Latin letters from them all, "not one of which [had] failed to please [him] thoroughly." More was troubled, however, by Gonnell's suggestion that only Elizabeth of all the students, save their mother *(absente matre),* demonstrated the proper modesty. The modesty theme prompted a lengthy disquisition on the supremacy of piety and morality to letters for their own sake. "If moral probity should be separated out, what else does literary fame bring but noted and noteworthy infamy?" More asked. Moving from general to gendered terms, he considered that the problem of fame was particularly acute for women, "whose erudition, like a new thing and challenge to cowardly men" left them vulnerable to the accusation that the "natural" moral deficiencies traditionally attributed to women were now being transferred to the world of letters. Far better, More continued, that his daughters prove to be good women with moderate learning than brilliant scholars with doubtful morals. More counsels their tutor to exhort all of them to seek wisdom rather than praise. He demonstrates an especial concern with his daughter Margaret's "high and lofty spirit," which her tutor found charming but which her father cautions him to direct toward "the true good" (contemplation of moral virtue) rather than the "shadows of the good" (praise and fame). For all of his children-students, More set the syllabus as "virtue first, then letters as second in the order of the good," with three ultimate goals of "piety towards God, charity to everyone, modesty and Christian humility with respect to themselves."[52]

Returning to his argument concerning women's education, More wrestles with the received gender paradigm. On the one hand, he had called men who criticize learned women "cowardly," but, on the other hand, he had urged Gonnell to curb Margaret's tendency toward intellectual pride. Now he returns to his more positive argument, rejecting the notion that women's only concern should be piety. Arguing that if both men and women are "human," then both have "reason," More claims that therefore "knowledge of letters, by means of which reason is cultivated, is fitting for both."[53] Against the biblical and Aristotelian conceptions of womankind as corrupt by nature—which prompted "many men to argue against educating women" because their works would be like poisonous fruit from a pernicious plant—More reasons that "all the more diligently should the female mind be cultivated by letters and good disciplines, in order that the defect of nature may be corrected by industry."[54] The authorities that he cites on this point are St. Jerome and

St. Augustine, who corresponded with "those most honest maidens and optimal mothers, who were not only called to seek out learning but even . . . to explicate diligently the abstruse points of Scripture." More continues, "The girls, moreover, wrote such erudite letters, which even mature men and professed doctors of holy letters could hardly read well, missing so many points that the girls understood. These works, most learned Gonnell, for your goodness you will take care that my little girls read thoroughly."[55]

Margaret More and her sisters, then, should read works that championed chastity (Jerome) and pious self-searching (Augustine). By the end of the letter, however, More modified this Christian syllabus, authorizing Gonnell to continue assigning Margaret and Elizabeth readings in Sallust, explaining, "These two girls seem more mature than John and Cecily." He also compromises his own contention that he would be happy to have pious daughters of only moderate learning. Like Bembo, More posits a reciprocal relationship between paternal affection and literary excellence. "At any rate," he concludes, "my children, first by the law of nature dear, then dearer for letters and virtue, you will make most dear by effecting their increase of doctrine and good morals."[56]

In the several letters addressed to "my school" and "my children," More takes an altogether less sententious approach: he encourages their study of Latin first and foremost, mentioning morality only in passing. In 1517 he wrote to Margaret, Elizabeth, and Cecilia and Margaret Giggs to praise their "elegant letters" *(elegantes epistolae vestrae)* and to urge them to be diligent in "dialectic exercises, making declamations and composing songs."[57]

Although More, unlike Bembo, seldom drew direct comparisons between his children, nonetheless he was not entirely above stirring up a bit of competition between John and his sisters. In 1522 More wrote "to his dearest children and Margaret Giggs, whom he count[ed] among his children," that he was once again delighted by their elegant Latin epistles, but he added extra praise for John to spur his daughters into making a greater effort.[58] "There was not one of your letters that failed to delight me," he declares. "But still, with a view toward speaking just as I feel, I will say that I was especially pleased with John's letters, because they were longer than the rest and, in that sense, revealed a bit more effort and study on his part. For he not only described things well, offering piquant examples of dialogue for everyone, but he even joked with me subtly and cunningly—pretty effectively answering back my own jokes . . . Now I expect daily letters from every one of you. Nor will I accept any of the usual excuses about time pressure, or the lack either of paper, or of subjects to write about; *John* doesn't try any such ruse!"[59] More pulled a "reverse Bembo," taking his daughters to task for laziness and goading them with their brother's good example. More appears to have been a more demanding father-teacher than his Venetian contemporary, however, as More expected daily letters—Bembo assigned Helena only weekly letters.

More took serious care to provide his children with practical assistance in developing their skills as Latin-letter writers (that is, as humanists.) He suggests that they write everything in English first, then translate the composition into Latin. In the ensuing instructions More, in essence, offers in one paragraph to his own children what contemporary pedagogical theorists like Roger Ascham and Johann Sturm devoted books to explaining only to their rarified circle of colleagues:

> It will not hurt anything if you write everything in English first, which afterwards you can translate into Latin much more easily and with much less effort—that is, compose without hunting for words, but only focusing upon eloquence. [As to proofreading,] ponder your general meaning first, then examine individual sections. This way, if you detect any solecisms, you can easily remove them. When these things have been tidied up, and the whole letter rewritten, examine the whole composition again, lest you nodded somewhere. Since it often happens that, as we revise, the errors which we had just corrected reappear.[60]

This passage illustrates that the More household academy involved not only weighty considerations of Christian ethics but also practical training in humanist eloquence, which the students developed largely through correspondence with More himself.

Of all his student-children, however, his daughter Margaret was unquestionably the favorite. Although almost nothing of her Latin juvenilia has survived, there are four extant Latin letters to her from More that address her developing skills in humanist epistolary. As with his other letters to his students, and in contrast to the moralizing of his letter to Gonnell, More's letters to his daughter exhort her to intellectual virtuosity more than to moral virtue. In one case, he expresses his delight at her cunning use of fine Latin prose to wheedle additional spending money out of him.[61] In another instance, he praises Margaret's mastery of the liberal arts and urges her, "Apply yourself for the remainder of your life to medicine and sacred letters, so that no supports to the fullness of human life will be missing for you (for as it should be a healthy mind in a healthy body). You have conquered letters and the other fundamentals already, and so no faculty for building upon them will be missing." He even insists that she attempt to surpass her husband in learning: "Now I who always was accustomed to persuade you to yield to your husband in all things, with a contrary command I make it that you should strive to surpass this husband in matters of learning."[62]

The students also engaged in "practica" beyond their letters to their father-teacher. In doing so, they moved along family networks much as we witnessed in the case of Isotta and Ginevra Nogarola, who wrote first to scholars already known to their family. Margaret and her siblings wrote first to their father's close friend Erasmus. It appears that Margaret and John were the great Dutch humanist's more frequent correspondents, as he dedicated works of his own to them in 1523/24. But Erasmus also commented to Margaret, "I have been put on my mettle *so often lately* by letters from you and your sisters—such sensible, well-written, modest, forthright and friendly letters," which suggests that More's other daughters also wrote to him with some regularity.[63]

Widening the ambit of Margaret's connections among the intellectual elite, More served not only as a father but as a kind of literary agent. He describes "accidentally" showing one of Margaret's Latin letters to the bishop of Exeter. More writes to his daughter of his having attended a state dinner recently, at which he found himself seated next to the bishop, "a man both learned and most reliable in the profession of all things." In the course of their conversation, More intended to pull from his pocket the schedule of the evening's events, but "by chance brought out [Margaret's] letter from [his] pocket instead." This letter produced keen interest on the part of his interlocutor, who "having snatched it up, began to inspect it." More continues, "When from the greeting he ascertained it to have been written by a woman, he started to read it yet more avidly. So novelty attracts him. But when he had read this and (if I had not confirmed it, he would not have believed it) been convinced that it was written with your own hand, the letter, as I will say no more, enough of such things—although why should I not tell you what he said?—such Latin, so well written, so erudite, so replete with sweet sentiments, he eagerly admired it."[64] The "accidental" pretext of this event was, of course, a thin veil for parental pride. The sentiments of this letter, as of the others to his students and as of his poem on choosing a wife, position More on the feminist side of the debate on women: far from extolling silence and chastity, he champions the learned woman. His reasons were both theoretical and personal. He was a humanist father proud of his daughter's skill in Latin.

More also showed Margaret's work to Reginald Pole, a prince of royal blood and a leading humanist, who was at the time studying abroad in Italy.[65] More expresses fatherly pride in once again challenging prejudices concerning women's intellectual merits, writing that it took all of his effort to persuade Pole that the letters were not written by Margaret's tutor but by Margaret herself.[66] These prejudices may be exaggerated in Pole's case, as he was to become a close friend and admirer of Vittoria Colonna, another influential early modern learned woman.[67] More's potential exaggeration notwithstanding, this letter offers further evidence that More made a considerable effort to publicize his daughter's intellectual excellence to learned men of his acquaintance.

More did not conceptualize female virtue in terms of chastity and silence. Many scholars have contended that the pursuit of learning placed women in a traditionally masculine sphere, thus leaving them in a liminal state. The learned woman, as an oddity, was potentially vulnerable to being perceived as a "virago" or even to being accused of sexual promiscuity.[68] In this view, to preserve her reputation, a woman should abandon all thought of education (beyond basic literacy, some mathematics, and plenty of religion) to maintain a perception of chastity, her greatest virtue.[69] Yet the concept of virtue was much more contested in Renaissance Europe than any totalizing definition for either sex would have us believe. As John Martin puts it, "in fashioning their religious, social, even personal identities, Renaissance men and women could draw on two distinct, even opposed virtues. On the one hand, there were those who embraced what I have been describing as a Renaissance notion of the prudential self (a rhetorical posture that subordinated honesty to decorum); on the other, there were those who favored the ideal of sincerity (which subordinated decorum to honesty)."[70] More and Bembo, as fathers, urged their daughters to embody the virtue of erudition first and foremost—what might be termed the "prudence" side of the Martin model. This was not the only sort of virtue that More and Bembo urged upon their daughters, however.

More does caution Margaret against the vanity of worldly ambition—as he puts it, "seeking to feather yourself with others' plumes" or, perhaps closer to the point, seeking "to adorn yourself with others' pens" *(te alienis plumis ornares).* He urges her instead to pursue knowledge for its own sake and to be prepared to content herself with the small but appreciative audience of her father and husband:

> But you, sweetest Margaret, are to be praised far and wide by that name, such that although you cannot hope for certain praise of your efforts, nonetheless you should persevere (with that outstanding virtue of yours) in joining more refined letters to the study of the good arts. Contented with the fruit and pleasure of your conscience, you will not seek fame; nor will you, given your modesty, wish to embrace freely what is offered but, because of your surpassing piety, you will find us more than enough and we shall be your constant audience, your husband and I.[71]

More articulates several different kinds of virtues in this passage; the first is the virtue of joining letters with the good arts—in other words, erudition. He cautions her against vanity and urges discretion ("not embracing freely what is offered") and finally piety. Nowhere does More mention chastity, nor does he state that she will not (or should not) gain a public reputation for learning, only that she "cannot not hope for *certain* praise of [her] efforts." He is not relegating her in any sense to obscurity, merely cautioning her against ambitions that may not be fulfilled.[72] Even the exhortation to modesty is mitigated by More's suggestion elsewhere that Margaret has been, if anything, too demure in her writing. In one instance, he notes that she too modestly and timidly *(nimium pudenter et timide)* asked for money; in another, he assures her that there was no cause for her to hesitate in sending her compositions, as they were so excellent that they needed neither the excuse of her sex nor the indulgence of a loving parent to bolster their merits.[73] There is of course a tension, if not an outright contradiction, between the call for modesty and that of confident learnedness, but this is a standard humanist dichotomy. As Margaret King notes in the context of another humanist father's grief over the death of his young son, the boy is praised for two almost contradictory sets of virtues. On the one hand, he was "gifted beyond the standard of his age with the greatest reason, grandeur of soul, moderation, prudence and eloquence," but on the other he exhibited "modesty and self-restraint, the greatest of all virtues."[74] The same dichotomy is present in More's exhortation to Margaret.

Although More was aware of the additional complication that Margaret's sex would present to her as a public humanist, he does not frame his comments in gendered terms. On the contrary, he urges her toward learning for its own sake (a standard trope in humanist rhetoric).[75] Morality and conscience, moreover, are articulated within the context of avoiding vanity, not cultivating chastity, silence, obedience, or any of the other female virtues that contemporary theorists and modern scholars assume were women's province.

When imprisoned in the Tower, More corresponded with his daughter in English, and the subject matter was literally a matter of life and death rather than pleasantries on the beauty of learning that occupied the Latin letters of earlier years. In this later correspondence, More relied upon his daughter as his means of communication with his wider circle of friends. He sent Margaret detailed accounts of his "interviews" with Henry VIII's officials and his own reasoning for refusing to swear the Oath of Supremacy.[76] As Margaret was the only one of her father's circle who was able to secure visiting privileges from the king, More wrote in a letter addressed to all his friends that they should consider his "well-beloved daughter Margaret" his official emissary and to "regard and tender" any request that she might make to them with as if "[he] moved it unto [them] and required it of [them] personally present [himself]."[77]

For her part, Margaret wrote to her imprisoned father of the pleasure his letters had offered her and the encouragement she wished to give him. There is every reason to believe that Margaret was sincere, but even in these heightened circumstances her prose is carefully crafted:

> It is to me no little comfort, since I cannot talk with you by such means as I would, at the least [to derive some pleasure] in this bitter time of your absence, by such means as I may, by as often writing to you, as shall be expedient and by reading again and again your most fruitful and delectable letter, the faithful messenger of your very virtuous and ghostly mind, rid from all corrupt love of worldly things, and fast knit only in the love of God . . . which I doubt not, good father, holdeth his holy hand over you and shall (as he hath) preserve you both body and soul *(ut sit mens sana in corpore sano)*.[78]

Her short Latin quotation in this particular letter adds the final touch to what is in any case a most elegant way of expressing pleasure in correspondence and offering him encouragement.

As Richard Trexler has argued, in Renaissance correspondence, "content and form were in a dialectical relationship to each other. There was no sincerity without form and no form without sincerity."[79] John Najemy also contends in his examination of the Machiavelli-Vettori correspondence that "the wide gulf between private, domestic letter writing and the humanist epistolary tradition may not be unbridgeable. The Machiavelli-Vettori correspondence may itself constitute one of the bridges between these two epistolary worlds."[80] Indeed, the sets of correspondence under investigation in this chapter suggest a fusion of the humanistic and the domestic, with the added dimension of gender: it is fathers and daughters who are building the bridge between the public and private—if indeed that distinction is in any sense meaningful.[81]

The merger of private correspondence and public positioning finds particularly intriguing expression in Margaret Roper's letter to her half-sister, Alice Alington.[82] This lengthy epistle belongs to the genre of literary dialogue. It contains "scripts" for both daughter and father—the daughter presenting an increasingly complex series of arguments that urge her father to think better of his scruple of conscience and the father offering rebuttals to each of the arguments that she adduces. Despite the somber setting of More's cell in the Tower of London, this piece of literature is full of elaborate puns and a pervasive sense of elaborate intellectual gamesmanship on both sides. The question of authorship for this epistolary set piece remains a source of scholarly debate. Elizabeth Rogers, editor of More's correspondence, attributed it to Margaret, but R. W. Chambers was less certain. Chambers noted that the letter's length was approximately equivalent to Plato's *Crito,* which it imitated in other ways, and that when it was printed after the death of More, his own colleagues could not decide whether the writer was father or daughter: "And the letter remains a puzzle. The speeches of More are absolute More; and the speeches of Margaret are absolute Margaret. And we have to leave it at that."[83]

We must not "leave it at that." The ambiguity surrounding this letter's authorship is most telling and speaks in particular to Margaret Roper's status as an intellectual. "Margaret" is a shrewd interlocutor. Richard Marius has argued that More's letters to his children were one means by which he "fashioned an image of himself before a public audience."[84] His letters to Margaret from the Tower do describe what was happening to More and what his self-justifications were, but while the letters were addressed to his daughter, they were intended for his circle more broadly. In this particular instance, "Thomas" and "Margaret" collaborated in setting the record straight; whether the letter to Alington was written by More, Roper, or both of them, it accomplished this objective.

"Margaret's" arguments begin with her fear that "if he stands still in this scruple of conscience (as it is at least called by many that are his friends and wise) all his friends that seem most able to do him good either shall finally forsake him, or peradventure not be able indeed to do him any good at all." She goes on to remind her father of his already dubious health and then proceeds to raise the plight of his family as a consideration to dissuade him from his obstinance: "I pray God, good Father, that their prayers and ours, and your own therewith, may purchase of God the grace that you may in this great matter (for which you stand in this trouble and for your trouble all we also that love you) take such a way by time, as standing with the pleasure of God, may content and please the King."[85] "Margaret" reworked her arguments as the dialogue moved forward, and "More" responded to them with increasingly elaborate rebuttals.

When pressed by "Margaret's" persuasiveness, he calls her "Mistress Eve," a characterization that has prompted scholars to the patently misguided assumption that More, in the final analysis, was himself a participant in the so-called "misogynist tradition."[86] Some scholars have begun to challenge this interpretation, noting the difficulty in ascertaining whether "More's" epithets were serious or playful.[87] It is not, however, all that difficult to tell in this case. Whenever "More" calls "Margaret" "Eve," he smiles. Early in the letter, "Margaret" writes, "With this my father *smiled* upon me and said: 'What, mistress Eve? . . . [have you come to] tempt your father again, and for the favor that you bear him labor to make him swear against his conscience?'"[88] Near the end of the dialogue, when she realizes that her father remains unpersuaded, she writes, "When he saw me sit with this very sad . . . he *smiled* upon me and said 'how now daughter Marget? [*sic*] What now Mother Eve? Where is your mind now? Sit not musing with some serpent in your breast, upon some new persuasion to offer Father Adam the apple once again.'"[89] The final reference to Eve moves from smiling to laughter: "'Why should you refuse to swear, Father? For I have sworn myself.' At this he *laughed* and said, 'That word was like Eve too, for she offered Adam no worse fruit than she had eaten herself.'"[90] Every reference to Eve begins with a smile or a laugh; "More" was clearly joking. Discrediting a woman's intellect through invocation of "Eve's sin" was indeed a common enough technique among some of his contemporaries, but More doubtless saw this as a joke, or he would not have educated his daughters. That "More" shares this as a jest with "Margaret," whose namesake was More's literary protégée, suggests no less.

The letter to Alice Alington is unquestionably a small work of literature—a "fiction" meant to convey a particular point. Humanists like More were keenly aware that their letters would affect their public perception. Margaret Roper was her father's "test case" for his own views on women's education.[91] In this light, the letter of Alice Alington, whether it was written by More or Roper, remains significant for its representation of the daughter as a skilled debater, the intellectual peer of her father.[92]

Margaret More Roper represents the first example of what would become a strong English tradition of "filiafocality" that both mirrored and reinterpreted Italian models. She was the most famous but by no means the sole "graduate" of her father's household academy. Her siblings, male and female alike, were celebrated for their erudition. And the Morean academy produced a second generation of learned women. Of all her five children (Thomas, Anthony, Elizabeth, Mary, and Margaret), Roper's daughter Mary most clearly continued the family business of humanism. Scholars from Thomas Fuller (*Worthies of England*, 1662) to modern historians (Elizabeth Rogers) have mistakenly attributed the translation of Eusebius's *Ecclesiastical History* to the senior Margaret Roper, but the extant autograph manuscript and its lengthy dedication to Queen Mary Tudor proves that it was actually the work of her daughter, Mary Roper Clarke Basset.[93] In her own day, Mary Basset was known as the translator of More's last work, a treatise on the passion of Christ, written while he was in prison. Like her mother, Basset was not only schooled by her intellectual family but published by it. Much as her mother's translation of Erasmus (a family friend) was published by a family member (Richard Hyrde), so Mary Basset's translation of her grandfather's treatise (a family text) was published by William Rastell, her father's friend and biographer, husband of her cousin by adoption Winifred Clement, and also a close friend of her second husband, James Basset.[94]

Like her mother, then, Mary Basset was the product of an extended intellectual family. Her early schooling in Latin can probably be credited to Margaret herself, whom More's biographer Nicholas Harpsfield termed a "double mother" to her children—that is, both biological mother and educator. "Not content only to bring them forth into the world," according to Harpsfield, she also "instructed them herself in virtue and learning."[95] One of Basset's tutors in Greek was the Oxford don John Morwen. She also enjoyed substantive early instruction from a John Charrice, whom she remembered in her will as "once my schoolmaster" and to whom she bequeathed the large sum of twenty pounds.[96]

Margaret Roper hired her children's tutors, and she aimed at the top. A letter of Roger Ascham (tutor to the future Queen Elizabeth) to Mary apologizes for refusing her mother's request that he tutor Mary and her siblings. He explains that he is writing now not only because he wishes to express his admiration for her but also because he had once been asked to instruct her: "I am the one whom your mother, Margaret Roper (a woman most worthy to be the daughter of such a father), once asked to instruct you and the rest of her children in the Greek and Latin languages; but at that time I was unable to extricate myself by any means from the Academy [Cambridge]."[97] At this point, both Ascham and Basset were working for Queen Mary Tudor. Ascham was one of the royal secretaries, and Basset served as a lady-in-waiting in the Privy Chamber. Basset probably gained this position, in part, by dedicating her manuscript translation of Eusebius to Queen Mary.[98] The post was important in personal terms as well: it was at court that Mary Roper Clarke met her second husband, James Basset, a member of the Queen's Privy Council.

Ascham's letter attests the importance of the connections that Basset was making at court; the letter frames her engagement with this literate society as an expansion of her learned natal family to a learned political "family." Basset herself mentions both kinds of association in her will. On the one hand, she notes that she enjoyed largesse from Queen Mary and the prince consort, Philip II of Spain, who had favored Basset's eldest son Philip with "a gilt cup with a cover [which] King Philip gave him at his christening." Basset bequeathed this item to her son, along with "[her] best ring of gold that King Philip gave [her], which has a great ruby set in it."[99] On the other hand, among her wide networks of kin (most often recipients of rings of remembrance), Basset also honors enduring connections with her natal intellectual kin. To Bridget Clement, "[her] god-daughter, Doctor Clement's daughter," Basset bequeathed ten pounds. Extended intellectual kin also appear in the will, such as "[her] god-daughter Mrs. Twiste, Master Tuche's daughter" and "[her] god-son Reynold Frier, Doctor Frier's son." In bequeathing money and property to other "intellectual affines," Mary followed a pattern evident in her own father's will. William Roper left a portion of his estates in Eltham, Kent, to "the use of the two daughters of Mr. James Good, Doctor of Physic," whom Roper also made one of his executors.[100]

The link between Mary Basset and her father was the most important connection that she possessed after her mother died (1544). Basset made her father the coexecutor of her own will—a service he duly performed when she predeceased him—along with her priest, Thomas Welles. By the time she drafted her will in 1572, she was once again widowed and deeply concerned that her two sons, Philip and Anthony (both from Basset), receive the right sort of upbringing. She states at the end of the will (the place of greatest importance), "I do make and ordain my most dear father, Mr. William Roper, Esquire, and Mr. Thomas Welles, Priest, executors of this my present will and testament, committing unto them the bringing up of my two children till they come to their full age, most heartily praying them according to the trust I put in them to take pains in the performance of the same."[101] Both sons ended up in a great deal of trouble, precisely because of their upbringing in the old faith, which reminds us that the intellectual family as articulated by and emanating from the More household academy might well have suffered deleterious association with Rome, making women's advanced education merely a footnote to the history of recusancy. But while the generations of learned More relations coming after Mary Basset did "retreat into continental convents," there were reformist examples to hand.[102]

The Cooke Family

Sir Anthony Cooke of Gidea Park, Essex, a man of strong reformist principles, spent the Marian reign (1555–1558) as a religious exile in Italy and Zurich. But Cooke's household academy had the same structure and goal as Thomas More's. Cooke shared More's view that daughters as well as sons must learn the humanities. Although Cooke was not himself a university man, and despite the fact that his writings do not show him to have been in any sense a humanist of either More's or Bembo's quality, nonetheless he valued rigorous training in classical languages.[103] From his domestic academy came four women widely celebrated as humanists and champions of the godly cause: Anne (wife of Sir Nicholas Bacon), Mildred (wife of William Cecil, later Lord Burghley), Katherine (wife of the diplomat Henry Killigrew) and Elizabeth (later wife of Sir Thomas Hoby). These women's sterling marriages among the intellectual elite during the Elizabethan period guaranteed that this household academy endured for generations. It was commemorated with the same fervor with which More's biographers touted the learned female graduates of his "school."

Marjorie MacIntosh has made a persuasive case that Cooke learned the humanities alongside his children.[104] Although Cooke's self-imposed exile made his presence intermittent during the youth of his daughters and sons (Richard and William), religious scruple would give way to fatherly ambition when it came to his daughters' preferment at court: both Anne and Mildred were ladies-in-waiting to Queen Mary—intriguingly, at the same time Mary Basset served in this capacity. Later, the Cooke daughters, especially Anne and Mildred, would follow their father's reformist example, serving as patrons to learned divines and campaigning vocally for further reformation as translators of godly devotional material. They were able to do so, however, because of the educational foundation offered them by their father.

Unfortunately, little is known about who the sisters' tutors were. The writings of Anne and her sisters reveal extensive training both in Latin and Greek, languages which their father read and with which he filled his library.[105] The fact that Cooke did not himself write in either language may suggest that his own training in them was less complete than his daughters'—further evidence for the notion that he learned alongside his children and served as colleague to them rather than as teacher in the Morean sense. Cooke's will proves that he considered his daughters his intellectual heirs, if not in fact his equals. He gave them first choice among his classical library, specifying, "Of my books, my daughter Burghley [Mildred] shall have two volumes in Latin and one in Greek, such as she will chose, of my gift; and after her choice . . . my daughter Bacon [Anne] shall have other volumes in Latin and one in Greek, such as she will choose; and after her choice, . . . my daughter Russell [Elizabeth, later Hoby] shall have other two volumes in Latin and one in Greek, such as she will choose; and after her choice . . . my daughter Killigrew [Katherine] shall have other two volumes in Latin and one in Greek, such as she will choose."[106] The rest of his library went to his sons, suggesting that while they got the most, they did not get the best volumes.

We also know that Cooke served as a tutor to Edward VI. Edward did not mention Cooke in his diary alongside his other tutors (Richard Cox and John Cheke), but John Hooper characterized him as a royal tutor in 1550, the same year that Cooke was awarded the robust lifetime annuity of one hundred pounds for teaching the king "good letters and manners."[107] Although his role as a royal tutor appears to have been informal, it nonetheless seems probable that Cooke would have taken a similar role in supervising his own children's instruction. It is beyond question that he supported their studies. Part of his approbation can be seen in his marriage strategies for his daughters. And, certainly, it is important that contemporaries credited Cooke directly with their education.

His confessional allegiance excepted, Cooke shared a great deal with Thomas More. His actions confirm his own commitment to the education of daughters, though Cooke does not seem to have left any extended disquisitions on the theme as More had. Was this attitude toward education characteristic of learned "new men" in sixteenth-century England? Quite possibly. While More's father had been a judge, an occupation that carried with it some intellectual cachet, before Thomas More the family had garnered no humanist credentials. The More family history reveals no trips to Padua like those of other English men with humanist ambitions; rather, their Mores' principal context was the Inns of Court. Sir Anthony Cooke's background was similar. The important distinction in Cooke's case, however, was that he was the first member of his country-gentry family to obtain any intellectual credentials whatsoever. The most noteworthy of his direct ancestors was his grandfather, Sir Thomas, who made a fortune as a draper and became Lord Mayor of London. Other progenitors included wealthy wool merchants and sheep farmers—no male or female scholars.[108] Cooke's pursuit of the humanities and encouragement of his children to do the same suggest an avid desire to shift the public perception of his lineage toward the "learned virtue" that was clearly a preoccupation of Pietro Bembo but may also have been a motivation for Thomas More. Cooke's particular aim, however, was to build an intellectual household that would, in turn, serve the godly cause. He made this aim visually manifest by covering his house (literally) with scriptural quotations in Latin, Greek, and Hebrew.

As to the daily routine of the Cooke household academy, tutors may have been responsible for some of the instruction of the children, but Cooke himself was ultimately responsible for planning and supervising their studies.[109] And he seemed to favor his daughters' education, perhaps because they proved more capable than their brothers. Cooke's younger son, William, entered Gray's Inn in 1554, but his subsequent career leaves no evidence of learned pursuits. William and his older brother, moreover, were granted master of arts degrees at Cambridge during a royal progress but did not actually attend the university.[110] Unlike the extended family of the Morean academy, the presence of other students (beyond biological children) in Cooke's household academy is more difficult to gauge. It is possible that Lady Jane Grey and the son of the lord protector (Somerset) may have taken part in the proceedings.[111] The curriculum, however, can be ascertained from the Cooke sisters' later writings. In addition to Latin and Greek, the sisters learned French and Italian. The sources upon which they later drew were largely devotional works (especially those of Gregorius Nazarensis, whom their father translated and often cited in his letters) and the writings of continental divines. Although the Cooke family read the secular classics, none of the Cookes emphasized these studies in the way that Italian humanists did.

In addition to providing his daughters with their fine education, Anthony Cooke also introduced them to scholars whom he met while in Italy and Zurich. Among the friendships that he made during his Marian exile and continued well into the Elizabethan reign was Bernardo Ochino, whose sermons Anne Cooke Bacon would translate in 1560. Similarly, Theodore Beza (Théodore de Bèze), whom Anthony Cooke met in Geneva, dedicated his *Christian Meditations* to Anne Cooke Bacon in 1581.[112]

The Fitzalan Family

Another domestic academy on the Morean model and one that offers a closer look at pedagogy is the household of Henry Fitzalan (Earl of Arundel). Godson of Henry VIII and later a governor of Edward VI, Fitzalan

possessed sterling humanist credentials: he was trained in the humanities at Henry's court and later at Cambridge. Fitzalan ensured that his
daughters, Mary and Jane, received the same training in the classical languages that he gave his son, Henry. As with Anthony Cooke's writing,
almost nothing remains of Fitzalan's own writing, but Fitzalan was certainly a humanist in the sense of being a reader and collector of classical
texts: he accumulated one of the finest Latin and Greek libraries in England. Fitzalan also hired tutors for his children, but they viewed their father as the final academic authority in the household. All three gave him
as New Year's gifts their translations and collections of moral maxims, as
"proof" of their progress in learning during the past year. On one occasion, for instance, his younger daughter, Mary, wrote in her dedication,
"This year, most illustrious father, I am reading certain Greek maxims at
the advice of my tutor."[113]

Fitzalan, like More, collected several unofficial wards who also enjoyed the status of "student" in his household academy. Among these
was a John Radcliffe, whose translation of the Roman emperor Alexander Severus's letter to the senator Gordianus appears alongside Mary
Fitzalan's Latin translation of an English biography of Severus.[114] Like
Mary and her siblings, Radcliffe dedicates his work to Fitzalan, whom
Radcliffe constructs as a father, signing the composition, "your son, most
obedient to Your Lordship."[115] Another ward-student was John Lumley,
who later married Fitzalan's daughter Jane—further evidence, like the
marriages of Margaret and William Roper and and Margaret Giggs and
John Clement, of endogamy within a Catholic intellectual family. To
judge by the extant documentary record, most of the academic work
taking place in the Fitzalan household was accomplished by Jane, Mary,
and Henry Fitzalan, together with John Lumley. One catalog of the
Lumley manuscripts includes John's translation of Erasmus's treatise *On
the Education of the Christian Prince,* which Lumley dedicated to his adoptive father. In addition, there is also mention of a collection of juvenilia
that included Lumley's work alongside that of his future brother-in-law
(Henry Fitzalan, later Lord Maltravers) and wife (Jane Fitzalan, later
Lady Lumley): "Exercises in Greek and Latin of the Lord Maltravers,
the Lord and Lady Lumley, done when they were young, of their own
writing, bound together."[116] This group of students was bound together
in more than one sense. Fitzalan would become Lumley's father-in-law,
as noted above, and Fitzalan's final will (written after the death of his

son Henry) made John Lumley the heir to his estate, including the vast library.[117]

The Fitzalan children, biological and adopted, were engaged in a common intellectual enterprise very much like that of the More household. In its more Italianate syllabus and mission, however, the Fitzalan academy diverged from the More and Cooke models: its students undertook diverse readings of Latin and Greek moral philosophy, with no special emphasis on Christian antiquity.[118] Unlike Margaret Roper or Anne Cooke Bacon, who read Sallust and Livy as preparation for appreciating Jerome and Augustine, Jane and Mary Fitzalan read Cicero and Seneca as preparation for translating Isocrates and Euripides. The Fitzalan curriculum certainly included ethical development, which Italian humanist pedagogues also stressed, but the aim of the Fitzalans' education extended well beyond achieving a deeper understanding of Christian doctrine.

The Italian character of the Fitzalan household academy was doubtless enhanced by the presence of the Florentine scholar and illuminator Francesco Ubaldini (1524?–ca. 1600). Ubaldini, a Protestant exile, joined Fitzalan's circle of protégés around 1550, and it seems likely that he became a member of the household from then until 1562, the year in which Fitzalan introduced him at court. In his *Lives of Illustrious Women in the Kingdom of England* (1591), Ubaldini described Fitzalan as "my Maecenas," a term which implies financial remuneration as well as public-relations patronage. Moreover, to judge by the autograph exercises of Jane and Mary, who wrote a distinctly Italianate calligraphic hand, Ubaldini was probably one of their tutors. The period between 1550 and 1562 is also the time frame in which the Fitzalan children were being educated: in 1550 Jane and Mary would have been thirteen and ten years old, respectively. Ubaldini's possible role as tutor is also suggested by several of his manuscript copybook extracts in Italian, entitled "his examples of writing very fair" and dedicated to young Henry Fitzalan (Lord Maltravers).[119]

Whoever served as their instructors, the children considered their father to be the final judge of their academic progress. All of their dedicatory epistles stress the desire to demonstrate to Fitzalan the progress that they are making in writing Latin versions of English material and then in translating Greek material into Latin. Jane, for instance, presented him with her translation of Isocrates' letter to Demonicus: "[I present these] as some example of my studies, partly because I know you to take particular delight in things of this sort and to be a student of doctrine, and also partly so that I might practice translating Greek into Latin."[120] Mary, similarly, offered her father one of her early translations (a biography of Alexander Severus): "an example of my ingenuity [this] New Year, by which you might discern how far I have advanced in letters."[121] Their brother Henry, likewise, dedicated his reflections on Cicero's *De senectute* to his father, writing, "by which fruit of my studies you might see my progress in good letters."[122]

Jane and Mary, much like Margaret Roper, continued their studies well after their marriages. Jane signed her translations "Joanna Lumleya," and Mary's four sets of exercises divide evenly between those written in her youth and those during her married life: her two sets of translations from English to Latin are signed "Maria Arundell"; her two later and more sophisticated collections of moral maxims, translated from Greek to Latin, are signed "Maria Norfolke." In fact, the dedication in which she mentions her tutor comes from the years after her marriage. Moreover, Jane Lumley's translation of Euripides' *Iphigenia at Aulis* (her most important composition) was similarly work that was undertaken by the author as a married woman. Marriage, then, in no sense presented an obstacle to the Fitzalan daughters' intellectual lives. Nor did childbearing, in Mary's case, interrupt her studies. She bore her husband, Thomas Howard (Duke of Norfolk), two children (Philip and Anne) before Mary's premature death at the age of seventeen (1557). We cannot say how childrearing would have affected Jane, who was childless to her death at the age of thirty-nine (1576). Her desire to become a mother, however, served as a melancholy incentive for study: she transcribed the portions of Mattheus Sylvaticus's *De lapide aquilae* that give specific advice on the use of minerals for increasing fertility and preventing miscarriage.[123]

Recurring Themes

As we have seen in several fifteenth-century Italian cases, dissociation from the traditional "mother" and cooperation between siblings seem also to have obtained in English household academies. In discussing these issues, however, I wish to follow up the Bembo story. Helena and Torquato Bembo seem to have enjoyed a civil relationship, despite their father's propensity for playing favorites. As we have already seen, Bembo encouraged Helena to write to her brother if she wished. Given Bembo's pedagogical technique of using his affection for Helena to goad Torquato, one might reasonably anticipate that there would be resentment or hostility between brother and sister. To judge by one letter of Bembo's to Helena after her marriage and the birth of her son, however, she seems to have positioned herself (at least by this point) as a buffer between her brother and her father. "You have done well," Bembo avers, "to have kept Torquato with you an evening more than I ordered. If he is as modest and polite as you say he is, I'm pleased—and let it be to his good."[124] Although we might wonder how Torquato viewed his father-mandated trip to visit his sister, she had evidently made some effort to convince Bembo that Torquato was not quite the hopeless case that their father insisted on making him out to be.

There are no contemporary references (direct or mediated) to Margaret Roper's relationship with her siblings, but her daughter maintained close bonds with diverse members of the interlocking More-Roper-Clement family. Basset's principal beneficiaries were, naturally, her sons. But she left "to [her] brother, Thomas, [her] pomander enclosed in gold, and to [her] sister, his wife now, a ring with a little ruby." Basset similarly bequeathed ruby and emerald rings to her brother Anthony and his wife, as well as to several of her godsons. As noted above, Basset also left bequests to her goddaughter, Bridget Clement (daughter of John Clement, her uncle by adoption).[125]

Among the equally profuse Cooke descendants, it seems that the sisters were on good terms—especially Katherine Cooke Killigrew and Mildred Cooke Cecil. There does not appear to remain any indication of their attitudes toward their brothers or vice versa. Certainly, however, Anne Bacon was a frequent correspondent of her brother-in-law William Cecil in her zeal for further reformation.

The Fitzalan family group appears to have worked harmoniously as well. None of the children reflect upon each other; rather each writes exclusively to their father without reference to their sibling-classmates. All three emphasize their filial piety. This is never done with explicit comparison to each other but exists only in their extensive use of obedience tropes and, for the daughters, in the superlative form. Writing to Fitzalan, Mary terms herself "your daughter, most devoted to Your Lordship."[126] In a slightly less formal mode, her elder sister closes her dedications to him with "your daughter, most dedicated to you."[127] Henry, by contrast, finishes his composition with a simple "farewell." In closing, however, he does acknowledge his dependant status by repeating his father's title: "Now you have, most cultivated Lord Father, the argument [of *De senectute*] in brief . . . which I very much pray and beg that Your Lordship take with equanimity."[128] Henry emphasizes his obedience in political rather than emotional terms.

The member of the Fitzalan household eloquent in her absence is once again the mother. Catherine Gray, Fitzalan's second wife and mother to all three children, does not appear in this manuscript collection. A manuscript biography of Henry Fitzalan, probably composed by a member of Fitzalan's circle, notes only that he "had two wives, the one being the daughter to the marquess of Dorset and mother to all his Lordship's children."[129] There is no further comment on Catherine's contributions to the Fitzalan household academy. The image of the learned mother could and did apply to the contemporary reception of women like Margaret Roper and the image of the learned and godly wife applied to the women humanists of sixteenth-century England in general. What might be termed the "first-generation mother," however, remains on the sidelines.

Pietro Bembo's companion, Faustina Morosina della Torre, whom he called "la Morosina" in some of his published letters to his nephew, certainly held Bembo's affection. In his will, Bembo underscores their affective bond in specifying that he wishes "very much to be buried at the body of Morosina, mother of [his] children."[130] But it is unclear in this case what role she may have played in raising Torquato and Helena. It is particularly unfortunate in this regard that we have no writings by Torquato (apart from his will) or Helena.

There are, similarly, few references to Margaret Roper's mother, Jane Colt. More's biographers note her "learning and virtue" only in passing.[131] Dame Alice, More's second wife, elicited more frequent comment, but of a mocking nature. Erasmus dubbed her role in the household academy as "taskmistress," emphasizing her effectiveness as an overseer rather than a participant in this school of geniuses.[132] William Roper, More's son-in-law and one of his biographers, even lampooned Dame Alice's visit to her husband in the Tower. "At her first coming," Roper relates, "like a simple and ignorant woman, and somewhat worldly, too, with this manner of salutation bluntly saluted him: 'What the good year, master More,' quoth she, 'I marvel that [you] have been always hitherto taken for so wise a man, will now play the fool to lie here in this close filthy prison . . . when you might be abroad at your liberty . . . I muse what [in] God's name you mean here still thus fondly to tarry.'"[133] To More's poetic wisdom in replying with the question, "Is not this house as near heaven as my own?" Roper has Dame Alice exclaim "after her homely fashion, 'Tyle valle. Tylle valle.'"[134] Roper used Dame Alice as a literary device. She contrasts not only to his father-in-law's moving detachment but also to the erudition, gravity, and piety of Roper's own wife, Margaret More Roper. Immediately before recounting Dame Alice's visit, Roper describes several "Tower episodes" in which Margaret and Thomas exchange godly comforts with all conceivable decorum.[135]

Mary Basset's will, in terms of the the third generation, does make one passing reference to her mother. In the event that both her sons should die, Basset specifies that her valuable estate should be directed to charitable works that will benefit the souls of herself, both her husbands, her father and mother, her brothers and sisters, and all those whom she felt "most bounden to pray for."[136] Margaret Roper had been dead for twelve years by the time Basset wrote this document, which may well account for the perfunctory nature of her mother's inclusion among "all such as in my time I have been bounded to pray for." By contrast, as we have seen, her living father and executor warranted the epithets "dear" and "most dear."

Anne Fitzwilliam, Anthony Cooke's wife and the mother of all seven of his children, was the daughter of William Fitzwilliam, a London merchant who settled in Essex.[137] Her children do not comment upon her, and the epitaph that Anthony Cooke wrote in her honor praises her only for having been attractive—but not so stunning that her beauty interfered with his studies. He also mentions her in a brief poem, commending her skills as a mother and housekeeper.[138] She is not mentioned in his will but may have died before he wrote it. Haddon's encomium to Cooke's academy, in which Haddon witnessed the "studies of women" flourishing, does not mention Anne—though even Erasmus troubled to note that Dame Alice More at least contributed to the Morean academy as its "taskmistress."

The role of the mother in these learned English families, then, seems to have evinced both the silence and ambivalence that we found concerning fifteenth-century Italian women humanists.[139] Here again, the textual distancing of the traditional matriarch may suggest the same desire on the part of participants and contemporary observers to create a contrast between customary "femininity" and a new type of intellectual women begotten by humanist fathers and surrounded by learned siblings.

Even within other sectors of what we might term educated but not humanistic society, women authors tended to associate "father" with books and "mother" with piety. For instance, Rose Hickman Throckmorton, reflecting at the age of eighty-five (ca. 1610) upon her reformist family's history of suffering under Queen Mary, commends her mother for seeing to her daughter's religious awakening. "My mother," she writes, "in the days of King Henry VIII, came to some light of the gospel by means of some English books sent privately to her by my father's factors overseas; whereupon she used to call me, with my two sisters, into her chamber to read to us out of the same good books very privately, because those good books were then accounted heretical [so] my mother charged us to say nothing of her reading to us for fear of trouble."[140] Throckmorton's ability to write, however, and her mention of the sources she has consulted in crafting her family history indicate that she received a great deal more than oral instruction.

Throckmorton's family chronicle, though by no means an "elite" text of the sort that her humanist contemporaries produced, shared the same instinct to foreground paternal connection. Throckmorton begins the work by associating her father, Sir William Locke, a wealthy merchant of Cheapside, with her reading practices. "Of my father," she declares, "In Hollinshed's Chronicle I find this story." The story was that William Locke, mercer of London, stopped the "curse" put upon the king and realm by the pope after King Henry divorced Catherine of Aragon. Locke was duly rewarded by the king with one hundred pounds a year and made a gentleman. "Now I, his daughter, Rose," she continues, "widow, late wife of Simon Throckmorton and first the wife of Anthony Hickman, a merchant of London, reading this of my father have thought good to leave to my children this addition to it." Her first impetus to write, then, was specifically to immortalize her father's achievements. In the process, she notes that she not only read Hollinshed's *Chronicles*—as a continuation to which she situated her own work—but also mentions that "Mr. Richard Hakluyt, in his second printed volume of English voyages to the south and southeast parts of the world" [that is, Hakluyt's *Voyages*] gave testimony to the "note and fame" that her first husband and her brother accrued for their successful joint merchant ventures.[141]

In short, although Throckmorton seems to have been taught principally scripture by her mother, she nonetheless read and wrote in the interest of immortalizing her male relatives. She was particularly proud of her father's godly social mobility, attesting that his rise in the king's favor and thus in civic importance was unprecedented for a man of his otherwise middling station. She observes in this regard that the king "made him a gentleman of his Privy Chamber and he was the king's mercer; moreover, he was knighted [and made] sheriff of London and so was never any Londoner before him." Her father also, and here she invokes the authority of first-person recollection, told her about his voyages abroad and how Queen Anne Boleyn "caused him to get her the gospels and epistles, written on parchment in French, together with the Psalms." By contrast, Throckmorton presents her mother's greatest achievement as dying in the grace of God.[142]

Even in this rather different kind of family setting, then, the female author associates "father" with books and "mother" with piety. I say "rather different" kind of family, since Throckmorton's extended networks of kin included a number of highly literate women. Among the more prominent was her sister-in-law, Anne Locke (fl. 1530–1590), who was a close friend and correspondent of John Knox and published her translations of French devotional works, including John Calvin's sermons on the book of Hezekiah (1560) and Jean Faffin's treatise *On the Marks of the Children of God* (1590).[143]

Throckmorton's reminiscences stayed within her family until the nineteenth century, when they were presented as a gift to the British Library, and they remain in manuscript. Her correspondence, however, moved from the domestic context into the wider world of learned divines in a way reminiscent of Margaret More Roper's. Throckmorton mentions writing to certain "bishops of Oxford" (possibly Latimer and Ridley) on the validity of Catholic baptism.[144] Her connections with these men, she notes, were formed thanks to her husband's hospitality. And it certainly appears that "evangelical" learning was a Throckmorton family business in much the same way as humanism was the family business of the More, Cooke, and Fitzalan household academies.

Beyond Exceptionality

Studies of learned women in early modern Italy and England customarily contain a disclaimer to the effect that such women were "exceptions" when compared to other women of their eras. No intellectual historian would apologetically introduce an edition of Pico della Mirandola's writings, for instance, by reminding the reader that most men did not enjoy Pico's latitude for literary contribution, because most men did not happen to be the count of Concordia or anywhere else. Rather the task would be to situate Pico's writings in relation to the work of other humanists. Yet women authors must, it seems, be compared to all other women, most of whom did not enjoy the good fortune of being born to liberal-minded fathers. Most women, we are informed, were taught only to cook, sew, and pray.

In her recent edition of Annibale Guasco's *Discourse*, written to his eleven-year-old daughter Lavinia (ca. 1585), which describes the careful way in which he taught her himself and hired numerous tutors for her in preparation for securing her a post as a lady-in-waiting at the Sabaudian court, Peggy Osborn follows form in noting that this was an "exceptional father-daughter relationship in late sixteenth-century Italy."[145] Osborn considers Lavinia Guasca's literary and musical education as perhaps "unique," as most young women of the age "were brought up to be pious, chaste and domesticated in preparation either for marriage or the cloister." Osborn similarly frames the *Discourse* itself as "a landmark in the history of women's education," because it is founded on the premise that a young woman who was talented should be encouraged to develop her skills. "Seen against the backdrop of an age when girls were educated for a life of self-effacement and narrow domesticity," Osborn explains, Guasco's view is "astonishingly far-sighted."[146] Osborn's assessment is accurate when the comparative referent is all other women in early modern Europe. When compared with the growing number of highly educated women, however, Lavinia Guasca becomes another success story, not an exception. Her relationship to her father evinces many characteristics common to learned women we have been discussing. Annibale Guasco was indeed farsighted in planning a career for his daughter, but he was very much with the times in being a humanist who educated his daughters alongside his sons.

The household academy made women intellectuals familiar and appealing figures in the literary landscape of sixteenth-century Italy and England. By 1580 there was an established tradition of learned women in both contexts who were neither nuns nor courtly patrons but the heirs of "new men." Collectively, women humanists redefined female capability and the boundaries of normative female activity. Positive celebrity is one barometer of their historical significance: almost without exception, contemporaries and later observers applauded the emergence of this new order of female stars and presented them as models for other women to follow.

3

The Biographical Tradition

MARGARET King contends that, a few enlightened fathers aside, "male hostility to female learning [was] widespread." She argues that early modern society viewed women who stepped beyond the parameters of the reproductive economy or (alternatively) the cloistered hermitage as having become "what women must not be: they become men, and turn men into women."[1] Stephanie Jed has even stated that "the idea of a woman writer made no sense" to early modern men, who viewed the terms "woman" and "writer" as mutually exclusive.[2] While any general argument concerning reception is bound to confront contrary evidence, two factors make these negative assessments problematic. First, "public opinion" (then as now) was contingent, responding to different categories of writers in different ways and shifting according to the literary genre of the response itself. The weight of evidence for claiming that early modern society feared learned women rests upon a few overdetermined prescriptive texts, such as Leon Battista Alberti's *On the Family* and Francesco Barbaro's *On Wifely Duties*. By contrast, a broad examination of reflections upon women humanists reveals a pervasive discourse in which educated women were understood as women and acclaimed as active contributors to their families' intellectual honor.

In Italy, numerous defenses of women and collections of female biography celebrated the "learned virtue" of the fifteenth-century women humanists, alongside a vast array of vernacular poets. English biographers focused more upon the nine women humanists of the More, Cooke, and Fitzalan clans as the daughters of paternal erudition, as well as the wives and mothers of extended intellectual families. North and south of the Alps, there were positive labels for educated gentlewomen, labels that blended "feminine" domesticity and "masculine" scholarship. Italian encomiasts favored what I have been calling the "Hortensian hermeneutic"; English observers praised women humanists both as pious daughters and "learned matrons."

Italian Biographical Compendia

Scholars have recognized that the Venetian women humanists appear in collections of "famous women" but have not studied the biographies themselves in any detail. Examination of several important biographical compendia published in Venice reveals that the contemporary mind set understood these learned women as participants in the family business of education, who brought honor both to their natal families and to the larger civic family of their native cities.

Within the wider world of Italian letters, erudition was considered a Nogarola family business—and specifically the business of the Nogarola women. Giuseppe Betussi's translation from Latin into Italian of Boccaccio's collection of 106 biographies of mostly pagan women (*De mulieribus claris*, 1362), to which Betussi appended his own biographies of more recent illustrious women, ensured the Nogarola legacy. Betussi's translation enjoyed at least four editions within fifty years. Published three times in Venice (1545, 1547, and 1558) and reprinted with new biographies for the Florentine printer Filippo Giunti in 1596, it ranked among the most popular sixteenth-century collections of women's biographies.

Betussi and his numerous imitators merged the categories "learned" and "virtuous," obliterating Boccaccio's connection of female accomplishment and sexual promiscuity. All of Betussi's forty-nine new biographies exemplify this interpretive shift, but his biographies of Angela, Ginevra, and Isotta Nogarola make the most powerful case for the moral benefits that women derive from humanistic study.

Betussi describes Angela Nogarola as a "most learned woman, who lived at the time of Pope Pius II. Nor was she only considered illustrious in her own region [Verona], but was esteemed and valued throughout Lombardy and all of Italy." Noting that she was the daughter of "that most noble cavalier Antonio Nogarola and wife of Antonio d'Arco," Betussi praises Angela for a host of excellent "feminine" qualities: beauty, spiritual virtue, kindness, modesty, and chastity. In addition to possessing this last and "principal virtue," however,

> she was considered a veritable oracle where doctrine in literary terms is concerned. In reasoning she showed infinite knowledge, in citing examples she gave proof that she had seen as many books as anyone could possibly study, and in argumentation to have applied herself to the pursuit of more than one branch of knowledge. This woman was particularly fond of holy Scripture, the mysteries of which she explained [largely] in spiritual poetry . . . With such skill did she write certain Eclogues, that without fear of exaggeration one could compare her to Cornificia of Rome, who as Saint Jerome writes, wrote holy compositions in verse, most excellent divine things, much prized in her day.[3]

Betussi steps up the rhetoric as he goes on to describe Isotta's sister Ginevra, "daughter of Cavalier Leonardo Nogarola, a gentleman of no small valor at the time of Pope Pius the Second." Betussi describes Ginevra as, like her aunt, renowned not only in northern Italy but throughout the peninsula. Praised as the magnanimous wife of the Brescian nobleman Brunoro da Gambara, Ginevra appears as the epitome of the generous patroness: gentle, kind, courteous, and "of infinite merits" *(infiniti meriti)*. The striking difference between Ginevra's biography and that of her aunt is Betussi's excitement concerning not just Ginevra's "wisdom" but her schooling. "As far as letters are concerned," he declares, "she was not just passingly expert, but thoroughly, since she was taught by the best and most learned men and in many branches of knowledge she demonstrated no small wisdom to the most worthy minds of the time. Of this we have clear evidence in her many epistles, full of doctrine and fine sentiment, whose style is considered grave, pure, full of sweetness, such that not just a woman, but every scholarly spirit would be proud of having written such letters." Betussi dismisses gendered categories of praise for women in calling her achievements worthy of any "scholarly spirit," rather than complimenting her as Boccaccio would have done for accomplishments "beyond her sex." In closing her biography, however, Betussi emphasizes her moral virtues of charity, mercy, and all qualities that pertain "to a true Christian."[4] Fusing intellectual virtuosity with Christian virtue makes the case that surpassing erudition in no sense compromises traditional values, even when the subject was female.

Isotta's biography follows Ginevra's. Betussi makes a point early on that Isotta, "most learned and most wise," had decided to remain un-married. Although this decision was only finalized at her midcareer point and well after her father's death, Betussi nonetheless preferred to make it seem all the more laudable by noting that she confronted paternal op-position: "However much her father urged her to take a husband . . . so firmly was chastity rooted in her heart that there was no shaking her from that praiseworthy resolution of hers." In order to avoid the danger of idleness that might arise if a woman was free from household duties, Betussi reasons, she "gave herself completely to the study of letters, in which she made such great profit that one could truly say that the an-cient Latin language had returned in full force; indeed, with no small dignity, she bettered it."[5] For all his talk of chastity, Isotta ultimately served as proof that ancient letters had returned—the very point of the humanist enterprise.

Isotta, like her sister, "showed herself the equal of the most schol-arly men of that age." Betussi adds to Isotta's luster, however, by giving her mind *(intelletto)* the adjective of highest praise for the era: *divino*. As supporting evidence, Betussi recounts a famous episode from Cardinal Greco's visit to Verona. As the story goes, the cardinal, having read her orations, conceived a curiosity to see the woman herself. Having "seen her and heard her, his admiration rather grew stronger than otherwise, such that he judged her to be not mortal, but divine." Along with this episode appears a summary of her collegial relationship with Ludovico Foscarini and their collaboration on the *Dialogue*. Isotta gets the credit, however, for her theological understanding; it was she who "had St. Au-gustine and Jerome as familiar friends." Brought to a certain rhetorical pitch by this achievement, Betussi intrudes as author into his narrative, stating, "Truly, I cannot say enough about her merits, which were of such a sort and so many—each of them rare enough to encounter indi-vidually, let alone in conjunction."[6]

Ten pages later, however, Betussi finds a subject even more merito-rious than Isotta Nogarola, to judge by his frequent authorial intrusions: Cassandra Fedele, like himself a native of the Veneto. "I think," he be-gins, "that it would be better to have recorded just her name, so that by saying little I would not seem to defraud her worth of its right, since she herself has given the clearest testimony to the world of how great her virtues were."[7] But he will tell us anyway.

First in the order of narration, as with the Nogarola women, comes her family and especially her father. She was first "Cassandra Fedele, the Venetian, daughter of Angelo Fedele" and then became "a light of all branches of knowledge, an ornament of the Muses, whom one could say had gathered and reintegrated every kind of study which had become extinct and been almost abandoned by the female sex." Like Isotta Nogarola, Cassandra Fedele improved upon the ancients, surpassing even the famous orator Hortensia: "With both a sure facility in composition, and also a great aptness for oratory, she was judged to have exceeded both Hortensia and all the other ancient and most eloquent Roman women."[8]

Fedele bested not only her ancient predecessor but also her modern antecedent. Whereas Nogarola's mind was merely "divine," Betussi considers Fedele's genius to have been "more than divine" (*più che divino*). Fedele's mastery of philosophy and theology, her skill in disputation, brought honor not only to herself but to "Venice, in which was born such a rare and excellent woman."[9] Betussi formulates her intellectual family in this instance not as a nuclear but rather as a civic entity. The learned woman constituted a tribute to Renaissance culture in general and a particular honor to her birth city. Whereas scholars point out that lavish praise of the Boccaccian type presented accomplished women as exceptions to the rule, it is important to note that Betussi uses the adjective "rare" (*rara*) to describe even these pinnacles of learned virtue.[10] Unlike Boccaccio, Betussi and those following him avoid terms like "unique" or "exceptional" in describing women's achievements. By implication, then, it may be unusual for other women to follow her example, but it is not inconceivable.

Betussi also provides testimony from Fedele's male contemporaries as evidence of her success. "From many extremely learned and scholarly men," he observes, "she was greeted with letters and poems, proof of which is even today clear when one looks at the infinite number of letters written to her, and in many other places where she is celebrated and remembered." In his customary fashion, however, Betussi moves from her fame among men to her feminine virtues, surrounding her unusual status as a public orator with paeans to her chastity and modesty. Here again, he intrudes as author to underscore Fedele's triumphs, both in scholarship and morality: "I do not see how, given her infinite merits, for which I have judged this Cassandra to have been most noble and illustrious, I could keep quiet about them."[11]

Betussi then recounts one highlight of Fedele's career, an invitation by the Venetian senate to perform a Latin oration. He mitigates the potentially unsavory implications of a young woman declaiming at an assembly of older men by noting that "she came together *with her father* . . . into the presence of many orators, philosophers and theologians, who had also been invited." Eradicating any remaining sense of impropriety, he adds that "the wise and learned young woman, blushing in the pleasing hues of chastity and modesty, made a Latin oration with such grace and fluency that we remember it even to this day."[12]

On other occasions, Betussi continues, Fedele debated philosophical and theological principles with the most celebrated male intellectuals, and she even lectured publicly at the *studio* of Padua. But she also loved chastity and (he mistakenly asserts) never married; rather, she kept herself from idleness (like Nogarola) by study and the practice of music. Differing here from the way he treated Nogarola, however, Betussi troubles to provide in this instance a particular quotation from the famous humanist Angelo Poliziano rather than the mere assurance that many men admired her accomplishments. "Among her other admirers was Angelo Poliziano," Betussi avers, "[who] with infinite praise remembered her, and exalted her, whom he said had taken up books instead of the spindle and the pen instead of the needle, and the stylus instead of the distaff, and has written such fine Latin epistles. Similarly he wrote at the beginning of another letter to her the following words of praise: 'O honor of women and light of Italy . . . who has condescended to honor me with your letters.' Certainly such faith and love could not accrue to anyone less than a woman—but why should I say woman?—to a girl, rather, and a virgin of celestial merit and such infinite value."[13]

Scholars have contended that encomia such as Poliziano's transformed learned women into abstracted icons of humanist endeavor.[14] Betussi's object in adding "modern" women to Boccaccio's compendium, however, was to historicize literary convention. In order to keep the tone of his translation and additions even, Betussi mimics Boccaccio's grandiose rhetoric to a certain extent. Yet he also makes a point of his subjects' historicity. Placing Fedele, for one, in a long tradition of ancient women philosophers and poets—familiar but scantily documented—Betussi avers that she, by contrast, "enjoyed writing and has left a record of the truth of the things that she found." And here again he speaks in the first person: "Since I would become excessively prolix in recounting her merits, which I do not think I know as well as I would like; in any case, I will leave the honorable task to a more worthy mind than mine."[15]

Betussi's text went a long way toward ensuring Fedele's continued presence in Italian letters. Redactions and translations of Boccaccio were reliable profit-makers for any early modern printer, to be sure, but Betussi's translation and indeed reinvention of *Concerning Famous Women* found its own substantial audience. Most importantly, other authors published biographical compendia of famous women in Betussi's mold, as well as works of pedagogical theory that made at least a few pointed references to the fifteenth-century women humanists whom Betussi had commemorated. Among such women, Fedele is the most consistently cited.[16]

In 1547 Betussi's contemporary and fellow Venetian writer-editor Ludovico Dolce published the first of what would be five editions of his dialogue *On the Education of Women*. Dolce framed this text as a conversation between a woman and a man, thereby placing his work in the tradition of famous Venetian humanist Pietro Bembo. Bembo's dialogue *Gli Asolani* gives its female interlocutors substantive speaking parts—in striking contrast to the more passive roles played by the women of Castiglione's *Courtier*.[17] Dolce's purpose in this dialogue is not to recount the biographical details of every woman who had ever written but rather to argue that the full instruction of women in the humanities, outlined in book I, serves as a foundation for the many moral and domestic virtues that constitute the bulk of his discussion in books II and III.

Dolce's interlocutors, Flaminio, a mature widower, and Dorothea, a young widow with a daughter to raise, are principally concerned with deciding how best to form a perfect daughter. Her education, they decide, must prepare her for becoming a good wife and mother, but the groundwork for domestic virtue will be a broad foundation in the humanities. In this text, the quattrocento women humanists live on as "state's exhibit A" for learned virtue in good family women. Although Isotta Nogarola does not receive explicit discussion, her *Dialogue* is mentioned, and other Nogarole (Angela, Ginevra, Laura, and Caterina) are praised as erudite matrons. Cassandra Fedele receives frequent reference as the heir of ancient women philosophers and orators, most of whom, both Greek and Latin, represent their fathers' excellence reborn in a chaste female form. In fact, Dolce begins by mentioning various royal women who exemplify learned virtue, but in moving toward women of what he terms "private station," his first example is "Cassandra Fedele of [his] city."[18] Dolce thereby presents the coupling of erudition and morality in non-regal women as a Venetian specialty.

"This modest woman," Dolce continues, "was so learned, that more than once she disputed publicly with very great honor, and among Poliziano's epistles I have read one that he wrote to her, in which that famous man shows how much he had esteemed her virtues."[19] Following his testimony to Cassandra's worth, Dolce lists among others Vittoria Colonna and another Venetian woman of letters, Veronica Gambara (later Countess of Correggio), for being "learned in humane and divine letters, and both equally exemplars of piety and chastity."[20]

In 1586 the cleric Tomaso Garzoni published a collection of women's biographies drawn from scripture, to which he appended a brief in defense of secular women.[21] Dedicated to the Duchess of Ferrara, Margherita Gonzaga, this text evidently ingratiated him with the Ferrarese court, since her husband, Alfonso II d'Este, served as patron for Garzoni's better-known publication, *La piazza universale di tutte le professioni del mondo (The Universal Marketplace of Every Profession on Earth)*, printed the following year (1587). That a cleric wrote "biographies" of scriptural women is not in itself novel. His defense of women, however, follows Betussi's new model in praising secular women intellectuals. In argumentative strategy, Garzoni follows Henricus Cornelius Agrippa's influential *Declamation on the Nobility and Preeminence of the Female Sex* (1529). Like Agrippa, Garzoni asserts the nobility of women on seven premises. The first six depend on bending material from the book of Genesis in order to present Eve as more dignified than Adam in terms of her efficient cause, name, place, material, and the form of her creation. For his seventh and final premise, Garzoni adduces women's "habits of knowledge and virtue." He contends that "the principal index of women's greatness and nobility is in their habit of knowledge and the virtues of the mind, for in these alone is a person's true nobility revealed, as Plato affirms in his book, *The Republic*, when he says that 'Feminae & vir aeque ad omnia apti' [Women and man (*sic*) are equally fit for all things]."[22] As proof of this postulate, Garzoni lists in quick succession many of the ancient women celebrated by Boccaccio.

Cassandra Fedele constitutes Garzoni's first "modern" example: "Angelo Poliziano praises to the heavens Cassandra Fedele, a young Venetian woman, with these words: 'She busied herself with the book, not the spindle; the pen, not the needle; the stylus not the distaff.'"[23] If Poliziano and his ilk made the learned woman into a myth, she was certainly a myth that subsequent writers took pains to perpetuate.[24] In Fedele's case, it is also worth noting that she is no longer placed in the category of "holy virgin" but rather is cited as an example of the praiseworthy act of trading "feminine" sewing gear for "masculine" intellectual apparatus.

Garzoni assumed that his patron and readers would already know about other women of Fedele's stamp and mentions them via a series of rhetorical questions. "What should I say about Isotta Nogarola," he asks, "or Ginevra [Nogarola]? or Costanza Sforza? or Battista Malatesta? Are not all of them commended by [Poliziano] for being scholarly women, adorned with a host of beautiful letters? Shall I fail to add these, who are lights of our own age: Vittoria Colonna, Laura Terracina, the other Battifera, Tarquinia Molza, and a thousand others, who fill up the whole universe with their fame?"[25] Garzoni tempers this potentially unsavory attribute, "fame," with the usual profusion of moral virtues. He was no statistician, but his comment that there are "a thousand" other women in his time who exemplify learned virtue represents a crucial departure from the Boccaccian exceptionality trope.

Twenty-three years later (1609), a Spanish expatriate canon, Pietro Paolo di Ribera, modified Garzoni's "thousand." Ribera considered only 845 women of classical antiquity and modern times illustrious enough for his compendium.[26] Ribera's text was published by a Venetian printer, Evangelista Deuchino, who probably solicited it. Deuchino's dedicatory letter to Valeria Bonomi, abbess at a convent in Trieste, expresses the wish that this publication may serve to repay his personal debt of gratitude for the care of his sister, Tranquilla Deuchina, who was a nun at the same convent. "I always thank the Divine Majesty," Deuchino explains, "for having granted Sister Tranquilla Deuchina, my sister, the grace to be situated in this sacred place [the convent], which one might call a terrestrial paradise . . . where I cannot number the favors that my aforementioned sister has received and receives from your charity—favors which redound superabundantly upon me, too, since I am myself favored thereby, and so remain indebted to Your Reverence."[27] When women's writing or works praising women appear, family connections and motives are often nearby.

Ribera's treatment of his subjects parallels Betussi's in that Ribera emphasizes women's paternal pedigrees and marital connections, as well as the mutually sustaining dynamic of virtue and learning. Like Agrippa and Garzoni, moreover, Ribera gives learned women pride of place by making them the final category for consideration in his wide-ranging compendium.

Erudite women were not hasty last additions but rather frame Ribera's whole composition. In his prefatory "Consolation to Women," Ribera advocates women's advanced instruction on the grounds that the ancients (especially Plutarch) had approved the practice of teaching women various branches of knowledge. Ribera's final sentence goes to the Agrippan extreme in positing women's supremacy over men in matters of the mind: "In closing I say that the Ancients, considering women's knowledge and aptitude, depicted the sciences and liberal arts as women, by which convention they tell us that women are more able, talented, ready and disposed than men to learn them."[28]

Ribera's organizational decisions reveal striking hermeneutics of association. Within his overall thematic category of "Learned and Eloquent Women," he most often groups the biographies into subject specialties, such as scripture, astrology, or poetry. When possible, however, Ribera privileges regional and familial association over field specialty. This decision forces him to create broader categories, so as to encompass women from the same part of Italy or the same family whose interests were diverse. This is particularly striking in the case of the Nogarola women, whose biographies appear in succession under the banner "women expert in various branches of knowledge" *(donne dottissime in varie scienze)*. The intellectual honor of the family group, then, takes precedence over its individual members: Isotta, who was a virginal rhetorician; Ginevra, who was a devoted wife, charitable patroness, and humanist letter-writer; and Angela, who turned her scriptural understanding into Latin poetry.

Cassandra Fedele appears in Ribera's subcategory of "women excellent in oratory," alongside two classical figures. The first is Eumenia, described in one sentence as "no less eloquent than her father." The other is Hortensia, the learned daughter who embodied her father's eloquence. Such was the skill of her oration to the Senate on behalf of the Roman matrons, unfairly taxed by the triumvirs, that the audience "seemed to hear in such facility the excellence of her father."[29] These three are the only biographies in this category. Female accomplishment in public speaking, especially in Latin, brings the father connection back to center stage.

At many levels, women's speech was a source of anxiety for early modern culture. Even farsighted humanists like Bruni, who advocated teaching women the humanities, excepted the study of oratory. Theoretically, the argument for women's silence derived from the Pauline injunction against women preaching in the Church, as well as the older classical association of women in public with "public women"—already persuasive enough in luring men from the path of virtue. The notion of women speaking in public presented the most overt challenge to "feminine" mores. Authors like Ribera, who sought to legitimize even women's speech, "domesticated" the female orator. Rather than explicating the political implications of Hortensia's taking up the cause of her fellow Roman matrons, Ribera makes the moral of the story the father's rebirth in his daughter's oration.

This same instinct to domesticate the female orator appears in the *Charming and Learned Defense of Women in Verse and Prose*, by Luigi Dardano, humanist and chancellor of the Venetian Republic. His grandson, Hippolito, published this text in 1554, with Dardano's brief treatise on the education of children. In this latter work, Dardano does not advocate instructing daughters in anything other than household skills and religion. Yet, in canto III of the earlier *Defense*, he urges his audience (which he presumes female) to disregard male criticism and focus instead on modeling themselves upon virtuous and heroic ancient women. Before exemplars of wifely virtue and chastity appear the women orators, among them "Tullia, whom Cicero so loved / of whose rare doctrine he filled his pages, / and who perpetuated her father's honor."[30] Tullia stands as the final example in this section, preceded by Hortensia, whose story Dardano recounts in several stanzas and whose rhetorical excellence he explains as a perpetuation of her father's intellectual honor: "She, eloquent, with talent immense / Because she maintained her father's excellence / Negated the law with marvelous sense."[31] Dardano's brief poetic references demonstrate the appeal of a Hortensian paradigm, even in the mental landscape of a man whose "syllabus" for women included praying, cooking, and childbearing. He would not teach women to write in Italian, let alone speak in Latin, but he could still admire the female orator as "her father's daughter."

In 1620 a Piedmontese, Francesco Agostino della Chiesa, published his *Theater of Lettered Women, with a Brief Discourse Concerning the Preeminence and Perfection of the Female Sex.*[32] Introducing himself as a doctor of laws from Saluzzo and otherwise an author of ecclesiastical biography, Chiesa presented the next step in collective female biography: a tome devoted to literary women alone. Chiesa's "theater" is remarkable not only for its thematic focus but also for its scope and international sensibility. His 499 biographies include a balanced mix of Italian, French, and German authors, with a few Spanish and a fair number of English examples. The text is organized alphabetically by first name and includes ancient, medieval, and "modern" examples in more or less equal proportion— though the modern examples get more extensive treatments, by virtue of the greater availability of source material. Chiesa will receive more extended discussion hereafter as an admirer of sixteenth-century learned women like Margaret Roper, Lucrezia Marinella, and Moderata Fonte. For the moment, however, it must be stressed that, even two centuries after they died, the quattrocento women humanists remained important figures in the world of Italian letters.

By restricting his collection to literary women, Chiesa offered his readers a far more comprehensive cast of characters in this field than had his predecessors, who attempted to populate every category of "virtue" with examples. Chiesa is the first writer in this genre to make note of Christine de Pizan. He was evidently unaware of her familial background but at least noted her prominence as an author at the French court and cited two of her compositions: the *City of Women* and *Le chemin de long estude.*[33]

Laura Cereta, whom even authors with Venetian biases like Betussi and Dolce did not mention, also reappears in Chiesa's treatment. He found her name in a catalog of the best modern astrologers and had also heard that "at 22 years of age, she had already written very beautiful Latin letters and some poems in the vernacular." From these pieces of information, Chiesa extrapolates that she was also known for her excellence in moral philosophy, oratory, and Tuscan poetry.[34] The same short biography of Cereta reappears five years later (1625) in Cristofano Bronzini d'Ancona's dialogue, *On the Dignity and Nobility of Women.*[35]

Chiesa amplifies the treatment even of Cassandra Fedele, who already enjoyed consistent citation by feminist authors. Chiesa followed Betussi in general narrative arc and in his mention that Fedele was accompanied by her father when she delivered her oration to the Venetian senate—a point that neither Dolce nor Ribera mentioned. Chiesa added somewhat more careful scholarship to her biographical tradition, although he mentions nothing of her marriage. Indeed, the connection between virginity and expository prose or oratory remained prevalent in discussions of Italian women humanists well into the seventeenth century. However, Chiesa did note Fedele's status as prioress at San Domenico and her final oration for the senate, information about her later life that moved her out of the child-prodigy category.

The Nogarola legacy also expands in Chiesa's treatment. Underscoring the family theme, Chiesa brings forward four further "letterate" of this Veronese lineage in addition to the more famous Angela, Ginevra, and Isotta: Antonia (dated 1330), Giulia (dated 1490), Lucia (dated 1550) and Nostra (dated 1340). The treatments of Antonia and Nostra are brief, as is common in works like this for any subject born before the sixteenth century. Chiesa does inform the reader, however, that Antonia came from the Veronese branch of the family, married Salvatico Bonacolti of the Mantuan nobility, and, finding herself already "a rival for the most learned men of her age, wished to deepen her knowledge, whereupon she soon became expert in all sorts of doctrine and was reputed an ornament not only of Verona, but also of Mantua."[36] Jacopo Sansovino's book on the Italian nobility, Chiesa explains, provided the information about Nostra, "who married into the Brescian household of the Martinengo and who is said to have been renowned for her sublime intellect and for the great understanding that she had of letters."[37] Giulia Nogarola, noted as Veronese but not as noble, is described as a nun at Santa Chiara in Verona and a "beata" venerated for her knowledge of philosophy and scripture.[38]

Chiesa pauses in his brief description of Lucia Nogarola to comment on the honor of the household itself, notable equally for its valorous men and for its numerous learned women. Lucia, he informs us, was from that noble Veronese "family from which—almost as if from a Trojan horse—have emerged an infinite number of valorous cavaliers, and many wise matrons."[39]

Cristofano Bronzini's defense of women, mentioned above, appeared in Italian and French editions in 1625, five years after Chiesa's compendium. The arguments of the feminist Onorio (the character who, as Bronzini states explicitly on the frontispiece, represents his own viewpoint) and various male and female interlocutors rehearse the prominent themes of the *querelle des femmes,* which was now over two hundred years old: the perfidious nature of men who malign women for their own faults, contrasted with women's excellence in every kind of virtue; and male jealousy as an explanation for excluding women from "publicity"—an exclusion that men attempt to secure by denying women the kind of education that would prepare them for public roles. Yet the hopes of the malignant have always and ever foundered, so the story goes, when confronted by paragons of learned virtue. The defense of womankind had, since Boccaccio's initial foray, depended upon biographies of women. Even in a dialogue, nearly three centuries later, the art of persuasion necessitated citation of numerous ancient and "modern" illustrious females. Though the dialogue as a genre cannot encompass direct reference to Garzoni's "thousand," Ribera's 845, or Chiesa's 499 examples, nonetheless the headliners remain.

Bronzini's text also posits a new hermeneutic for learned women. Whereas authors had previously given learned women contemporary to themselves ancient predecessors like Hortensia, Bronzini sometimes links women of his own day to fifteenth-century success stories. Bronzini admired two of his contemporaries, the Venetian writers Lucrezia Marinella and Moderata Fonte, above all others, to judge by the sheer word count that he devotes to them, as well as his encomiastic fervor. We will revisit his dialogue in due course, but for the moment it is important to note that the precedent he adduces for Moderata Fonte's excellence as wife, mother, and intellect is not an abstracted classical heroine but rather Ginevra Nogarola:

> How great was the worth, the courtesy and the knowledge of Ginevra one discovers from her own works, since she earned an immortal name on account of her wisdom. I mention in passing that for Beauty, Prudence, Liberality, she became famous throughout the whole world, and that beyond all this, she was very kind and charming to every sort of person, that for the infinite merits that compounded in Her, everyone revered and esteemed her. Concerning letters, she was well versed and on that account became exceedingly famous, and she gave no little example of her great knowledge in many fields, even to the most worthy minds of her time. Her letters testify this, written copiously, full of good teachings and precepts, with a style so grave, pure and full of sweetness that they would cause not just a woman, but any great scholarly man to glory in

them. In her other actions, whether public or private, she was beyond compare: she cared greatly for works of mercy and often visited the infirm, gave assistance to the poor, succored the needy—indeed, she never failed to perform any act that befits a true Christian.[40]

The heir to this example of the learned woman who was also a good family woman and Christian is Moderata Fonte, who appears next in the text. "Of what sort, and indeed how great," Onorio continues, "were the goodness, prudence, and knowledge of Modesta Pozzo, otherwise called Moderata Fonte, her works and her compositions give ample testimony to the world."[41]

Taken together, these biographers and encomiasts of illustrious women were the first specialists in "women's studies." Fascinated with the woman intellectual, they sought to find a suitable category for her that would appeal to their more conventional contemporaries. Antique precedent gave the female subject cachet; lineage gave her substance and credibility.

Capitalizing upon the growing interest women of the pen, Jacopo (or Giacomo) Filippo Tomasini (1595–1655) wrote extensive biographies of both Cassandra Fedele and Laura Cereta. His innovation was to move beyond the genre of biographical compendium toward the modern critical edition. Tomasini's editions of both women humanists comprise detailed biographies, complete works of the authors, and careful attention to contemporary reception. A Paduan by birth, a canon by profession, and a prolific scholar of his native city's intellectual history by vocation, Tomasini produced his credentials as a historian of women in 1636 and 1640: his publication of the works by Cassandra Fedele and Laura Cereta might be considered the first volumes in the Other Voice in Early Modern Europe series insofar as they are serious, scholarly works that link women's biographies to their writings and reception.[42]

In the letter to the reader that prefaces his edition of Fedele's letterbook and orations, Tomasini contextualized the Venetian prodigy by reference to three other illustrious women Latinists of the Most Serene Republic: Isotta and Angela Nogarola, and Laura Cereta. He tantalized the reader with the prospect of providing edited volumes for all of them.[43] Four years later, he posited in his note to the reader that he considered Laura Cereta to be "in the society of learned women like Cassandra Fedele who, because of her surpassing fame for erudition, [became] an ornament among the most learned women of her age."[44] Tomasini enunciated a historical tradition of learned women.

Fedele and Cereta contributed to the luster of their native cities and to the women of their age, in Tomasini's view, but above all they served as worthy heirs to their intellectual families. After discussing various branches of the Fedele family in northern Italy, Tomasini positions Cassandra in the tradition of her well-educated progenitors, especially her Venetian progenitors: "From this Venetian lineage, Cassandra was indebted to the genius of her fecund mother and kindly nurse [the household], to Angelo, the best sort of father and a man famous for his expertise in the languages among princely men of great authority, to her grandfather and great-grandfather, concerning whose erudition she herself said: . . . I apply myself to study of the best arts, lest I seem unworthy to my great-great grandfather, my great-grandfather and our most famous ancestors."[45] He makes a particular point that Angelo, "an admirer of Cassandra's ability to conquer the laziness customary to her age and sex, took pains to ensure that she be instructed." Tomasini continues, "But she, after learning the first rudiments of grammar, so excelled in Latin and Greek language that it seems she thought chiefly of complying with the hopes of her father, who marveled at her surpassing genius. And alongside domestic duties, his principal concern was that her mind be encouraged in good letters by means of frequent discussion with her teachers; in which she made such progress that, having barely reached the age of twelve, she was fluent in Latin."[46] Tomasini thus makes it clear that Cassandra's remarkable academic talent was nurtured by her learned father within the household and alongside her "domestic duties." She was a good daughter, in short, in addition to being a credit to her learned lineage.

Tomasini situates Laura Cereta in context of her native Brescia, remarkable "not only for its preeminent men, who have ornamented various European nations with their speech and writings, or whose fame for sanctity was remarkable, but . . . also [for] its women of surpassing piety and doctrine, whose names have received passing mention on the old monuments: as the worthy Ludovico Cendrata of Verona is quoted as saying by the historian, Capreolus, Brescia 'will be known as an Academy, not only of Men, but also of Women.'"[47] Among women like Lucia Albana (an expert in law) and Veronica Gambara (the learned vernacular poet), Tomasini found Laura Cereta the most remarkable. As he does with Fedele's background, he highlights the tradition of learning present in Cereta's male ancestors, who included an important doctor of medicine (fl. 1430–1465) and her father, Silvestro, "notable in public works."[48]

Underscoring the domestic theme again, Tomasini paraphrases Cereta's own narrative concerning her name. "Since the first child born [to Silvestro] was a daughter," he explains, "he gave her the name of Laura in memory of a laurel tree that had for many long years withstood the injuries of winter in the household garden."[49] Moving from the image of the tree that flourished despite adversity within the "household garden," Tomasini describes how its namesake flourished in her household academy: "[She] drank in piety with her first lessons in grammar. After she reached the age of seven, she was given to the Holy Sisters for instruction. Here she, who was already progressing in letters and in needlecraft, perfected both arts with remarkable speed. Two years later she left [the convent], having been called back home, where she devoted herself to the study of rare documents and her father took pains that she be instructed in the finer points of grammar and in the more subtle aspects of letters. By virtue of her versatile and ready genius, she was successful in joining deeper study to the administration of domestic matters."[50] Here again, Tomasini presents the young female talent as a dutiful daughter who exemplifies learned virtue.[51]

From biographical encyclopedias and defenses of women to edited texts, there are a variety of documentary lenses for gauging the reception of learned women in sixteenth- and seventeenth-century Italy. Contemporary responses to learned women in England, in contrast, must be assembled from male humanists' letters, biographies of male celebrities, and encyclopedias of statesmen. English presses would begin to publish collections of female biography in the late seventeenth century, but in the sixteenth century encomia were closely tied to individual women scholars and their networks of erudite male kin.[52] Women's education was thus neatly categorized as a "family affair" during the age of English humanism.

Celebrations of English Women Humanists

In 1523 Erasmus sent Margaret Roper his commentary on two hymns of Prudentius as a Christmas present and in commemoration of the birth of her first child. As was his characteristic approach to the dedicatory epistle, Erasmus toyed with layered meanings, wrapping them in his thorny Latin. The particular sport to hand in this instance, in honor of the season, was rhetorical play upon the various meanings of human and divine kinship. Erasmus opened his letter by praising Margaret's learning. The terms of his compliment, however, were familial. "I have been put on my mettle so often lately," he wrote, "by letters from you and your sisters—such sensible, well-written, modest, forthright, friendly letters—that even if someone were to excise the headings I would be able to recognize the 'offspring true-born' of Thomas More."[53] Erasmus thus made biological and intellectual pedigree coterminous.

Compatibility in marriage came next in Erasmus's exordium. He compares Margaret and William Roper's praiseworthy mutualism as husband and wife to that of a sister and brother. "William Roper," Erasmus observes, "a man of such high character, such charm and such modesty that were he not your husband he might be taken for your brother, has presented you—or, if you prefer, you have presented him—with the first fruits of your marriage, and most promising they are. To put it more accurately, each of you has presented the other with a baby boy to be smothered in kisses."[54]

Finally, Erasmus arrives at the dedication itself, which explores the connection between intellectual and biological "issue," as well as divine and human family. "Here I am sending you another boy," he writes, "who brings more promise than any other: Jesus, born for the Jews and soon to become the light of the gentiles, who will give the offspring of your marriage a happy outcome and be the true Apollo of all your reading, whose praises you will be able to sing to your lyre instead of nursery rhymes to please your little ones."[55] In this passage, Erasmus conflates Margaret's intellectual and physical motherhood. At the beginning of the letter, she is a "virtuous maiden," whose letters prove her to be her father's daughter; by the end, however, she is a learned matron, singing Latin hymns about the Christ child to her own children.

Scholars believe that Margaret Roper also served as the model for the "learned lady" who intellectually defeats the pompous clergyman in Erasmus's dialogue titled *The Abbot and the Learned Lady.*[56] In his own correspondence, Erasmus certainly served as a publicist for the More intellectual family project. In a letter to Guillaume Budé, he claims that although he once agreed with his contemporaries that it was pointless to educate women, "More has driven this thought completely from [his] mind."[57] This epistle does far more, however, than make passing reference to More's success in proving the utility of women's advanced instruction. Erasmus uses this letter to rehearse the debate on women systematically, particularly the debate on women's education, using the More household school as conclusive evidence in favor of the feminist side of the argument. Given that Erasmus's letters circulated throughout the known intellectual universe, the importance of this document cannot be overstated.

Erasmus urges Budé, his younger colleague, to cultivate a relationship with Thomas More, since More was at the right hand of King Henry, who was himself a comparable figure to the famous patron of literature in Augustan Rome, Maecenas.[58] Erasmus then devotes one hundred lines to explicating the achievement of his English friend in the education of his entire family—an achievement that Erasmus expects others to imitate. More is by no means alone in his intellectual excellence, Erasmus explains, "because he himself, a most learned man, openly favors all educated people and, what's more, is ensuring that a universal family of letters [*universam familiam literarum*] develops by means of honest studies. [His is] certainly a novel case to date, but one that many will follow, and soon, unless I am mistaken. So far, he succeeds happily." More's four learned daughters prove the measure of this success. "From their infancy," Erasmus narrates, "[More] took care to imbue all of them with chastity and holy conduct first, then with very polished letters. To the three biological daughters he has added a fourth little girl [Margaret Giggs], whom the grace of his goodness favors so that she might be a friend to them. He also has a ward [Alice, later Alington]—a girl of admirable beauty and rare genius (married some years ago to a young man who is himself not unlettered), but her morals defy comparison."[59]

Moving from this general description, Erasmus describes another way in which More served to publicize his household school. "Around New Year's," he begins, "it occurred to More to show me some example of how far the daughters were coming along in letters. He ordered that all of them write to me . . . neither giving them topics, nor correcting their language in any way. When they gave their compositions to their father to be corrected, he just pretended to be outraged at their sloppy compositions and ordered them to rewrite everything more accurately and perfectly. And when this was done, without changing so much as a syllable, he sent the unsigned letters to me." Erasmus attests that he has "never admired anything more," because their letters constituted impressive compositions, in which "there was nothing clumsy or childish," and even more striking is the fluency of their language, which was so well-developed that "you would think that they spoke Latin every day." Although Erasmus's visit to the Chelsea household occurred long before the children began their studies, he nonetheless shifts toward an eyewitness account to highlight the image of the learned young women devoting themselves to study. He testifies that "you won't see even one of the girls lazing about, not one of them engaged in idle womanly pursuits. Titus Livius is in their hands. For in Livy they are so far along, that they're now reading others of his quality and understanding them without resorting to glosses, unless they happen to run into a word that would have stumped even me."[60]

In 1550, six years after Margaret's death, John Coke published his treatise titled *The Debate betwene the Heraldes of Englande and Fraunce,* in which England and France each argue their superiority as countries, with Lady Prudence sitting as judge. England claims pride of place with regard to the "gentlewomen" who possess knowledge not only of scripture but of Greek and Latin as well. He cites three such women: Mistress More, Mistress Anne Cooke, and Mistress Clement. First on the list was Mistress More.[61]

The comments of Erasmus and Coke serve as one indicator of Margaret Roper's reception and her intellectual legacy. Her own husband, however, offered similar testimony in his *Life of Sir Thomas More.* William Roper wrote this text around 1557, and by 1598 there were several manuscripts in circulation. By 1626 a print redaction of the *Life* appeared, and the work enjoyed reasonably wide readership thereafter. Roper's biography, as Richard Marius puts it, was "[filled] with quiet praise of his wife."[62] Largely, this praise involved extended explication of the emotional bond between More and his daughter. Most famously, Roper recounts an episode in which Margaret had fallen ill. He describes More's hours of prayer in his private chapel for her recovery, More's vision from God that she needed an enema, and her miraculous recovery after receiving the same—with the touching final statement, quoted in direct statement from his father-in-law, that if Margaret had died More would "never after have meddled in worldly affairs." Roper also stresses his wife's filial devotion during her father's imprisonment and the way in which she abandoned conventional manners by running to hug and kiss her father good-bye on the night before his execution. Thus at one level Margaret appears as a pious daughter.

Yet Roper emphasizes his wife's "virtuous learning," a theme that connected More to his children as much as emotional affinity did. Explaining his father-in-law's shift from semimonastic devotion at the London Charterhouse to married life, Roper observes that it was only the "honest conversation and *virtuous education*" of the three daughters of Master Colt that made More begin to think of marriage.[63] It was the same combination of virtue and learning that More aimed to instill in his children. More had by his wife "three daughters (and one Son), in *virtue and learning* brought up from their youth, whom he would often exhort to take *virtue and learning* for their meat and play for their sauce."[64] As we have already seen, More himself placed these "subjects" on the syllabus in that order: virtue first, learning second. In fact, in his concluding remarks to William Gonnell, he stated that his paternal affection, although present according to the law of nature, would increase in direct proportion to their progress through learning and virtue toward spiritual perfection: "My children, first by law of nature dear, and then dearer for their learning and virtue, you must make by this increase of doctrine and good morals most dear."[65]

While Roper's *Life* only hints at Margaret's erudition, his epitaph presents her as a quintessential "learned matron." The inscription itself, supposedly once in the chancel of St. Dunstan's, Canterbury, no longer exists.[66] Even if it is an invention, however, the language of the putative epitaph nonetheless highlights Margaret Roper's tripartite mythos: learned daughter, ideal wife, and dutiful mother. It also suggests that a learned wife proved an asset to her husband, especially if education was central to his own self-presentation:

> Here lies the venerable man William Roper esquire, son and heir of John Roper, esquire, and Margaret, wife of this same William, she who was most learned in Greek and Latin letters and daughter of Thomas More, once the greatest knight of the English Chancery; this same William succeeded his father in the office of protonotary in the supreme college of the King's Bench, in which he has faithfully served for 54 years and which office he has left to Thomas, his first-born son. This William was generous, tender and merciful at home and abroad, the protector of pris-

oners, the oppressed and the poor. He had from Margaret his wife (who was the only wife he had) two sons and three daughters, from these he has seen in his lifetime grandchildren and great-grandchildren but his wife died while still young, and he was made a widower of a most blameless woman, who was then only 33 years old. However, having finished his days in peace, he died at a ripe old age (something to be desired by all) on the fourth day of the month of January in the year of our savior Christ 1577, at the age of 82.[67]

The description of Margaret, in the Latin, emphasizes the degree to which she encompassed her father's learning. She is described first as Roper's wife; this is followed by a clause noting her status as More's daughter; finally, her gifts in Greek and Latin are emphasized. In this epitaph, then, Thomas More stands literally at the center of his daughter's persona. It is she, in turn, who links her husband to higher levels of intellectual and social prestige. William Roper "armiger" and "protonotarius" associated himself with More "milites" by marrying his "doctissima" daughter.

Explicit testimony that she was both a biological and an intellectual mother to her children derives from Nicholas Harpsfield's biography of Sir Thomas More (1557). "To her children," Harpsfield observes, "she was a double mother, as one not content to bring them forth only into the world, but instructing them also herself in virtue and learning." As supporting evidence for Margaret's "double motherhood," Harpsfield relates a memorable anecdote. During her husband's brief imprisonment, Henry VIII dispatched certain men to search Roper's house. What they found, running into the house "upon a sudden," was Margaret, "not puling and lamenting, but full busily teaching her children: whom they, finding nothing astonished with their message and finding also, besides this her constancy, such gravity and wisdom in her talk as they little looked for." The end result was that the king's officials were "much astonished" and "in great admiration"—to the extent that afterward they spoke nothing but good of her "as partly [Harpsfield had] heard at the mouth of one of them."[68]

Harpsfield's propensity for hyperbole is well known. Yet his close connection with William Roper, evident in his dedication of the *Life* to Roper, suggests that when matters of his patron's household were concerned, he would at least keep to the representational mode that Roper approved. Indeed, Harpsfield announces that Roper had asked him to undertake the biography and acknowledges his own great debt to his dedicatee's earlier work. Elsewhere, Harpsfield mentions receiving anecdotal information in conversations with Roper himself.[69] Given these circumstances, it is safe to assume that Harpsfield's account of Margaret tutoring her children was not, or at least not wholly, his own invention.

Alongside Harpsfield's encomium to the virtuous and learned Margaret Roper appear similar accounts of her sister Margaret Giggs (wife of the physician John Clement) and daughter Mary Basset. These three portraits, taken together, form a triptych that manifests the powerful appeal of socially normal educated women in sixteenth-century England. Harpsfield's argument regarding all of these women is that erudition reinforced what we now term "family values." The latter point arises repeatedly in his systematic description of the More household but focuses upon Margaret first, who was, Harpsfield declaims, "to her father, and to her husband, such a daughter, such a wife, as I suppose it was hard to match her in all England."[70]

In his estimation, Margaret-the-consummate-daughter was best evinced by her behavior during her father's imprisonment. She not only visited but offered him "wise and godly talk," which, together with "such letters she sent him," made her "the chief and almost the only worldly comfort Sir Thomas More had. To whom he wrote . . . that to declare what pleasure and comfort he took of her said letters, a peck of coals would not suffice."[71] For Harpsfield, the most important qualities that sustained her father during his affliction were her "wise and godly talk" and her letters. Learning sustained filial piety.

Next appears Margaret-the-consummate-wife. Harpsfield blends his own assessment with Roper's confirmation that she was an excellent wife: "Her husband thought himself a most happy man that ever happened upon such a treasure—a treasure, I may well say, for such a wife incomparably exceeds (as Solomon says) all worldly treasure. Surely, the said Master Roper had her in such estimation, or rather admiration, that he thought, and hath also said, that she was more worthy for her excellent qualities to have been a Prince's wife." As if this were not testimony enough, Harpsfield cites Erasmus, who "for her exquisite learning, wisdom and virtue . . . called her the flower of all the learned matrons in England."[72] Erasmus wrote to the educated world. To that world he praised Margaret as a wise and virtuous "matron." Far from being dissociated, by virtue of her education, from contemporary culture, Margaret Roper was the best among a collectivity of educated women.

Harpsfield spoke to a vernacular English audience, but he nonetheless demonstrated his own humanist credentials in adducing a list of illustrious learned women from the pagan and Christian traditions. Picking up where Erasmus left off, he concludes, "To say the truth, she was our Sappho, our Aspasia, our Hypathia [*sic*], our Damo, our Cornelia. But what speak I of these, though learned, yet infidels? Nay, rather she was our Christian Fabiola, our Marcella, our Paula, our Eustochium."[73] This impressive list made three interrelated points: learning sustains wifely excellence; learning produces optimal motherhood; learning teaches the Christian virtues that make the best wives and mothers.

Harpsfield's story concerned the perfect marriage of virtue and learning. Thomas More, as the principal subject, was of course the hero. The subplot, however, was the transmission of More's perfection of human excellence to his descendants. Margaret was the next best thing to Thomas More himself, but the rest of the household also received due mention.

In particular, Harpsfield focuses on the Clements as representative of the same conjunction of virtue and learning—this time, that learning being medical rather than scriptural. For Harpsfield, women underscored the "field specialties" of the men with whom they were most closely connected. As Thomas More was a scholar and martyr, so his daughter possessed a "wise *and godly*" kind of intelligence. Because John Clement was a renowned physician, so his wife Margaret Giggs had, in addition to her skills in Latin, Greek, and Hebrew, a remarkable gift for "physic."

The Clements varied Harpsfield's theme of the More household as a utopia of godly erudition. Directly following his account of Margaret's excellences, Harpsfield exhorts the reader to "now see some other that were of the family of this worthy man, Sir Thomas More." He continues, "Among other, Doctor Clement, also his wife (a woman furnished with much virtue and wisdom, and with knowledge of the Latin and Greek tongue, yea, and physick too, above many that seem good and cunning physicians) were brought up in his house." Harpsfield recounts that More took Clement into his household from St. Paul's School and that the young man did not disappoint his patron's hopes in letters (especially Greek), medicine, or virtue. Margaret Giggs Clement exemplified her husband's academic and moral virtues. Harpsfield describes, in particular, her youthful precocity in medicine. About fifteen years before his execution, More fell ill with a "tertian fever," one symptom of which was to feel hot and cold at the same time—a malady that baffled his physicians, who insisted that this was impossible and that he must have dreamed the sensation. "[But] Mistress Clement," Harpsfield narrates, "being at that time a young girl, whom a kinsman of hers had begun to teach physic, told Sir Thomas More that there was such a kind of fever indeed, and forthwith showed [him] a work of Galen, *de differentiis febrium*, where Galen affirms the same."[74] Harpsfield justifies Margaret Giggs Clement's medical expertise on two domestic premises: first, her marriage to a physician husband; second, her education in medicine "from a kinsman."

Wary of secularizing More's household utopia, Harpsfield shifts to the couple's Catholic piety. The Clements lived "full blessedly together" and were "besides all [their] other excellent qualities . . . notable for their great constancy in the Catholic faith; for the which they voluntarily and willingly relinquished their country, and banished themselves in the late reign of King Edward the Sixth."[75] Time and again, Harpsfield returns to the connection between virtue and learning.

Demonstrating the enduring legacy of this connection within the More family and complimenting his patron, Harpsfield also offers a laudatory sketch of Mary Basset's virtue and virtuosity. In his dedication, he stated that Roper was dignified by his illustrious family—natal and, above all, conjugal: "You and your family are by no one thing more adorned, [made illustrious] and beautified, than by this worthy man, Sir Thomas More, in marrying his daughter, the excellent, learned and virtuous matron, Mistress Margaret More." So, too, Roper's children constituted significant assets in the More-Roper portfolio of intellect and piety. Harpsfield gives only a brief notice of Roper's sons being "brought up and learned in the liberal sciences and the laws of the Realm," but he comments extensively on his patron's daughter. He notes her familial connections as "late wife to Master Clarke, and now wife to Master Bassett, one of our gracious Sovereign Queen Mary's Privy Chamber," and then proceeds to enumerate her many scholarly achievements:

> This Mistress Bassett is very well expert in the Latin and Greek tongues; she hath very handsomely and learnedly translated out of the Greek into the English all the ecclesiastical story of Eusebius, with Socrates, Theodoretus, Sozomenus and Evagrius, albeit of modesty she suppresses

it, and keeps it from the print. She hath also very aptly and fitly translated into the said tongue a certain book that Sir Thomas, her grandfather, made upon the passion, and so elegantly and eloquently penned
that a man would think it were originally written in the said English
tongue.[76]

Like his patron, Harpsfield further dignified his principal subject by
praising the women of the More family to the second generation. Far
from being a one-act about Thomas More, Harpsfield's account was a
play in three full acts, including characters not only running along the
main agnatic line but extending to More's adopted daughter and her
husband, and to More's grandchildren.

Harpsfield's praise for Basset's skill as a translator followed the
prefatory praise offered by William Rastell in the original publication.
Having specified her occupation and pedigree, informing the reader that
the text is "an exposition of a part of the passion of our savior Jesus
Christ, made in Latin by Sir Thomas More, knight (while he was pris-
oner in the Tower of London) and translated into English, by Mistress
Mary Basset, one of the gentlewomen of the Queen's Majesty's Privy
Chamber, and niece to the said Sir Thomas More," Rastell highlights the
connection between kinship and authorship.[77] In his words, Basset's
translation "goes so near Sir Thomas More's own English phrase that
[she is as near] to him in kindred, virtue and literature, [as] in his English tongue: so that it might seem to have been [written] by his own pen,
and not at all translated: such a gift hath she to follow her grandfather's
vein in writing."[78] These are terms similar to those used by Erasmus
when he called the letters of Margaret Roper and her siblings "the 'offspring true-born' of Thomas More."[79]

For Harpsfield, Margaret Roper remained the pivotal player in the
transmission of More's legacy, because she "did prick nearest her father,
as well in wit, virtue and learning, as also in merry and pleasant talk."[80]
And Margaret would, despite Harpsfield's and Rastell's attempts to highlight the full range of talent in the More household, continue to inspire
comment when her siblings and indeed her own children did not.

As late as Thomas Fuller's *History of the Worthies of England* (1662),
Margaret Roper retains costar billing in the Morean drama. An account
of her directly follows the entry on her father. Fuller apologizes to his
reader for "placing a lady among men and learned statesmen" but justi-

fies his apparent affront to gender boundaries on the basis of "her unfeigned affection to her father, from whom she would not willingly be
parted (and for me shall not be) either living or dead."[81] As a doctor of
divinity, however, Fuller was also interested in Margaret as a blend of
learning and virtue. He reports that in her father's house she "attained
to that skill in all learning and languages that she became the miracle of
her age. Foreigners took such notice hereof, that Erasmus hath dedicated some epistles unto her."[82] Fuller relates her insight into a corrupted passage of Cyprian, also noted by Harpsfield, but mistakenly
attributes the translation of Eusebius to her, thereby conflating Margaret
with her daughter.

While later authors, like Fuller, would remember only Margaret's
achievements, nonetheless the story of the mid-sixteenth century was
not about this woman alone but rather about the household as academy.
Harpsfield not only accentuated this theme in providing detailed testimony to the excellence of several generations of More-Ropers but made
the notion of the household academy explicit:

> Surely, if a man had seen and fully known the order [and] trade of
> [More's] children, and of this young Clement, and the aforesaid maid that
> was after his wife, and of his other family, he would have taken great
> spiritual and ghostly pleasure thereof, and would have thought himself
> to have rather been in Plato's Academy—nay, what say I, Plato's? Not in
> Plato's, but in some Christian well-ordered academy and university, rather
> than in any layman's house. Everybody there so beset himself and his
> time upon such good and fruitful reading and other virtuous exercises.[83]

The family as academy (or university) served Harpsfield's principal purpose of demonstrating the "ghostly and spiritual" benefit of any connection with his principal protagonist. Yet this image of the household
academy also connects closely to the social realities of sixteenth-century
Englishwomen's education. Women in England and indeed in premodern
Europe as a whole had no access to public institutions of higher education; with the dissolution of the monasteries under Henry VIII, Englishwomen lacked even the provisional option of a convent education.
Thus, if they were to receive any instruction in letters or the arts, it would
necessarily take place at home. If a woman's humanistic learning, moreover, were to be understood by contemporaries as in any way appropriate despite its novelty, it needed to be surrounded with the legitimizing

framework of familial—and particularly patriarchal—sanction. All of this being said, however, it is striking that contemporary authors did not represent household academies as inferior to public institutions. On the contrary, their domestication of the Platonic paradigm, a translation of this eminent pagan institution into a Christian framework, was one of the distinctive inventions of the age.

Learned English women seldom appear in the collections of female biography published in Italy. Francesco Agostino della Chiesa, however, commemorated several of the More women in his *Teatro delle donne letterate* (*Theater of Lettered Women,* 1620). Among the non-Italian figures whom he commemorates, Chiesa mentions a number of women from the More family. Although his account is not without peculiarities and a few errors, Chiesa nonetheless underscores the achievement of the household as a unit. As for the work's peculiarities, rather than offering a biography of Margaret Roper (surely the most famous of her siblings), he includes her in a short paragraph under the heading "Cecily More and her two sisters, 1530": "Cecily, daughter of Thomas More of London (the most important city in England) and the Great Chancellor of the kingdom, as well as her sisters Margaret and Elizabeth, were raised by their father in ways appropriate for the daughters of such a man. Most importantly, he had them instructed in Latin and Greek, believing that this was the best way to keep women from wicked thoughts."[84] Chiesa devotes a longer section to Margaret Giggs, whom he designates as the wife of "Thomas" Clement (Clement's name was, of course, John)—an "English nobleman" (Clement was not noble). Interested in this Margaret as a Catholic exile, Chiesa gives a brief biographical sketch and also includes his translation of the Latin epitaph that Clement supposedly wrote for her:

> Margaret, wife of Thomas Clement, a noble Englishman, was extremely learned in Greek and Latin, and quite expert in medicine as well. Finding her self twice banished from her fatherland on account of her constancy to the faith (that is, in the reign of Edward and Queen Elizabeth his sister), she moved to Flanders, where she lived admirably, maintaining her aforementioned piety and constancy of mind until her death, which happened at Medina, in Spain. Above her tomb her husband placed a Latin epitaph which, translated into verse, says: "Here lies Margaret Clement / A wife beyond compare, / Married to me for forty years / A model and everlasting mirror of modesty. / She taught her sons and

daughters / Greek and Latin, but even more to fear God. / . . . / Rest in peace now, my Margaret. / Of conduct and piety a true mirror/ Rest in peace father, sons and daughters, / And pray for me without cease."[85]

Following this account, Chiesa mentions another Englishwoman named Margaret from the same period, whom he recognizes as having been called "Gis" [i.e., Giggs]. Uncertain if this is the same woman that he has just described, he mentions in passing that this woman also "fled from the same island because of religion" and was similarly "most learned in every branch of knowledge, and ornamented with a marvelous eloquence." Chiesa continues, "Finding herself at the court of the most powerful King Philip II of Spain, she recited a most beautiful Latin oration in his presence."[86]

Until the accession of Elizabeth I, the English household school derived its academic and moral cachet by association with Thomas More. Subsequently, this same association—now dangerously "Romish" rather than laudably "godly"—might have proved disastrous. But, as discussed in the previous chapter, the Cooke family presented a reformist example of the same kind of well-knit kinship networks and intellectual production. One scholar has even suggested that "Cooke's greatest contribution historically was the impetus which he gave to the education of women through the training of his own daughters, women whose accomplishments were magnified through the importance of their husbands and sons."[87]

The Cooke women were not so subsumed into the personality of the patriarch as were the More women. Upon graduating from the Cooke family school to successful marriages with learned men, the individual identities of Cooke's daughters emerge with greater clarity than those of Margaret Roper or her siblings. Contemporaries viewed More's female descendants, above all, as case studies for his pedagogical theory, embodiments of his own intellectual excellence, and support players in the story of his martyrdom. Cooke's daughters, conversely, constituted the most important chapter in their father's intellectual history.

Thomas Fuller devotes almost all of his entry on Anthony Cooke to his learned daughters. Covering Sir Anthony's heritage, his enhancements to the family manor, and his tutoring of Edward VI in a few lines, Fuller moves immediately to Cooke's daughters. Cooke was "happy in his daughters, [who were] learned above their sex in Greek and Latin . . .

Indeed, they were all most eminent scholars (the honor of their own, and the shame of our sex) both in prose and poetry."[88] Fuller goes on to offer an example of Katherine and Mildred's Latin learning, quoting a letter of Katherine that "catches" her in the praiseworthy act of enlisting her sister's aid in protecting Henry Killigrew from a dangerous embassy to France.[89] Fuller provides no evidence of Sir Anthony's own poetic skill and learned endeavors, beyond tutoring the young king. Thus, Fuller suggests that Katherine and Mildred are the most important evidence of their father's humanistic career.

Fuller followed in a tradition of praise of the Cooke daughters. Their contemporary, Walter Haddon, Regius Professor of Civil Law at Cambridge and a longtime friend of Anthony Cooke, played an Erasmian role in publicizing his friend's domestic academy. In his 1552 *Exhortation to Letters,* Haddon praises Cooke himself in general terms as a man with "deep knowledge, a keen sense of literature, various areas of expertise and a truly remarkable memory."[90] Haddon reserves especial praise, however, for the education of women taking place at Cooke's household, which was "really more like an Academy" *(domum . . . imo parvam quandam potius Academiam).* "When I visited," he writes, "I felt myself to be living among the Tusculans—the only difference being that, in this Tuscany, the studies of women were thriving. Indeed, I certainly discovered more wholesome and fruitful teaching, more dedication to the education of children and fatherly effort, than it seemed possible for domestic walls of this kind to enclose."[91]

Haddon's "Tuscan" simile hints at the degree to which English humanists gauged their excellence by comparison (and indeed by contrast) to what their Italian counterparts were doing. Haddon's contemporary, the pedagogical theorist Richard Mulcaster, also posited women's education as a point of national pride, in his essay "On the Education of Girls," which appears as part of his larger treatise on education, the *Positions* (1581). His attitude, however, was slightly different than Haddon's insofar as Mulcaster demonstrates some concern that the "studies of women" in Italy might be flourishing too much. "Do we not see," Mulcaster asked, "in our own country some of that sex so excellently well trained and so rarely qualified, either for the tongues themselves or for the matter in the tongues, as they may be opposed by way of comparison, if not preferred as beyond comparison, even to the best Roman or Greekish paragons, be they never so much praised; to the German or French gentlewomen, by late writers so well liked; to the Italian ladies, who dare write themselves, and deserve fame for so doing, whose excellency is so geason [forward] as they be rather wonders to gaze at than precedents to follow?"[92] Women publishing their works struck Mulcaster as going a step too far, but he heartily approved of educating women, which he represents as a widespread practice in his own country. "Is it to be called into question," he concludes, "which we both daily see in many and wonder at in some? I dare be bold, therefore, to admit young maidens to learn, seeing as my country gives me leave, and her custom stands for me."[93]

Mulcaster parallels Haddon in situating women's advanced education within the household. Mulcaster makes the particular point that he is not advocating the presence of girls in public grammar schools—"a thing not used in my country"—but rather considers it appropriate that daughters be tutored at home, especially in languages, "which their parents [will] procure for them, either as opportunity or circumstance will serve, or their own powers extend unto, or their daughter's towardness doth offer hope, to be preferred by, for singularity of endowment, either in marriage or some other means."[94] Education, Mulcaster suggests, might well serve as a form of dowry—rewarding the parents for their expenses or their own efforts at tutoring. It is the latter possibility that Mulcaster highlights in discussing who should teach young women. "There [sic] own sex were fittest in some respects," he reasons, "but ours frame them best, and with good regard to some circumstances will bring them up excellently well, [e]specially if their parents be either of learning to judge or of authority to command, or of both to do both, as experience hath taught us in those which have proved so well."[95] The examples in Mulcaster's mind, though he does not name them, would surely have been the More or Cooke families.

Mulcaster began his discussion by announcing that he was an unabashed partisan of women, whom he intended to champion "tooth and nail." But he was making a purely intellectual point about women's education. Haddon, by contrast, seems to have had a more personal stake in the Cooke family, and one of the daughters in particular, which contributed to his unequivocal stance regarding their case as an example to be followed. There is one extant Latin letter (still in manuscript) from Anne Cooke to an unnamed sister, in which Anne plays go-between in favor of Haddon's romantic suit. It is unclear whether Haddon dictated the letter to Anne directly, but at all events the hand is hers. "My sister," it begins, "while I was at Cambridge, I saw your Haddon, whom you will love when you learn that he is wholly yours."[96] The problem was that, despite Haddon's many excellences, he was cash poor, and for that reason Anthony Cooke was opposing this sister and Haddon's evidently mutual wish to carry on a courtship: "But father's will resists you—it will be difficult to find ways and means."[97] Anne closes by offering whatever services she can to help in the matter.[98]

What this document reveals is that Haddon, a career intellectual, entertained hopes of linking himself to one of the most celebrated female intellectuals of his day. Paralleling the cases so far adduced of learned men exerting themselves to ensure that their daughters possessed educations commensurate with their own, Haddon's inclination toward a learned wife suggests that More's advice on choosing a wife and Mulcaster's idea that an educated daughter might make a particularly good match ("be preferred by singularity of endowment . . . in marriage") resonated with the preferences of men within the educated elite. Above all, this shadowy Haddon episode helps to explain why all of the Cooke women married men within the upper ranks of intellectual society: all their husbands were university men; in fact, all of them were Cambridge men, like the unfortunate Haddon.

The received wisdom about Anthony Cooke's marriage strategies for his daughters was that he did consider his excellent daughters to be "their own portions"—that is, their suitors should desire to make matches with these women for their accomplishments and not the promise of rich dowries. At least this is what David Lloyd, writing more than a century after the fact (1665), considered Cooke's attitude to have been. Lloyd, until very recently, had been the expert on Cooke and, as Marjorie McIntosh notes, created in his *Statesmen and Favourites of England* a biography of him that constituted the definitive version until MacIntosh herself revisited the documents. Lloyd observed, "[Cooke's daughters were] their own portion: parts, beauty and breeding bestow themselves. His care was that his daughters might have complete men and that their husbands might be happy in complete women: never promising, yet always paying, a great dowry."[99] This statement says more about attitudes of the late seventeenth century than about what happened in the 1540s, when Cooke's daughters were marrying, but it nonetheless suggests that the "learned marriageability" of the Cooke women endured as an image.

Two poems by Sir Nicholas Bacon (husband of Anne Cooke and Queen Elizabeth's lord keeper of the seal), unpublished until the early twentieth century, reveal another learned man who indeed considered his wife's erudition to be a crucial asset. One is a translation of an ode by Horace, designated as having been "at the desire of [Bacon's] Lady, his Lordship's wife."[100] The second is a poem that Bacon wrote after a long sickness, and it touches more directly on the comfort and satisfaction that his wife's learning brought him. This poem might easily be a first-hand account of More's advice on choosing a wife, rehearsing as it does the benefits of a learned woman's sober counsel, her excellent conversation, her ability to recall her husband to philosophical composure:

> Calling to mind my wife most dear
> How often you have in sorrows sad
> With words full wise and pleasant cheer
> My drooping looks turned into glad,
> How often you have my moods to bad
> Born patiently with a mild mind,
> Assuaging them with words right kind.[101]

Bacon expresses particular pleasure, however, in Anne's ability to read edifying things to him when he is ill or otherwise in danger of becoming idle:

> Thinking also with [what] a good will
> The idle times which irksome be
> You have made short through your good skill
> In reading pleasant things to me,
> Whereof profit we both did see,
> As witness can if they could speak
> Both your Tully and my Seneca.[102]

Bacon considered his marriage, in a sense, as that of two philosophical schools.

In 1581 Theodore Beza (Théodore de Bèze) dedicated his *Christian Meditations* to Anne Cooke Bacon, whom he considered the embodiment of all that was best in her family. Beza explains that he put this little work aside after his original dedicatee, a princess, had died. "[Yet] at the arrival of Monsieur Anthony Bacon your [Anne's] son," he recounts, "seeing that he took pleasure in this little work, and besides that knowing as I do from the Latin letters with which you have seen fit to honor me the great, signal, and extraordinary graces that God has given you (virtues of which I recognize a true portrait in your aforementioned son)—[all of these things] have persuaded me that you would not be displeased to receive this little booklet, bearing your name on the front, presented to you as testimony of the honor and reverence that I bear to your virtue and that of your family."[103] Having situated his new patron by connection with her son, Beza goes on to praise her learning. At the same moment, however, he links her with her husband. Beza writes, "Now in your widowhood . . . after the decease of that exceptionally virtuous and deservedly renowned Lord, Monsieur Nicholas Bacon, your husband . . . you might find some consolation, after reading the great and holy Greek and Latin doctors who are your familiar friends, in strengthening yourself more and more by meditating upon spiritual matters."[104] In so doing, Beza thought, this learned widow could then fortify the Christian patience and constancy that God had already given her and for which she was already well known. She might also add to these the "magnanimous courage" exemplified by her father "during both the great public calamities of the realm and the particular ones that affected him and his whole house."[105] Beza, then, dignifies his potential female patron by connecting her with the three crucial male figures in her familial life: first her son, who serves as an image of his learned mother's virtues; then her deceased husband; then her renowned father.

An unknown partisan of Jane Lumley utilized similar familial categorizations in commemorating her. A volume of funerary monuments, compiled in the seventeenth century, contains for the most part simple pen-and-ink drawings that depict the funeral processions of notables, including Anne of Cleves; Sir Christopher Hatton; Mary, Queen of Scots; Henry Radcliffe (Earl of Sussex); and Queen Elizabeth.[106] Lady Lumley's procession stands out in two respects. It is one of only two sections for which the illustrator used large figures, for each of which a name appears underneath, as well as full color and volumetric shading. The other procession of this more elaborate type is Queen Elizabeth's. Lady Lumley's section, however, trumps even the Queen's in that it also incorporates textual material. The folio that opens this section comprises a manuscript sheet, on the left side of which appears a poetic encomium (supposedly taken from the epitaph penned by John Lumley, her husband) in English and Latin; on the right side appear her favorite prayers, in Latin.

The encomium fashions Lady Lumley as a quintessential "father's daughter" and "learned matron." As she was childless, the text emphasizes her roles as daughter *(filia)* and as wife *(sponsa)* en route to praising her learning. This emphasis is particularly clear in the Latin transcription, in which the initial word on each line appears in bold capital letters.

Daughter pious to her venerable father and obedient to him from her
  earliest youth
Wife faithful to her husband, chaste, dear, living always without blame
Whose modesty, despite her nobility, was a thing marvelous and rare
In letters both Latin and Greek she exceeded her sex.[107]

Bolstering her status as a wife, a brief testimonial follows, ventriloquizing her husband: "I, her unhappy and bereft husband, have known all these things and more besides to be true, not empty flatteries for decorating a tomb."[108]

In their own day, the achievements of English women humanists were commemorated in a diverse assortment of letters and biographical encyclopedia. Collections of specifically female biography began to appear in the seventeenth century, however, and by the eighteenth century England began to catch up with their Italian predecessors in publishing biographical encyclopedia devoted exclusively to extolling the illustrious lineage of learned Englishwomen and to presenting them as inspiring examples for women of the compilers' own time and acquaintance.

A particularly rich volume of this type is a massive 480-page encyclopedia detailing the lives, writings, and reception of sixty-two learned Englishwomen of the fifteenth, sixteenth, and seventeenth centuries that was published in 1752 by George Ballard (1706–1755), a clerk at Magdalen College, Oxford. Ballard's *Memoirs of Several Ladies of Great Britain* is the first English text that exhibits the passionate commitment to historical recovery characteristic of Ballard's continental predecessors—especially Tomasini, Chiesa, and Ribera. Indeed, Ballard cites Ribera and Chiesa explicitly as his inspiration. Lamenting in his dedication to a Mrs. Talbot of Warwickshire that England's illustrious women have been overlooked by "our greatest biographers," he suggests that this oversight has kept England from taking its rightful place in the pan-European world of letters—especially "when it is considered how much has been done on this subject by several learned foreigners," including "Boccace Betussi [Boccacio and Betussi], Peter Paul de Ribera [and] Augustin della Chiesa."[109]

Ballard's encyclopedia is a work of thorough and careful scholarship. Published by the subscription of 394 interested parties, each listed by name in the prefatory material—a roll call of eighteenth-century British feminists of both sexes and from every rung on the social and academic ladder, which would reward analysis in itself—Ballard's *Memoirs* was the first English *City of Ladies*. His biographies are, with very few exceptions, factually sound. Indeed, apart from its rhetorical force, this text is remarkable for its scholarly rigor: Ballard cited women's writings explicitly, provided both foreign language texts and English translations of their compositions when the original sources were likely to be inaccessible to his readers, and included a thorough critical apparatus for his secondary sources. If literary society was in danger of forgetting Margaret Roper, Mary Basset, Jane and Mary Fitzalan, Anne and Mildred Cooke, and their numerous peers, Ballard stopped that process by immortalizing them all.

In a wide variety of sources, then, early modern authors celebrated women intellectuals and ensured that their achievements would be remembered. The household academy made "woman as intellect" a familiar and appealing figure in the literary landscape of sixteenth-century Italy and England. By 1580, in both contexts, there was an established tradition of recognized female scholarship and a growing presence of female authorship in print. But what did these authors write? And did their publications make any kind of collective argument?

4

Models of Feminist Argument

RICHARD Mulcaster exhorted English men to be proud of the learned women in their country, who were "so excellently well trained, and so rarely qualified" in the ancient languages, and to marvel at the Italian women of his era who "dare[d] write themselves."[1] By the 1580s, when Mulcaster was writing, there were scores of women writers in Italy publishing their treatises, orations, letterbooks, dialogues, and poetry under their own names. In England, there was a strong tradition of women translators, who would soon be followed by a growing number of women writing original works of poetry, autobiography, family advice, moral philosophy, and pedagogy. While Mulcaster was partially right to represent his contemporary countrywomen as less bold than their Italian counterparts, insofar as sixteenth-century English women did not usually put their full names to their works nor offer explicit contributions to the debate on women, it is nonetheless clear that in both contexts women were daring to write themselves. "Woman as intellect" had arrived on the literary scene. But what did that mean?

The first secular women of the pen and their supporters should be understood as contributors to "Renaissance feminism." Scholars have long defined the feminism of this era as a literary defense of womankind, or a pro-woman argument.[2] This definition, however, has the infelicitous effect of excluding women writers (for instance, all English women writers of the sixteenth century) who did not explicitly nail their colors to the mast but who, by doing the scholarly work hitherto the sole province of men, prompted contemporaries to think in new ways about female capability.

Three levels of feminism exist in women's writing and writing about women of the fifteenth and sixteenth centuries. The most apparent, and that which has already drawn scholarly attention, is a direct critique of the patriarchal order that seems to prefigure nineteenth-century political feminism. Siep Stuurman, following Karen Offen and Nancy Cott, has offered a useful shorthand for the constituent elements of what I will call "explicit" feminism: a sustained critique of misogyny and male supremacy, the belief that women's place in society does not correspond to natural law (that is, that biological determinism is a self-serving male discourse), a positive revaluation of womankind, and an articulated desire to offer women as a group a public voice.[3] To this formulation of explicit feminism I would add the tendency of women writers not only to consider women as a group but especially to explore the possibilities of female community and, above all, to argue for the suitability—even necessity—of women's education.

In addition to overt or explicit feminist argument, however, there are two other ways in which learned women contributed to the history of feminism. The first might be termed "celebratory" feminism. In emphasizing their particular status as scholars, undertaking various forms of self-writing (from prefatory self-fashioning to literal autobiography), and celebrating other learned women, female authors strengthened the new category "woman as intellect."[4] The second contribution that women intellectuals made was their direct engagement with men in literary culture, what I am calling "participatory feminism." Whether or not the woman writer made a point of the fact that she was doing the same authorial work as men, her participation in the world of letters made a case for the equality of the sexes in matters of the mind. This formulation of gender parity, albeit provisional, created the first chink in the armor of ancient, as well as Judeo-Christian, misogyny. Women such as Margaret Roper and Anne Cooke Bacon, who in no sense took an explicit feminist position, nonetheless became authoritative models for later writers like Bathsua Makin, who cited them alongside the eminent example of Queen Elizabeth to bolster an overtly feminist claim for women's right to an advanced education and the pious benefit to the state that this education produced.

Renaissance feminism was born at home. Successful women intellectuals benefited from the legitimacy that their "intellectual families" afforded them. The domestic paradigm made room for the female voice in the world of literary exchange; ironically, however, what many of these female voices said and what contemporaries said about them constituted a serious critique of literary misogyny and even the patriarchal order itself, as well as a call for more active female participation in society and culture. To judge by the praise that women from Christine de Pizan to Anne Cooke Bacon received and by their substantive publication histories, the literary world was listening.

Italian Women and the Querelle des Femmes

Christine de Pizan was an explicit feminist: she offered an unapologetic articulation of herself as an intellectual, defended womankind, and made a case for women's education. She was also one of the most popular and internationally recognized authors of her day. Christine capitalized on her good fortune in being born to a forward-thinking father and on the connections that his status as an intellectual and intimate of the king brought her at the French court. Building upon her initial success as a poet, she ultimately wrote in all the major literary genres, from history and biography to political and moral philosophy. It is on the subject of women, however, that Christine moved from participation to invention.

Christine's writings on womankind, which spanned much of her career, have rightly been termed "landmarks in women's history."[5] At the vanguard of the first effort to redefine woman as an ethical being and a positive member of society—the so-called "debate on women"— Christine engaged with the prominent intellectuals of her day in creating a new literary genre to which countless authors (male and female) would contribute for the next three hundred years. From 1399 to 1403, Christine participated in a heated epistolary debate on an antiwoman allegorical romance, the *Roman de la rose*—a popular work that distilled every deleterious image of women inherited from antiquity. The female figures of this work embody the traditionally "feminine" vices, especially deceit, lust, vanity, and greed. At best, the female figure is an object for male sexual conquest. These initial volleys in the debate drew upon a long antique and medieval tradition of devaluing marriage. Written largely by clerics, the medieval antiwoman literature articulated a characteristically misogamist position: in order to prove the superiority of celibacy— clerical celibacy itself being an innovation of the Middle Ages, one that required justification—the *Roman de la rose* attacked marriage.[6] To malign a state sanctified by God in the Bible, however, required taking a misogynist position: women, corrupt by nature, prevent men from achieving divine grace.[7] The courtly love tradition flourishing in Christine's era presented a different kind of theoretical dilemma regarding womankind. On the one hand, the poetics of courtly love presented woman as a worthy object of men's love and admiration; but on the other, it underscored the notion that women were faithless in marriage—a centerpiece of traditional misogyny. Either way, the early volleys of the debate on women worked within the traditional syntax of male argument. The issues at stake were the hypothetical merits or defects of womankind and the married state relative to men.

In 1405 Christine de Pizan's *Book of the City of Ladies* reinvented the terms of this debate. Whereas the question had formerly been in what sense women might play any kind of positive role in male society, Christine instead created a female society. Her literary edifice contained a history of female accomplishment and a potent argument for womankind's intrinsic merit. This work, considered by many to be "the first example of what we now call 'women's studies,'" because it "reorganized knowledge from a feminist point of view," offers an especially rewarding lens for exploring the initial boundaries of Renaissance feminism.[8]

The *City of Ladies* champions the notions that women should be proud of their illustrious predecessors (both classical and Christian) and, most importantly, that it is fitting for women to have access to the kind of advanced education that Christine received. In Christine's city dwell only "virtuous" women, but this is the sole exclusionary premise. The walls otherwise encompass women of every state and estate: daughters, wives, widows; noble, bourgeois, and lower class. The cloister had traditionally offered one positive vision of female society, legitimate by virtue of its seclusion, pious objective, and male supervision. Christine's city, in contrast, is a civic gynecocracy (ruled by a queen, the Virgin Mary), and it is militant. As Judith Kellogg argues, Christine reconstituted the body politic itself, quintessentially male, as a female space, "a political structure in which the marginalized become the center of the social system and responsible for its governance": "Her city represents a gendered body politic, which becomes literally embodied, for in the end, Christine's city is an idea meant to be 'mapped' into individual female bodies—to be internalized to function as protection and fortification within the social spaces that they actually inhabit."[9]

The *City of Ladies* is also a fortress against misogyny, built on the "Field of Letters" *(Champ des Lettres)*.[10] The bricks and mortar are the masculine vocabularies of warfare, law, and civil government. Lady Reason terms misogynists women's "jealous enemies" and "boors who have pelted women with so many arrows," whose victory against womankind is nonetheless hollow, because it has been "handed over without resistance." Continuing in martial and legal terms, Reason asserts that even "the strongest city will fall immediately if it is not defended and even the most unjust law case will win by default if the plaintiff pleads unopposed." The time has come, Reason announces, "to take away women's just suit from the hands of Pharaoh." The new fortress and court are different aspects of the city that Christine will construct: "a city that you [Christine] have been chosen to build and enclose—a stronghold amply fortified with our help and advice."[11]

What are Christine's qualifications for this task of literary warfare, jurisprudence, and architecture? She is Boethius remodeled female. Representing herself as the philosopher oppressed by adversity to whom a celestial female figure appears (in Boethius's case, Lady Philosophy), Christine's own status as a praiseworthy intellectual serves as the cornerstone of her literary edifice.

The *City of Ladies* begins with a complex articulation of Christine-as-philosopher. "According to my habit and the discipline which has regulated the course of my whole life," she narrates, "that is to say, the indefatigable study of the liberal arts, I was one day sitting in my study completely surrounded by books concerning every imaginable subject." Intending to refresh herself with some poetry, she describes finding by chance a volume by Matheolus that, like so many other books, presents womankind in the worst possible light. Relating how she perused this book, she comments, "Despite the fact that it possessed not the slightest authority, nonetheless immersed me in a profound lucubration within my very soul. I asked myself what the causes and reasons could be that have driven so many men, clerics and others, to slander women and to reprimand their conduct—whether in speaking, or in their treatises and writings."[12] Thus the problem is set: do we trust "authority" to answer a question, or instead depend upon our own powers of reason? Christine-the-philosopher initially chooses the former.

Examining her own character and the habits of the many women whom she had known personally, "not only princesses and great ladies, but also women of the middling sort and those of no rank" *(tant princesses et grandes dames que femmes de moyenne et petite condition)*, she cannot reconcile the negative theoretical assessment of womankind with her own experience of women's exemplary conduct. But literary authority will, for the moment, retain the upper hand: "I still persisted in reproaching womankind, reasoning with myself that it would be highly unlikely that so many illustrious men, so many great scholars, who possessed such a profound and pellucid understanding of everything (or so it seemed to me) could have spoken in a manner so erroneous."[13] Deciding that she must be too simpleminded to perceive her own faults and those of other women, she will take male authority at its word.

Christine's decision to trust theory instead of experience puts her into a profound depression. "In the midst of these reflections," she recounts, "I was plunged into such disgust and consternation that I came to disparage myself and the entire female sex as if Nature had made us all monsters." She asks God why she was not permitted to be born a man: "All of my faculties might [then] have been directed to your service, and so that I would never make a mistake and would be able to achieve that great perfection that men are said to have." She comments to her readers that "in this folly of [hers]" she lamented that God had made her so unfortunate as "to make [her] be born in a female body."[14]

The Ladies Reason, Rectitude, and Justice then appear to Christine-the-temporary-misogynist. Contravening the self-hatred and hatred of womankind that the day's reflections have produced in the author, these feminized images of "masculine" virtues call her "dear daughter" *(chère enfant)*. With the aim of recalling her to philosophical composure, they remind the author (and her readers) of her own intellectual credentials. Reason, Rectitude, and Justice validate the author as an authoritative philosopher, worthy of their ministrations.

"Dear daughter, what has happened to your good sense?" Lady Reason inquires. "Have you forgotten that it is in the melting pot that one purifies gold, which neither changes nor loses any of its properties but, on the contrary, the more it is worked and stretched, the better refined it becomes? Similarly, don't you know that the truly important issues are the ones discussed and debated the most?"[15] Parading her familiarity with Aristotle's *Metaphysics*, Augustine, and patristic scholarship, "Christine" reminds herself in the voice of Lady Reason that she has often witnessed these seemingly unassailable philosophers contradicting each other, which proves that no authority (however esteemed) is irrefutable: "You have yourself seen in Aristotle's *Metaphysics* that he criticizes and refutes the opinions of Plato and the other philosophers whom he cites. And note, moreover, that Saint Augustine and other doctors of the Church have done just the same with certain passages of Aristotle, whom one nonetheless calls the Prince of Philosophers and to whom one attributes the most elevated tenets of natural and moral philosophy."[16] As for poets who criticize women, Lady Reason says, "One can perceive their use of the rhetorical figure called *antiphrasis,* which indicates—as you know perfectly well—that something called bad is actually to be understood as good and vice versa."[17] Christine thus begins by asserting, through Lady Reason, her own status as a scholar and woman of letters.

Lest this point be missed by her readers, Christine underscores her scholarly credentials once again at the conclusion of Lady Reason's second speech, which addresses the purpose of the three figures' appearance. "We do not frequent just any place, nor do we appear to just anyone," Reason explains. "But as for you, my beloved Christine, by virtue of the great love that you have demonstrated for seeking truth by means of perpetual and avid study, which has taken you from the world and left you thus in solitude, you have earned our friendship and proved yourself worthy of our visit, which is meant to ease your distress and confusion and to bring clarity to your understanding of those matters that disturb and unsettle your spirit by dimming your reasoning."[18]

Throughout the work, moreover, Christine cites her own writings in the voices of Lady Reason and Lady Rectitude. Discussing the trope that one cannot fault something good simply because someone put it to a bad use (the "good thing" being, in this case, women), Lady Reason notes that this is an issue that "[Christine has herself] explicated effectively elsewhere in [her] writings." Similarly, Lady Rectitude observes in discussing male inconstancy and abuses of power that Christine has herself "treated this subject exceedingly well in [her] *Letter to the God of Love.*" Later, when treating the related argument that women are more commonly faithful in love, Lady Rectitude remarks, "My beloved daughter, I do not know what more to say to you concerning these accusations concerning women's infidelity, since you yourself have sufficiently refuted the charges in your *Letter to the God of Love* and in your *Letters Concerning the Romance of the Rose.*"[19] Indeed, throughout this work, Christine deftly uses self-citation to situate herself as a philosopher and an author with proven credentials.

Assisted in turn by Lady Reason, Lady Rectitude, and Lady Justice, Christine populates her "New Kingdom of Femininity" *(nouveau royaume de Feminie).*[20] This kingdom is a loose allegorical framework for a biographical encyclopedia of famous women. Collectively, it is a history of female achievement. The kingdom is filled with illustrious women, whose biographies are divided into the three basic categories of "virtue." Book I describes the city walls and foundations. Through discussion with Lady Reason, Christine adduces women who have exhibited virtue in the sense of *virtù:* achievement in politics and warfare, as well as in the arts and letters. The subjects of book I are all pagan, for the most part taken from Boccaccio's *Concerning Famous Women*—though Christine does not belittle their merits in the way that Boccaccio often seems to do. Book II concerns the horizontal civic space, built in consultation with Lady Rectitude and populated by a mixture of classical and Christian women (some from Christine's own time) who have demonstrated moral virtue, such as reverence for the divine, filial and wifely piety, generosity, and charity. Book III describes the construction of the highest towers, under the guidance of Lady Justice. The residents of this most elevated part of Christine's city exemplify specifically Christian virtue: biblical heroines, female martyrs, and the women who, while not themselves saints or martyrs, served the male apostles and saints.

This lineage of illustrious female figures supersedes all prior models of female community inherited from the literary tradition. In particular, Christine's city will be "altogether more perfect than the Amazon kingdom of old, since the women installed here will not have to leave their lands to conceive and give birth to their heiresses in order to secure the transmission of their estate within their rightful lineage. Indeed, those women whom we now settle here will remain for eternity."[21]

Along the way, Christine discusses the problem of marriage, a centerpiece of the *querelle des femmes*. Through a series of questions posed to Lady Rectitude, Christine outlines the scholastic argument in favor of male celibacy, the chief components of which are that "husbands are routinely assailed with the mighty storms that rage on account of women's peevishness and spiteful bitterness" and that "many books have counseled wise men to avoid marriage so that they might sidestep or, better put, ward off such affronts, attesting that not one woman, or at least very few, are faithful to their husbands."[22]

Lady Rectitude replies that the real victims in marriage are women. The point can certainly be taken as feminist, whatever the era, and the vitriolic stridency of Christine's language represents a marked departure from the contemporary debate on marriage. "I am persuaded," Rectitude contends,

> that if one wished to study carefully the subject of domestic disorders, with a view toward writing a book that bothered with the facts, one would hear an altogether different story. Ah, dear Christine! You yourself know how many women one could point out who, on account of a cruel husband, gasp out their wretched existence in the shackles of a marriage in which they find themselves even more abused than the slaves of the Saracens. Ah, God! How many wives are practically broken on the rack with beatings—without cease and without justification! Oh! The indignities, the denigrations, the abuse, injuries and outrages that so many good and courageous women suffer without the least complaint.

Tempering this feminist permutation of misogamy, however, Rectitude notes that there are counterbalancing factors, such as many excellent husbands. Christine's own husband, Etienne du Castel, appears here as the principal example of a virtuous, intelligent, and loving man. This reference both cools the furor of the foregoing diatribe and also makes the author seem impartial: although Christine herself had an excellent husband, she nonetheless sympathizes with the plight of many women who have not been so fortunate. Rectitude also admits the existence of some immoral women. She will not discuss these cases, however, "since women of that breed are technically no longer women, but rather should be classified as monsters."[23]

Championing through example the myriad women from classical and Christian antiquity who demonstrate the principal "feminine" virtues of wifely devotion, and loyalty to family interests, in addition to "masculine" virtues such as courage, fortitude, and prudence, Christine characterizes the species "woman" as equal in merit to men. Christine unites different categories of women, emphasizing the transcategorical worthiness of womankind. Lady Justice remarks, concluding her disquisition on holy (though noncloistered) women, "I do not know what else to say to you, dear Christine; I could adduce an infinite number of women from all walks of life and all points in the life cycle—maidens, widows and wives—in whom divine power manifested itself with a singular force and extraordinary constancy." All kinds of women will be included in the City of Ladies, which is ultimately unveiled as a new City of God. Shifting reference from Augustine's city to Christine's, Lady Justice exclaims, "Glorious things be said of you, city of God."[24]

Learned women, however, stand as especially important proof of female virtue. The discussion of intelligent women's service to society is a dominant theme in books I and II and serves as a kind of Ariadne's thread for the whole work, uniting Christine's status as author with her illustrious female subjects and the overall argument for a reevaluation of womankind's contributions to history. In book I, "Christine" asks Lady Reason a theoretical question concerning whether women possess sufficient intelligence to understand the more obscure branches of knowledge. Reason replies that indeed women have equal intelligence to men, despite what some men say. "If it was customary to send little girls to school and to teach them all subjects systematically as one does in the case of boys," she explains, "the girls would learn and understand the finer points of all the arts and sciences just as well as the boys can."[25] The classical examples that follow include Cornificia, Proba, Sappho, Leontium, Manto, Medea, and Circe. Lest the debate remain merely on the question of women's ability to work in male-dominated fields, "Christine" asks a related question concerning whether women have themselves invented or discovered any branches of knowledge. The answer, according to Lady Reason, is that they have: Nicostrata invented Greek literature; Minerva invented technology and science; Ceres invented agriculture; Isis created horticulture; Arachne invented weaving, and Pamphila first had the idea of cultivating silk; Timarete, Irene, and Marcia innovated in the visual arts; and Sempronia took Latin and Greek composition to new levels of excellence.

Hearkening back to this Boccaccian list in book II, Christine underscores women's status as active contributors to the progress of culture in her discussion with Lady Rectitude. "My lady," she begins, "I certainly see that women have made many positive contributions. And even if we grant that some wickedness has been perpetrated by certain corrupt women, it nonetheless seems to me that if we consider the boons bestowed, both in the past and today, by virtuous women—and especially by those learned women, trained in letters and sciences, whom we mentioned before—these are really the more important things. And so I am amazed at the opinion advanced by some men, who claim that they would not want their wives, daughters, or other female relatives to study, for fear that their morals would be corrupted." Lady Rectitude replies that this belief is simply idiotic. Far from corrupting female students, education "without a doubt improves and ennobles them. How could anyone think or believe that she who pursues good teaching and doctrine would be corrupted by it? That is wholly irrational and may therefore be dismissed."[26]

Lady Rectitude cites three examples of father-daughter dyads, which prove that education "betters and ennobles" the female student: Hortensius/Hortensia, Giovanni Andrea/Novella, and Tomas/Christine de Pizan. These examples, discussed at length in Chapter 1 as the means by which Christine made space for herself as a woman intellectual in the historical record, exemplify her central rhetorical strategy of making coextensive self-justification, a defense of learned women as a category, and the reevaluation of womankind as a class. The forward-thinking father associated with each of these women represents a new kind of "authority." Pitted against the illogicality of male detractors and misogynist texts, these fathers provide a culturally legitimate foundation for her feminist project. Patriarchal sanction strengthens her case for expanding the boundaries of female achievement. Asserting in the negative that one may "dismiss" the erroneous opinion of some men presents a less forceful argument than positively demonstrating that other fathers' decisions to train their daughters in the humanities produced successful results.

Christine de Pizan invented women's history. Her *City of Ladies* owed a debt to Boccaccio, but she transformed his curiosity cabinet of exceptionally famous and infamous women into a cohesive argument about womankind's long-standing contributions to culture and society, the obstacles they faced, and the necessity of understanding female capability in a new way. Similarly, she drew upon the hagiographical tradition, particularly in book II's lengthy rehearsal of the female saints and martyrs. She is at pains, however, to make it clear to her readers that her history is inclusive, not exclusionary, and that women from all walks of life must build upon the accomplishments of the female lineage that she has charted.

Putting aside the dialogical literary device in her conclusion, Christine directly addresses her female readers. She envisions her readership, "all women," as a unified class within which social status has no importance: "Let us praise the Lord, my most revered ladies! For behold our City, built and finished. All you who love virtue, fame and renown will be received here with the greatest honors, since this city was built for and dedicated to every honorable woman." She makes explicit her intention that class boundaries will not obtain in this civic space, exhorting, "All of you, my ladies—whether you are women of great, middling, or humble station—above all else be on your guard and be vigilant in defending yourselves against the enemies of your honor and virtue. My dear friends, you see how on all sides these men accuse you of heinous vices! Let the luster of your virtue make liars of them." While Christine accepts the prevailing definition of female "honor" as chastity and good conduct, she departs sharply from precedent in suggesting that women from every walk of life will "increase and multiply our City" by cultivating virtue and avoiding vice. In short, even women from a humble station may be able to become the kind of exemplary figures that she has documented. Ending in a liturgical mode, Christine prays, "[May God] forgive my great sins and receive me into eternal joy—the very same grace that I wish for you all. Amen."[27]

Christine's *City* established itself in the Western literary canon during her own lifetime. From the time she wrote it, the *Book of the City of Ladies* was a popular work, constituting a significant portion of the fifty extant manuscript presentation copies of her work made while she was still alive (and some in her own workshop)—a manuscript collection that surpasses those of all her male contemporaries.[28] There are sixteen such manuscripts in France, one in England, two in Germany, and one in Switzerland.[29] The *City* also comprises a substantive portion of the 150 manuscripts dated after 1418 that demonstrate continued interest in her work.[30]

Moving our attention into the world of print, Nadia Margolis observes that early modern editors "working closely with printers, quickly fixed upon her most popular works, such as the *Epistre Othea, Cité des dames* and *Trois Vertus*."[31] Bryan Anslay's first English translation of the *Book of the City of Ladies* was printed in 1521. This same year, a John Skot printed Christine's *Book of Policy*, which was the first female-authored work of political philosophy. As Charity Canon Willard notes, these publications built upon previous interest in Christine's writings: "Christine had scarcely established herself as a court poet during the final years of the fourteenth century when Thomas Hoccleve, one of Chaucer's disciples, produced an English version of her first long poem, 'L'Épître au Dieu d'Amour.' Somewhat later, William Caxton translated and printed two of her works, *The Book of the Fayttes of Arms and Chyvalerye* (1489–90) and the *Morale Proverbes of Christyene* (1478)."[32] Following the edition of the *City*, Richard Pynson reissued the *Moral Proverbs* in 1526, and Robert Wyer published her *History of Troy* in 1549. To put these six early English publications of Christine's works in perspective, the *English Short Title Catalogue* lists only ten editions of Baldassare Castiglione's *Courtier* printed in Britain during the sixteenth and seventeenth centuries. In this sense, although her works seem to have fallen out of favor in the mid-sixteenth century, Christine nonetheless stands up well in the publication record of works by continental authors printed in England in the early modern period.

In the world of early French printing, Christine's most popular work was her sequel to the *City of Ladies*, the *Treasury of the City of Ladies* (or *Book of the Three Virtues*), which went through three printed editions in France between 1497 and 1536.[33] There is no known French printing of the *City of Ladies* itself before the modern era, but it is worth noting that she remained an important figure in the French literature until tastes changed in the mid-sixteenth century. Christinian works issuing from Parisian presses during the late fifteenth and early sixteenth centuries include *L'art de chevalerie* (1488), *Le tresor de la cite des dames selon dame Cristine* (1497), *Les cent histoires de Troye* (1499/1500), *Le tresor de la cite des dames de degre en degre: et de tous estatz selon dame Cristine* (1503), *S'ensuyt l'epistre de Othea deesse de Prudence moralisee . . . par Christine de Pisan* (ca. 1518 and ca. 1521), *Les cent hystoires de Troye* (1522), *L'arbre des batailles et fleur de chevalerie selon Vegece* (1527), *L'epsitre de Othea deesse de Prudence moralisee* (before 1534), *Le tresor de la Cite des dames, selon Dame Christine de la Cite de Pise* (1536), *Le chemin de long estude de Dame Christine de Pise* (1549). There was also a printing (date unknown) of her early works against the *Romance of the Rose*, which appeared under the title *Contre rommant de la rose*.[34]

Christine de Pizan would have literary successors in her adoptive France by the sixteenth century, but it was within her native Italy that colleagues, albeit probably unknown to her, first appeared. One of Christine's younger contemporaries, the Veronese humanist Isotta Nogarola, was the first to match her literary productivity and level of international acclaim. Eugenius Abel based his first complete edition of Nogarola's collected works (1886), including her letters, orations, and her *Dialogue* (which will be the focus of my discussion), upon three major manuscripts now held in Verona, Vienna, and the Vatican.[35] Margaret King and Diana Robin have noted, furthermore, the "impressively wide diffusion of Nogarola's works, which are often embedded in humanist miscellanies including works by the leading humanists of the Renaissance," contributed "as much as the praise of contemporaries to her great reputation and influence."[36] Paul Oskar Kristeller's exhaustive bibliographic research has uncovered no fewer than ninety fifteenth- and sixteenth-century manuscript copies of Nogarola's writings, ranging from a single letter to her complete works, now held in libraries and archives from Seville to Helsinki.[37] In the last period of the manuscript book, Isotta Nogarola was a celebrity who held her own alongside the illustrious male humanists with whom she frequently shares parchment space in these volumes: Leonardo Bruni, Coluccio Salutati, Guarino Guarini, Francesco Filelfo, and Francesco Barbaro. Nor did transcriptions of her writings cease with the advent of print: scribes continued to copy her works into their manuscript collections well into the sixteenth century, by which time her *Dialogue* was also in print.

As King and Robin trenchantly observe, Nogarola "was a pioneering woman's voice—the voice of the gendered 'other'—at the opening of the Renaissance and early modern era. With her older contemporary, Christine de Pizan, . . . she launched the tradition of learned women in the early modern period, setting up the framework within which learned women expressed themselves over the next several centuries."[38] Nogarola's role in the intellectual history of women has received substantive scholarly treatment from the seventeenth century to the present day.[39] Her contribution to the history of feminism, however, requires further explication. This Veronese prodigy of humanism took up Christine de Pizan's "pick of reason" and continued, in her own way, to deconstruct the foundations of literary misogyny.

Isotta Nogarola did not envision a female body politic as Christine had done. Nor did she argue explicitly for women's right to an education as Laura Cereta and her literary descendants in Italy would assert with increasing vehemence. Yet Nogarola belongs to the history of feminism for two reasons: the first is that her influential status as a female intellectual made her a prominent figure in defenses of women and collections of female biography. Nogarola would also become an important precedent for feminist writers such as the English pedagogue Bathsua Makin. Such was Nogarola's "participatory" feminism. Her argument for the exoneration of Eve in her *Dialogue on Adam and Eve* represents the second factor that supports her inclusion in the history of feminism. While Nogarola does not overtly argue for a more positive evaluation of womankind, this contention is implicit. Eve served metonymically for the "natural" defects of all women; to defend the first mother was to defend the female sex.

Nogarola's defense of Eve as less culpable than Adam in disobeying God's commandment contributed to the growing force of the debate on women by returning to a central piece of "evidence" adduced in anti-woman literature. The arguments in this unresolved debate between Nogarola and her friend and patron Ludovico Foscarini circulated widely in manuscript during the fifteenth century and were published in 1563 at the prestigious Aldine press in Venice.[40] Nogarola's strategy, using Genesis and the patristic commentators against these same commentators, would be taken up by numerous subsequent defenders of women. Among these was the highly influential humanist Henricus Cornelius Agrippa, who would similarly warp material from the Book of Genesis to "prove" not only the equality of the sexes but female "preeminence."[41]

Before we proceed to the particular contentions that the characters "Isotta" and "Ludovico" bring forward, it is crucial to note that the structure of this text in itself announced intellectual equality between the sexes. The genre of the academic dialogue had hitherto been quintessentially male, whether in the classical or in the Christian context. The major precedent for a female-authored dialogue, Marguerite Porete's *Mirror of Simple Souls*, concerned mysticism, not scholarly interrogation.[42] And while Boethius engaged a "female" interlocutor in his *Consolation of Philosophy*, Lady Philosophy is a feminine personification of an abstract concept, not a human woman. Christine de Pizan pushed the dialogue a step further in the *City of Ladies*, by representing herself as a philosopher in discussion with similar female abstractions, but these quasi-academic debates occur in the literary distance of an imagined female community. By contrast, Nogarola's *Dialogue* is a theological debate between a man and woman who are represented as scholars of commensurate abilities.

Nogarola presents this conversation as a collection of letters, which begin when "Ludovico" invites her to undertake an epistolary exchange with him concerning the respective gravity of Adam and Eve's sins. Although she gives him the last word, there is nonetheless no clear "victor" in the debate, which ends with the suggestion that the correspondents will continue the discussion in person, beyond the parameters of the page. We might think of this literary setting as an initial prefiguration of what Diana Robin aptly terms the "virtual salons" in late sixteenth-century Italy—that is, a torrent of published dialogues and anthologies of poetry that transcribed for an eager public the conversations of erudite and most often reformist women and men taking place in "real time" gatherings sponsored by enlightened women patrons.[43]

Nogarola's text, portraying a theological debate between a female and male scholar, offers a potent image of "woman as intellect." The title page announces that the conversation is taking place between "the Famous Lord Lodovico Foscarini of Venice, Doctor of Civil and Canon Law, and the Eminent, Most Learned and Divine Lady Isotta Nogarola of Verona."[44] There are essentially four stages to the text: "Ludovico's" invitation, "Isotta's" first argument, "Ludovico's" rebuttal, "Isotta's" restatement and clarification, and finally "Ludovico's" concluding remarks. The dominant theme throughout is the depth and sophistication of Nogarola's learning. While the readers are left to choose for themselves whether to side with "Isotta's" defense of Eve or with "Ludovico's" argument in favor of Adam as the lesser sinner, the point that cannot be missed is that this is a discussion between intellectual equals.

The central plank of "Isotta's" argument is that God made Eve an imperfect creature, less intelligent and therefore less accountable than Adam, upon whom God bestowed every perfection, including a thorough understanding of all things. In flouting his full knowledge of God's injunction against eating the forbidden fruit, Adam exhibited contempt for divine law, whereas Eve merely fell prey to her imperfect understanding and "natural" gullibility. This contention, which demeans the first woman, seems a paradoxical way to defend her. The issue at stake for Nogarola, however, was an Aristotelian return to first principles and causes: for centuries, original sin was understood to have derived more from Eve than from Adam. It was Eve who, like Pandora for the ancient Greeks, brought continual hardship, suffering, and death into the world. As the first cause of sin, Eve shouldered more of the blame than her husband. Because his sin derived from hers, he was therefore more of an accessory to rather than an agent of the Fall.

Nogarola, in order to make a persuasive argument, had to use her culture's own terms. A modern scholar might contend that the Bible is a male-authored text, which uses conceptions of gender inequality to justify patriarchal domination. This kind of reasoning was, of course, not intellectually available in the fifteenth century. Nogarola's argument should, however, be understood to be similarly subversive insofar as she was the first to use assumptions about female inferiority (paradoxically) to defend her sex: by partially exonerating the First Mother, Nogarola challenged the logic of considering all womankind, the "daughters of Eve," as just so many reiterations of originary female depravity.

The greatest weapon in Nogarola's arsenal is philology. She uses close textual analysis to display her erudition and positions herself, in the manner of Christine de Pizan, as a worthy interlocutor. On the point that Adam is more guilty by virtue of his greater contempt for God's command, Nogarola uses the grammatical precision characteristic of the early humanists as a means to unravel textual ambiguity. She observes that God's commands are all directed at a singular subject, the man, and not at a plural subject, which would have denoted Eve's equal participation in the divine injunction. "Isotta" notes,

> In Genesis II. one finds that the Lord admonished Adam, not Eve, since the passage reads: "thus the Lord God took the man and put him in a paradise of delight, so that *he* might cultivate and guard it." It does not say, "so that *they* might cultivate and guard it." Furthermore, "God warned *him* (and not 'them'): you (in the singular) may eat from every tree (not 'you' in the plural)." And later it says, "for whenever you (in the singular) eat of it, you (in the singular) will die"—not "you will die" in the plural sense. And this was because God rated the man higher than the woman.

Nogarola similarly argues, based on her reading of Corinthians, that if Adam had not sinned, then Eve's sin would have had no consequences. She observes that Paul does not write, "If Eve had not transgressed, then Christ would not have been made man," but rather, "If Adam had not sinned" and "Adam, being the father of all succeeding generations of humankind, was also the first cause of their ruin."[45]

"Ludovico" engages "Isotta's" arguments seriously. "You defend Eve's case with the utmost subtlety," he begins, "and so much so that if I had not been born a man you would have completely brought me over to your side." In rejecting "Isotta's" contention that Eve's intellect was flawed, though he imputes the greater share of blame to Eve, he nonetheless seems more "feminist" than "Isotta" insofar as he attributes equal cognitive skills to both original parents. He cannot understand why his interlocutor faults the mental capabilities of Eve, given that "her intelligence was formed in paradise by God, the sole inventor of all that exists." Arguing that the severity of punishment is the key to understanding the gravity of the transgression, he furthermore contends that Eve's sin must be understood as the greater, because she not only suffers the penalties inflicted on both of them, such as a life of toil, the certainty of death, and the loss of paradise, but receives two additional punishments peculiar to herself: the pain of childbirth and subjection to her husband. As to the discourse of first causes with which "Isotta" began, "Ludovico" maintains that Eve caused Adam to sin and was the example of his sin; those who follow are partly excused. "Ludovico" concludes by returning the reader's attention to Nogarola's status as a worthy interlocutor. "Farewell," the section ends, "and you should not be discouraged. Rather, be bold and argue further, since you have studied all this material thoroughly and you write with superlative erudition."[46]

"Isotta's" second statement expands upon her first, employing a wider range of sources to bolster her central contentions. Whereas her initial argument referred only to the *Sententiae* of Peter Lombard, the book of Genesis, and 1 Corinthians, her second statement deploys all four Gospels, the book of Psalms, Romans, and Ecclesiastes. Other authorities that she either cites explicitly or uses tacitly are Ambrose (*Expositio in Lucam* and *De paradiso*), Aristotle (*Metaphysics*), Augustine (*On Nature and Grace* and *The Literal Meaning of Genesis*), Gregory (*Moralium libri*), and Isidore of Seville (*Etymologiae*).

Although the final section, "Ludovico's" concluding remarks, does not give "Isotta" the ultimate academic victory of persuading him to her view, it nonetheless gives her the ultimate literary victory of awarding her humanist skills pride of place with his own. One means of making this statement in favor of the woman intellectual is his reconstruction of the debate itself as a source of ongoing discussion between scholarly equals. Foscarini held degrees in both civil and canon law, and the way in which this conclusion validates his interlocutor's credentials cannot be overestimated:

> You have explicated everything in such an inspired manner that we could believe that your writings have descended from heaven and not

arisen from philosophical and theological sources. In this sense, your works warrant praise altogether more than rebuttal. However, lest you be defrauded of the profit in continuing the discussion that we have begun, take into advisement these few points that can be made for the opposing position, in order that you might then disseminate these honey-sweet seeds of paradise, which your readers will adore and [which] will embellish you with glory.

In his final comments, "Ludovico" persists in viewing Eve as culpable, by virtue of her unimpaired mental capability. He also taxes "Isotta" for "pushing too far Aristotle's views on first causes" and even impugns womankind for its natural "deceitfulness." Yet, at the end, he returns to the issue with which he began these concluding remarks: "Isotta's" learned virtue. He once again emphasizes her intellectual equality, which, unlike Eve's, is altogether praiseworthy: "I have articulated these things in brief, in part because I was obliged to respect the page limit and in part because I am speaking to you, an expert. Indeed, I have no desire to play tour guide for you along the fine road where, by virtue of your surpassing excellence, everything is clear to you. Really, my sole intention has been to point a finger (as they say) at the documents available to us here on earth, which are like the shadows of a more perfect world."[47]

The conclusion awards Nogarola the highest degree of authorial agency. "Ludovico" gives "Isotta" the responsibility of publicizing their debate. He thereby entrusts their mutual scholarly glory to her writing, which he considers superior to his own. "For some audiences," he admits, "my writings might labor under the impediment of obscurity, but if you, a celebrated woman, collect and join them to both your and my previous works, they will become well known—shining and gleaming in the darkness. And if my contributions prove awkward, you will make them worthy of your talent, virtue and honor by means of your own scholarly zeal."[48]

Foscarini's encomiastic letters to Nogarola, discussed in Chapter 1, suggest that her representing him in her *Dialogue* as an ardent admirer is consistent with the views he himself expressed. He was proud to number this stellar woman intellectual among his friends and peers. Nogarola's argument in defense of Eve as the lesser sinner is not explicitly feminist. Yet her status as a woman intellectual and especially her representation of herself as a theologian gave a new force to the category "woman as intellect" in early Renaissance Italy.

Men other than her friend Foscarini considered Nogarola an asset to their literary circles. The Venetian nobleman, soldier, and literary patron Jacopo Antonio Marcello invited her to contribute to an elaborate volume he was preparing in commemoration of the excellence and tragic death of his eight-year-old son, Valerio. Nogarola's brilliant letter of consolation (1461) was her last known composition. As Diana Robin has noted, this letter attests that the literati who counted considered Nogarola a humanist of excellent credentials.[49] Scholars recognize Nogarola's letter to Marcello as a triumph in the genre of the *consolatio*. Full of elaborate praise for Marcello—father and son—as well as a panoply of classical and biblical references, all of which exhort the father to bear his grief with patience and fortitude, Nogarola's letter does precisely what this kind of piece should do: it honors both the deceased and the bereaved.[50]

Nogarola's "feminine" pride, however, departs from consolatory convention. First of all, she is proud to be Marcello's discursive daughter. Employing the father-daughter metaphor common to the quattrocento women humanists, she speculates that her consolation may be more effective than those offered by his male friends: "Your lordship will recognize that I have hereby served the office of a proper daughter, risking accusations of boldness and immodesty by everyone except you, most beneficent father, and those who are aware that since my extreme youth . . . I have been deemed your most obliging daughter, on account of your remarkable love for me and the Nogarola family, as well as my reverence for you."[51]

More striking, however, is Nogarola's pride in being a woman. She follows form in reminding Marcello of men and women celebrated by classical writers for their stoic resignation when their children died—a trope meant to inspire "manly" (moderate) grief in the recipient. Nogarola departs from the script, however, in stating, "I myself, who feel no shame in being a woman, and as a woman (albeit I am also bolstered by the authority of myriad ancients and Christians) I declare that these figures should be likened more to giant marble statues than to humans . . . For what human being could be so greedy for renown, so unfeeling, so stern, or so cruel that the death of a parent, child or friend would not make them weep?"[52] To the best of my knowledge, no female writer before Isotta Nogarola (not even Christine de Pizan) flatly stated that they were not ashamed to be female or to speak "as a woman." This is a potent articulation of female authorial identity. Nogarola was the only woman author represented in Marcello's 426-page commemorative volume. Her contribution appears alongside works by many contemporary humanists, such as Francesco Filelfo, Niccolò Sagundino, Pietro Perleone, and George of Trebizond.[53]

Nogarola's point was that weeping, though customarily coded feminine, should not in all cases be considered unmanly. Rather, a balance must be struck between unreasonable stoicism and excessive sorrow. She notes that Christ himself wept, as did the male apostles and saints. For her classical examples, however, she makes some intriguing choices. Cato represents one case of immoderate male lamentation, as he "took the death of his brother more to heart than was deemed suitable for a philosopher." The second pagan example is Cicero, who "attests that he had always battled fortune and won; yet even he acknowledges that when he lost his dearest daughter, he was vanquished by fortune."[54] Cicero's grief fits thematically, as it concerns a father lamenting the loss of a cherished child. One might, however, read more into this choice. Given the contemporary propensity to use the example of Tullia as "her father's daughter" with reference to her skill in oratory and as a justification for women's education, Nogarola may have used her example to rework the consolatory paradigm in such a way that it accommodated at least a subtextual statement about the value of women—especially learned ones.

In 1469, three years after Nogarola died in Verona, a new voice in the history of feminism emerged in Brescia, a provincial town at the westernmost edge of the Venetian dominion. The voice was that of the sometimes conflicted but always forceful Laura Cereta. Although Cereta's works did not enjoy the widespread recognition that those of Christine de Pizan and Isotta Nogarola received, nonetheless her writings circulated both within and outside of Italy during the fifteenth and sixteenth centuries. There are at least five different manuscript volumes that include works by and about Cereta in collections now held in Italy and in northern Europe.[55] Jacopo Filippo Tomasini's edition of her complete works (1640) brought her once again to the attention of the literary world, as did the seventeenth-century biographical encyclopedias that publicized her membership in a historical tradition of learned women.

Laura Cereta's letterbook demonstrates her mastery of humanist epistolary. Concomitantly, her letters distill an intensity of feminist critique hitherto unseen in Western literature. Steeped in Latin and Greek literature under the auspices of her father, Cereta held her own as a writer in displaying the depth and breadth of her erudition, but, like Christine de Pizan, this graduate of the household academy used her father-sponsored education in the service of feminism.

Diana Robin has offered a thorough analysis of the feminist themes in Cereta's writings and it will therefore be helpful to outline her claims before proceeding. Pointing in particular to Cereta's letters concerning women and marriage, and her argument for women's advanced education, Robin demonstrates that Cereta was recognizably "feminist," even by modern standards. First, Cereta concerns herself with reimagining the role of women in society as a group. In much the same manner as Christine de Pizan, she revises Boccaccio's classifications of illustrious women, challenging his paradigm of exceptionality and his emphasis upon rape, incest, and sexual transgression as common to the tradition of illustrious women. As Robin notes, however, Cereta's most distinctive contribution on the theme of women, marriage, and the family was to assert the importance of "the maternal as an emblem of women's natural loyalty and strength." Much as Christine had done, Cereta overturns the misogamist tradition that held women to be the ones who benefited from marriage, whereas men only suffered. As Robin summarizes Cereta's position, "the advantages of matrimony are all on the male side . . . Women debase themselves like animals in marriage and the end they meet is widowhood, poverty and grief."[56]

In an essay concerning liberal studies for women, Cereta's principal line of attack is upon Boccaccian exceptionality. Robin notes that "learned and intellectually gifted women like [Cereta] are not exceptions to the rule among women, as Boccaccio claims. Instead, a long history of brilliant women thinkers, philosophers, writers, and prophets precedes her. Learned women, she asserts, have had a long and noble lineage: a *generositas*. Much as Christine de Pizan uses the metaphor of the city, its walls, and buildings to suggest that gifted women have had a tradition of their own, Cereta employs the image of a 'family tree of women geniuses.'"[57]

More striking still, Cereta posits that education is the right of all human beings ("naturam discendi aeque omnibus unam impartiri licentiam"). As Robin observes, Cereta's concern with the "right" *(licentia)* to an education and her concept of a "Republic of Women" *(Res publica mulierum)* push Christinian argumentation to the next level of advocacy. Also innovative was Cereta's decision to take women themselves to task for refusing the opportunities available to them for education. As Robin summarizes, "while she attacks the typical attitude of her male contemporaries in the person of her correspondent Bibolo Semproni, for his erroneous assumption of women's inferiority, she blames women's lack of schooling on women themselves rather than on either 'nature' or society and its institutions."[58]

Building upon Robin's arguments, I posit that the aspect of Cereta's feminism that rewards further examination is her argument concerning women's education. Cereta's theoretical examination of the learned woman as a character appear in two invective letters addressed to fictional opponents or at the least to antagonists whose names she changed. Either way, Cereta freed herself from the strictures attendant to "real" conversation, thereby allowing her feminism greater scope.

Cereta's most important contribution is her forceful argument against the notion that she, as an intellectual, was exceptional. As in Christine de Pizan's view, justification of the self, womankind, and women's education were one and the same. This stance reinforces the innate gifts that womankind as a category possesses, which Cereta bolsters by citing a historical tradition of women like herself. In her letter "Against Bibolo Semproni, a Defense of the Liberal Education of Women" *(Laurae Ceretae in Bibulum Sempronium De liberali Mulierum institutione Defensio)*, she constructs the woman intellectual as a familiar figure. Ignoring the famous tradition of female erudition parades both the misogynist's injustice and his poor scholarly credentials. "Your accusations beat my weary ears," she begins, "in which you claim (indeed shout from the rooftops) that you not only marvel, but also grieve, to learn that I exhibit an incredible genius, the kind that only the most erudite man might possess. You seem to deduce, as if from plausible grounds, that until our own times such a woman had rarely appeared in human society. Both planks of your argument are erroneous."[59]

Cereta invokes two masculine discourses in combating her opponent: institutionalized justice (court and law) and personal justice (vendetta). She initially lends force to her declamation by situating her contentions in a courtroom setting (writing, "as if you had deduced from reasonable grounds"). Following this, however, she represents herself as unable to stomach Semproni's poisonous logic. She will combat him in a more primal sense with her anger, using her mind and her pen as weapons in this imagined fight. He has implicitly attacked womankind and thereby "goaded a spirit thirsty for vengeance, roused a dormant pen to inexhaustible pages." Cereta writes, "Thanks to you, burning rage now unleashes a wrath that years of silence have hitherto contained."[60] Ann Rosalind Jones has argued that a characteristic technique of sixteenth-century women poets was their "negotiation" of the male erotic idiom.[61] She contends that retaining the dominant features of masculine discourse served ultimately to contain the woman writer—that is, the rules of the game were still set by men. Yet women writers can also be seen to empower themselves by appropriating masculine vocabularies. This is what Cereta accomplishes when she deploys the language of courtroom and vendetta against her imagined male opponent. Literally, she fights fire with fire.

Having vented her anger, Cereta returns to legal metaphor. "This cause is just," she announces, "by which I am driven to demonstrate how much virtue and literary fame has been left behind by that eminent female lineage which I bear in my heart and which intelligence (generous patroness that *she* is) has always and ever glorified. In point of fact that hereditary possession is indisputable and legitimate, which has descended eternally from one age to the next and all the way to me."[62] As Robin notes, Cereta's terminology derives from property and inheritance law: she has inherited "the intellectual and cultural legacy of generations of learned women," just as she might take possession of land, money or goods rightfully bequeathed to her.[63]

Her intellectual patrimony (or in her formulation "matri-mony") includes the achievements of a host of women prophets and scholars from classical and Christian antiquity. Cereta claims the sibyl Amalthea; the Babylonian prophetess Eriphila; Nicostrata, mother of Evander; Isis (understood as in Boccaccio to be a human female gifted in prophecy and occult studies); the ancient queen Zenobia; as well as Manto, Pyromantia, Pallas-Athena (again taken, in Boccaccio, to be a human female who invented the arts, technology, and science). In addition, Cereta "owns" the legacy of women writers such as Phyliasia, Lasthenia, Sappho, Leontium, and Proba. Moving to the women orators, Cereta lays claim to the erudition of Hortensia, Cornificia, Tullia, and Cornelia. She is able to strengthen her point about the continuous genealogy of learned women in a way that Christine de Pizan could not do, as Cereta had modern examples other than herself to hand, chiefly "Isotta of Verona, and Cassandra of Venice."[64]

In battling the notion that accomplished women are rarities, Cereta's first strategy is to situate herself in an unbroken line of illustrious women intellectuals. Concomitantly, she brings forward her notion that all human beings share the freedom to learn: "Nature bestows one license upon everyone and in equal measure: that of acquiring knowledge." Clarifying the relationship of this "licentia" (a term that seems to prefigure the much later discourse of natural rights) to the problem of exceptionality, Cereta notes, "One point alone remains in doubt, and that is my uniqueness. Choice makes all the difference, since choice alone determines conduct." She reasons that most of her female contemporaries choose leisure and hollow entertainment instead of the long hours of study in which she herself routinely engages. However, lest she belie her own argument by setting herself upon a Boccaccian pedestal, she subsequently states, "Compared with the dazzling acclaim that other women have earned, I am nothing more than the tiniest little mouse."[65]

The subject of other women's accomplishments prompts Cereta to make a Pizanian promise: she will devote her literary skill to championing honorable women. Cereta envisions her task not as constructing a defensive citadel, however, but rather as waging an active campaign against male detractors. Attesting that she is a selfless lover of virtue, she vows to "file [her] pen down to a nub in contravening these windbags, who are inflated by the hollow celebrity that their lies bring." She continues, "What is more, I will be an immovable roadblock on their every insidious path and will fight to annihilate the reprehensible slander of these noisy morons with my weapons of vengeance. For some disreputable cretins and madmen, egged on by this kind of nonsense, make rabid assaults upon the Republic of Women, which instead deserves reverence."[66]

Cereta's invective reveals the expanding boundaries of the thinkable in early modern Italian feminism. In building her own imagined female community on the Field of Letters, Cereta politicizes Christine de Pizan's "City of Women" and "Kingdom of Femininity" as a "Republic of Women" *(Respublica muliebris)*. Her notion of women's education also takes a step beyond the precedent set by Christine, who made the point that learned women are praiseworthy, using her own example and that of other liter-

ary women from history, but offered no explicit argument about pedagogy. Cereta, in contrast, contends that women, like men, have a natural
"right" to be educated. Finally, while Christine maintained a Boccaccian
paradigm in presenting her histories of women as an encyclopedia to be
read, Cereta internalized her predecessors, whom she envisioned as dwelling literally within herself. In coming years, this awareness on the part of
the learned woman—that she belongs not merely to a literary collection
but to a historical tradition—bolstered the advocacy of new institutions
for female education, advocacy characteristic of seventeenth-century feminists like Bathsua Makin.

Cereta also broke new ground in lambasting misogyny in both
sexes, not just in men. Elaborating upon the idea adumbrated in her letter to the fictitious Bibolo Semproni that what separates a learned from
an ignorant woman is a matter of individual choice, she directed an
equally scorching invective to an imaginary female opponent, Lucilia
Vernacula. This letter assails female misogyny, or women who attack
other women for accomplishments that exceed their own. In this formulation, it is the lack of female solidarity that destabilizes the *Respublica
muliebris*. "Eminent and distinguished matrons always praise me with
decorous speeches," she attests, "[but] mental rust disturbs certain psy-
chotic mothers—or, better yet, Furies—who cannot bear to hear so much
as the very expression 'learned women.'"[67]

Cereta spends much of this invective insulting and mocking the
"Latinless" *(vernacula)* female misogynist, but Cereta's combat strategy is
far less clear here than in her war against perceived male opposition. Ultimately, she reiterates her postulate from the letter to Semproni, reminding her readers that the only real prerequisite for scholarship is
determination. "Learning does not pass down to us as if from a will," she
lectures, "nor is it a matter of good luck. We ourselves are responsible for
obtaining virtue; nor indeed can women achieve an understanding of
complex matters if they waste their minds in the fetid swamp of sensu-
ality, or else in stupefying sloth." Restating the point in the positive,
Cereta concludes that "the path to intellectual expertise lies wide open
for those women who appreciate the fact that indefatigable devotion to
study will win them definite commendation."[68]

One woman of Cereta's time who received "definite commendation" was her older contemporary and fellow denizen of the Venetian
Republic, Cassandra Fedele. Cereta was arguably the more inventive

writer, and she was certainly the more outspoken feminist. In order to emphasize these close links to the precedents set by Christine de Pizan and Isotta Nogarola, I have broken with chronology and discussed Cereta before Fedele. It is important to note, however, that in terms of publication record and influence, Fedele surpassed her younger and more radical colleague. Whereas Cereta's works exist in only six Renaissance-era manuscript collections, Fedele's writings appear in twenty-five different collections dating from the late fifteenth to mid sixteenth centuries.[69] And while none of Cereta's works appeared in print during her lifetime, Fedele's "Oration for Bertuccio Lamberto" was published three times between 1487 and 1489.[70] Nor were Fedele's writings devoid of feminist sentiment. Her letters to female patrons celebrate in the clearest terms her recipients' learning and influence.

Cassandra Fedele presents a classic case of participatory and celebratory feminism. Although she did not herself enter the debate on women in the way that Christine de Pizan, Isotta Nogarola, and Laura Cereta did, her esteemed position as a humanist made its own case for the intellectual equality of the sexes. Fedele's letters to and about Alessandra Scala, for instance, suggest that Fedele was aware of their shared participation in the new category "woman as intellect." As we saw in Chapter 1, Fedele thanked Alessandra's father, Bartolomeo, for producing another woman like herself, whose virtue and erudition adorned "our sex" and "our age as well."[71] Fedele's celebration of Alessandra's excellence and the letters that the two women exchanged created at least a microcommunity of women intellectuals; her letters to female patrons enhanced both the scope and luster of this society.

Fedele's correspondence with Isabella, the queen of Castile, Aragon, and Sicily, reveals a shared feminist hermeneutic: they praise each other as honors to their sex on account of their "learned virtue." In 1487 Fedele wrote to Isabella, praising the queen's myriad and famous achievements, by means of which "[their] sex [was] being supported, recovered and restored" across Europe and even in the non-Christian world.[72] Isabella replied within the same syntax of celebratory feminist compliment. Having discerned Fedele's "outstanding erudition" *(egregiam doctrinam tuam)* from her letters as well as from the comments of a trusted male courtier, Isabella wrote of her certainty of Fedele's importance: "Thanks to you, our sex and our age will enjoy precisely the pitch of praise for literary excellence that the Amazons once enjoyed for military valor on account of Penthesilea."[73] Making a practical offer of her compliment, Isabella invited Fedele to her court—an offer that Fedele accepted joyously, but which her illness and later the military unrest in northern Italy prevented from coming to fruition.

The same mode of compliment appears in Fedele's correspondence with Beatrice, Duchess of Bari (later Milan). Writing first to congratulate Beatrice on the birth of her son, Fedele made the usual excuses for writing to a powerful figure unbidden. Beatrice responded not only with noble courtesy but with warmth and reciprocal compliments. "Not only am I disinclined to chastise you for daring to write to me," she began, "but rather I offer my thanks, just as I should do. For you, whom I love on account of your surpassing *virtù*—by which I mean the way that you, with your knowledge of letters, have single-handedly glorified womankind in our age—you have demonstrated that you possess a dual zeal that I should know you and know that you love me. I do not merely find this gratifying, but deem it altogether amazing."[74]

Beatrice of Aragon (Queen of Hungary) similarly elicited Fedele's praise as a woman with intellectual credentials. Here again, the language of compliment extols the learned woman as a triumph for womankind and a testament to the excellence of the age. Fedele fears, "I might with my inelegant expressions deafen your most learned ears and offend your greatness of intellect, which is expert in both book learning and true wisdom, in addition to many practical skills."[75] While Beatrice's brilliance presented one reason not to write, it also offered an incentive: "Your lofty intellect ensured that I did not shudder at the thought of sending this to you, and all the more since I have discovered that your will inclines toward *literati*, and especially women writers. But above all, when I heard that you should be put first on the roster of womankind, not only to those now alive, but to all women who have ever been or will ever be, I was veritably set on fire to introduce myself to you."[76]

Eleonora of Aragon, Duchess of Ferrara and a woman of considerable learning, celebrated Fedele's "learned virtue" in 1488.[77] Like her predecessors on Fedele's roster of women patrons, Eleonora praises the Venetian humanist as an honor to her sex: "In our estimation you deserve the highest commendation. You are happy and lucky, who find yourself abundantly endowed with such celestial and divine talent, and grace as well, that even so young, you honor our sex."[78]

To be sure, stating that an accomplished woman honored or adorned the female sex was a trope, but embedded in this seemingly standard compliment is a fundamentally new attitude toward being female. Since when was womanhood a point of pride? Since when had the woman intellectual served to dignify the female sex as a whole? This late-quattrocento celebration of woman as a positive contributor both to history and to contemporary society suggests that Christine de Pizan's initial redefinition of female capability was being revised and indeed intensified in Italy in the decades following Christine's death. The previous chapter has explored similar modes of praise with which male writers heralded the entrance of learned women onto the literary stage. To find this style of celebration here in letters by women to women suggests their growing courage in asserting their membership in this group.

Christine de Pizan, Isotta Nogarola, Cassandra Fedele, and Laura Cereta differed in the pitch of their feminist arguments. What they shared, however, was an insistence upon their own status as intellectuals. This scholarly self-identification connects reticent English women to more-radical thinkers like Laura Cereta. English women would only begin to explore the possibilities for something like Cereta's *respublica muliebris* at the close of the seventeenth century, but the sixteenth-century English women humanists and their supporters deserve more credit than historians and literary critics have given them for making it possible to conceive of secular communities of learned women—for instance, girls' schools with serious intellectual agendas. Seventeenth-century women writers like Bathsua Makin and Mary Astell would not only consider but establish these communities.

English Women and Scholarly Piety

Scholars have lamented the fact that educated Englishwomen of the sixteenth century were translators rather than authors of original works. Mary Ellen Lamb has even argued that, because women could and did translate, translation was then coded "feminine" and that male intellectuals therefore found the work demeaning. Lamb remarks that "translation, especially of works by males, was allowed to women because it did not threaten the male establishment as the expression of personal viewpoints might" and that "any competence [women] displayed could be dismissed by denigrating the task of translation itself."[79] Her principal evidence for this claim is a comment by John Florio in the dedicatory letter of his translation of Montaigne's *Essays*, in which Florio terms his edition "defective (since all translations are reputed females)" and "delivered at second hand." He continues, "And I in this . . . serve but as Vulcan, to hatchet this Minerva from that Jupiter's big brain."[80] Florio's evident anxiety concerning his role as surrogate "father" might well derive from the fact that he was working only in the vernacular (French to English). Translation from the Latin and Greek, in contrast, defined the Italian humanist enterprise. North of the Alps, moreover, scriptural and devotional translation constituted one of the most prestigious genres of intellectual production. Erasmus, for instance, devoted much of his career to translating and paraphrasing scripture; no one seems to have thought that he was engaging in "women's work."

Translation as a genre involves not only scholarly skill but also creativity in the choice of text to reproduce and in the choice of words for making foreign syntax and content legible to an altogether different socioliterary milieu.[81] Beyond this issue, it is important to note that prefaces and dedicatory epistles accompanied most works, including translations. These paratextual artifacts constitute crucial repositories of women translators' highly original self-presentation. The prefatory material associated with English women's translations also served as a vehicle for men to offer celebratory feminist reflections on "woman as intellect" as a positive contributor to society and specifically to revealed religion.

The presentation of self is a creative act. The secular woman scholar was a new character in sixteenth-century England, but women scholars themselves crafted an effective persona that mitigated the danger inherent in their novelty. The central elements in this persona were the mask of modesty and the rhetoric of family. English women used kinship to sustain their authorship, bolstering their status as writers with their familial connections, most often to their learned male relatives. Male encomiasts recognized both the serious scholarly contributions that women were making and the need to legitimate such novelty by means of the culturally sanctioned domestic referent.

English women humanists, in other words, were active participants in the history of feminism. What the women translators of sixteenth-century England share with their explicitly feminist colleagues in Italy is a clear sense of their own status as scholars and writers. While neither

Margaret Roper nor her daughter Mary Basset nor any of the brilliant Cooke sisters wrote epistles denouncing misogyny, or even works celebrating their female predecessors and contemporaries, a recurrent theme in their writings and contemporary "reception" is their importance as translators. In the parlance of the day, these women were "learned matrons" engaging with "well-learned men" in the most important genre of scholarly endeavor: finding the right words to express scriptural truth.[82] English women's feminism is best understood as participatory. Feminist themes become explicit, however, in contemporary works written about the achievements of these women, works that present them as examples for other women to follow.

The feminism of the English Renaissance was, like its humanism, not an end in and of itself but rather a servant of the Word. English women humanists, legitimate graduates of household academies devoted to the propagation of divine truth, made the female intellectual a recognized and praiseworthy character in English literature: they charted an initial trajectory that their countrywomen would take in new directions during the seventeenth century.

Mary Basset and the Editorial "I"

Mary Basset followed and indeed bested the scholarly example of her mother, Margaret Roper. Whereas Roper earned the respect of the literary world for translating Erasmus's short Latin treatise on the Paternoster into English, Basset translated the first five books of Eusebius's *Ecclesiastical History* from Greek into Latin and English. Basset's virtuoso manuscript, composed during her first widowhood, demonstrates the highest skill in Greek as well as in Latin and English prose composition. The first sentence of her dedicatory epistle, however, foregrounds her paternal heritage and cultural normality. She announces herself as "Mary Clarcke . . . most humble oratrix widow, and daughter to William Roper, Esquire."[83] Given that it was her mother who had been the direct heir of Thomas More's intellectual legacy, it stands to reason that she might also have mentioned being the daughter of "Margaret Roper, virtuous Latinist." As biological legitimacy followed the patriline, however, so too did intellectual credentials.

While the English translation comprises the greater part of the manuscript, Basset also included her Latin translation of book I. She explained that there were two principal reasons for undertaking the Latin translation: the first was private knowledge ("for mine own exercise in the Latin tongue"), but the second, public scholarship, required further explication.[84] The original Latin translator of Eusebius, she explained, had lacked sufficient understanding of the historical sense attendant to certain Greek words. This defect produced numerous inaccurate renderings. He also had omitted sentences and (worse still) added others of his own devising. As she put it,

> I thought this kind of study should be to me no small furtherance toward the attaining of the true sense and understanding of the author, and especially for as much as Rufinus by whom this work was (as far as I ever could hear) first translated into Latin (I mean not here anything to speak to his dispraise, for if he had not taken pain thereabout, the Latin Church of likelihood this eleven hundred years and more . . . should have lacked the knowledge of so godly and profitable a story) doth not in all points thoroughly perform the office of a true interpreter; sometimes altering the very sense, sometimes omitting whole sentences together, sometimes adding and putting to of his own.[85]

Her only reason for interrupting her full Latin translation was that, immediately upon finishing the first book, a friend had informed her that "a great learned man had the whole translation thereof fully finished already, whereupon I (as me thought was mete) left off this my foresaid enterprise."[86]

Basset used the humility trope to good effect at several points in her dedication. She claimed, in the first place, that her undertaking had begun as a private exercise, but that friends had prompted her to make the work public. Most intellectuals, male or female, utilized this rhetorical device as a means to circumvent criticism. For women, however, it was a particularly critical element in their authorial persona. Confronting more restrictive bounds of propriety than their male colleagues, women writers depicted themselves as demure, prompted to action only by the demands of their "friends" or their sense of duty to their patron. Above all, the "feminine" trope of humility emphasized deference to male authority.

Basset takes a confident stance, conversely, when she reflects upon the act of translation and advances her scholarly credibility. As we have already seen, she tells us that she embarked upon her translation in the interest of public knowledge. Parenthetical niceties aside, she called the first translator a hack, whose sloppy work she aimed to correct. Furthermore, she attests to passing through a due process of male scholarly review. Fearing that her friends (their sex unspecified) might have been overindulgent in their praise of her translation, she explains, "[I submitted it to] more than one or two very wise and well learned men, desiring their advice and judgment therein, being such of themselves, as I well knew were neither with favor borne toward me likely to be corrupted, nor again for their wit, erudition and knowledge unable to compare my translation with the Greek, and soon perceive where I had swerved or varied."[87] Continuing on the theme of her reviewers' objectivity, she claims that she only "waxed somewhat bolder" once these men "had leisurely perused, examined, liked and allowed the same."[88] At one level, she rates male approbation higher than her own talent. Yet this anecdote also serves as a positive statement of her own academic rigor. The end result is a self-authored letter of recommendation: her translation has been sanctioned by an unbiased committee and should therefore be considered reliable.

Similarly, Basset "admits" her lack of learning but in so doing underscores her familiarity with classical philosophy. Describing her reservations about showing her work to a noble and learned patron rather than to her indulgent friends, she at once compliments Queen Mary, disparages her own merits, and proves her status as a scholar. Her intended patron, Basset states, was so royal and so learned that "any man were he so eloquent as Cicero or Demosthenes, as profoundly learned as Plato or Aristotle, with as great prudence and wisdom endowed as Solon and Licurgus [sic], might well be abashed to presume to present any work of his unto so honorable, so virtuous, so wise and well-learned a princess, as [her] grace is." Basset continues, "Then on the other part, [I recalled that] I myself was, one neither for wit, erudition, learning, nor any other like quality mete to take upon me, so great and weighty an enterprise as it should be, much less *my simple rude translation* to dedicate unto your highness, since that besides all other inabilities, I was also but a woman, whereas the translating of such a work (in my opinion) required rather the diligent labor of a wise, eloquent, expert, and in all kind of good literature, a very well exercised man.[89] "My simple rude translation" was a time-honored humility trope for translators. William Caxton, for instance, likewise begged pardon for his "simple and rude reducing" of a French courtesy book into English.[90] The way in which

Basset catalogs the great philosophers of antiquity, moreover, under-scores the proud subtext of her ostensible humility. In the very act of denying her erudition, she proves it.

As a patronage seeker, Basset relied not upon her own merit but rather upon the good nature of her intended patron. Only the "remem-brance of [Lady Mary's] most gentle nature, which (as all men report) taketh in good part any present, be it never so simple, that proceedeth of good will and unfeigned affection toward [her] grace," could give Mary Basset the requisite courage to "publicize" her work.[91]

Basset's dedicatory epistle thus deployed the three most important tools in the rhetorical workshop: humility, classical flourish, and flattery. Where she departs from other women writers—including her mother, who never explicitly claimed authorship for her translations—is in the unequivocal association of her name with her work. Also distinctive is her extended "specialist" reflection upon the act of translation, including citation of the external review that guaranteed the credibility of her text. A woman orator needed a platform from which to stake such claims. In Basset's case, as in the numerous others that this study analyzes, the so-cial self legitimized the scholarly self from the outset. The translator was legitimate because she was a proper family woman—a humble widow and the daughter of William Roper, esquire.

Unlike many contemporary English women authors, Mary Basset was named as the translator of one printed text: her grandfather's trea-tise on Christ's passion, which Thomas More wrote while in prison. William Rastell, publisher of More's complete works (of which the trea-tise is one section), makes a point of attributing the translation to Basset, who, being an expert in Latin, was both intellectually fit for the job and an especially appropriate translator of the text because she was a rela-tive. In Rastell's words, Basset's translation "goes so near Sir Thomas More's own English phrase that [she is as near] to him in kindred, virtue and literature, [as] in his English tongue: so that it might seem to have been [written] by his own pen, and not at all translated. Such a gift hath she to follow her grandfather's vein in writing."[92]

For her own part, Basset connects credentials and consanguinity in her marginal comments. She does not explicitly equate her bloodline with her scholarly ability but rather suggests the link in reminding the reader that she had her grandfather's text to hand: "I have not translated this place as the Latin copy goes, but as I judge it should be, because my grandfather's copy was for lack of leisure never well corrected."[93] Similarly, she asserts, "This prophecy, I will strike the shepherd etc. was not written in my grandfathers copy, and therefore I do [only] guess that this or some other like he would himself have written."[94]

Translators' choices and contributions are sometimes occluded. Basset, however, makes her editorial work apparent. In one instance, where More took "pray without ceasing . . . pray ye without intermission" to be Jesus's injunction to his apostles, she notes, "Thessa[lonians].5. Albeit these words here (pray ye without intermission) be Saint Paul's words, yet in effect did our savior say the same. Luke.18."[95] In another instance, she alerts the reader to a turn of phrase that was chosen in the interest of readability but that diverged from the Latin text. This passage chastises Christians for failing to follow Jesus's example and spend the night in prayer, instead remaining awake to brood on worldly affairs or else to sleep and allow their minds to be "occupied with mad fantastical dreams." Basset comments on this phrase: "Whereas the Latin text hath here *somnia speculantes Mandragore,* I have translated it in English, 'our minds all occupied with mad fantastical dreams,' because Mandragora is an herb, as physicians say, that causes folk to sleep, and therein to have many mad fantastical dreams."[96]

This explication suggests three important elements in Basset's conception of her role as a translator. First, she wishes to avoid unjustified deviations from the original text of the kind that she imputed to Eusebius's first Latin translator. She also considered translation to be a form of intellectual bravura. The vernacular reader would not have required evidence of the original Latin phrase or adduction of the current medical understanding concerning the mandrake root's soporific properties in order to understand this passage on the merits of constant prayer. Rather, Basset's explication constitutes a moment of superfluous scholarly flourish. Like her other interventions, moreover, this comment suggests that she wanted credit for her performance. Each of these protofootnotes is in the first person, presenting an unabashed editorial "I" to the reader.

It is unclear whether the impetus to print Basset's marginalia was hers or Rastell's. In either case, however, the decision would be his as publisher. Although he had described the translator as modest and initially unwilling "to have [the work] go abroad, for that (she says) it was first turned into English, but for her own pass-time and exercise, and so reputes it far to [*sic*] simple to come in many hands," nonetheless he himself felt free to praise her learning.[97] In this regard, he employed Basset's own strategy: couching a bold departure from precedent in the rhetoric of feminine modesty. Mary Basset wished to be seen as a thorough scholar. One strategy toward this end was to remind the reader of her skill with the ancient languages. The other strategy, the one most evident in her translation of More, was to present herself the intellectual heir of England's most famous humanist.

Apart from direct reference, certain practical decisions supplemented women authors' self-fashioning, among them the choice of mediator with the publisher. Richard Hyrde published Margaret Roper's translation (at the press of Wynkyn de Worde, 1526?), which he prefaced with a long dedication to "Lady Fraunces," a young gentlewoman whose own education Hyrde claimed to sponsor and who was, in his terms, "a near kinswoman" of Roper. Once again, the dangers inherent in "publicity" for a woman author are here mitigated by the context of the intellectual family. Hyrde negated the potentially unsavory association with print culture, which in this era possessed connotations of incontinence, by framing Roper's scholarship as more akin to manuscript circulation. Roper's text remained within an imagined community of intellectuals.[98] Similarly, Mary Basset's translation of her grandfather's treatise was published by William Rastell in his edition of Thomas More's complete works. Rastell also happened to be Basset's cousin by marriage. In this sense, as in the choice of text, Basset maintained a paradigm of domestic discussion, even in the act of publishing. In her case, this context was even more important, as the translation was directly attributed to her— her name, however, was surrounded by the illustrious members of her pious and erudite lineage.

The women of the More and Roper families were the first celebrated members of the category "woman as intellect" in England. Their younger contemporaries, the four daughters of Sir Anthony Cooke, not only added to this category but went a long way toward saving it from extinction in the fast-moving culture of political and religious change under Edward VI and Elizabeth I.

The Cooke Women and the Progress of Reform

The Cooke sisters were all busy in the reformist cause. Elizabeth Cooke Hoby and Katherine Cooke Killigrew have left less extensive documentary records than Anne Cooke Bacon and Mildred Cooke Cecil, but their extant writings suggest that they, too, made good use of the domestic paradigm to situate their compositions. Elizabeth's translation of a French devotional book, published in English as *A Way of Reconciliation* (1605) is dedicated to her daughter, then Lady Herbert. Elizabeth's other known composition is a Latin inscription commemorating the death of her two infant daughters. Katherine was best known in the early modern period for a Latin letter (quoted by Thomas Fuller in his *Worthies of England*) that epitomizes wifely affection. Fearful of the dangerous embassy to France with which Henry Killigrew had been commissioned, she begs her sister, Mildred, to ask her own husband, Sir William Cecil (later Lord Burghley) to excuse Killigrew. Katherine was also a supporter and long-time correspondent of the Puritan preacher Edward Dering. Having been forbidden to preach in public, Dering seems to have used this correspondence as an outlet for theological expression.[99]

Anne Cooke, of all her sisters, put her humanist education to the most professional use. Her first major translation was a collection of sermons by one of her father's friends, Bernardo Ochino (1548 and 1551?). She also translated John Jewel's *Apologie on the Church of England* from Latin into English (1564), a translation that Jewel himself would later use in his own theological disputes and that also became the official version of the text, distributed in churches throughout England for parishioners' edification.[100]

Cooke, under the initials A. C., wrote her own dedication for Ochino's sermons. This dedication both invokes and confronts the domestic paradigm. "A. C." dedicated these pious translations to her mother, "Lady F[itzwilliam]," and employed tropes of filial humility throughout. Much as we found with Christine de Pizan and Laura Cereta, however, the attitude of Anne Cooke to the maternal figure appears ambivalent, especially in matters of learning. Her mother, she observes, considered the study of Italian useless, if not indeed dangerous, where piety was concerned. Cooke is therefore at some pains to position herself as a dutiful daughter, when these translations from the Italian so obviously confronted her dedicatee's "motherly injunctions."

Written by a "G. B.," the prefatory comments to the reader, like Hyrde's address to "Lady Fraunces," justify female translation on the grounds of the translator's exemplary piety. Unlike Hyrde's unequivocal support of women's education within the family context, however, "G. B." uses the family in part as legitimation for Anne Cooke and in part as an excuse for any possible errors in the translation itself. If there are any errors, he cautions, then readers should keep in mind that it is a woman's translation—indeed, "a maiden's, that never gadded farther than her father's house to learn the languages."[101] On the one hand, then, the translator appears appropriately within "her father's house" (private); on the other hand, by virtue of that same commendable context, she lacks the professional credentials of a "public" education.

The same ambivalence toward, yet use of, the family paradigm appears in Cooke's dedication "to the right worshipful and worthily beloved Mother, the lady F." Cooke begins by stating her wish to demonstrate that she honors her mother's "careful and motherly goodness" and her "most godly exhortations"; but immediately the problem of Italian arises, "as it hath pleased [the mother] to reprove [the daughter's] vain study in the Italian tongue, accounting the seed thereof to have been sown in barren, unfruitful ground (since God thereby is no whit magnified)."[102]

Cooke ultimately resolves the tension by using the material itself— "the excellent fruit [herein] contained, proceeding from the happy spirit of the sanctified Bernardin, which treat[s] of the election and predestination of God"—as justification for her study of Italian. Her pursuit of these themes demonstrates that "your so many worthy sentences touching the same have not utterly been without some note in my weak memory" but rather "yielded some part of the fruit of your Motherly admonitions in this my willing service." As a servant of revealed scripture and evangelical zeal, then, if not precisely as a student of Italian, Cooke is able to end her epistle in good conscience as her mother's daughter "most boundenly obedient."[103]

Obedient not only to her mother but also to the time-honored humility trope, Anne Cooke's elaborate self-deprecation also suggests (as did Basset's) that modesty was a critical ingredient in authorial self-presentation. To follow form, Cooke acknowledges that her translations are "not done in such perfection, as the dignity of the matter doth require; yet [she] trust[s] and know[s] [her mother] will accept the humble will of the presenter, not weighing so much the excellency of the translation" but rather accepting what Cooke calls her own "small labor . . . at [her mother's] hands, under whose protection it is committed with humble reverence." Sincerity and humility serve as credentials for one who is reluctant to claim Ochino's "high style of theology" and must instead acknowledge their relative "debility."[104]

For all her talk of humility and even "debility," however, Cooke does not express these concepts in gendered terms. While Cassandra Fedele, for instance, referred to herself as an "unlettered little woman" in opening her oration at the *studio* of Padua, Cooke does not posit her weakness as specifically feminine. But then again this task had already been performed for her by "G. B."

Cooke did not write a dedication for her translation of Jewel's *Apologie,* which she made after her marriage to Sir Nicholas Bacon. The prefatory encomium by Archbishop Matthew Parker, however, represents a marked shift away from "G. B.'s" condescension. As we will see later in this chapter, Parker treats her as a thorough professional and adduces her status as a "learned matron" (in contrast to "G. B.'s" emphasis upon her as "only" a maiden) and as an example to other women of "learned virtue."

Mildred Cooke Cecil was less prolific than her sister Anne, but she too enjoyed a scholarly career that continued after her marriage. And the extant manuscripts certainly attest that she was also a gifted translator. Indeed, Mildred Cecil is ultimately the more impressive scholar, in that she specialized in Greek. Cecil's translation (ca. 1550) of a sermon by Basil the Great underscores her skills and the degree to which she shared the interests of the leading male intellectuals of her time.[105] Cardinal Reginald Pole, for instance, was similarly preoccupied with the writings of St. Basil as a prefiguration of a central concern for Christian humanism: learning as the handmaiden of divine grace.[106]

Mildred Cecil dedicated her translation of St. Basil's sermon to Anne Stanhope, the second wife of Edward Seymour, who had long depended upon the political assistance of Cecil's husband.[107] In her dedication, she displays more of a literary and even an ironical sensibility than her sister Anne does. Much of the dedication plays upon the various meanings of debt in such a fashion as to suggest a shared joke between translator and patron:

Like as poor debtors, most honorable and my very good Lady, desiring to pay what their poverty keepeth back, and taking [what] they would use for the continuance of their creditors' favor, either to pay some small part, or to prolong the remnant, or to intercede by friends to diminish the debt, so I Your Grace's humble servant and debtor, knowing in heart my earnest zeal to serve your virtuous content[ment], and seeing indeed the weakness of my thin power unmeet to answer the same, thought mete with these few leaves thus by me translated to move your goodness either to take them as some small part of the service I owe, or instead of some mean friend to entreat for my debt.[108]

Fiscal metaphor is common among dedications of this period, as it lends itself so readily to the economy of patronage—that is, the debts incurred by humble authors/artists/musicians, which by virtue of their humility they can never repay but only partly defray by making "gifts" of their works to the mighty patron. The laboring of the metaphor in this case, however, suggests a sense of rhetorical play and even familiarity.

Far from praising her own skill or elegance, Cecil adopts a humble stance. "Albeit my labor herein," she continues, "be indeed neither worthy to serve either the one or the other [i.e., the debt, or else friendly intercession for the debt], yet I trust the Author, whose commendation my words can finally enlarge, will claim such favor that by my labor coming in his company be thought as welcome for his sake as my good will meant to send it for his own. Whereof the one I hope through Your Grace's gentle acceptance, the other I doubt not through the author's worthy deserving."[109] Alongside the predictable profession of her inadequacy comes a poignant reflection on the intellectual fellowship between her patron and the author, Basil the Great: Stanhope would be "coming into his company" through Cecil's labor as translator. Cecil disparages her linguistic credentials far less than her sister does. In part, the greater sense of confidence may be attributed to the medium: manuscript circulation was less "public" and therefore less dangerous than print—perhaps all the more so in this case, as she is offering her work to one other woman rather than the wider (ostensibly) male readership that print brought. At least those were the conventions. Perhaps also, like Mary Basset, Mildred Cecil was aware of the cachet attendant to expertise in Greek, the province of not just humanists in general but only the most proficient of that already rarified group. Even a humanist as capable as Pole seems to have preferred consulting St. Basil in translation.

Cecil also parallels Mary Basset in describing her philological method. Much as Basset emphasized the need to translate with a view toward the meaning of the Greek words in their historical context, so Cecil states that she has "somewhat superstitiously observed the nature of the Greek phrase, not omitting the congruity of English speech, but rather the use, that the treatise of so good an Author should not in too much serving the English tongue lose his own efficacy and value, thinking it less fault that the author should speak Greekish English, and save his own sense, than English Greek and confound it with a doubtful—in this showing the property of the tongue, in the other the verity of the matter."[110] In preferring the niceties of the original language to a smooth translation, Cecil and Basset set themselves in the camp of earlier humanist philologists (paradigmatically Lorenzo Valla), for whom rendering the precise meaning of ancient words in their own context was the top priority, and somewhat against the grain of sixteenth-century humanist theory, which was making moves toward prioritizing modern readability over the historical sense of the original text. Largely, the distinction broke down over genre: Basset and Cecil, like their predecessor Valla and their contemporary Erasmus, were working with scripture and parascriptural material; thus, accuracy of the "word" was of the utmost importance. It was truth, not elegance, that counted in this context.

Indeed, the theme of "truth" versus "words" pervades the sermon itself, which is an extended consideration (twenty-three folios) of the need to moderate speech, examine one's thoughts at all times, and be prepared to receive godly counsel. The exordium is as follows, in Cecil's translation:

> God, who made us, gave unto us the use of speaking to the intent that we should discover one to another the councils of our hearts, and by the communicating of our nature deal them to our neighbors, bringing forth our purposes out of the secret places of our hearts, as it were out of certain storehouses . . . but if the noise from the hearers do blow against the speech, like a rough storm, the speech is straightaway wrecked and broken in mid-air. Therefore make a calm for my words with your silence.

Moving then to the principal matter, Moses's exhortation in Deuteronomy 15 ("Take heed to thy self, lest at any time the secret and still word hid in thy heart become wickedness"), the sermon continues as a complex reflection upon inner truth, thought, and communication (the "word" in all its senses): when to speak, when to listen in silence.[111]

The theme of meticulous self-examination would resonate with those who were the "hotter sorts of Protestants," as Mildred Cecil and her sisters were. Yet her choice of text also suggests a concern particular to women intellectuals of her era and especially to those working within the field of theology: the problem of silence. The Pauline injunction against women preaching, which contemporary theorists across Europe often cited, circumscribed the female religious writer only to a certain degree. The boundary was permeable. Rather than writing a treatise on Deuteronomy 15, for instance, which might have raised brows, Cecil translated the views already presented by a male theologian. Yet translation is not reproduction.

Historians have posited that women writers of sixteenth-century England were, in Margaret P. Hannay's influential phrase, "silent but for the word." That is, women translated but were not acknowledged for their work; and they translated, rather than writing original works.[112] Yet, the example of Mildred Cecil alone suggests the limitations of this model. On the one hand, her work remained in manuscript, so its readership was limited to members of her immediate circle. On the other hand, her accomplishments were a matter of public record. The eminent pedagogical theorist Roger Ascham, for one, praised her in his published letters (alongside his particular favorite, Lady Jane Grey), as the most learned woman in England.[113] Indeed, translation was not original literature; it was scholarship. Many first-order intellectuals throughout Europe engaged in translation as a critically important aspect of formulating an accurate canon. In our own time and academic world, translations count virtually nothing toward tenure or promotion—a modern prejudice that has perhaps led to misunderstandings of the situation in early modern England. That Cecil and other women translated and were lauded for their efforts shows that the female scholar was a respected figure in the republic of letters.

Mildred Cecil staked her claim to this scholarly status within the intellectual elite by means of connections formed through her husband. For instance, she dedicated a multilanguage Bible to William Cecil's alma mater, St. John's College, Cambridge. Her dedicatory epistle, in Greek, positions Mildred as learned benefactress engaged with her husband in a common project of intellectual patronage.[114] A Burghley memorandum indicates that he donated thirty pounds a year to the college, and among the Burghley papers is also a letter from Robert Wright of July

1580, reporting his progress in study at Cambridge, signed "devoted to your Lordship," which suggests support from Burghley.[115]

This movement from textual translation to practical action constitutes another important dimension of English women's "participatory" feminism, their direct engagement with men in matters of religion, during the late Tudor period. In addition to her work as a translator, Anne Cooke Bacon, like her sister Mildred, was an agent in promoting further reformation. Over the course of her career, Bacon also protected a number of Puritan preachers, among them Percival Wyborne (whom she made her chaplain at Gorhambury), William Dyke, Richard Gawton, and Thomas Wilcox. She was the dedicatee of the radical Puritan apology *A Parte of a Register,* the collaborative effort of Wyborne, Gawton, and Wilcox, and it may indeed have been written under her roof or at least with her financial support. Similarly, Wilcox turned to Bacon to "countenance" his 1589 *A Short Yet Sound Commentarie* (on the proverbs of Solomon). When William Dyke was ousted from his parish of St. Michael's, Bacon prevailed with her son Anthony to get Dyke a vicarage at Hemel Hampstead and a license allowing him to administer the sacraments.[116]

In 1572 Bacon collaborated with her sisters in writing a set of verses supporting the preacher Edward Dering, who had been so impolitic as to accuse Queen Elizabeth of being insufficiently attentive to the spiritual well-being of the nation and to do so in a sermon delivered to the queen herself. As Alan Stewart has shown, Dering had the Cooke sisters to thank that this serious breach of protocol lost him only his license to preach. Lady Bacon herself was also an important patron of the preacher John Walsall, who dedicated one of his published sermons (1578) to her. Walsall's dedication underscores her importance in his mind as a sponsor of religious reform. He was indebted equally to her and to her husband for his employment as tutor to their sons and for the living that they awarded him, but nonetheless associated his published work with Lady Bacon alone. Lady Bacon also intervened directly in the Lambeth Conference controversy of 1585. Through the mediation of Cecil (her brother-in-law), she was personally present in Commons during the debates, and unsatisfied with the negative resolution concerning Puritan preachers, she wrote to Cecil to urge renewed discussion. In addition, she also sent considerable financial support to Geneva and specifically to Theodore Beza (Théodore de Bèze), her encomiast, in 1590.[117]

All of which is to say that English women humanists can be seen to abandon the partial anonymity of their initials and to put their literary reputations to active use. The role of women as protectors of priests and patrons of preachers is more recognized by scholars than women's influence as intellectuals. In their own day, however, these two spheres of activity were intertwined—if not coterminous.

Examples to Follow: Margaret More Roper and Anne Cooke Bacon

Italian defenders of womankind used numerous examples of learned women to bolster their argument for the reevaluation of women's roles in society. As we have seen, Italian biographers pointed to the several Nogarola women, Laura Cereta, and, above all, Cassandra Fedele as proof that advanced education produced "learned virtue" in women. While the genre of collective female biography did not appear in England until the eighteenth century, early modern English men demonstrated in their own way the notion that the learned woman was not only respectable but worthy of emulation. In the first place, learned men such as William Cecil and Nicholas Bacon chose to marry women humanists. This decision in itself stands as compelling evidence that learned women were not only respectable but indeed desirable, at least among men whose principal self-definition was intellectual. More broadly, however, English authors of a feminist persuasion used particular examples, such as Margaret Roper or Anne Cooke Bacon, to make the same point as their Italian contemporaries about the positive ethical results of women's education in the humanities.

Richard Hyrde, editor and publisher of Margaret Roper's translation of Erasmus's treatise on the Lord's Prayer, exemplifies this strategy. His dedicatory letter to one of Roper's distant female relations offers a lengthy and tightly argued case for women's education in Latin and Greek, using only the examples immediately to hand: the female translator, "a young, virtuous and well-learned gentlewoman of 19 years of age," and his dedicatee, "the most studious and virtuous young maid Fraunces S[taverton]"[118] Women's education was Hyrde's field specialty: he was also the first English translator of Juan Luis Vives's influential treatise *On the Education of a Christian Woman*.

Hyrde begins his explicitly feminist reflection on the broader applicability of Margaret Roper's example by outlining his antithesis. Many men, Hyrde explains, believe that educating women, if such a thing were even possible, would only create more outlets for womankind's "natural" vices: vanity and presumptuousness. Education, in short, would make daughters and wives even more troublesome to their male relations than they already are. Hyrde accuses men who hold this view either of failing to think before they speak, or of being "for the most part unlearned, [so that] they envy it and take it sore to heart that another should have the precious jewel, which they neither have themselves, nor can find in their hearts to take the pain to get."[119] The chief motivations for misogyny, according to Hyrde, as according to his numerous predecessors on the Continent, were envy and a desire to foist upon women the faults more often found in men.

Having asserted that women are, if anything, more discreet, humble, and constant than men, Hyrde returns to the theme of education. "Now as for learning," he explains, "if it were cause of any evil as they say it is, it were worse in the man than in the woman, because (as I have said here before), he can both worse stay and refrain himself than she. And moreover than that, he comes more often and in more occasions than the woman inasmuch as he lives more forth abroad among company daily, where he shall be moved to utter such craft as he has gotten by his learning." Given that women, in contrast, remain for the most part busy at home, there is as little harm in their reading Latin and Greek in this private context as there is in their reading "books of English and French, which men both read themselves for the proper pastimes that be written in them . . . and so can bear well enough that women read them if they will." Yet, Hyrde continues, how much better it is to spend leisure time reading Latin and Greek, in which form and content "are far better handled than in any other language, and in them are many holy doctors' writings, so devout and efficacious, that whosoever reads them, must needs be either much better or less evil."[120]

Mocking the notion that a husband should worry about his wife using Latin or Greek to arrange assignations with priests and friars, Hyrde argues that linguistic skill serves instead to arm women against clerical insinuations. "I suppose nowadays," he remarks, "a man could not devise a better way to keep his wife safe from them, than if he teach her the Latin and Greek tongue[s] and such good sciences as are written in them: the which now most priests abhor and fly from—yes, as fast as they fly from beggars that ask for alms in the street!" Hyrde also dismisses the fear of some men that learning would make women danger-

ously "witty" and "crafty." Such men show themselves to be not only ignorant, disparaging education for its principal positive effects, but also
mad, because any man that prefers a foolish wife to a wise one proves
himself to be "worse than twice frantic." Echoing the views of Juan Luis
Vives and Erasmus, Hyrde reminds his male audience that learning oc-
cupies a woman's mind completely and therefore insulates it from objec-
tionable fantasies even better than handiwork, in which "the body may
be busy in one place and the mind walking in another." And, in any
case, those women who are "evilly disposed will find means to be naught,
though they can never [read, or make] a letter on the book, and she that
will be good, learning shall cause her to be much the better."[121]

As Hyrde moves from a general defense of women's education to the
particular paragon of learned virtue that he wishes to praise, he notes in
passing, "I never heard tell, nor read of, any woman well-learned that
ever was (as plenteous as evil tongues are) spotted or infamed as vicious." Hyrde has noted the contrary, writing, "Many women by their
learning have taken such increase of goodness that many may bear
them witness of their virtue, of which sort I could rehearse a great number, both of old times and of late. Saying that, I will be content as for
now, with one example of our own country and time, that is: this gentlewoman, who translated this little book hereafter following, whose
virtuous conversation, living, and serious demeanor may be proof evident enough what good learning does, where it is surely rooted."[122] This
paragon is, of course, Margaret Roper.

Not content merely to praise Margaret Roper, however, Hyrde
makes the crucial point that her brand of "learned virtue" should be
imitated by her countrywomen, and especially by his own dedicatee.
Learning augmented Roper's beauty and made her an optimal wife:

> [From her] other women may take example of prudent, humble and
> wifely behavior, charitable and very Christian virtue, with which she has
> with God's help [endowed] herself, no less to garnish her soul, than it
> hath liked his goodness with lovely beauty and comeliness, to garnish
> and set out her body. And undoubted it is, that to the increase of her
> virtue, she has taken and takes no little occasion of her learning, besides
> her other manifold and great commodities taken of the same, among
> which commodities this is not the least: that with her virtuous, worship-
> ful, wise and well-learned husband, she has by the occasion of her learn-
> ing and his delight therein such especial comfort, pleasure and pastime

as were not well possible for [an] unlearned couple either to take together or to conceive in their minds what pleasure there is therein.

Having set this sterling example of learned virtue before Fraunces, Hyrde exhorts her to ignore "the lewd words of those that dispraise [women's education], as verily no man does, save such as neither have learning nor [know] what it means." He reminds her that the best and wisest sort of men (though never the majority), such as the Church fathers and Plato, have always upheld the notion that learning benefits both men and women. He encourages her to put her trust in this noble minority rather than the base majority and to pursue her studies with undaunted courage: "Take you the best part and leave the most; follow the wise men and regard not the foolish sort; but apply all your might, will and diligence to obtain that especial treasure, which is delectable in youth, comfortable in age and profitable in all seasons: [from which] without doubt comes much goodness and virtue."[123]

Hyrde also tantalizes his young female dedicatee with the idea that erudition will make her even more appealing as a prospective bride. Much as Pietro Bembo urged his daughter Helena to "beautify" herself with letters and as Richard Mulcaster suggested that education might serve a daughter in terms of social mobility, so Hyrde considers whether knowledge of Latin might enhance Fraunces' marriage prospects. Moving beyond the philosopher Diogenes' famous comment that learning and virtue can make an ugly man handsome, Hyrde suggests that Fraunces will be even more ravishing than she already is if she cultivates "this precious diamond and ornament" of intellect, which will "flourish and lighten all [her] other gifts of grace and make them more gay." Neglecting her mind, conversely, will "dark and blemish sore" all her other excellences. Rounding out the comparison, Hyrde asserts that even if Fraunces had no other attractions save the "beauty" of her intelligence, this would nonetheless earn her "greater love, and more faithful, and longer to continue of all good folks than the beauty of the body, be it never so excellent."[124]

Putting his exhortations within a domestic framework, Hyrde situates Fraunces in a virtuous household academy. Hyrde has no doubt that she will persist in her studies and succeed, seeing as she was "naturally born unto virtue and having so good bringing up of a babe, not only among [her] honorable uncle's children—of whose conversation and company they that were right evil might take occasion of goodness and amendment—but also with [her] own mother, of whose precepts and teaching and also very virtuous living, if [Fraunces] take heed . . . [she] can not fail to come to such grace and goodness as [he had] ever had opinion in her that [she] should." Hyrde suggests that he had himself contributed to Fraunces's education, adding, "I have ever in my mind favored you, and furthered to my power and profit and increase thereunto and shall as long as I see you delight in learning and virtue, no kind of pain or labor refused on my par[t] that may do you good." As a testament to his avuncular concern for his dedicatee's continued growth in learned virtue, Hyrde presents her with Margaret Roper's translation. He specifically notes that it is "turned out of Latin into English by your own forenamed kinswoman," who is herself an incontrovertible example of learned virtue. Hyrde declines to itemize the multitude of the translator's virtues: "It were a thing superfluous to spend many words unto you about the matter, which your self know well enough by long experience and daily use." He continues, "[I] would eschew the slander of flattery, howbeit I count it no flattery to speak good of them that deserve it, but yet I know that she is as loath to have praise given her as she is worthy to have it."[125]

While he refrains from commenting upon Margaret Roper's personal virtues, Hyrde nonetheless takes pains to explicate her intellectual virtues. "As touching the book itself," he comments, "I refer and leave it to the judgments of those that shall read it, and unto such as are learned, the . . . name [alone] of the maker puts out of question the goodness and perfection of the work." Much as William Rastell had made kinship and authorship coterminous in his praise of Mary Basset as a credible translator by virtue (in part) of her blood ties to her learned grandfather, so Hyrde suggests that Margaret Roper's name underwrites her scholarly credibility. In case a name were not sufficient articulation of intellectual credentials, however, Hyrde adds that the work could not, to his own mind, "be amended in any point." He writes, "And as for the translation thereof, I dare be bold to say it, that who so list and well can confer and examine the translation with the original, he shall not fail to find that she has showed herself not only erudite and elegant in either tongue, but has also used such wisdom, such discrete and substantial judgment in expressing lively the Latin, as a man may peradventure miss in many things translated . . . by them that bare the name of right wise and very well learned men."[126]

Hyrde interweaves "masculine" learning and "feminine" behavior in the representation of the woman intellectual in a manner akin to that of the Italian biographers. The male feminist challenged the gender paradigm in commending the learned woman for exceeding the skill even of the most learned men. For instance, there was nothing "womanly" about Cassandra Fedele's Latinity in Betussi's estimation; just so, there is nothing "womanly" about Margaret Roper's abilities as a translator in Hyrde's assessment. With a view toward persuading the recalcitrant, however, the encomiast posed his challenge in terms palatable to his contemporaries: he followed his rehearsal of the learned woman's intellectual credentials with a renewed emphasis on her "feminine" modesty and on the domestic context of her literary activity.

Hyrde concluded his defense of women and of Margaret Roper as a translator with another invocation of the household academy. He announces that his gift of Roper's translation is an homage to Fraunces's mother "unto whom [he is] so much beholden, of whose company [he takes] so great joy and pleasure, in whose godly communication [he finds] such spiritual fruit and sweetness that as often as [he talks] with her, so often [he thinks he feels himself] the better." This mother, however, appears as more than godly: she, too, serves as an example of "learned virtue." Hyrde urges Fraunces to follow her example alongside that of Margaret Roper: "[It would be] a great shame, dishonesty and rebuke unto you born of such a mother . . . to degenerate and go out of kind. Behold her in this age of hers, in this almost continual disease and sickness, how busy she is to learn and in the small time that she has had, how much she has yet profited in the Latin tongue, how great comfort she has taken of that learning."[127]

A self-proclaimed "friend" of Fraunces, Richard Hyrde used his lengthy prefatory letter not only to encourage her own studies but also to praise learning in women generally.[128] Although Hyrde does not provide long lists of accomplished women from ancient and modern times as the Italian biographers and defenders of women did, nonetheless his rehearsal of "querelle" arguments concerning the utility and even necessity of women's advanced education, together with his praise of particular learned women as examples for others to follow, places him directly in the Italian tradition.

Matthew Parker (1504–1575), the archbishop of Canterbury, similarly commended and recommended Anne Cooke Bacon's English translation of John Jewel's Latin *Apologie on the Church of England* in his prefatory letter to her. Like Hyrde, Parker set the female translator as an example of scholarship for other women to follow. Printed with a text found in most parish churches, Parker's letter, together with Bacon's translation, made a strong case that learned women served the public good in Elizabethan England.

Like Mary Basset, Anne Cooke Bacon submitted her translation to be reviewed by men expert in the classical languages. She thereby conducted herself as a professional intellectual, a stance that Parker highlights in his letter "to the right honorable and virtuous Lady A. B." He begins by thanking her for doing him the honor of making him a "judge" of her work. Emphasizing that his letter is not in praise of these "private respects," however, he immediately moves to Bacon's contribution to the public good. He does praise her "accustomed modesty" in submitting her work for male review but states that "therein is [her] praise redoubled, since it has passed judgment without reproach." Not only does Parker himself approve her translation, but "the chief author of the Latin work and [Parker], severally perusing and conferring [her] whole translation, have without alteration allowed of it."[129]

Modern scholar Alan Stewart has recently pointed out Parker's disingenuousness. The *Apologie* was one of two Latin pieces originally commissioned by William Cecil and was therefore (in Stewart's terms) anything but "a spontaneous englishing by a pious and leisured lady"; on the contrary, it was a commissioned work.[130] However, Parker had good reason to establish a framework of impartiality, which masked his personal debt of gratitude to Bacon, to whom he had turned during a falling out with her husband.[131]

Lest the readers suspect either Parker or Jewel of gallantry, however, Parker makes a point that it is on scholarly terms alone that they have both approved her work. Friendship aside, their principal motivation was an "unwillingness—in respect of [their] vocations—to have this public work not truly and well translated." There can be no greater validation for scholars, whatever their sex, than to be told that their work has contributed to the public good.

Parker challenges gender categories by posing the female translator as a professional intellectual worthy of emulation by men and women alike. "Besides the honor you have done to the kind of women," he continues, "and to the degree of Ladies, you have done pleasure to the author of the Latin book in delivering him by your clear translation from the perils of ambiguous and doubtful constructions and in making his good work more publicly beneficial. [Your good example] must needs redound to the encouragement of noble youth in their good education and to spend their time and knowledge in godly exercise, having delivered them by you so singular a precedent."[132]

It is on the point of "precedents" that Parker links Bacon, the quasi-private translator, to the behemoth public example of women's "learned virtue" and political influence: the currently reigning Queen Elizabeth I. Parker concludes, "God (I am sure) does accept and will bless with increase [Bacon's scholarship], so our and our most virtuous and learned Sovereign, Lady and Mistress shall see good cause to commend, and all noble gentlewomen shall (I trust) hereby be [l]ured from vain delights to doings of more perfect glory." Parker is certain that both God and Queen Elizabeth will approve of Bacon, and although he only "trusts" that other gentlewomen will follow suit, he vows, "[I will] exhort other[s] to take profit by your work and follow your example."[133]

Historians of women have long struggled to assess the real effects of Queen Elizabeth's reign on the women of her time and specifically on the education of women. Even as Elizabeth's erudition and effective rulership were trumpeted by many Renaissance feminists in their defenses of women and may well have inspired subroyal families to educate their daughters, her status as the sovereign makes us question how broadly applicable her example of excellence might have been. Like Boccaccio's famous women, did her status as a queen put her into an "exceptional" category that prevented association with other women of her time? Pamela Benson contends that contemporary male writers most often considered Elizabeth as a singular case, an "extraordinary woman" and not an "exemplary woman" who belonged to a broader category of accomplished women.[134]

Parker, however, had no difficulty in forging a connection between Elizabeth's role as a paragon of "learned virtue" and the comparatively minor "precedent" of Anne Cooke Bacon. Nor was Parker alone in this regard. Richard Mulcaster went so far as to justify his whole argument for women's education on the basis of Queen Elizabeth and the other learned women of the English intellectual world. From a theoretical standpoint, he urges that women in general possess the ability to learn the higher subjects and that doing so provides both "care to themselves" and "comfort to us" their countrymen. "What foreign example," he asks, "can more assure the world than our diamond at home?" He immediately follows this reference to Elizabeth with assurance that "we have besides Her Highness, as undershining stars, many singular ladies and gentlewomen, so skillful in all cunning, of the most laudable and loveworthy qualities of learning, as they may well be alleged for a precedent to praise." Mulcaster is uncertain if the example of Elizabeth and (by implication) of women like Margaret Roper or Anne Cooke Bacon, the queen's "undershining stars," will prove "a pattern to prove like by," but he expresses hope on this point. Provided that "nature be no niggard" and that "education do her duty," other women will indeed model themselves on these illustrious examples, even though such "precedents be passing."[135]

In essence, Mulcaster's program of women's education is implicitly designed ("if education do her duty") to create more women of Queen Elizabeth's excellence. A vocal admirer of the queen, Mulcaster ends his chapter on women's education with a triumphant rhetorical question that allows for education as a means to prepare women (like men) not only for living better lives and being more beneficial to their families but also for assuming public leadership roles. Because women are, in his words, "our mates and sometimes our mistresses," he concludes, "[and] considering they join always with us in number and nearness, and sometimes exceed us in dignity and calling, as they communicate with us in all qualities and honors, even up to the scepter, so why ought they not in anywise but be made communicants with us in education and training, to perform that part well which they are to play, *for either equality with us or sovereignty above us?*"[136]

Not all were as sanguine as Mulcaster about female equality, to say nothing of gynecocracy. Indeed, his views were forward-thinking in almost every aspect. In addition to exhorting his countrymen to make young English gentlewomen in general as learned as their queen, he also advocated the education of impoverished boys at the state's expense. Still, his views demonstrate that Queen Elizabeth's reign provoked a further intensification of "querelle" arguments on the equality of the sexes in matters of the mind.

In other words, Queen Elizabeth served as a crucial point of reference for English men and women who took an explicit feminist position from the late sixteenth century onward. Her illustrious example, often in conjunction with the more accessible "undershining stars" like Margaret Roper and Anne Cooke Bacon, made the learned woman a focus of nationalistic pride. Elizabeth also served as a useful recent example for women writers who, like their Italian counterparts, sought to justify their own membership in the category "woman as intellect" by pointing to a historical tradition of female contribution to culture and society. The seventeenth-century poet Anne Bradstreet (ca. 1612–1672), for one, drew strength from Elizabethan precedent. In a poem of 1650, she asked,

> Now, say, have women worth? Or have they none?
> Or had they some, but with our Queen is't gone?
> Nay, Masculines, you have thus taxed us long,
> But she, though dead, will vindicate our wrong.
> Let such as say our sex is void of reason
> Know 'tis slander now, but once was treason![137]

Bathsua Makin and a National Canon of Learned English Women

The seventeenth-century antiquarian Sir Simonds D'Ewes wrote a lengthy autobiography in which he described the processes by which he became the paragon of erudition and godliness that he considered himself to be. In the course of explicating his brief time (1614) as the pupil of Henry Reginald, schoolmaster of a private grammar school in St. Mary Axe Parish, London, D'Ewes mentions in passing that this teacher's reputation was founded more upon his famously learned daughter than upon his own skills in the classical languages. "[Reginald] had a daughter named Bathsua," D'Ewes remarks, "being his eldest, that had an exact knowledge in the Greek, Latin and French tongues, with some insight also into the Hebrew and Syriac. Much more learning she had, doubtless, than her father, who was a mere pretender to it; and by the fame of her abilities, which she had acquired from others, he got many scholars, which else would neither have repaired to him, nor long have stayed with him."[138] D'Ewes' assertion, as one scholar has noted, voices the bias of a schoolboy—and a particularly solipsistic schoolboy at that.[139] Nonetheless, "Bathsua" did indeed prove a prodigy of classical erudition. And she became one of the first explicitly feminist writers in England.

Bathsua Makin's most famous work, *An Essay to Revive the Antient Education of Gentlewomen* (1673), took a central argument in the now three-hundred-year-long debate on women to the next level. While writers such as Christine de Pizan had long contended that education made women better and some, such as Laura Cereta, had posited that women had something like a "right" to an education, Makin, herself a governess and tutor to Princess Elizabeth (daughter of Charles I), outlined a clear model for a new institution: the girls' school.

Makin's *Essay* details the program of such a school, which she claims to have established in a London suburb. "If any enquire where this Education may be performed," she writes, "such may be informed that a School is lately erected for Gentlewomen at Tottenham High-Cross, within four miles of London, in the Road to Ware, where Mistress Makin is Governess, who was sometimes Tutoress to the Princess Elizabeth, Daughter to King Charles I; Where by the blessing of God, Gentlewomen may be instructed in the Principles of Religion and in all manner of Sober and Virtuous Education—more particularly in all things ordinarily taught in other schools." Following this statement is a syllabus. Half of the students' time will be spent in dance, music, singing, writing, and keeping accounts, with the other half "employed in gaining the Latin and French tongues." Those students who wish might also "learn Greek and Hebrew, Italian and Spanish, in which this Gentlewoman has a competent knowledge." Allowing that some might think it sufficient that their daughter learn to read and write only English, Latin and French might be put aside in favor of "only Experimental Philosophy and more, or fewer, of the other things aforementioned." Lest any reader dismiss Makin's pedagogical initiative as a daydream, the final lines of this text urge doubters to obtain further details concerning this school "every Tuesday at Mr. Mason's Coffee-House in Cornhill, near the Royal Exchange; and Thursdays at the Bolt and Tun in Fleet Street, between the hours of three and six in the Afternoons, by some Person that Mistress Makin shall appoint."[140]

In her dedicatory epistle, written to "all Ingenious and Virtuous Ladies, more especially to her Highness the Lady Mary, Eldest Daughter to his Royal Highness the Duke of York," Makin posits that the education of women "may glorify God, and answer the end of [their] creation, to be meet helps to [their] Husbands." Acknowledging the more strident strain in the *querelle des femmes*, the argument for women's innate superiority to men, Makin sets her sights not at the theoretical extreme but at a practical middle-ground. "Let not your Ladiships be offended," she urges, "that I do not (as some have wittily done) plead for Female Preeminence. To ask too much is the way to be denied all." She does make the argument, however, that women's education ultimately serves the interests of the English nation. If women should be educated in the manner of the ancients, she asserts, "I am confident the advantage would be very great: the women would have Honor and Pleasure, their Relations Profit and the Whole Nation Advantage."[141]

Makin's models, the examples upon which she justifies this broad curriculum in ancient and modern languages, logic, history, geography, and mathematics, bring forward again a number of the famous cases that we have been discussing. She contends that England must build upon the precedents it has for female excellence in letters, so as to better compete with its rivals on the European literary stage—and especially so as to trump the Dutch and the Italians. Acknowledging the well-earned fame of women like the sixteenth-century Italian poet Olympia Fulvia Morata, a Protestant and "tutress to the Empress of Germany" renowned for her understanding of French, Latin, Dutch and for her being "so good a Grecian that she read publick Lectures in that Language," Makin nonetheless aims to show the superior skills of her countrywomen. "The Lady Jane Grey excelled Morata in this," she argues. "She understood the Hebrew also. There is a large discourse of her Learning (in which she took great delight) and Piety, in the Book of Martyrs." Similarly tipping the scale toward English excellence, Makin adduces "the present Duchess of Newcastle [who], by her own Genius rather than any timely Instruction, overtops many grave Gown-Men," and also two of her own pupils, the Countess of Huntington and Princess Elizabeth, as well as a Mrs. Thorold, Lady [Grace] Mildmay, and a group of women she terms "Dr. Love's Daughters." While Makin praises the illustrious Petrarchan poet Vittoria Colonna for writing "largely and learnedly in the praise of her dead Husband," she observes, "I may rank [with Colonna] (if the comparison I do not underprize) the beautiful and learned Lady Mary, Countess of Pembroke, the worthy sister to that incomparable person Sir Philip Sidney."[142]

Makin similarly gives due credit to the illustrious "Isola Navarula" (Isotta Nogarola), for her "many eloquent Epistles" and her great proficiency "in Philosophy and Theology, as appears by that Book she wrote by way of a Dialogue between Adam and Eve, which sinned first and most; and by diverse other books." Makin posits, however, that in general terms Italian men have not permitted their female contemporaries to follow Nogarola's example. "The Italians slight their wives," she explains, "because all necessary knowledge that may make them serviceable (attainable by institution) is denied them; but they court, adore and glory in their courtesans, though common whores, because they are polished with more generous breeding."[143]

Makin provides a brief biographical compendium of illustrious learned women, which includes thirty-nine Greek examples, twenty-six Roman cases, ten Hebrew/Old Testament heroines, seventeen early Christian/New Testament women, and two Saxon women. Her modern examples represent England as numerically ahead in continuing this historical tradition, as it can boast seventeen recent women of letters whom she deems worthy of mention, whereas Italy has only eight, France only one (Catherine de Médici), Germany two, Sweden one (Queen Christina), and the Dutch Republic the glorious, but singular, example of Anna Maria van Schurman.

Many of Makin's seventeen English cases are the female relatives of Sir Anthony Cooke. Aware of them through Sir John Harington's commentary on Ariosto, Makin cites "the four daughters of Sir Anthony Cook, [otherwise known as] the Lady Russell, the Lady Bacon [and] the Lady Killigrew, giving to each of them, for Poetry, a worthy character." Mildred Cecil and Katherine Killigrew get separate and somewhat erroneous mention as well. Seduced by the Hortensian hermeneutic, Makin represents Mildred Cecil as one of "Lord Burghley's Daughters," who received from her sister, called here "Silesia" instead of Katherine, the Latin poem begging that her husband might be excused from an embassy to France.[144] Confused though some of her information is, Makin could invoke a lineage of learned women to bolster her argument for establishing girls' schools with serious intellectual agendas.

Continuing the theme of learned marriageability prominent in the writings of Thomas More and Richard Mulcaster, Makin attests that the education of women will ultimately serve "their relations and the state" at a practical level: education supplements women's dowries, or "portions." She expresses the hope that her *Essay* might therefore "persuade some Parents to be more careful for the future Breeding of their daughters. You cark [fret] and care to get great portions for them, which sometimes occasions their ruin. Here is a sure portion, an easy way to make them excellent. How many born to good fortunes, when their wealth has been wasted, have supported themselves and their families too by their wisdom?" Answering the potential objection that men might not want learned wives, she echoes Richard Hyrde in claiming that such men are either "silly" or "themselves debauched," but learned men, in contrast, "will choose such the rather, because they are suitable." She notes that "some men marrying wives of good natural parts, have improved themselves in Arts and Tongues, the more to fit them for their converse," and that "many women formerly have been preferred for this very thing." Such women include, once again, the illustrious Roman matrons Hortensia and Tullia, who would never have been "married to such brave men, had not their Education preferred them."[145]

Makin capitalizes on the long-favored Hortensian paradigm, but also she departs from it in citing the most important modern examples of women whose advanced educations brought honor not only to themselves and their families but in fact to the nation. Like Mulcaster before her, Makin construes women's education as a point of national pride. Her best example in this regard is Queen Elizabeth, who in fact receives the highest number of references throughout the work (ten)—more even than Hortensia and than any of Makin's other favorite examples. More concerned with religion than Mulcaster, Makin considers the queen's real contribution to have been not merely to humanism or to government but specifically to the institutionalization of Reformed religion. Lest anyone doubt the godly benefits of instructing girls, she contends, "Our very reformation of Religion seems to be begun and carried on by Women . . . Henry the Eighth made a beginning out of State Policy, his Feminine Relations acted out of true Piety; this stuck in the Birth till his Daughter Queen Elizabeth carried it to the height that it is now at."[146]

George Ballard would take Bathsua Makin's Anglocentrism to a new level in his *Memoirs of Several British Ladies* (1752). Whereas Makin gave credit to continental women writers (especially Anna Maria van Schurman), Ballard was unabashedly nationalistic in setting forth his sixty-two biographies of brilliant English women, who substantiated his claim "that England [had] produced more women famous for literary accomplishments than any other nation in Europe."[147] Much as Italian biographers of the sixteenth century emphasized the honor that learned women brought to their native cities, English biographers of the seventeenth and eighteenth century made the illustrious lineage of British women intellectuals a point of national pride.

Assessing the Contributions of Women Humanists

Scholars observe that the end of the sixteenth century marks a turning point in the history of women intellectuals in Europe. Noting that women writers of the seventeenth century wrote almost exclusively in the vernacular, some have suggested that the women humanists failed insofar as the movement died, with Queen Elizabeth if not precisely because of her, around 1600.[148] Yet we must question the degree to which humanism itself, as an intellectual movement, existed in any meaningful way in the seventeenth century. To be sure, Latin remained the language of prestige in the seventeenth-century republic of letters, but humanism as textual emendation and the dogged imitation of Ciceronian rhetoric were no longer ends literary society pursued in and of themselves. Rather, literary society became more interested in hearing new things well said in the vernacular. That women Latinists were increasingly rare should not, therefore, be understood to prove the failure of women humanists but rather to reflect the changing priorities in the broader community of knowledge.

The contribution of the women humanists in the period 1400–1580 was to create a viable space for the female voice in literary society. The positive celebrity of the best-known women humanists made the educated woman a popular figure, despite the challenge to masculine cultural hegemony that she might be seen to represent by doing the same literary work as men, and despite her sometimes explicitly articulated attack on the patriarchal organization of society.

By 1600 the European literary world had hosted two hundred years of the *querelle des femmes,* which had from the outset included female voices. The Italian cultural elite was celebrating a lineage of women intellectuals, and English men of letters were touting the godly contributions of their Queen and her "undershining stars." The illustrious learned women of the Italian and English Renaissance constituted precedents to admire and to follow. In other words, women humanists gave force to literary arguments about female capability—regardless of whether or not they themselves explicitly entered the fray.

The literary descendants of the fifteenth- and sixteenth-century women humanists capitalized on their predecessors' examples. So, too, they employed the domestic rhetoric that had proved so useful in making the unusual, and indeed the feminist, acceptable and praiseworthy. I have argued so far that the "household academy," headed by a learned father and supplemented by father-patrons, produced the first generations of secular women intellectuals and the first audible articulation of feminist theory. In Italy, criticism of patriarchy and celebration of new forms of female accomplishment pervaded literary culture, but even within the more conservative English context, Renaissance feminism made its appearance. Pamela Benson has remarked that men like Thomas More and Richard Hyrde "did not question the political division of the sexes as the Italians did, but they did challenge the intellectual division and they encouraged women to develop the autonomy that would enable them to act on that challenge."[149] Whereas Benson locates this feminism in male-authored prescriptive literature, I find it at the intersection of theory and practice: forward-thinking men put their support where their rhetoric was. The result was a canon of women writers who laid the foundation upon which successive generations of learned women would build.

II

THE HOUSEHOLD SALON, 1580–1680

5

Learned Wives and Mothers in Italy

WOMEN had an honored place in literary society by the end of the six-teenth century. A lineage of writers and translators, associated with vir-tuous household academies and represented as paragons of "learned virtue," had proved to the intellectual elite that education made women not domestic liabilities but instead positive contributors to family honor and literary culture. Women writers of subsequent eras required less justification. Fathers and father-patrons continued to be important sources of educational opportunity and encouragement for women writers. The father figure also remained a crucial referent for women who explicitly criticized the social order. Yet many women writing at the close of the Renaissance era represented themselves and were wel-comed by contemporaries not only in a filial role, what we have been calling the "Hortensian hermeneutic," but as mature, married women. Literary culture was ready for the learned wife and mother.

The changing contours of the intellectual family drove this concep-tual transformation. By the close of the sixteenth century, the house-hold academy had begun to resemble a salon. Diana Robin has shown that the "woman-led salon was the primary vehicle by which elite women first entered the commercial print world of sixteenth-century Italy."[1] As her study also shows, these salons and the collaborative work taking place within them exerted a powerful influence on Italian litera-ture throughout the century—especially the development of reformist religious thought. But it is important to recall that the salon was based in the household, and this aura of domesticity (even when purely rhetorical) served women writers well in establishing themselves as "proper" women. The household salons under investigation here, however, did present a more flexible framework than the household academies that preceded them. New characters played increasingly important roles in women writers' lives and rhetorical strategies: the husband became a colleague, and children were presented as extensions of maternal excellence.

This second part of our story begins with two Venetian writers, Moderata Fonte (Modesta da Pozzo; 1555–1592) and Lucrezia Marinella (1571–1653). At the turning point between the filial learned virtue of "Hortensia" and the maternal learned virtue of "Cornelia," these women capitalized on the support of their fathers and father-patrons. Equally important for them, however, were their successful marriages to learned men. Both women were also culturally normal mothers of sons and daughters. Marinella, the more "scholarly" and also more vigorously feminist, preferred the filial persona, but also married and had children. Fonte's patrons and admirers emphasized her status as a wife and mother—a prefiguration of the household salons that would foster the next generation of women writers.

Women began to adopt new personae as the sixteenth century continued. While their predecessors used domestic and "feminine" vocabulary to establish their credibility, Fonte and Marinella adopted "masculine" rhetorical stances. In most cases, they presented themselves as writers with proven credentials instead of as devoted daughters; they also flattered their patrons in political, rather than filial, terms. It is only in their works in defense of women, particularly in Marinella's treatise that asserts women's inherent superiority to men, that domestic rhetoric reappears to establish the writer's credibility. Indeed, father-daughter rhetoric remained crucial for feminists of Marinella's scholarly type through the seventeenth century, as two cases outside the Italian context will illustrate: the French author Marie le Jars de Gournay (1566–1645) and the Dutch humanist Anna Maria van Schurman (1607–1678).

The "household salon" incipient in Moderata Fonte's case came to fruition in the lives and careers of one married literary team: the northern Italian author-actors Isabella (1562–1604) and Francesco Andreini (1548–1624). Like Fonte, Andreini enjoyed the support of a learned husband, who promoted her career. Contemporaries also heralded Andreini as a pinnacle of literary, wifely, and maternal excellence. The shift away from the father-daughter model toward an acceptance of learned women like Andreini as full members of the reproductive economy shows a dramatic expansion of the range of possibilities for Italian women writers at the dawn of the seventeenth century.

Moderata Fonte and Lucrezia Marinella

The two most celebrated women authors of late-cinquecento Venice were Moderata Fonte and Lucrezia Marinella. As scholars have argued since the 1980s, Fonte and Marinella redirected the "querelle" from theoretical arguments about women's inherent "merits" toward a systematic exposition of the gender inequalities that constrained women's social roles.[2] This intensification of explicit feminism will be discussed at length in Chapter 7. It will be useful, however, to begin by situating these remarkable women within their intellectual families and to consider the full range of their compositions, rhetorical strategies, and reception. Rather than understanding these authors to be exceptional voices in the *querelle des femmes,* I present them as part of a lineage of women writers and as members of a new generation, whose biographies and techniques of representation exhibit an illuminating dialectic between continuity and change.

Fonte and Marinella exemplify the broader trend in Italian letters toward classically informed vernacular composition in a wide range of genres, including epic, pastoral, and arcadian poetry, as well as the feminist dialogue and treatise. Both came from educated families of the upper middle class in urban Venice. Fonte's father (who died during her infancy) was a lawyer; her grandfather and adoptive father, Prospero Saraceni, were poets; and Niccolò Doglioni, a family friend and later her patron and biographer, held a respected place among Venetian humanists. Lucrezia Marinella's male relatives, both natal and marital, were physicians. Her father, Giovanni Marinelli, was a celebrated author of medical works and a natural philosopher (much like Tomas de Pizan). Marinelli's published works include treatises on controlling the plague (*De peste et de pestilenti contagio,* 1577), on Italian grammar and compositional elegance (*La prima e seconda parte della copia delle parole,* 1562), and on women's beauty and health (*Gli ornamenti delle donne,* 1562, and *Le medicine partenenti alle infirmità delle donne,* 1563). Marinelli enjoyed considerable respect in the literary and medical communities, but his "nobility" was purely figurative. Marinella's brother, Curzio, was also a physician, as were her husband, Girolamo Vacca, and her patron, Lucio Scarano. Like their predecessors Cassandra Fedele and Laura Cereta, Moderata Fonte and Lucrezia Marinella belonged to families of the cultural but nontitled Venetian elite.

Early Education and Family Dynamics

Unlike their predecessors, details of the educations of Fonte and Marinella are scarce. Biographers and their own literary representations of women's education, however, do offer a general picture of their early studies. Niccolò Doglioni's biography of Fonte, which serves as the preface to her feminist dialogue *Il merito delle donne* (*The Worth of Women*, 1600), notes that she received some education as a boarding student at the convent of Santa Marta in Venice, where the nuns adored her and she charmed everyone with her performances in their sacred plays *(sacre rappresentationi)*.[3] Elissa Weaver has shown that convent plays were often sophisticated works that demonstrate a high degree of education, as well as a determination to provide young women with an outlet for creative expression.[4] But this is not the picture that Doglioni paints in Fonte's case. He sets her convent years in a negative light, noting that she had been placed there not by her guardians (Saraceni and his wife) but by another relative who had essentially kidnapped her.[5] Doglioni is also vague about what subjects the nuns taught, stating only that Fonte learned their specialties or, literally, "their things" *(quelle lor cose)*. All of which directs the reader to consider the substantive portion of her training to have taken place after she returned to Saraceni's household:

> As [Saraceni] greatly enjoyed literature and particularly poetry, the little girl, in imitation of him and in competition with him (as if she were born to the task), set herself to suiting his taste and composing verses of her own; for a child of her age, she succeeded amazingly well. Thus Saraceni, who recognized her natural inclination and wished to encourage her all the more, kept offering new topics for her to discuss, and seeing to it that she did not lack books to read and study as well as she could. She would even (a thing marvelous to relate) bother her brother the moment he returned home from grammar school, making him show her and tell her about what he had been taught and what he had learned. She etched all this in her mind in such a way that she profited far more from his lessons than he did.[6]

We might dismiss Doglioni's attitude toward her convent instruction as a humanist's condescension, but Fonte herself had been silent on the subject. Indeed, she made no reference to convents, even in the portions of *Il merito* that discuss the plight of superfluous daughters. When Fonte discussed women's education, for instance in her popular chivalric romance *Tredici canti del Floridoro* (1581), she (like Doglioni) set it in a domestic context. As Virginia Cox and Valeria Finucci have noted, the often self-referential Fonte juxtaposes the negative effects of a traditionally "feminine" education in her femme fatale, Biondaura, with the positive results of the "modern" education given to her warrior heroine, Risamante.[7] Kidnapped by a magician as a child and educated by him in letters and the military arts, Risamante represents a pinnacle of excellence. Lest the point be missed by her readers, Fonte intrudes as author to explain that Risamante proves that the capabilities of men and women are equal and that any differences between male and female achievement are therefore the result of "nurture," not "nature." Fonte argues that "if, when father has a daughter, he should put her with his son to the same tasks, she would prove just as capable as her brother, however deep or delicate the endeavor—whether he should train them in military exercises, or set them both to learning the liberal arts. But a daughter is taught other things and, because of this difference in education, she receives little esteem."[8]

Lucrezia Marinella presented herself as another Risamante, educated by a forward-thinking father. Marinella's writings, devoid of references to women educated in convents, instead make repeated mention of fathers training their daughters in the liberal arts. An admirer of her older contemporary, Marinella cites the foregoing passage from Fonte in her own feminist treatise, *La nobiltà delle donne* (*The Nobility of Women*, 1601).[9] Marinella also created another "modern woman" in Erina, the warrior heroine of her epic poem *Henry, or Constantinople Conquered* (*L'Enrico overo Bisantio acquistato*, 1635). Erina, like Fonte's Risamante, received an unconventional humanistic education from her father. In this case, the paternal figure is a natural philosopher, Fileno. "And countless times," Erina narrates, "while I was still a little girl, he took me with him up the mount . . . and of his knowledge imparted to me what was beautiful and good; and I, like a new Aurora, grew to virtue in the sunshine, and under the benign influences of the heavens, friend of Apollo, the God of Delos."[10]

While Marinella's father may not have been quite as heroic as this literary figuration, his views on women were bold; indeed, they were feminist. Giovanni Marinelli dedicated his *Gli ornamenti delle donne* to all "chaste and young women," in the device of repaying a debt of gratitude to them for showing such interest in his previous work on Italian grammar. "I have seen," he explains, "how much valorous men and equally valorous women have esteemed my writings, and so seeing that I have been granted such authority and honor, and my works read and heard with so much more affection than they deserve . . . it has occurred to me to explain something new, and something so important that it will give all gentle people material for discussion."[11] As Letizia Panizza has pointed out, this handbook of advice on women's health and beauty presents a striking departure from the contemporary tendency to stigmatize women's concern with their physical appearance as vanity.[12] Making an explicit point of his feminism, however, Marinelli also prefaced his text with a brief defense of women, which rehearsed the prominent features of the *querelle des femmes* and underscored his status as a humanist contributing to this pervasive literary debate.

Fonte and Marinella both made use of their extensive family networks in their careers. Doglioni was a close friend of Prospero Saraceni, Fonte's grandfather, and would marry Saraceni's daughter. At the age of sixteen, Fonte moved into Doglioni's house, and it would be he who arranged her marriage to the tax lawyer Filippo di Zorzi, in addition to seeing her works through to publication. Marinella, similarly, had a patron closely connected to her natal family: Lucio Scarano was a friend of her father and brother. Marinella, for her own part, also married a man of considerable education, the physician Girolamo Vacca.

Brothers were also important figures in the intellectual families of both women writers, though the relationships worked very differently. Marinella's relationship with her brother, Curzio, appears to have been harmonious. She mentions him prominently in dedicating *La nobiltà* to her patron, Scarano, who she hopes will consider her work a worthy offering because he has already praised her in his lectures and "because of the great friendship that you, sir, had with that most excellent Signor Giovanni my father and because of that which you have now with that most excellent Signor Curtio [*sic*] my brother."[13]

Conversely, Fonte's relationship with her brother, Leonardo, was competitive. The theme of competition for the family's intellectual patrimony occurs in her literary work, as we have seen. It also appears in Doglioni's description of Fonte "stealing" knowledge from him. The rivalry also played out in property disputes. Leonardo complained in his will that Fonte's husband was in possession of the Pozzo family library: "Filippo Zorzi my brother-in-law has many writings of our house and in particular the books."[14] It thus appears that Fonte had inherited the library instead of her brother and that the books then passed to her husband, according to Venetian property law. It is also possible that Zorzi pulled some sort of trick to get hold of the Pozzo library. The will of Moderata's father does not specify a bequest of books, but only that his brother, Vettore Pozzo, be universal heir, successor, and commissary and that this Vettore should divide all the property equally among the legitimately married male heirs.[15] Vettore's will, in turn, leaves his brother Girolamo as commissary and heir, specifying that his own estate, including the books, be sold to create a fund for his nephews—sons of their third brother, Lorenzo, who had died by the time of this will (1566).[16] Both brothers, then, emphasized that the patrimony go in toto to male heirs. So it seems that Leonardo had grounds to complain about being defrauded of his library.

For Fonte's part, her will is devoid of references to her brother. It was common practice among female testators to divide their possessions among wide networks of kin and friends, both male and female. And so this testamentary cold shoulder might well be further evidence of a strained relationship.[17]

Whatever may have been the situation with her brother, Fonte's will gives pride of place to her "elective" kin. Her bequests to Doglioni and his family are one way in which she underscored her connection to this intellectual family; the other is in her penchant for using terms in the Venetian dialect that help to classify extended and even invented kinship. She makes it clear in both ways that she considered her marital and adoptive families her real family. Fonte characterizes herself as the "daughter of the excellent Messer Hieronimo da Pozzo, doctor" and "wife of the excellent Messer Philippo di Zorzi"—citing relationships to men that are the usual self-identifiers for women.[18] She also designates her husband as her commissary "for the most part," but to Niccolò Doglioni, "notary and [her] *barba*," she leaves ten ducats "as a sign of love." To Madonna Saracena his wife, "[her] dearest *ameda*," she bequeaths five ducats, again as a sign of love. The terms *barba* and *ameda* mean "uncle" and "aunt" in the literal sense, but they can also be used figuratively to signify older authority figures who are not blood kin.

Fonte's first repository of trust for the governance of her children and estate is her husband, whom she terms both *marito* (husband in the legal sense) and *consorte* (husband in the affective sense). Filippo's role as the children's governor, however, is contingent upon his remaining a widower after her death. Although she wrote this will in 1585 and would not die until 1600, Zorzi did not, in fact, remarry. "Should he wish to remarry," Fonte continues, "I don't bequeath to him anything except the third of my dowry, which he for his kindness gave to me." In this event, "all of my goods, together with the governance of my children should go to Messer Zuan Nicolo [*sic*] Doglioni and Madonna Saracena his wife."[19]

For its own part, the Doglioni family clearly viewed their adoptive daughter, the learned Modesta, as one of their own and perhaps as a female role model. Doglioni named his biological daughter Modesta (Moderata's given name), a tradition that continued for several generations after his death.[20] Invented kinship became real kinship within this cultured family. Not only did the Doglioni family incorporate Moderata, but they also cared for her daughter, Cecilia, who apparently never married.[21]

Leonardo Pozzo testifies to this tangible dimension of invented family—but in a very different sense. Apart from complaining about the books in Zorzi's possession, he makes a point of his disgust with the way in which Doglioni handled Leonardo's affairs when he (like his sister) was "in his [Doglioni's] power." Leonardo demands that his executors obtain three hundred ducats from Doglioni, who had accumulated them during the period 1583–1585, when he "was managing [Leonardo's] houses, and furniture, and various other things."[22] According to Leonardo, this sum remained unpaid, although he had confronted Doglioni about it "more than once" and had tried "to resolve the debt in a friendly way." Despite Leonardo's best efforts, the debt remained unpaid: "When it came time to pay up, he always put me off from one day to the next, and in the interest of not breaking completely our family bond, I've remained in this muddle to this very day; but I beg my executors to finish this matter that I haven't yet been able to resolve."[23]

Nor is the three-hundred-ducat debt the only complaint that Leonardo raises against the man whom he, like his sister, called *barba*. Leonardo expresses further resentment about some bad investment advice that Doglioni had given him. "The aforementioned Doglioni," he continues, "in the time that I was in his power, made me make a donation of the aforementioned benefice [*benefitio*] in that same time, '83 and '84 . . . With great travail, finding myself at Sacile in his villa, where I was supposed to be paid back, I was induced to make that donation; but I leave it to my executors . . . to do what has to be done, seeing as I have never had any profit from them [Doglioni's family] save in words, but instead much ingratitude and disgust in the encounter. And that's all I have to say on the matter."[24]

Leonardo's discontent offers a new perspective on the father-patron in a case in which the sister was clearly favored over her brother. It was Doglioni's opinion that Modesta/Moderata surpassed her brother in matters of education, and the careful attention of her *barba* to her publishing career underscores his favor. Leonardo was an ambitious young man, but his ambition tended toward the family's political status more than its literary fame. He applied in 1589 to the Avogadoria for ennoblement but was denied.[25] Usually, denial implied insufficient funds to push the paperwork through. Perhaps this is why Leonardo was particularly angry about the financial bad blood between himself and his sister's patron. At all events, given Doglioni's overt campaigns on behalf of Fonte and her own ambitions, we may safely read more into the remark of Leonardo that he "never had any benefit from them, save in words" than the lack of repayment alone.

Fonte, for her part, praises Doglioni not only in her will, entrusting him with her children and estate in the event that her husband remarries, but also in her published writings. The generally acid-tongued character Corinna in Fonte's *Il merito delle donne* pauses in her disquisition on astrology to compliment "one [astrologer] with whom [she is] acquainted, a Signor Giovanni Niccolò Doglioni, a most noble intellect who, beyond his other singular talents, possesses his own peculiar merits of generosity and astonishing loyalty—characteristics which one seldom finds in men."[26] That Fonte would portray Doglioni as generous and loyal—the antithesis of Leonardo's portrait of him as greedy and unreliable—suggests that the beauty of the intellectual family was found in the eye of the favored child.

Doglioni did exert himself on Fonte's behalf. He saw *Il merito* through two printings. He also gave both the author and her text a ringing humanist endorsement in his prefatory "Vita." We are told that the author "devoted herself to studying humane letters with the help of grammar books, which she both read and memorized, as well as to mastering the *arpicordo* of Saraceni; soon she became so proficient that she understood every book in Latin very well and also wrote tolerably well in that language."[27] Doglioni was a humanist of substantial credentials and therefore a good judge of Fonte's skills. His lukewarm praise for her compositional abilities in Latin lends credibility to his account: the "Vita" is not panegyrical.

Fashioning Fonte's public image to suit the changing ideals of "elite" education in the late sixteenth century, Doglioni emphasizes the diversity of Fonte's talents. In particular, taking a leaf from Castiglione's *Courtier,* he stresses that Fonte was proficient not only in letters, arithmetic, and handwriting but also in music and art. Doglioni also notes his protégée's precocious talent in drawing, playing the harpsichord and lute, and singing. Feminizing this portrayal somewhat, he also mentions her skilled needlework.

Although Fonte and Marinella shared a similar socioeconomic background and many of the same interests (spiritual poetry, feminism), nonetheless Doglioni's portrait shows us a rather different sort of training than Marinella received—at least to judge by the skills she displays in her writings and her literary representations of young women learning. What can we make of this?

The cases of Fonte and Marinella suggest that women's education followed the broader patterns of literary culture, refracted through the family's specialties. Fonte received what might be termed a "gentlewoman's" education in the humanities, with a particular emphasis upon poetry, art, and music. Marinella was trained according to the intellectual commitments of her progenitors: expository prose, medicine, and natural philosophy. Her writings also reveal a thorough familiarity with arcadian poetry. Where Marinella differs most sharply from Fonte (at least in terms of representation), however, is that she does not mention, nor was she understood by contemporary observers to have received, any training in art or music. Her education, mirroring her father, was scholarly. Marinella certainly read Latin. In her own feminist work—a treatise and not a dialogue, as is Fonte's—Marinella intersperses her vernacular composition with numerous Latin quotations. *La nobiltà* also displays Marinella's thorough knowledge of scripture and the patristic commentators. Marinella's epic-length poem, the *Life of the Virgin,* demonstrates her familiarity with theological argumentation, which she displays especially in her dedication and the prose summaries that appear throughout the work. Marinella's comments concerning women's health and beauty in *La nobiltà,* moreover, suggest her mastery of classical medical texts, such as Galen and Aristotle; they also reveal (as Letizia Panizza points out) her assimilation of her father's work on the theme.[28]

Marriage and Motherhood

Unlike their Venetian predecessors and similar to the English cases that we have examined, Fonte and Marinella were both married and mothers at the time when they were most active in their writing. Both began their literary careers before marriage, and, in fact, both married late relative to their contemporaries: Fonte at age twenty-eight (1583) and Marinella at about thirty (ca. 1601). But both continued to write subsequent to their marriages. Fonte's premarital compositions include her *Tredici canti del Floridoro* (Venice, 1581); *Le Feste: Rappresentazione avanti il serenissimo prencipe di Venetia* (Venice: Guerra, 1582); and *La Passione di Christo descritta in ottava rima* (Venice: Guerra, 1582). The works she completed subsequent to her marriage were her poem *La Resurretione di Giesu Christo* (Venice: Domenico Imberti, 1592) and *Il merito delle donne* (Venice: Domenico Imberti, 1600). While the birth of her four children accounts for the significant gap (1593–1599) in Fonte's oeuvre, nonetheless marriage and childrearing did not stifle her productivity. In fact, her husband, Filippo Zorzi, was a collaborator.

Zorzi certainly supported his wife's career. First of all, Fonte was an established author when he married her. In seeking out a learned woman as a wife, Zorzi was in good company, including the husbands of Fedele and Cereta, as well as those of all the most famous English women humanists. Zorzi also wrote a prefatory poem in honor of Fonte's *La Resurrettione di Giesu Christo* (1592), in which he praises the work and gives its author a striking degree of spiritual agency. In his formulation, Fonte has offered Christ a second resurrection by commemorating his first so effectively: "Behold, now Christ arises again to a new life, / And gives hope, and shows a way through this errant world / To rise with him; he calls, waits and beckons."[29] Zorzi's celebration of his wife's achievement foreshadows the marital collaboration that would characterize the household salons of Isabella Andreini, Esther Inglis, and Mary Beale, as we will see.

Lucrezia Marinella increased her literary productivity after marriage. Whereas before the wedding she had published only her *Life of the Angelic and Glorious Saint Francis* (*Vita del serafico et glorioso S. Francesco*, Venice, 1597) and the first edition of *La nobiltà* (1600), after her wedding she published her epic poem on the Virgin Mary (*L'Imperatrice del mondo*, Venice 1617), another spiritual allegory in verse (*Amore innamorato et impazzito*, Venice 1618), a revised edition of *La nobiltà* (1621), her epic poem *Enrico overo Bisantio acquistato* (Venice, 1635), and the *Essortazioni alle donne* (1645). Marinella also had two children, Antonio and Paulina, both of whom she mentioned with affection in her will.[30] In her literary work, however, Marinella never made a point of her marriage or motherhood. And neither of her children seems to have followed her in scholarly pursuits.

By contrast, to judge by Doglioni's encomium, Fonte played a role akin to that of Margaret Roper's in continuing the intellectual family tradition. In particular, Doglioni laments the early death of his protégée, because it impeded her children in developing their precocious talents. "They have been raised by her," he stresses, "with all possible diligence to make them become excellent in the most rare accomplishments . . . The boys and the girl at that age were writing Latin very conscientiously by the book; they were reading sheet music and playing on the viola— each one playing or singing their part to the admiration of everyone . . . Now that they no longer have her governance and teaching (since the father has to attend to his civic business) they cannot arrive as quickly at the summit of *virtù* which, had she lived, they would long since have reached."[31] Doglioni presents a complete woman writer: a good daughter, good wife, prolific author, and prolific mother, all at once.

Doglioni established a new paradigm of reception in his biography of Fonte. Seventeenth-century authors such as Pietro Paolo di Ribera and Cristofano Bronzini, whom we have already encountered as admirers of fifteenth-century women humanists, followed Doglioni in representing Fonte as a consummate intellect and exemplary wife and mother. Ribera highlights Fonte's wifely and maternal excellence by placing her biography directly after his treatment of Cornelia, the Roman matron credited with teaching her sons (the Gracchi) their famous eloquence. For Ribera, Fonte was "glorious and famous for her literary skill in [their] own times, and proved the equal of all those ancient women," but she was also exemplary for her "honorable marriage to a certain Filippo

Zorzi, a most learned and clean-living man, with whom she lived for twenty years before she died giving birth."[32] Cristofano Bronzini reproduces this encapsulation of Doglioni's biography word for word.[33]

Lucrezia Marinella remained only a daughter in contemporary biographical sketches. She herself never made a point of her status as a wife and mother, and neither did her friends or patrons. Representing Marinella as a direct descendant of the fifteenth-century women humanists, biographers emphasized her filial excellence. Ribera makes a point that Marinella came from a most learned family, whose example she followed. He specifies that she was the "daughter of Giovanni Marinello, a most famous physician, one of the wisest men of his time" and sister of "the learned and most excellent Curtio [*sic*] Marinello, also a physician and one who did not depart one jot from his father's excellence in the field." Marinella, having benefited from such inspiring company, "devoted herself to imitating their virtues and wisdom, albeit in her own fields of interest."[34] Unaware of Marinella's marriage, Ribera mistakenly asserts that she chose to remain a perpetual daughter. "Because of her love for spiritual things," he states, "she quietly dedicated her virginity to God."[35]

Cristofano Bronzini is more voluble concerning Marinella's publication history than he was concerning Fonte's. He devotes several pages of his dialogue in defense of women to the learning, poetic skill, and wisdom of Marinella's diverse compositions. And while he follows Ribera in describing Marinella as an imitator of the excellence of her father and brother, Bronzini reworks the phrase to give her more credit than Ribera had given her. While Ribera stated that it was her brother who maintained his father's excellence, Bronzini claims that "the marvelous and truly learned Lucrezia Marinella maintained the standard of excellence set by her father and brother."[36] Bronzini does, however, reproduce Ribera's mistake in claiming that she remained "a most chaste virgin" *(vergine castissima)*.[37]

The cases of Moderata Fonte and Lucrezia Marinella represent a turning point in the contemporary Italian understanding of the learned woman. In the absence of any emphasis on her status as a wife and mother by the woman herself or her male associates, even seventeenth-century encomiasts perpetuated the filial paradigm. Yet Fonte's case attests that observers readily incorporated a new image of a learned wife and mother when a textual authority represented her as such, as Doglioni did.

Changing Personae

Fonte and Marinella also underscore a significant shift in the ways in which women presented themselves. While their humanist predecessors most often emphasized their "daughterly" qualities, women intellectuals from the late sixteenth century onward reserved father-daughter rhetoric as a tactic to situate their most overtly feminist works. Otherwise, women writers began to present themselves in a more "masculine" mode, using only the sparest form of political rhetoric to flatter patrons.

Dexterity in self-representation was a defining characteristic of the Renaissance intellectual. Erasmus, for one, knew the power of an image. Through portraits, voluminous correspondence with editors and colleagues, and his selection of long-term projects (especially the letters of St. Jerome), Erasmus became the quintessential "man of letters."[38] Women such as Moderata Fonte and Lucrezia Marinella used many of the same basic techniques, in particular the manipulation of letters (both correspondence sets and dedicatory epistles) to highlight their own intellectual "charisma" and that of their literary milieu. As we will see hereafter, however, the acclaimed actress-author Isabella Andreini was perhaps the most original in shaping her image for public consumption.

Moderata Fonte offers a useful starting point for a discussion of the changes in women's self-presentation around 1600. While Fonte's patron, Niccolò Doglioni, situated her feminist dialogue within the customary rhetorical safe zone of domesticity, she ignored domestic rhetoric in her other publications, which were all works of poetry, most of them religious poetry. Her decision to use a pen name may have given her more freedom of expression, though "Moderata Fonte" (meaning perhaps "restrained fountain") was so close to her given name "Modesta Pozzo" ("diffident well") that it hardly obscured her identity. In fact, she may well have chosen "Fonte" to invoke the humanist commonplace *ad fontes* ("return to the sources") and thereby claim membership in the intellectual elite.

The frontispiece of her chivalric romance *Tredici canti del Floridoro* (1581) indicates that she dedicated this work to the Grand Duke and Grand Duchess of Tuscany, but it lacks a dedicatory letter. Even the prefatory poems to this work, written in Fonte's honor by a Bartolomeo Malombra and by her patron, Niccolò Doglioni, do not praise her in domestic terms. Malombra calls her "a friend of the Muses," which was the standard mode of compliment for all poets, male and female, since antiquity. Doglioni does, however, pay tribute to her poetic excellence in conjunction with her feminine propriety. He considers that her creativity would be amazing enough in a learned man, who would be free to seek out texts at whim, but are altogether astonishing in Fonte, who "sings everything perfectly" despite being "a little maiden, / Hemmed in by close-pressing walls."[39]

Fonte dedicated her first work of religious poetry, *La Passione di Christo* (1582) to the current doge, Niccolò da Ponte. Her dedicatory epistle makes a striking departure from the rhetorical strategies that we have hitherto witnessed women writers using: at no point does she feminize her achievements. Instead, she offers her composition to him in the standard format used by male patronage-seekers. Her rhetoric is political, not domestic. Fonte situates herself in the political economy of Venice with an extended metaphor of the city as a sea and herself as a tributary to the doge, the ultimate source of power in that aqueous world. "In the way that all rivers," she begins, "knowing that they originate from a vast and profound sea, hold that sea as their Prince and leader and pay the greatest tribute to him that Nature allows them; just so do I, knowing that my origin is this marvelous and blessed City, recognize that she is my Mistress. And since Your Serenity is her Prince and leader, I offer you the tribute that I owe."[40] The tribute is, of course, her poem. Where we might have expected her to forestall potential criticism by adducing her "feminine" weakness, she states simply that she offers the best gift that she can, saying, "in view of my scant abilities," *(rispetto le forze mie debili),* which is how men phrase this standard disclaimer.

The following page of Fonte's dedication proceeds in ungendered terms. She justifies the worthiness of her offering on its subject matter: what could be more appropriate to give anyone than a reminder of Christ's suffering for the redemption of humanity? Fonte also justifies her choice of patron in standard fashion. Who better to receive this work, she inquires rhetorically, than this most serene prince, "in whom one sees united all the virtues and gifts, which can only be found separately in others?"[41] In closing, she asserts her status not as a "daughter," or "little woman," but rather as the doge's client. "I beg that you deign to accept this work," she concludes, "in the way that you, by virtue of your innate goodness, have already accepted my other compositions, which (whatever they were) have been deemed worthy to be read and

heard by Your Serenity."[42] She signs herself as his "most humble servant" *(humilissima serva)*.

Fonte wrote a more extensive dedicatory epistle for her second major religious poem, *La Resurrettione di Giesu Christo* (1592), which she
dedicated to Margarita Langosca, Countess of Bastia and wife of the
Savoyard ambassador. While Cassandra Fedele, for instance, exalted her
illustrious female patrons as "honors to their sex," Fonte pushes this
type of feminist compliment to a new level: she treats Langosca like a
male patron, praising her noble family and exalting her political acumen
without categorizing her recipient's excellence as specifically female.

Fonte makes bold at the outset in addressing Langosca as "my most
honored Lady and Patron."[43] It was more common to employ a euphemism such as "friend," rather than making the politics of the relationship transparent by using the term "patron." She praises Langosca as a
paragon of nobility and piety, as one might expect of an author dedicating a religious work to a noblewoman. Fonte asserts, however, that she
knows of Margarita's "divine merits" not from mere rumor but from
"the most excellent Signore Oratio Guarguante, a most learned physician, considered the most perceptive man of our days, an illustrious
philosopher and most talented poet, who has given [Fonte] more than
once a marvelous report of [Langosca's] abundant genius and most honorable habits." Fonte constructs Margarita, first and foremost, as another
member of the category "woman as intellect" celebrated by a reliable
male intellectual. Only then does she return to her patron's piety, noting
also, "[Guarguante has] revealed to me particulars of Your Ladyship's
spiritual devotion, which had already made me eager to include myself
among those who so faithfully and sincerely serve you."[44]

The two pages that follow praise all the members of Margarita's illustrious family ("on both your father's side and your mother's") as exemplars of pious nobility and devotion to their political responsibilities.
Fonte disavows the ability to express Langosca's "lofty genius, which is
apt not only to run [your] own household, but to govern kingdoms and
empires." While Fonte, in her conclusion, praises Langosca's religious
zeal and charity, qualities appropriate for a female patron, the majority
of the dedication emphasizes the genius and political talent of her subject more than her "feminine"' virtues. And Fonte presents herself at the
end as Langosca's "most devoted servant," the same phrase that she used
in closing her dedication to the Venetian doge.[45]

The only domestic referent in all of Fonte's prefatory material is the brief laudatory poem written by her husband (discussed above), which follows Fonte's dedication to Langosca. Where has the father-daughter rhetoric gone? Fonte did not deem it necessary to justify her religious poetry in these terms, but this might be explained by the fact that piety and devotion were subjects often considered appropriate for women writers. It is more striking, in this sense, that her chivalric poem, *Il Floridoro*, also avoided the domestic framework. Her patron did note in his prefatory poem that the author was a "little virgin," but that was all. Fonte's case suggests, then, that by the late sixteenth century, women intellectuals required far less justification.

Feminism, however, did require justification. The posthumous publication of Fonte's *Il merito delle donne* (1600) offers a carefully crafted image of the author as a proper family woman. The particulars of this dialogue's feminism will be explicated in due course, but here it is important to note that a pointed attack on misogyny and the patriarchal order necessitated the rhetoric of domesticity. Doglioni's biography, as we have seen, stressed that Fonte's erudition had patriarchal sanction and that she put her learning to use in the service of family interests. To complete the picture of Fonte as a dutiful mother who had raised optimal children, the prefatory material also includes a dedicatory letter written by Fonte's daughter, Cecilia, to the Grand Duchess of Tuscany, as well as two poems concerning Fonte's "learned virtue" written by her son, Pietro.

These editorial decisions were made by Fonte's male patron and might therefore be dismissed as paternalism, albeit well intended. The parallel case of Lucrezia Marinella, however, suggests otherwise. Much as Fonte eschewed domestic rhetoric in all her works that were not explicit defenses of women, Lucrezia Marinella positioned herself in ungendered terms as a poet, intellectual, and even theologian in all of her publications except her feminist treatise *On the Nobility and Excellence of Women and the Defects and Vices of Men* (1600, 1601, 1621). In this case, Marinella built her propriety and credibility on a domestic foundation.

Marinella dedicated her defense of womankind to her patron, Lucio Scarano. A respected intellectual and founding member of the newly resuscitated "Venetian Academy," Scarano had also been a close friend of her father.[46] Marinella puts Scarano *in loco patris* as a defender of the woman author herself. She hopes that he will approve her composition not only because of his earlier praise for her in his lectures but also on account of "the great friendship that you, sir, had with that most excellent Signor Giovanni my father and because of that which you have now with that most excellent Signor Curtio [*sic*] my brother." Signing her dedication, "from *home* . . . as from a *little daughter*," Marinella replicates the filial rhetoric that her fifteenth-century predecessors found so effective.[47]

The daughter persona remained important for "scholarly" feminists like Lucrezia Marinella through the mid-seventeenth century. The Utrecht prodigy Anna Maria van Schurman (1607–1678) employed the same technique in framing her Latin *Dissertatio logica,* generally titled *Whether a Christian Woman Should Be Educated* (1632). Schurman's work is a scholastic exercise that argues, through a rigorous series of major and minor premises, that girls should be educated in all the learned (and particularly biblical) languages, philosophy, science, and mathematics, as she herself had been at her father's instigation. Schurman had read and admired Juan Luis Vives's *De institutione foeminae Christianae* (*On the Education of a Christian Woman,* 1524), and while her argument broadened Vives's conceived curriculum, she retained his focus upon preparing women to read scripture.

Schurman's treatise was intricately connected with her correspondence with André Rivet (1595–1650), a Leiden theologian who later served at The Hague as tutor to the future prince of Orange. In an early exchange, Schurman thanked Rivet for his public praise of her treatise, and he responded by emphasizing his hope that other women might follow her example.[48] A debate ensued between them concerning how many women either could, or should, seek to attain Schurman's prodigious skills in Latin, Greek, Hebrew, and the modern languages. At first, Schurman contended that many women should be trained as she had been. Later, however, she yielded to Rivet's view that only a select few ought to aspire beyond the literacy necessary for reading holy works in the vernacular.[49] While Rivet was no defender of women as a category, he nonetheless proved an avid patron for Schurman, introducing her into correspondence with two other notable women of learning: Princess Elizabeth of the Palatinate and the French author Marie Le Jars de Gournay (of whom more below).[50] His public approbation for Schurman's treatise, despite their disagreements, was an important contribution to her already significant intellectual cachet. Notwithstanding Schurman's own ambivalence on the question of the broader applicability of her example, she cultivated Rivet's patronage.

The correspondence between Schurman and Rivet highlights once again the processes of creating discursive intellectual kinship. Regarding their newly established epistolary acquaintance, Rivet observed, "I realize, moreover, that I benefit from this as well—I who certainly take pride, not undeservedly, that a girl of such genius and such piety should seek out my friendship of her own accord, and so courteously provoke me to this correspondence. For which favor I feel myself so moved, that although we have not met face to face, nonetheless I respond with such paternal affection—would that I might one day be able to produce its effect! If God should wish it, an opportunity will be granted for me to open my heart to you in person, and to behold the face that such an elegant mind embellishes."[51] Responding to the paternal cue, and perhaps scuttling the hint that Rivet harbored a bit more than paternal affection, Schurman in her reply addressed him (who was not a member of the clergy) as "a father to be honored in Christ"—repeating the epithet twice in her opening lines.[52] She also made a point of sending her regards to his wife, just to keep the exchange situated within a tidy familial framework.

Rivet got the message. He addressed her in the next exchange as "the most noble virgin who is most perfect in every kind of virtue" and rejoiced "that such a daughter [had] befallen [him] from [his] own wish and her consent, whom [he] embrace[d] with true paternal affection and esteem with the respect that her virtues merit."[53] Closing her response with another invocation of the father-daughter metaphor, she answered, "Farewell, father dear to me in many ways, Anna Maria van Schurman, who depends completely upon your approbation."[54] Correspondence between a man and a woman who were not related by blood, particularly if the subject of their exchange was an explicit feminist argument for women's advanced education, required a legitimate foundation. Rivet and Schurman therefore fashioned their discussion as a chaste and praiseworthy exchange between father and daughter.

The French feminist Marie le Jars de Gournay (1566–1645), author of *The Equality of Men and Women* (1622), was far less concerned with feminine decorum than was Schurman, with whom Gournay corresponded. (Schurman herself cited Gournay in one exchange with Rivet.)[55] Yet Gournay also valorized her own intellectual pursuits by creating a discursive father—in her case, no less a luminary than Michel de Montaigne.

Her father having died while she was in her early teens, Gournay solicited and received Montaigne's mentorship. After his death in 1592, she lived for a year with his widow and daughter, who gave her the *Essays* to edit and republish in accordance with his intent. In the preface to her edition of the *Essays*, Gournay stressed that Montaigne had considered her his protégée and indeed his "adopted daughter."[56]

Describing their first meeting, Gournay stated, "After the *Essays* had made me long to meet him for two years, I first saw the author of the *Essays* himself, whom I am so honored to call Father, display the eager solicitude that—no surprise—many have experienced."[57] The only direct reference to Gournay in Montaigne's own work appears at the end of "On Presumption": "I have taken pleasure in making public in several places the hopes I have for Marie de Gournay le Jars, my covenant daughter *(fille d'alliance)*, whom I love indeed more than a daughter of my own, and cherish in my retirement and solitude as one of the best parts of my own being. She is the only person I still think about in the world. If youthful promise means anything, her soul will some day be capable of the finest things."[58] As Tilde Sankovitch argues, it is likely that Gournay interpolated these comments, thereby constructing herself as Montaigne's daughter. Gournay's first will (1596) extended the metaphor: she addressed Montaigne's biological daughter, Léonore, as "my adoptive sister" *(seur d'alliance)* and bequeathed to her 20 percent of her own property.[59]

The use of father-daughter paradigm by Marinella, Van Schurman, and Gournay confirms the general European utility of domestic discourse as an effective tool for feminist writers of the late Renaissance. For Schurman and Gournay, neither married nor cloistered, it may have seemed their best strategy for signaling both "feminine" propriety and authorial credibility. Yet the case of Gournay also suggests that, by the late sixteenth century, the domestic referent could function metaphorically. Lacking the support of a biological father, Gournay invented one in the figure of Montaigne. Gournay was not alone in this. For early modern Europeans, kinship counted—whether substantiated by blood, marriage, or metaphor.

Isabella Andreini: An "Illustrious Daughter of Padua"

Among the most remarkable cases of a woman intellectual who lacked the "prerequisite" of a learned father or father-patron but who nonetheless forged a successful literary career is Isabella Andreini (1562–1604), who exemplifies the new range of possibilities open to literary women at the turn of the century. Contemporary observers celebrated Andreini as an actor, poet, humanist, and mother of seven children. Late-cinquecento literary society was equally drawn to her actor-author husband, Francesco, and their first-born son, Giovanni Battista, who followed in his parents' footsteps in sustaining a double career on the stage and in print. Giovanni Battista even surpassed his parents' achievements: he was a leading figure in the commedia dell'arte. In short, the Andreini carved out a respected place within the cultural elite, but their success had nothing to do with social status or wealth (they had neither); it was the result of a brilliant discursive masque.

This learned family, united by affection, talent, and intellectual passion, also collaborated in a project of mutual legitimation. The marriage of Francesco and Isabella built a monument of literary nobility upon the inauspicious foundations of prison, possible illegitimacy, and the theatrical profession itself, which Counter-Reformation zealots condemned as demonic. How was Isabella, in particular, able to maintain her reputation for "virtue" while serving as the "prima donna innamorata" (leading lady) of the Gelosi—and indeed while forging a literary career? Marriage brought with it a sense of propriety. As one scholar has observed, Isabella's reputation for virtue "was verified by the constant presence of her husband."[60] But there is much more to explaining Andreini's success than this. What we find, in fact, is a complex system of collaboration and mutual appreciation binding together the entire household salon: mother, father, children, fellow actors, and literary colleagues. Adept at performing for theatrical audiences, the Andreini also enacted a compelling scenario for European literary society: the scenario of the intellectual family, which erudition and morality made unassailable. In life as on the stage, however, the prima donna got most of the attention.

Silence accompanies Isabella Andreini's origins. Contemporary epithets classify her as Paduan: she was always "Isabella Padovana" in the frontispieces of her published works, and a three-hundred-year tradition of Paduan self-congratulation claimed her as one of its "illustrious daughters."[61] We also know that her father's name was Paolo. It is speculated that this Paolo belonged to the Canali family of Venice, but examination of family documents at the state archives in Venice and Padua has produced no link between Isabella and any of the contemporary Canali.

In any case, it is unthinkable that a patrician family would have permitted a fifteen-year-old female relative to join a theatrical company hundreds of miles away from family control, as Isabella did in 1577 when she joined the Gelosi in Bologna. She may have been illegitimate. But in that case, like many illegitimate patrician daughters, she would probably have been placed in a convent, in the interests of family honor. Perhaps she ran away from home. Whatever the truth may be, her "official" history begins with her marriage at the age of sixteen (1578) to Francesco—a marriage that would cancel out both of their pasts.[62] This was no accident, but a considered strategy. Neither of them had tangible families; rather, they constructed one together under Francesco's stage name of "Andreini."

We know somewhat more about Francesco's background. He was born in Pistoia around 1548, probably to the Cerrachi family, which was later called Dal Gallo. At twenty, fighting in a naval battle (probably on a galley of the Order of San Stefano), Francesco was captured and spent eight years in Turkish captivity. Escaping in 1576, he returned to Pistoia and began his new career as an actor by joining the company of the Gelosi in 1577/78, shortly before marrying Isabella, who was barely half his age. He played the role of the young lover at first but later specialized in a variety of characters. Some roles required considerable erudition to perform, including his most famous as the long-winded stoic "Capitan Spavento da Vall'Inferna." At intervals, Francesco also directed the Gelosi with Isabella until her death in 1604.

As in the case of his wife, Francesco's education remains mysterious. He was certainly fluent in French. Francesco's poetry, plays, dialogues, and theoretical writings also reveal his mastery of classical literature, at least in translation. Tradition has it that he composed in Latin on at least one occasion, the death of his wife, whose epitaph reads, "Isabella Andreina Paduan, a wife marked by her great virtue, a shining gem of probity, the honor of marriage and modesty, eloquent in her speech, fertile in her thoughts, religious, pious, a friend of the muses and head of the theatrical art, here she awaits resurrection."[63] A prolific author himself, Francesco took a great deal of pride in his wife's intellectual accomplishments, weaving them into her personification alongside the traditional wifely virtues of marital devotion, piety, and fertility. As with William Roper's epitaph in honor of his wife Margaret, the learned man derived considerable honor from a wife of his own stamp.

And it may well have been Francesco who introduced Isabella to "learned" discourse, as she published nothing until 1588, a decade after her marriage. The first product of her *mens faecunda* was a charming vernacular fable, *Mirtilla*. Fashioned to suit the contemporary taste for Neoplatonic allegory, *Mirtilla* enjoyed immediate success and a long publishing history: ten editions were printed by 1616. Written in ottave rime and loaded with classical allusions, this work of vernacular humanism occupied Andreini for much of her career. She revised it frequently before renewed publication. Nineteen years after *Mirtilla* was first published (1607), Andreini's *Lettere* appeared in print. Like *Mirtilla*, her *Lettere* were immensely popular, enjoying ten editions before a final printing, together with other fragments of her work, in 1652. In her dedicatory letter to Carl Emmanuel, Duke of Savoy, she comments that she had written *Mirtilla* "when [she] had just learned to read, so to speak."[64] The "so to speak" clause cautions us not to take her meaning too literally. A favorite humanist trope, derived from Cato, was to posit the distinction between the mechanical ability to read and the deeper meaning of reading as understanding. What she suggests, then, is that as of 1588 she was newly inducted into what she would term her "citizenship" in the world of learned discourse. Francesco took a great interest in extolling his wife's intellectual capabilities, what he termed her "glory," to his contemporaries. After her death, he retired from the stage to Venice and Mantua, devoting himself to publishing his own and his wife's works. One explanation for his keen interest in her legacy was that she had also been, in some sense, his student.

Isabella Andreini's ambitions extended well past the parameters of the stage. She possessed an avid desire for intellectual development, which was satisfied within her professional and household contexts, as well as her epistolary exchange. In 1601–1602, Andreini entered into an intense correspondence with a Dutch humanist, Erycius Puteanus (Henry de Put, 1574–1646), who was then resident professor of Latin at the Palatine School of Milan. Puteanus, the intellectual heir of Justus Lipsius, became one of Andreini's most ardent admirers, and he treated her as a humanist colleague.[65] While Andreini wrote to him in Italian, she had no trouble reading his Latin letters to her.

In one early letter to Puteanus, Andreini expresses the desire to further her education by corresponding with him. She envisions an epistolary tutorial of the sort that Thomas More's children enjoyed. "As much as my letters encourage Your Lordship's desire to write to me," she explains, "so much do your letters discourage me, not for any lack of love, but because of my insufficient understanding. Of all the reasons that induce me to write Your Lordship, then, there are these two: that writing to you gives me some patina of your own infinite *virtù* and teaches me, who lives so desirous to learn."[66]

Puteanus, however, treated Andreini as a colleague, not a student. He respected her as an academician and greeted her in his first letter just as he would a male colleague: "Isabellae Andreinae Academicae Intentae" (To Isabella Andreina, member of the Accademia degli Intenti [Pavia]). As Anne MacNeil has demonstrated, this Pavian academy provided Andreini with many of her most important patrons and colleagues. The interests of the Intenti encompassed both science and literature, and its members included, besides Puteanus and Lipsius, Carlo Emmanuele II; Cesare d'Este II, who was a patron not only of Isabella Andreini but also the Gelosi; Cardinal Cinzio Aldobrandini, nephew of Pope Clement VIII and dedicatee of Andreini's *Rime* (which would be published five times between 1601 and 1696); and Gherardo Borgogni, an author-publisher who, on at least five different occasions, included Andreini's poems with others by members of the Intenti, thereby augmenting her reputation as a master of lyric verse.[67]

Of all her academic contacts, however, Puteanus contributed the most to Andreini's sense of herself as an intellectual. He praised her erudition and observed that her skills in public speaking far surpassed his own. As Boccaccio had done in lauding the virile spirit of his female patron, Andrea Acciaiuoli, so too Puteanus gives the name "Andreini" the false Greek etymology of *andros* (genitive, "of man"). Unlike Boccaccio, however, Puteanus did not intend to categorize Andreini as a transgressor "beyond her sex"; rather, he indicated that she was a better "man" than he in terms of accomplishments. He states that Andreini represented all the best qualities of the ideal human being, being manly with respect to intellectual and artistic virtuosity but at the same time blessed with the female ability to "give birth" to *virtù*. He declares that she is certainly a "man" insofar as this is the only term (albeit itself insufficient) to encompass her level of achievement:

> To my mind, Andreina, you have corrected Nature's defect; for not only are you capable of manly glory, but you are its very sister. By no means

do you, casting aside your sex, turn yourself into a man for the sake of this same *virtù*. But if for the sake of argument "virtue" derives from "vir," then so much happier are you than a man—you who, as a woman, give birth to the fruit of virtue. But then again, if a man is a man by virtue of his *virtù*, then you deserve the reward of this better name, since you perform the official duties of "the better sort," by which I mean "men." Thus you are a man; a point which you will recognize too, if you consider the name "Andreini."[68]

Continuing in a vein reminiscent of Guarino Guarini's letter to Isotta Nogarola, Puteanus laments the general failure of contemporary men to devote themselves to the *studia humanitatis* but praises Andreini as a woman who shows lazy men how it should be done. "As much as I praise you," he observes, "so much do I blame the sloth of us men, who should respect the dignity of the name 'man' all the more. We men have been Trojans. Little by little we have now fallen away; having neglected (let me not say contemned) the cultivation of the mind, we pay lip service to form and rank with the most vapid flatteries. I grieve about this, but love you, since you love the studies and vows that we have betrayed."[69] After casting aspersions on men in general, he makes fun of himself in particular for failing to uphold Andreini's skill and boldness in oratory. Nervous about a lecture that he is soon to deliver, he wishes "that [he] might know [Andreini's] gracious goddess Persuasion and speak boldly and to the point!" He continues, "Both things are rather difficult for me . . . whether because my nature is inherently more timid, or that I am more inclined to be bashful. I will masculinize my spirit and make a special effort uphold the name of a man."[70]

Andreini responded immediately (19 November 1601) with reciprocal denigration of her own talent. She echoes his line of argumentation and even his phrasing as she offers her own reflections on the gendering of *virtù*. Andreini also demonstrates considerable pleasure that he had commended her recently published poetry:

If a mere wish could transform desire into effect, it would give me the courage to render thanks for praises. My dear Signore Erycius, if Your Lordship were truly right in constantly praising me as a genius, then happy me—but alas! How far I am from that desired happiness—as far, that is, as fact is from opinion! I know perfectly well that if *virtù* had not always derived from the word "man," then it would be necessary to coin

the term in that way now, since you are a man of such indisputable virtuosity that the term *virtù* should be made masculine in your honor. Oh!
Would that I were that famous Theano, wife of Pythagoras, who was so
wise, or that other Greek Theano who similarly wrote such worthy
things, since if I really were the kind of woman that you have made me
out to be, then I would be worthy of writing about you now, and I know
that this noble subject would give me the perfect opportunity to compose
verses that might perhaps be sufficiently lofty and glorious to warrant
those high praises with which it has pleased you to honor the poems that
I have already composed; but nonetheless I will attempt to sing our great
light, the resplendent sun of *virtù*, not caring that I remain dazzled by your
overwhelming splendor, or that I am at the moment devoted to working
on my *Lettere* which, as they are written in an altogether different style,
make it impossible for me to invoke the Muses for your contemplation.[71]

She expresses her hope that he will continue to honor her with his letters, which teach her what she so wishes to learn: "I could not have
more savory food that the fruits of your wisdom."[72] Commenting upon
his lecture, she concludes, "I have heard about the oration that you
are going to give and rejoice with you, certain that it will win the highest praise—of the sort that you garner in all your endeavors, and in particular like that which has accrued to your most beautiful eulogy on
my *Rime*, which is celebrated by everyone who reads it . . . I end with
this sheet by greeting you heartily with my husband and Signore Giovanni Paolo."[73]

A few weeks later (December 1601), Puteanus responded with a
lengthy letter and copy of his poem "to Isabella Andreini, Sulpicia of our
Age."[74] This letter is full of renewed praise for her learning. After a page
of assurance that she is the chosen avatar of all the Muses, he exhorts
her to continue writing and thereby win immortality: "Ha! Good! Read
and keep reading; build upon this foundation, so that in writing you
may beggar the praises even of literary pundits. Keep working, so that
you might increase posterity's coming admiration."[75] He also praises her
as a woman, equating her literary and biological productivity. "I exhort
and beg you all the more vehemently," he pleads, "for the benefit of
your heirs: keep writing no less than speaking, for in this you put Nature's benevolence before our eyes. We have seen your *Mirtilla, Eclogue,*
and now *Epigrams* [*Rime*]: give us more. Prove to be as fertile a writer as
you have been a mother."[76]

Underscoring his theme of literary inheritance, Puteanus insists that Andreini continue publishing as a service to the republic of letters. Specifically, he exhorts her to consider publication as the fulfillment of a duty to her "heirs," who are Puteanus himself and his contemporaries, as well as all subsequent generations of intellectuals:

> See to it, then, that you publish your *Reflective Letters,* infusing them with delightful comedy, divine tragedy and all the other hallmarks of elegance, in your beautiful handwriting: we will be your heirs and immediate successors, but you are always our lady and mistress. For from one point of view your writings are subject to Fortuna's whim, but from another they constitute the monuments of genius which, after you have gone, may be bequeathed from one heir to another such that you will never disappear, but will always be with us, since your works will be read. Indeed, since by a kind of law we have imposed upon your modesty, it is right that you, having publicly taken up the rewards of genius, should show yourself resplendent with such illustrious and extraordinary gifts for the benefit of this not ungrateful age. So, seize the laurel and the opportune moment . . . Think, O Goddess Persuasion, O Muse, of yourself, of us men and of the generations yet to come.[77]

Andreini responds to his compliments with a trope. She claims to be torn between the desire to write and the fear of displaying her ignorance. "For any number of reasons," she explains, "I should not write and chief among them is that the more I write, the more I reveal my ignorance. What should I do then? If I write, I show myself unlettered; if I don't write, I show myself badly bred. So, then, of these two evils I choose the lesser, which will be writing, since it is better, to my mind, to demonstrate oneself ignorant, owing to an imperfect education, than a bumpkin, defective by nature."[78] In a letter written shortly thereafter (January 1602), he echoes her sentiments. He states that he also wished to write but felt unequal to the task insofar as he could imitate her modesty but not her eloquence.[79]

Uncomfortable with the framework of equality that Puteanus established, Andreini preferred to play the part of his student. He had observed that the excellence of her letters cured him of an illness, a service which he hoped to repay with his own letters someday. She, however, was unwilling to speak of exchange in these egalitarian terms *(ma, che dic'io di cambio?),* because "exchange denotes things of equal value, which cannot apply to your works and mine, since mine are full of ignorance, whereas yours are full of wisdom." Rather, she positioned herself as his pupil, "eagerly awaiting the latest fruits of [his] most beautiful genius, to satisfy [her] hunger for learning" and sending her best regards, together with those of her husband and a mutual friend.[80]

In the course of this correspondence, it seems that Puteanus developed something of an infatuation with Andreini. Both refer often to love, which, though typical of the era's belles lettres, might nonetheless suggest some mutual amatory inclinations. De' Angelis takes this view, arguing that Andreini's increasing rejection of love metaphor and references to her husband in her later letters testify to her ultimate rejection of any potential dalliance. Andreini's references to Francesco served as a distancing mechanism, De' Angelis contends, because they "allude to the familiar, rather than private, nature of their friendly bond."[81] Yet Andreini mentions her husband even in the earliest letters.[82] Rather than using Francesco's name to end an epistolary affair, Isabella employs this marital referent from the beginning to set the boundaries of propriety. Like the father-metaphor so useful to fifteenth-century women humanists, Andreini's invocations of husband and their mutual male friends represent her as a respectable woman—an especially important issue, given her status as a "public" actor.

Full of admiration for Andreini, Puteanus attempted to forge a connection between her and his own teacher, Justus Lipsius. Puteanus wrote a lengthy letter to Lipsius in 1602, describing the stimulating intellectual and literary exchanges taking place in northern Italy, of which Lipsius was an admirer and indeed a participant. Like Puteanus and Andreini, Lipsius belonged to the Accademia degli Intenti. Puteanus cites his friend, Isabella Andreini, as evidence of the salubrious intellectual climate in northern Italy. "I make so bold as to insinuate into your *amicitia*," he wrote, "a woman of excellent and well-developed intelligence, the favored child of the Muses and Goddess Persuasion, Isabella Andreina; in welcoming her you become a friend of the Muses and Persuasion."[83]

Nothing seems to have come of this introduction. Nor did Andreini, when she heard of her friend's efforts on her behalf, expect any benefit from them. Apparently Puteanus had communicated his intention to mention her to Lipsius, as she states in a letter predating his that such a serious man would at best dismiss her compositions as trifles: "As to the most learned Sr. Lipsius, I don't so much mock myself as fear that his perfect taste will find my writings insipid—or the sad and sour little children of my badly trained mind."[84] In a letter of 6 March 1602, Andreini wrote of her embarrassment in hearing that Puteanus had not only mentioned her to his exalted transalpine friends but also shared her letters with them. "I certainly blushed," she writes, "when I learned that you have not only deigned to read my letters (which I would by no means have sent if I did not have complete confidence in your generosity, which never rebukes my ignorance), but have even shown them to those most fortunate countries that can claim you and where you have friends." She hopes that his authority *(autorità)* will protect her reputation *(fama)* in "those frigid northern lands."[85]

Once again, Andreini chastises Puteanus for being too forward thinking—for treating her as he would a male colleague and circulating her work in the republic of letters. "When I met you," she cautions, "I did not appoint you as my friend, but as my patron. Nor could I choose you as a friend, since friendship [*amicitia*] can exist only between equals. Such equality does not exist between us, since you touch the heavens with the sublimity of your genius, while I am hurled to the ground, because of my humdrum intellect. And if I sometimes arise, it is only when you help me and when I think of your virtues, which drove me the other evening to write this sonnet, which I'm sending to you."[86] She renews her insistence that theirs is an unequal relationship of teacher and student or of patron and client. In her correspondence with Puteanus, she positions herself as a woman humanist. While Andreini did not use the filial paradigm, she still reproduced the notion of hierarchy intrinsic to that social script.

Writing to patrons and colleagues who were not career intellectuals, however, Andreini applied her humility tropes more sparingly. To Carl Emmanuel, Duke of Savoy and dedicatee of her voluminous collection of essays, titled *Lettere* (1607; reprinted 1617 and 1627), she played upon her academic nickname (*l'Accesa,* "the burning one") by emphasizing her burning desire for knowledge *(ardentissimo desiderio di sapere).*[87] Beginning her dedication with the theme of mankind's natural desire for immortality, she cites two urges that "Nature, our best mother and greatest means of self-perpetuation" implants in humankind. Nature instills in many the "ardent wish for children, grandchildren and great-grandchildren, in whose lives Fathers, Grandfathers and Great-Grandfathers, although dead, still happily live on as immortals."[88] But

Nature directs others "to the noblest arts" and especially to the search for knowledge, on account of which "man has been called Lord of inferior things, blood kin of the highest things, a terrestrial god, a heavenly animal and, finally, the triumph and miracle of this same Nature."[89] After noting the pre-Socratic philosopher Anaxagoras's belief that he had been born to contemplate the stars, she observes that every human "possesses at least the desire for knowledge."[90]

As Andreini develops this line of reasoning, she distinguishes herself from other women. Situating herself within the group of those whom Nature compels to find their immortality in pursuit of the noblest arts, she notes that the "Highest Creator" had called her to be a "Citizen of the World" *(Cittadina del Mondo)* and that she was born with a passion for learning that is "more ardent than in many other women." She concedes that other women "have discovered the virtues of many studies and a good number of them have even become famous and immortal" but claims that most women prefer to serve "the needle, distaff and spindle." By contrast, she herself has always been committed to nourishing her innate "burning desire for knowledge."[91]

Andreini considered herself not a woman, then, but a "Citizen of the World" devoted to her quest for learning. She complains that Fortune had been "stingy in bestowing upon [her] the means that would have been so helpful toward this end" and that her busy life leaves her so little peace: "I have not been able to say with Scipio that I ever saw an hour's rest."[92] It was only in the "little spaces of an hour" snatched from the exigencies of her double life as mother and actress that she pursued knowledge.[93] These disclaimers, however, are topoi characteristic of humanists in general and women humanists in particular. Andreini's invocation of continual responsibilities parallels a favorite theme in Laura Cereta's epistles. As Diana Robin argues, Cereta's presentation of domestic responsibility as an obstacle to her intellectual pursuits inaugurated a line of argument that would be crucial for later feminists, including Madame de Staël (1766–1817) and Mary Wollstonecraft (1759–1797).[94]

A woman studying was one thing; a woman writing was another. Andreini began to write, she explains, "in order not to betray that talent which God and Nature have given me and so that my life could not be called a perpetual slumber, knowing that I, like every good Citizen, am called to benefit the Fatherland as much as possible."[95] Ann Rosalind Jones has pointed to women poets' appropriation of the masculine erotic idiom as evidence of a broadening range of possibilities for female authorship in continental Europe during the sixteenth century.[96] Yet Andreini's adoption of masculine political discourse suggests that the boundary markers were wider even than Jones would allow. Indeed, Andreini follows this striking assertion of her "citizenship" with an unabashed statement of her aspiration to literary immortality, which she hopes her writings will ensure: "My intention was to save myself (to the extent that I was able) from death, having been taught how do so by Nature. Thus, it should not seem strange that I have sent, and if I still send, my writings into men's hands, since everyone naturally desires to have if not perpetual, then at least very long life."[97] She repeats this statement again, once she has requested the Duke's "heroic" patronage. Distancing herself from other authors, whose dedications "only obey custom . . . since these days not four lines get published without a dedication," and separating herself from common toadies who know where their bread is buttered, she reassures her potential patron that her rationale is what she stated before: under his aegis she will become immortal.[98]

Andreini appropriated the syntax of masculine desire for intellectual honor. The passions she emphasized—the desire for knowledge, fame, and literary immortality—were stock themes for male classical and Renaissance authors alike. Like Moderata Fonte before her, Andreini closed her patronage letter in the manner that most men closed theirs, using political rather than familial discourse. She termed herself "Your Exalted Lordship's most humble servant" without any gendered self-deprecation.[99]

In the *Lettere*, which were published without the names of recipients as essays on various themes, she adopted a full range of literary personae. The least incendiary of these essays were written in the female voice: a young woman infatuated with a faithless man; a learned woman exhorting a mature man to welcome the birth of his daughter; a woman of experience giving advice to a female friend. More striking are letters in which Andreini presents herself as a man. She experiments with the courtly love letter by writing as a man approaching his imperious (female) beloved. For her explorations of friendship *(amicitia)*, she adopts the persona of one young man addressing another. How did she get away with this?

At the same time that she stood like a man, Isabella stressed her maternity.[100] In the dedication of her *Rime*, she presented herself to

Cardinal Cinzio Aldobrandini as the doting "mother" of her poetic children. A theme foreshadowed by Christine de Pizan and developed at second hand by Doglioni in his life of Moderata Fonte, the connection of intellectual and physical fertility resounds in Andreini's self-presentation. She asks for the cardinal's indulgence regarding her tender attitude toward her poems: "I love [them] in that way in which one loves one's own children, cherishing not only what is beautiful and good in them, but even finding their errors and defects pleasant and charming. As much as a father burns to see his children become great and does everything he can to help, so much do I, who am Father, Mother, and Nurse to these my children . . . ; so pardon me this maternal piety, which always desires the best for her progeny."[101]

Male intellectual supporters collaborated in Andreini's project of domesticating audacity by providing her with encomia for her printed works, encomia that stressed her enviable talent, as well as her exemplary conduct as a wife and mother. Prefatory testimonials, a common feature of "learned" publication, established scholarly legitimacy when the author lacked official credentials. As Lisa Jardine has noted, Erasmus and other male intellectuals outside the university system often used "print citations" in place of diplomas and degrees.[102] The technique also served women intellectuals like Andreini, who lacked "official" academic validation. Indeed, testimonials became all the more important in the case of women writers, because publication put their domestic "virtue" no less than their literary *virtù* on the line.

A Latin poem of Puteanus, which appears opposite Andreini's portrait on the double frontispiece of her *Rime*, praises Andreini for embodying a triple perfection: beauty, eloquence, and marital fidelity. Andreini was "the Sulpicia of our age," upon whom the three principal goddesses—Venus, Pallas, and Juno—bestowed their several gifts. At birth, Venus "painted [her] face, brow and hair with the flower of loveliness," making Andreini another Venus—but specifically another Venus Genetrix, a "nurturing and chaste Venus, the mother of chaste Love."[103] Not to be outdone, Athena added "powerful genius and the seeds of Fame, covering [Andreini's] eloquent tongue with Pierian nectar."[104] Saturnian Juno provided "a happy marriage bed," and "Hymen himself sang the song."[105] Devoting the remainder of the poem to her marriage, the poet makes this observation: "Suffering the labors of Lucina, you, fertile, have brought forth a hearty brood for your dear husband . . . You are worthy of the marriage bond, and so too the husband to whom you have given the dear ring finger . . . I would call you a new Venus-Tritonia-Juno."[106] The printer was careful to specify that this praise of Andreini's virtue and eloquence came from a true expert, Erycius Puteanus, professor of eloquence at Milan.

Andreini's other academic admirers, whose poems also precede the posthumous edition of her *Lettere,* echoed Puteanus's sentiments. Francis Pola, member of the Accademia Filarmonica, iterated the "best of all goddesses" theme. Pola uses the famous bronze medal cast in Andreini's honor, the obverse of which depicted the goddess Pallas (Athena), as the premise of his theme: the fusion of beauty and genius. In one bronze coin shine "what you [the viewer] wish to see, whether beauty or genius"; the viewer can "recognize the one in the figure of the other," because "both are Pallas and both are Isabella."[107] Following Puteanus and Pola, the physician Leonardo Todeschi Medici added his own version of Andreini as at once Venus, Cynthia, and Juno.[108]

Apart from the allusion to her "worthy husband" that we saw in Puteanus's poem, however, Francesco Andreini seems barely visible in these laudatory verses. Where is the masculine legitimation that accompanied the learned women of the fifteenth and early sixteenth centuries? Andreini's contemporaries appear to have had little trouble praising her in autonomous terms, certainly once she was dead. And Isabella herself seems, at first glance, to have approached her literary and theatrical audiences without employing the patriarchal idiom. She tended to emphasize her professional credentials, especially her role as a principal actress with the Gelosi and her membership in the Accademia degli Intenti.

Francesco was of course "present" with her in their invented family name. Each of her publications and all of the poems and letters addressed to her categorized her as "Andreina." Unlike her contemporary Moderata Fonte, who used a pen name and was otherwise known by her patronymic, and also unlike Lucrezia Marinella, who retained her patronymic throughout her career, Isabella made her status as Francesco's wife her first credential. Yet it is significant that Andreini's writings otherwise avoid the emphatic domestic rhetoric that we have come to expect from women intellectuals.

Andreini took her honorable place in the literary world by dint of talent and a minimum of domestic rhetoric. The cultural cachet attached to the literary and moral aspects of her character were even powerful enough to ennoble the greatest liability in her life: the fact that she performed in public. Andreini's status as an actor ought to have elicited sexual slurs. The Catholic Reformation was nearing its apex. The theater was the devil's playground, and contemporaries often used "actress" and "whore" interchangeably.[109] The images of Andreini as a learned woman and dutiful wife, however, forestalled criticism. Indeed, the respect that she compelled had enduring effects long after her death. If she derived social legitimacy from being Francesco's wife and the mother of his children, both he and their eldest son, Giovanni Battista, used the accomplishments of "la divina Isabella" to enhance their intellectual and moral honor.

Collaboration, even posthumous, defined the Andreini. Francesco and Isabella Andreini worked together as actors and as spouses; they were also codirectors of the Gelosi. Francesco emphasizes their administrative collaboration in an early letter (13 April 1583), responding to a request from Vincenzo Gonzaga that the Gelosi perform another season in Mantua. Francesco apologizes for their inability to fulfill this request: "I find myself deeply obliged to the most beneficent favors of Your Serene Highness and cannot but with the greatest unhappiness thank you from the bottom of my most courteous heart of having done me, together with my wife, such a great honor as to invite us back into such honorable company."[110] While Francesco answered the Duke's letter, he made it clear that he and his wife together represented the executives of the Gelosi.

The Andreini partnership was also literary. In particular, Isabella's illustrious publishing history brought Francesco significant cultural capital. In his own works, which he began to print only after her premature death in 1604, Francesco emphasizes both his love for Isabella and the benefit of intellectual association with her. At the end of the Gelosi's celebrated tour in France, on the journey home to Italy, she suffered a miscarriage of her eighth child in Lyon and died from medical complications soon thereafter. Francesco immediately retired from the stage and began preparing her unpublished works for the press. At the same time, he began publishing his own works, sometimes together with hers.

Among the earliest of Francesco Andreini's publications was a compilation of the speeches that he had invented for his best-known character, "il Capitano Spavento." In these last days before the full articulation of the commedia dell'arte as a form—which would take place largely under the influence of Isabella and Francesco's son, Giovanni Battista— a hallmark of a virtuoso actor was the ability to craft (and often improvise) clever soliloquies or repartee. As with cadenzas in music, the performer's ability to be inventive, while keeping to the general outline of the written work, was considered one proof of his or her excellence. In 1609 Francesco published his most successful improvisations, *Le bravure del Capitan Spavento*, which would enjoy several editions.[111] He dedicated this work to a brother of the Duke of Savoy, who had been one of his wife's patrons. Following a standard rehearsal of his dedicatee's excellence, Francesco positions his wife as the foundation of his own literary hopes. "Because my wife Isabella had in mind to dedicate a compendium of her most beautiful *Lettere* to His Most Serene Highness, your brother the Duke," Francesco explains, "and since I myself want to follow her good wish, with the same affect and effect, I dedicate this, my little labor, to Your Excellence."[112]

Francesco ends his dedication with an explanatory note that the first work in this collection is a pastoral scene once enacted by himself as the character "Corinto Pastore; in lugubrious verses I have sung the honest marital ardor of my lovely Fillide, which was the name that my Dearest Wife took in these pastorals."[113] He leaves no doubt, then, that this work may be read not only as a scenario that he and his wife had enacted on the stage but also as a first-person testament to his grief. Among its most moving passages is a confession that it is only the thought of protecting their children that keeps the grieving husband from taking his own life. "Dear Soul," he exclaims, "my beloved Wife, the conjugal love that lives and always will live in my heart urges me to follow you. But the piety joined to this love—that is, for our tender little ones, our children—keeps me on course."[114]

Francesco's letter to the readers follows his lament. This second piece puts renewed emphasis upon the role that the memory of his wife has played in driving him to compose and publish his works, as well as hers. His self-presentation is dual: he reminds the reader of his most famous role, Capitan Spavento, and he portrays himself as the grieving widower of the Gelosi's most famous actress. Beginning with a long tribute to his company, "whose triumphal voices will never have a closing night," Francesco also informs his readers that in addition to his role as a performer, he has also devoted himself to "demonstrating for future thespians the true way of writing and performing comedies, tragicomedies, tragedies, pastorals, intermezzi, apparatuses and other theatrical inventions, as daily we see on the stage."[115] These principal occupations came to an end, however, with "the death of Isabella [his] most beloved wife, who was the very light and splendor of that virtuous and honorable company." When she died, he explains, many friends urged him to begin writing and publishing his own compositions, "so as to leave some tangible vestige of [himself] and to follow the honorable acclaim of [his] wife, who has left to the world, much to her glory and honor, her most beautiful poetry, her splendid pastoral fable, the *Mirtilla*, and a collection of her elegant *Letters*."[116]

In 1617 Francesco republished Isabella's *Rime* and brought out the first edition of her incomplete writings, entitled *Fragments*.[117] This collection of dialogues on love between male and female classical characters was a coauthored work.[118] He notes that some were his wife's and some his, without specifying the authorship of any individual piece. His letter to the reader further emphasizes that he founded his own authorial identity upon his wife's celebrity: "With my own compositions are intertwined a few writings, which I have put forward in the happy memory of Isabella the actress, and member of the Academia degli Intenti, my wife. Concerning these, I have devoted myself to serving her glory, in not leaving them in Fortune's power. These, my little labors, are all amorous and all of them concern honest love, so as not to display for the world, or introduce, wicked behaviors."[119] At pains to prove that the theatrical profession could be a vehicle for promoting virtue, Francesco asserts his Neoplatonic belief in the power of art to inspire "honest love." A crucial means to stake his claim to credibility in this field of endeavor was mention of his accomplished and virtuous wife.

Giovanni Battista Andreini followed in his father's footsteps. A celebrated actor, prolific author, and foundational influence on the commedia dell'arte, Giovanni Battista also turned to the image of Isabella Andreini as a paragon of learned virtue when he set out to defend the nobility of the theatrical profession. In his 1625 publication, *The Scourge: Second Treatise against the Accusations Leveled at the Theatrical Profession*, Giovanni Battista uses his illustrious mother as evidence that the theater was no hotbed of licentiousness but rather a vehicle for propagating the beautiful and the good.[120] In this text, Isabella Andreini stands as synecdoche for the merits of the theatrical profession itself. As Nevia

Buommino has observed, Giovanni Battista used his learned household as evidence of both his own "nobility" of character and that of the theatrical profession. The virtues of his natal household presented useful rhetorical ammunition against the most common criticisms of the theatrical profession—especially that beautiful actresses, as active and vocal agents, transgressed expectations of female passivity and that they drew the sexual attention of male audiences, which destabilized the nuclear family.[121]

Contemporary critics did indeed make actresses a focal point for attacking the theater itself. Against such notions, Giovanni Battista pitted his mother as an emblem, or mirror *(specchio)*, of everything wise, noble, and good. Isabella Andreini's learned virtue is the leitmotif of the entire work. Like the women humanists who used the paternal or domestic referent to contextualize and justify their status as intellectuals, Giovanni Battista canonizes his mother to legitimize himself, as well as his parents' literary and theatrical careers. The theater itself is a school for learned virtue, and his mother represents its finest lecturer. But both require, as women do, a chivalrous masculine defense against male detractors.

Giovanni Battista calls those who attack the theater stupid *(sciocchi)* and lacking in judgment *(privi di giudizio)*, because the greatest application of human intelligence is observing "the mirror of human actions, the Book of Virtue and the theater of events, all of which are, in short, the theater. The theater, in the guise of a transparent crystal, makes us look carefully at our actions in just the same way as a wise and learned book teaches us many strategies for coping with misfortune." He goes on to assert his role in defending this repository of the beautiful and the good, in gendered terms. "I have at all times acted in conformity with truth," he states, "and have had always had it in my heart to defend the honor of the meek. So, as the Theater is a Woman, having little power against her detractors, I have determined to take up the shield of reason, and fight with truth on behalf of an innocent damsel in distress."[122]

Although he disavows using "rhetorical colors," claiming that the simplicity of truth will be his only textual weapon, he nonetheless presents himself as a classically informed champion of this innocent damsel, the Theater. His argument for the utility of the theater as a school for virtue, he is careful to note, derives from ancient and modern authors of surpassing credentials. He cites Livy, Valerius Maximus, Horace, and an acclaimed modern poet, Torquato Tasso, in making the point that the ancient and modern theater have the same objective, which is to "save men from bad living and wickedness by leading them to a better life, and persuading them to adopt good habits; so as to sweeten the bitterness attendant to being reproved, we mix the lessons with delight, by which everyone is the better persuaded to listen to them."[123]

Continuing on the theme of the theater as a school, Giovanni Battista switches gender categories: now actors are understood to be masculine pedagogues and soldiers. Against the criticism that actors receive by virtue of accepting payment for their services, he asks, "Should physicians be ashamed of receiving money for their advice? Or lawyers for offering their arguments? Soldiers for wages earned in defending their Fatherland? Lecturers for teaching their students?" Just as it is only right that other types of male professional be remunerated for their services to society, he answers, so too should actors be paid for theirs. The last and thus most important issue in this periodic construction is the comparison of actors to "lecturers," which highlights his conviction that the theater should be seen as a school of virtue. "If lecturers deserve payment for teaching their students," he concludes, "then just so do actors warrant reward for trying to delight their audiences at the same time as they teach them."[124] Not only are actors positive contributors to society, like soldiers and teachers, but they participate in an even more ancient and noble profession, oratory, which Giovanni Battista defines as the art of persuading listeners to virtuous action.

The subject of oration brings Giovanni Battista to cite his mother. Demanding indulgence for his "filial ardor, the celestial commandment to honor one's Mother," he reminds his readers that his own mother had been "a fertile oratrix [*oratrice faconda*] admired in the world of the theater and immortalized by her writings." He further inquires, expecting an affirmative reply, "was she not always worthy, because of her earnest virtue, to be named an *Intenta*?" Isabella Andreini becomes a pivotal referent again when he argues that the theater was nothing like "Satan's Proscenium," as its actresses are the very antithesis of libertines.[125]

Women's theatrical roles, Giovanni Battista contends, discourage male lust, because the female speakers most commonly attack men for licentiousness. As pinnacles of good conduct within the context of the play—at least the plays that his company performs—the female characters champion normative domesticity. Those who attack actresses for public speaking, he continues, have evidently missed three hundred years of the debate on women. He encapsulates this debate for the benighted but adds his own emphasis upon actresses as compelling evidence of female excellence. He contends that, whatever some might think, actresses are indeed fit for teaching honor to the multitudes, because actresses are devoted "to books, to writing, to the vigils and hardships that attend their frequent contemplation, in private, of that which . . . they must perform in public." Who better, he asks, to teach women about clean living than another woman? The women of the theater are like the revered goddess Minerva, wise and courageous. As real women, however, actresses are especially "fertile" in their doctrine: "O women, as fecund with regard to children as you are intellectually fertile with respect to good teachings; full worthily was Minerva the Goddess both of War and of Books, by which the ancients indicated that in Woman, both courage and wisdom are conjoined. O Women, or rather Minervas or Bellonas all; since she was born from Jove's head, you are the head of all greatness, as glorious as you are wise. Actresses, you are the most fortunate of all, since you above all other women have been granted a world of sublime pursuits."[126]

This is all fine rhetoric, but his readers will want an example. Once again, he provides them with the example of his mother. This time, however, Giovanni Battista cites her own words concerning the preservation of honor: "Among all the other things that must be prized, a woman must value her honor. As Isabella, my dearest Mother of blessed memory, said in her *Letters*, 'clean living is as crucial for a woman as earth is for mankind, water for fish and air for birds.' And she goes on to say that 'I know that honor is more valuable even than life itself, since living is common to all animals, but living honorably is the sole preserve of the prudent man; and since this term 'man' is a general one, and indicates both men and women—'woman' being included in the same name—she must try to conduct herself prudently.'"[127]

This citation of his mother leads Giovanni Battista to a more general disquisition on actresses as good family women, who keep themselves busy attending to the needs of their husbands and children in addition to striving for perfection in their careers. If leisure leads to vice, he reasons, then actresses are the least prone to moral lapses, because they are the busiest of all women. Giovanni Battista provides a fascinating portrait of the actress at home. He does not name Isabella as the subject, but we may take her as such, as this passage appears between the quotation from her *Lettere* and his subsequent discussion of the Andreini household as a utopia of "learned virtue." In a breathless description, Andreini praises his learned mother as a consummate professional—driven at every moment to perfect herself. He begins this encomium by observing that "at the very moment that she retires to her room for some rest, she does nothing else but learn the wise discourses that she anticipates reciting; and she corrects her actions and chastises herself, and practices her gestures over and over." Lest she seem self-obsessed, however, Andreini describes how the talented wife and her husband rehearse together and then offer their children a preperformance of "what will make everyone marvel later." We follow this talented family through the hectic course of their days and nights, driven forward by Andreini's close-packed clauses but always focused on the prima donna—the mother—who fulfills her obligations as her children's governess even after a tiring performance: "Now exhausted she returns to her room and, despite the fact that she is completely worn out, nonetheless troubles to examine—O lynx-eyed matriarch!—the public acts of her household, and she is especially attentive to hearing and seeing what her little ones have been studying that day." Rounding out this cinematic itinerary of the theatrical matron, Giovanni Battista concludes by stating that she belongs to the ranks of the truly virtuous: "Putting on the bedside lamp (the custom of the virtuous), she illuminates still more brightly with her own excellence the study of the new material that she will perform soon, such that day by day she transforms the common perception of womankind with her ever-greater triumphs."[128] Giovanni Battista Andreini thus transformed the memory of his mother into compelling evidence that actresses (and, by extension, the theater itself) embodied society's most cherished ideals.

La ferza does introduce readers to other theatrical households that became schools of virtue. For instance, he gives credit to his colleagues Girolamo Garavini of Ferrara and his wife, Signora Margarita, who "above all else have educated so well Signor Carlo Amedeo and Signora Caterina, both their most honorable children—the son making remarkable profit in virtue by upholding at all times the true rule of good doctrine under the Reverend Jesuit Fathers, and the daughter having now taken the veil at the venerable convent of Migliarino."[129]

The best example of admirable excellence in a theatrical family, however, remains that of Giovanni Battista's parents. Andreini points to his father's sacrifices as a soldier but above all to the ideal household salon over which Francesco and Isabella jointly presided: "A soldier of about twenty years of age, [my father] was fighting in a naval battle when he was taken by the Turks; imprisoned for eight years, he later fled and became the husband of such a glorious Woman, no less dear to him than life itself. Every city that they visited celebrated them as the very image of tender marital love and heralded this beautiful pair of Virtuosi—these twin images of gentility—celebrating their dual success as excellent actors and superb teachers at home."[130] Explicating the glories of his parents, Giovanni Battista presents us with an image of a household salon, in which the learned married couple hosted the best and brightest of their day. "At every moment," he goes on, "this home was full of noble and learned people, who came to us with delight and left us with amazement." Noting that the most elevated minds of the age celebrated his parents' home, he still gives the greater share of the credit to his mother.

Isabella, Francesco, and Giovanni Battista Andreini articulated a complex image of their household as an academy, a theater for moral education and ultimately a salon of virtuosi. We are already familiar with women writers who created a legitimate space for themselves in the world of letters by approaching male patrons "as daughter to father" and who tightened their connections with friends and colleagues by appropriating terms of kinship. And this theatrical family's successful manipulation of the hallowed images of the virtuous learned woman, the spiritual bond of the perfect marriage, and the household as a site for the inculcation of "learned virtue" proves the continued effectiveness of domestic rhetoric in making the female leadership in the sphere of learning seem acceptable and even praiseworthy.

The case of the Andreini, however, also suggests an important change in the rules of engagement for Italian woman writers. Insofar as Isabella Andreini was an author and intellectual, she fit within the lineage of women intellectuals that fifteenth-century women humanists established and that learned sixteenth-century women such as Moderata Fonte and Lucrezia Marinella continued. Andreini's theatrical career, however, should have compromised her "virtue" and therefore her abil-

ity to claim membership in this category. Given the contemporary association between actresses and prostitutes, she should have been considered a learned courtesan, at best. Yet with only the slightest nod to her
status as a wife and mother, she garnered the same praise that accrued
to her more conservative predecessors. At least in Italy, literary culture
was prepared to honor any talented woman who could harness the
power of rhetoric.

Perhaps the most striking shift that appears in conjunction with
the Andreini family, however, is the symbolic potency of the learned
woman herself. This study has shown the success of women writers who
established their legitimacy on the foundation of patriarchal sanction,
whether real or rhetorical. We have become accustomed, in short, to
hearing women's voices mediated through the father figure. The case of
Marie de Gournay, editor of her "father"-patron's *Essays*, hints at a potential inversion of this relationship: Montaigne's voice was mediated
through his adopted daughter and literary executor. In Giovanni Battista
Andreini, we witness this inversion in the most precise sense. Here is a
male author who staked his credibility on the "learned virtue" of his
mother. He brought Isabella Andreini forward to bolster his personal
claim to intellectual "nobility" and his defense of the theatrical profession itself. Giovanni Battista's strategy suggests that, by the early seventeenth century, women intellectuals were beginning to exercise a form
of cultural leadership that previously had been possible only for enlightened patriarchs.

The increasing authority of learned women was by no means restricted to the Italian context. The Andreini model applies as well to the
educated elite of Britain at the turn of the century. But just as Isabella
Andreini was the star of her family and their theatrical company, it
would be the excellence of women themselves that took center stage in
the household salons of seventeenth-century Britain.

6

Collaborative Marriages in Britain

WOMEN intellectuals enjoyed a veritable golden age in seventeenth-century Britain. By 1580 a famously erudite woman sovereign, Elizabeth I, sat on the throne, and at least one playwright, Shakespeare, was fascinated with the character of the powerful and intelligent woman, as well as the instability of gender itself. Below the level of royalty and the most famous authors, we have witnessed the educated elite welcoming women humanists, most notably Anne Cooke Bacon, as Elizabeth's "undershining stars," embodiments of their families' intellectual honor and examples for other women to follow. The next generations of women writers capitalized on a new range of possibilities for literary contribution and invention.

Seventeenth-century English women writers defy categorization: they emerged across the socioeconomic landscape, wrote in a variety of languages, and worried far less about propriety. The famous sixteenth-century graduates of household academies had established a strong foundation in the English literary memory. A testament to their success is the facility with which subsequent generations of women writers from diverse backgrounds were able to make their voices heard.

These new voices spoke most often in English, by this time a recognized language of erudite composition and in fact far more suitable than Latin for expressing new ideas. As Margaret King has observed, by the seventeenth century, "the seeking and questioning female voice [was] heard in a new key."[1] A look at the sheer quantity of publications by women may suggest something of the changing contours of women's participation in literary culture from the sixteenth to the seventeenth century. As King notes for the English context, only eight female-authored works had appeared in print between 1486 and 1548. By 1640 ninety-five more had been printed. And while English women's printed works constituted only 2 percent of all published material by 1690, this admittedly small percentage suggests women's increasing visibility in print culture.[2]

Historians and literary critics have already devoted considerable attention to this era's prominent women of letters, among them Mary Sidney, later Countess of Pembroke (1561–1621), a poet, translator, and patron of literature; Elizabeth Grymeston (ca. 1563–ca. 1603), whose principal work, her posthumously published *Miscellanea, Meditations, Memoratives* (1604) parades her knowledge of classical literature, the Bible, the Church fathers, Latin, Greek, and Italian; and Maria Thynne (ca. 1575–1611), a letter writer and accomplished Neo-Latinist. Other celebrated women authors followed Grymeston's precedent in publishing works in the advice-manual genre. The most notable examples in this category are Elizabeth Jocelyn (1596–1622), whose posthumous publication, *A Mother's Legacie* (1624), reached its third edition within a single year, and Dorothy Leigh, author of *A Mother's Blessing*, which enjoyed its fourteenth edition in 1629.

Seventeenth-century England also witnessed a dramatic increase in women's translations, plays, and poetry. Consider, for example, Margaret Tyler (fl. 1578), translator of a lengthy Spanish romance by Diego Ortúñez de Calahorra (published in 1578 as *The Mirrour of Princely Deeds and Knighthood*), and the prolific playwright Aphra Behn (1640–1689), whose oeuvre comprises an astonishing sixty works, eighteen of which were plays performed frequently during the 1670s and 1680s. Two of the most notable poets were Anne Bradstreet (ca. 1612–1672) and Katharine Philips (1632–1664). Bradstreet was transplanted from England to America with her natal family, and her vast collection of poetry (published in London in 1650 and in America in 1678 as *The Tenth Muse, Lately Sprung Up in America*) represents the first major collection of female-authored poetry in the New World. Katharine Philips was celebrated for her translations and poetry. She first circulated her works among her "Society of Friendship"—a network of male and female correspondents who were all assigned classical names—and many of her works were also printed. Philips's best-known epistolary compositions were issued as *Letters from Orinda to Poliarchus* (1705 and 1729). In the years following her death, male colleagues also printed several editions of Philips's poetry (1664, 1667, 1669, 1678, and 1710).

Several female pedagogues also emerged in this century. We have already encountered Bathsua Makin's *An Essay to Revive the Antient Education of Gentlewomen* (1673). Preceding her was Mary Ward (1585–1645), an ardent advocate for women's education. Hannah Wooley (ca. 1623–1677) followed in the footsteps of Ward and Makin in her manual titled *The Gentlewoman's Companion* (1675), which offered a sharp critique of masculine hegemony in the realm of education, as did Mary Astell's *Serious Proposal to the Ladies* (1694).

As the project of historical recovery progresses, the ranks of women authors known to us continue to expand, making any statistic provisional at best. Statistics based solely upon printed material, moreover, become irrelevant when we consider the persistence of manuscript circulation within the cultural elite, as Harold Love, Margaret Ezell, and many others have done.[3] Indeed, male and female authors alike often chose what Love has termed "scribal publication" as their preferred medium throughout the early modern period. Demonstrating the vast amount of English women's writing that appears when scholars look beyond print, a recent anthology edited by Helen Ostovich and Elizabeth Sauer, *Reading Early Modern Women* (2004), has located over thirty women authors of the late sixteenth and seventeenth centuries who wrote epistles, treatises, plays, household advice, love poetry, history, and much else besides, but remain understudied (or altogether unknown) to modern scholars, as they chose to circulate their works among kin, friends, colleagues, and patrons instead of printing them.[4]

In order best to illustrate this climate of expansion, I turn now to women intellectuals who were not the most famous authors of their day. Here we will meet a prolific author of copybooks, Esther Inglis (1571–1624); a painter and moral philosopher, Mary Beale (1633–1699); and a painter and feminist author, Mary More (died ca. 1716). These women lacked the advantage of being born into the cultural elite, but their compositions parallel the works of their more exalted predecessors and contemporaries. Inglis, Beale, and More reveal the presence of women intellectuals among the "middling sort."

These case studies also underscore the broadening range of methodological possibilities available to women authors. A central theme that unites Inglis, Beale, and More is their use of scribal publication as a pre-

ferred venue for literary contribution. So, too, they show us the movement of classical learning from the realm of Neo-Latin to vernacular
composition. Latinity served to this point as a convenient justification
for terming women writers "learned." The erudition of these new cases,
however, appears in a more complex system of facilities and intellectual
priorities, chiefly, familiarity with classical literature (at least in translation), dexterity in expository prose, theoretical commitments emblematic of the humanist enterprise (especially an insistence upon education
as the bedrock upon which to build "virtue"), and a self-conscious assertion of authorial credentials.

In Italy, the decline of Latinity among women writers exemplified
the changing priorities of literary culture, which increasingly favored
vernacular humanism as the best means for disseminating ideas to a
broad milieu. The relative infrequency of female Neo-Latinists from the
late sixteenth century onward did not reflect the "failure" of women humanists but rather the generalized loss of faith in the power of mere classical imitation as a means to improve society and the individuals within
it. As Charles Nauert summarizes, "by the time of Montaigne, and certainly by the seventeenth century, sublime trust in the curative powers
of Antiquity had waned; but the critical spirit, the hope of improvement
(no longer just by 'rediscovering' Antiquity) survived as the enduring
legacies of humanism."[5] This attitude obtained in seventeenth-century
England as well, but with an important difference. Latin, as the official
language of Rome, labored under the negative connotation of popery
and connoted the occlusion rather than revelation of knowledge.

Emblematic of Latin's weakening hegemony, many prominent male
intellectuals of seventeenth-century England wrote largely, if not exclusively, in English.[6] Much as Michel de Montaigne represents the advent of
vernacular humanism in France, John Milton and the scientist and natural philosopher Robert Boyle represent the growing number of learned
English men who published their most important compositions in the
vernacular. Indeed, authors in seventeenth-century Europe embraced
the opportunity to gain the widest possible audience for their ideas.

Beyond the issues of numbers and media, however, I am concerned
here with charting the broad distribution of intellectual families in
seventeenth-century Britain and the emergence of the "household salon"
in this new era. William Petty (later Sir William Petty) was the son of
a clothier. Together with his wife, however, this self-made man created

a household academy for his sons and daughter akin to that which Sir Thomas More and Sir Anthony Cooke had forged in the previous century. But the Petty intellectual family also extended this model into the new level of the household salon, where Elizabeth Petty, her brother, her sister-in-law, and a range of tutors all participated in its cultural production. In this sense, the Petty family had more in common with the Andreini family than the "school" of Thomas More.

Within the household salons of seventeenth-century Britain, the father-daughter dyad remained important, but the narrative concerning seventeenth-century women of the pen came to focus upon marital collaboration and extended kinship networks. The rhetoric of filial piety, moreover, gave way to a more egalitarian discourse of friendship— especially friendship within marriage. The notion of equality in letters and marriage was already present in Erasmus's portrait of the relationship between Margaret More and William Roper. But Thomas More, "father" to both, sanctioned this striking image of parity. Expanding as a concept with the Andreini, *amicitia* (redefined as friendship between men and women) became pronounced for Esther Inglis and Bartholomew Kello, as well as for Mary and Charles Beale. In short, the story with which we are now concerned is the symbiosis of learned couples and their interdisciplinary creativity.

Much like the dialectic of continuity and change in the cases of Moderata Fonte and Lucrezia Marinella, however, the household academy and women's instruction in Latin remained important constants, even as its cast of characters began to change. Accordingly, our starting point will be a brief return to the feminist pedagogue Bathsua Makin, who exemplifies a continuing tradition of women Latinists trained by their learned fathers. The family of Sir William Petty, chief physician of Cromwell's army and author of a famous survey of Ireland, illustrates the shift toward a more expansive model of the household salon. Proud of his own erudition, Petty joined the tradition of enlightened patriarchs determined to see both sons and daughters educated in the classics. His autograph letters describing the education of his sons Charles and Henry, as well as his daughter, Anne, show us yet another academy on the Morean model. At the same time, however, Elizabeth Petty's letters concerning the children's education, as well as the satire she coauthored with William, suggest the theme of marital collaboration that characterized the creative lives of other learned women in Tudor-Stuart Britain.

A "Familiar" Classical Model: Bathsua Makin and Anne Petty

Long before Bathsua Makin published her 1673 *An Essay to Revive the Antient Education of Gentlewomen* in English, she established her reputation as the humanist daughter of her schoolteacher father, Henry Reginald. In 1616 the as yet unmarried Bathsua Reginald published an impressive compilation of the Latin and Greek poems that she had written for the royal family, titled *Musa Virginea (The Virgin Muse)*. The frontispiece announces that the author is "Bathsua R[eginald], daughter of Henry Reginald, a schoolmaster and philologist of London."[7] In her recent article on the *Musa,* Anne Leslie Saunders points to the pivotal role played by Henry Reginald in providing his daughter with a thorough classical education. Yet I would argue that Saunders overdetermines the father's role: she takes it for granted that Reginald himself wrote this byline with the intention of using his daughter as an advertisement for the quality of his school.[8] This is a plausible interpretation only when Bathsua Makin is situated as a singular case rather than as a participant in a lengthy tradition of women humanists, both in Italy and in England. When we consider the long and successful history of women humanists' frequent choice of a filial persona as a means to situate themselves, it seems far more likely that Bathsua chose to introduce herself to literary society as "her father's daughter."

In any case, Makin presents another example of a woman humanist who enjoyed a rich early education thanks to her father. She also follows in this tradition insofar as she, once graduated from her household academy, put her learning to use in the service of womankind. Like Margaret More Roper and Anne Cooke Bacon before her, Makin demonstrates that neither erudition nor even a public career proved fatal to a woman's marriage prospects: she married a courtier named Richard Makin in 1621, and the couple had several children.[9]

Bathsua Makin represents a turning point in the history of learned women in one important respect, however: her education won her employment as a governess. As we have seen, Makin asserted in her *Essay* that she had not only founded a school for girls but had been the governess and language instructor of Princess Elizabeth (daughter of Charles I). Prior to this post, Makin had also been a tutor for the Hastings family.[10] I have argued throughout this study that the authorial careers of learned women militate against a long-standing scholarly argument that women's advanced education served no purpose beyond the ornamental during the early modern period.[11] Makin's employment as a governess, however, constitutes a fitting conclusion to this line of reasoning: by the end of the seventeenth century, the role of the governess emerged as a career possibility for learned women. To be sure, it was customary among noble English families to send daughters to other households for instruction in social graces and household management—and some young women might well have received a humanistic education as well, if the lady of the house happened to be trained in these subjects herself. It was quite a different matter, however, formally to hire a woman as a tutor. As a testament to the potentially revolutionary effects of women's employment as governesses, Makin was not, it is worth noting, the only female pedagogue to become an explicit feminist: Mary Wollstonecraft also began her career as a tutor and governess of aristocratic children.[12]

Analysis of the new institutions for women's education and occupational possibilities for educated women that began to appear in the late seventeenth and eighteenth centuries lies outside the scope of this study. I have highlighted the figure of the governess here only to suggest a new phase in the history of women's education: the context remains the household, but the governess herself, as a paid employee, occupied a more professional role than that of the learned daughter or wife.

More firmly rooted in the seventeenth century was the tradition of home schooling in the classics by relatives, specifically, by the learned father. Literary icons such as Bathsua Makin enjoyed this benefit, but so too did women such as the daughter of William and Elizabeth Petty, Anne Petty, whose extensive education has not drawn scholarly attention by virtue of the fact that she did not take up an authorial career— or else her writings have not yet been identified. Anne Petty exists only as a subject of much discussion between her parents in the voluminous Petty papers, many of which remain in manuscript.[13] While she does not belong to this study, then, as any kind of feminist, her case underscores two points at the heart of this analysis: the first is the continuing tendency of learned men to offer their daughters advanced educations; the second is the suggestion that it may have been more common than scholars currently realize for women outside the exalted ranks of the nobility to be instructed in a range of subjects beyond religion and "housewifery." In this sense, Anne Petty serves as a useful introduction to the milieu of Esther Inglis, Mary Beale, and Mary More.

William Petty (1623–1687) was a prominent member of the English intellectual elite.[14] His remarkable career also demonstrates the social mobility that education afforded. Not unlike Francesco Andreini, Petty had humble origins, which hardly prefigured either his authorial celebrity or his knighthood. As Petty, never one to underestimate his achievements, emphasizes in his final will, he was a self-made man. Eschewing the pious preambles common to wills, Petty's "testament" begins with a ringing assertion of his greatest point of pride: his mind. "In the first place," he writes, "I declare and affirm that at the full age of fifteen years I had obtained the Latin, Greek and French tongues, the whole body of common Arithmetic, the practical Geometry and Astronomy."[15]

At the age of twenty-three, Petty had already published a treatise on education with Samuel Hartlib (1647). In 1650 he took a doctorate in medicine at Oxford and the next year accepted a professorship in anatomy at Brasenose College. Not satisfied with one subject alone, Petty also taught chemistry and even held a professorship in music at Gresham College. He resigned these posts in 1652, however, when he was appointed as physician general in Cromwell's army in Ireland, where he would live from 1667 to 1673. Among his most remarkable achievements is that Petty steered a course between his parliamentarian employment and the emoluments of royal patronage: he was knighted in 1662. Thereafter, Petty shifted from his post as private secretary to Henry Cromwell, lord deputy of Ireland, to a favored place in the courtly circle of Charles II.

But then again, Petty's obsession was knowledge, not politics. A fellow of the Royal Society from its incorporation (1662), he was a staunch Baconian devoted to the practical applications of mechanics and mathematics. Petty is credited with being the first to apply mathematics to developing economic models. Statisticians still make use of his survey of Ireland (1655–1656), commonly titled "The Down Survey," which earned its author the astronomical fee of thirteen thousand pounds and the admiration of Sir Hardress Waller.

Petty married Waller's daughter, Elizabeth, in 1667. This was a second marriage for both Elizabeth and William, and both already had children. Elizabeth's son, William Fenton, died in 1670, and Petty mentions him fondly in his own will: "[I leave] fifty pounds for a small monument to be set up in St. Bride's Church in Dublin, in memory of my son, John, and my near kinsman John Petty, supposing my wife will add thereunto for her excellent son, Sir William Fenton, Baronet, who was buried there."[16] In addition to his son from his previous marriage, Petty also had an illegitimate daughter, who became an actress. John Aubrey, a contemporary biographer of Petty, mentioned, "He has a natural daughter that much resembles him—no legitimate child so much—that acts at the Duke's playhouse."[17]

Aubrey also made note of the many excellences of Petty's wife and their three children, Charles, Anne, and Henry, whose education will constitute the majority of the following discussion. "In 1667," Aubrey notes, "[Petty] married on Trinity Sunday the relict [widow] of Sir Maurice Fenton of Ireland, Knight, and daughter of Sir Hardress Waller of Ireland—a very beautiful and ingenious lady, brown, with glorious eyes, by whom he has sons and daughters, very lovely children, but all like the mother."[18] Petty would certainly have disagreed. His letters to his wife present their children as extensions of his own excellence. Like Cicero and Thomas More, however, Petty viewed his daughter as the best embodiment of his own intellectual ideals. To judge by the dozens of instances in which he expresses the idea, Anne was also his favorite child.

During the 1670s and 1680s, Charles, Anne (or Marianne), and Henry Petty were often with their father in Dublin while their mother oversaw her own and her husband's properties elsewhere in Ireland and in London. It is most fortunate for historians that William and Elizabeth Petty were so busy: their frequent separations necessitated a constant flow of information by letter. This voluminous correspondence constitutes a rich repository of information about the upbringing and education of children in families of the cultural but not noble elite.

William Petty was proud of all his children, but his letters suggest a special bond with his middle child, Anne, who seems to have been every bit as ornery as he. He usually signifies his sons by name only, but Anne often receives the epithet "my dear girl." He writes to his wife in July 1679, for instance, about their eldest son, Charles, who was then about nine years old: "[He] is well lusty, active and well-coloured as ever or as need he be. He sleepeth and learneth well, has broke the neck of his Latin difficulty and does well in his writing and in all other exercises." Following this proud but somewhat distant rehearsal of his son's progress, however, Petty underscores the charming precocity of Anne (age seven at the time): "You ask what Anne learns; I answer that, do we what we can to the contrary, she learns the exercises of musket and pike and is very forward in beating the drum! But I must say she learneth all things else as well."[19]

Petty's affection for all his children rings out in his instinct to tease them. He terms Anne and Charles, for instance, as "[his] little Jade and Rogue, who are great comforts to [him]."[20] And one of Petty's so-called "poetical amusements" on the subject of his daughter mocks the hegemony of beauty and advantageous marriages in women's lives. His epigram of 1678/79 to Anne reads,

> My pretty Little Pusling & My daughter Anne
> That shall be a Countess if her Pappa can
> If her Pappa cannot, then I make no doubt
> But my little Pusling will be content without.
> If my Little Pusling prove an Ugly Carren
> Then it will be well enough
> If shee get but a Baron.
> But if her fortune should be so
> As to get but a Knight
> Then I trow her cake is dough
> And hopes are all beshite.[21]

Here Petty mocked his own station as "but a Knight" and, more broadly, the whole issue of status. In a letter to his wife of 1683, written after the then-teenagers Charles and Anne had just recovered from smallpox, Petty again makes light of excessive concern for women's beauty. He had been vitally worried for the lives of his children, but now that the danger was passed he emphasized the relative insignificance of the fact that the disease had disfigured them—especially Charles. "Tell Charles," Petty writes, "that I cannot but laugh to hear that he is the bottom and Anne the top of beauty among my children. I begged their lives of Almighty God and not their beauties, yet I believe 'tis such as they may be well enough contented with it. If not, let them repair this defect by some Noble acquisitions."[22] Much as Pietro Bembo before him, Petty maintained that accomplishments could be relied upon to titivate when physical beauty (or other worldly enticements) were either absent or marred.

Satire was Petty's alternate mode to academic discourse. In 1685 he and Elizabeth, as well as her brother, the poet James Waller, collaborated on an elaborate lampoon of their noble acquaintances, titled "Henealogie, or the Legend of Henhen and Penhen in Two Parts," the first part of which they characterized as "Twenty-Four Chapters of Raillery."[23] Inspired in part by Juvenal's *Satires* and in part by Ovid's *Metamorphoses*, this work is witty and coarse by turns. It is a small wonder that they did not print this often crude amusement, particularly in view of the fact that they specified "Henhen and Penhen" as "Lord Chief Baron Henry in Ireland and Penelope his Lady."[24]

Titles and pretension were fair game for mockery in the Petty household salon, but the education of their children was no laughing matter. Each of the children had several tutors, but William and Elizabeth also instructed them personally. William notes in a letter to Elizabeth of 1681, when they were having trouble with the children's principal tutor, Master Mesnell, "[Mesnell] was considerable only for French. You must be your children's tutor in the small morals yourself; I teach Charles every day. I take notice of what you say about Harry [Henry]—'tis to no purpose to deal with Master Tod unless we had a better way for the money. Master Baret is as well as any other." A few years later (1683), Petty wrestled with the competing impulses to avoid risking his family on the journey from London to Dublin and the desire "to enjoy [his] wife and children, and to assist in their Education." In this same letter, he asked his wife to "thank Anne for her wise letters." Still debating the problem of a sea voyage the next year, Petty at first left his wife to decide "which of the children [she would] bring and under what masters [she would] leave the rest," but a few weeks later wrote to inform her that all things were ready in Ireland and that if she could "be so valiant as to come thither, do so." He continues, "You shall be as welcome as I can make you. Bring dear Charles with you—I will not venture my whole in one bottom. Let Master Mesnell stay with the other two and forward them in their books and exercises."[25]

Petty took an intense personal interest in his children's academic development. His papers include treatises on pedagogy and the syllabi that he devised for Charles, Anne, and Henry. In 1686, with all of his children in their adolescence, William Petty organized their curriculum. Charles, for whom Petty envisioned a prominent career akin to his own, was to follow almost precisely the curriculum outlined in Castiglione's *Courtier:* he was to master music, dance, fencing, horsemanship, and the military arts; he was also to read broadly in the ancient and modern classics. Charles's reading list includes Justinian, Hobbes, Aristotle (especially on rhetoric), Cicero's *De officiis*, Erasmus's *Colloquies*, Caesar, Sallust, Tacitus, and Virgil's *Georgics*. For piety and polish, Petty also instructed Charles to read Genesis, Luke, and Acts 4; the plays of Molière; "Reynard" [probably *The Romance of Reynard*]; and Aesop. Henry, the youngest child, was neither old enough nor, it would appear, apt enough for most of this material. Petty conceived Henry's readings and activities only in such general terms as "Latin, Scripture, Chronicles, Writing and Arithmetic, Singing, Fencing and Riding."[26]

Anne Petty's syllabus, to be undertaken from her fourteenth to eighteenth year, is the most extensive. To the same list of texts assigned to her elder brother, Petty adds the poet Horace, as well as the Roman historian Suetonius and the Jewish historian Josephus.[27] It is also worth noting that Petty assigned Anne and Charles substantive study of anatomy (what he terms the "ars parva") as well as geography and topography—which suggests that he wished them both to perpetuate his own field specialties.

William and Elizabeth Petty also taught their children to write by the kind of "correspondence course" in belles lettres that we have witnessed in the More and Andreini letter sets. While the Pettys did not attempt to make their children into humanists, they were concerned that all the children learn to write with poise and elegance. In the summer of 1680, Charles was with his mother in London. Petty writes to his wife that he expects Charles to "write . . . an account of his proceedings & how he passes his time, what friends and interests he makes, etc." Petty would also underscore the point for all his children in writing to his wife that he wished them "to exercise themselves in writing to [him]. For they must 'ere long come to it in earnest."[28]

By 1681/82, however, Anne's progress in learning elicited the greater part of her father's attention and affection. "Let dear Anne have any money bestowed for her teaching," he exhorts his wife, "for I see she will learn as appears by her excellent Writing. I love her exceedingly."[29] A few months later, Petty wrote again to his wife, "I rejoice [to learn that] Anne is so good an Accountant, etc. I love her dearly."[30] Within the next three weeks, he sent two letters to his wife on this same theme of Anne's increasing profit by her education. He urges that Anne write to him again, "for [he takes] pleasure to see it." He adds thereafter, "I am ravished with Anne's Writing. I shall be glad to see the like progress in Arithmetic, for if God bless me I will give her somewhat to reckon. She shall not be bound 'prentice to a scrivener, but shall be her own Papa's steward and Secretary Mistress."[31] Petty's comment about giving Anne "somewhat to reckon" is a witty allusion to the large dowry that he was preparing for her. Two years previously, he had communicated to Elizabeth the financial bequests that he intended to offer his children: Charles was to have three thousand pounds per year, and Henry one thousand; and three thousand pounds were to be set aside for Anne's dowry "payable at sixteen years old." He hoped, however, to offer her six thousand pounds in the end.[32] As it happened, Petty found himself in very easy financial circumstances by the time he wrote his final will (1685): Anne received a dowry of twenty thousand pounds.[33] Once again, we see the close connection between a daughter's educational progress and her dowry. The two "endowments," while perhaps not absolutely proportional, were as linked in William Petty's mind as they had been in Pietro Bembo's. Ambitious fathers rewarded talented daughters.

Elizabeth Petty took just as much of an active role in her children's education as her husband. She wrote to them during those periods (especially 1684–1685) when she, William, and Charles were together in Ireland, and Anne and Henry were staying with relatives and friends in London. In one instance, she cautions Anne, "Read your Letters just before you answer them, & then you will be able to answer every particular. Let Mr. Banworth take care to buy you good ink, paper, pens & wax, & then you will take pleasure in writing. I would have you tell me everything that you hear, where you go, who comes to see you, what clothes you have and what your brother Harry does."[34] In February of 1684/85, Elizabeth praised Anne in particular for her careful account of current events, especially the king's death.

Lady Petty could also be stern about her children's studies—indeed, much more so than her husband. In contrast to William's consistent ebullience at Anne's progress, Elizabeth stepped in to scold when necessary. "Master Mesnell says that you will learn nothing," she wrote to Anne in June 1684, "and that your Brother not much more, and that you do perpetually affront him & his wife; you, on the other hand, say that they are cross at you. At this distance I can say, nor do, no more than I have already done, wherefore I have written to Master Mesnell that if you & your brother do not learn, then I have no further occasion for him & that he has his liberty to go when he pleases, as he desires. But let me tell you both, I believe you will scarce ever get a better [tutor], and one you shall have when it pleases God that I return." She notes in closing, "You tell me nothing of Master Isacke, nor Seigneur Bartlome; methinks Harry should be always present when you sing and dance." Lady Petty's concern was doubtless for propriety, but her suspicion of artistic education (not unlike Pietro Bembo's) also contained a measure intellectual snobbery—a distaste most evident in her attitude toward Anne's instruction in drawing, a study that her daughter seemed to enjoy and that William encouraged but that Elizabeth urged Anne to pursue "only as a diversion."[35] In her insistence upon academic rigor, Elizabeth Petty was a maternal figure antithetical to the image of Christine de Pizan's mother, who wished that Christine occupy her time only with "spinning and silly girlishness, following the common custom of women," and commensurate with the recollection Giovanni Battista Andreini had of his own mother, whom he termed with admiration a "lynx-eyed matriarch" in the supervision of her children's education. The learned mother had become an equal partner in the intellectual family.

Learning was a Petty family business in the fullest sense of the term: everyone seemed to participate with zeal and in a spirit of collaboration. We might expect Charles, as the eldest and a son, to remain somewhat aloof; yet he troubled to keep his brother and sister, no less than his parents, informed about his studies. For instance, he wrote to Henry and Anne that he was learning "to vault, to fence and to Ride," adding, "[One tutor] comes to me every day to teach me Latin & I am now pretty well advanced in it." He also responded to Anne's particular inquiries concerning his instructors in riding and fencing and solicited her help in restoring the faulty lines of communication between him and Master Mesnell, hoping that she and their shared tutor "will both be kind to [Charles] and let [him] do everything with [Anne]." He concluded the letter by saying, "Pray continue to write to me in Mama's letters. I am, Dear Sister, your humble servant, Charles Petty."[36]

Lady Petty also seems to have relied on Anne to transmit news, letters, and her husband's instructions. "My dear girl," Elizabeth begins one letter of May 1684, "your Pa-Pa [is] in very good health & much pleased with your pretty letters." She goes on to thank Anne for transmitting a letter from Master Mesnell, instructs her to let the tutor know that a response will be forthcoming, and observes, "Sir William desires Master Mesnell not to trouble Harry with the Latin yet, & my Dear Children learn with ease what is necessary for you, & you shall never be troubled with un-useful or Crab-eyed studies. I was much delighted with Harry's letter."[37]

Even Elizabeth's older sister, Bridget Cadogan, took part in the children's education. Cadogan spent many of these years either in London or in Dublin, assisting with various aspects of household management; she probably also served as an unofficial governess. Cadogan sometimes appends her own notes to the backs of letters written by Elizabeth to her children. In one instance, Cadogan writes to Anne, "I have persuaded your Mama to leave off writing that I may have room to tell you how greatly I think myself honored and obliged to you for your kind letters [that] I have had from you, which I should have thanked you for before, only my letters were not worth the postage." Cadogan's relatively unpracticed hand, her sometimes strange syntax, and frequent difficulties in spelling (even by the standards of the day) indicate that her level of literacy was not as high as Elizabeth Petty's or her children's. Yet Master Mesnell, the tutor, felt confident enough of Cadogan's abilities to enlist her aid. Cadogan asks Anne, "Present my service to Master Mesnell; and I assure him nobody would be prouder to serve him than I should and I thank him for his most ingenious and obliging letters, which I shall be ashamed to answer because I can say nothing well enough."[38] Given Mesnell's trust, Cadogan's self-deprecation seems less like honest revelation and more like a fondness for the humility trope.

Similarly, James Waller, Elizabeth's brother and William's frequent correspondent on matters of poetry, contributed his own opinions concerning the children's progress in learning. In one instance, he wrote to Anne and Henry of his "great satisfaction in [their] Letters": "I do expect [them] from you for all you write is so ingenious that all people admire that persons of your age are capable of so much understanding."[39] Here James Waller appears in a Morean role, ensuring that the work of a clever female relative circulated beyond her immediate kin.

In the end, the talented Anne seems to have provided a focus for much of this learned family's pride. Perhaps the greatest testament to this are the comments of her brother, Charles, who echoed the sentiments of both their father and uncle in praising his sister's abilities. "I have not written to you," he explains at the end of one of his mother's letters to Anne, "because I think you have too much business for one of twice your age; pray do not think it was because I do not love you, for I assure you I love and admire you, and there is none that has read your pretty letter but will do so, too."[40]

Anne Petty exemplifies the continuity of the intellectual family as a site for women's education and promotion. In this sense, she represents a latter-day Helena Bemba or Margaret Roper—the favorite child of a learned and forward-thinking father who invested a considerable proportion of his own intellectual honor in the education of his children, including (indeed, especially) his daughter. Anne Petty's apparent choice not to pursue an authorial career notwithstanding, her case suggests a fruitful avenue for further archival research: the degree of classical learning that may have taken place in many "upwardly mobile" intellectual families in seventeenth-century Britain. For our immediate purposes, however, Anne Petty also reveals the changing shape of the intellectual family itself. Unlike the mothers of Margaret More Roper or Anne Cooke Bacon, who seem to have played a limited pedagogical role, Anne's mother appears as her husband's colleague with regard to her children's instruction.

Esther Inglis

The career of Esther Inglis (1571–1624) offers one striking prefiguration of the collaboration that obtained in the Petty household. Scholars have studied the calligraphy and miniature paintings with which this Franco-Scottish writer adorned her astonishing corpus of over fifty manuscripts and have begun to explore the political implications suggested by her selection of material.[41] What has not been noted, however, is Inglis's intellectual creativity. Proud of her ability to write in Latin, Greek, French, and English, Inglis worked in the medium of scribal publication from 1586 to 1624. Her collecteana, transcriptions, and redactions encompass treatises, emblematic texts, collections of maxims from the Bible (especially the book of Psalms), and sixteen volumes of moral verses largely derived from the eminent French humanist Guy du Faur de Pibrac (1529–1584).[42] Her patrons ranged from British nobles and intellectuals to royalty: Queen Elizabeth I, King James VI (I), and even continental Protestant icons, including Prince Maurice of Nassau. Inglis contributed to the history of feminism by her creative appropriation of the strategies she inherited from female predecessors on the Continent and in England.

She capitalized upon her natal and marital connections to forge a successful Christian humanist career.

Like her predecessors, Inglis owed her technical skills and initial patronage networks to her father, Nicholas Langlois, who had been a schoolteacher in France. Fleeing the persecution of the Huguenots that culminated in the St. Bartholomew's Day Massacre, Langlois moved his family to Edinburgh around 1574. He became master at the French School, where he taught French and scribal handwriting—services for which King James VI provided him the generous annuity of one hundred pounds.[43] Inglis's mother, Marie Presot, a noted scribe in her own right, probably taught her daughter calligraphy.[44] Inglis obtained her first job through her father: in her teens, she served as a "writing mistress" at his school.[45] In her earliest extant manuscript, cataloged as the "Livret contenant diverses sortes de lettres" (1586), Inglis credited both parents with spurring her to write: "Both parents having bidden me, a daughter has written, breaking the tedium of exile with her pen."[46]

Her father's position on James VI's payroll facilitated her connection to the elite patronage networks that she would enjoy throughout her career. Her father also wrote Latin poems praising her skills, which she transcribed in several of her volumes. When she dedicated another early work to Queen Elizabeth, the "Discours de la Foy" (1591), Inglis displayed quatrains by her father that praise both the queen and his daughter. Ventriloquizing the psalms that Inglis had chosen to present in different calligraphic styles and with illuminations, Langlois asked the questions, "why we are now dressed in elegant apparel?" and "who could devise so many forms of clothing?" His answer was that "a French girl wove them with her pen," and he proudly signed himself as "Nicholas Langlois, Father of the Aforementioned Girl."[47]

In 1596 Inglis "graduated" from her household academy and married a learned man, Bartholomew Kello, clerk for foreign correspondence at James VI's court. After James became the king of England, Inglis and Kello followed him to London, establishing residences there and in Essex (where Kello obtained a post as rector) from about 1606 to 1615. Thereafter, the couple returned to Edinburgh, where they remained until Inglis's death in 1624.

Inglis and Kello provide a fascinating portrait of marital collaboration: she acted as his scribe; he served as her publicist and business manager. Kello also wrote dedicatory letters and poems praising the recipients of her manuscripts and celebrating his wife, which Inglis reproduced (like her father's Latin epigrams) in her prefatory material.⁴⁸ Proud of her skills, Kello signed himself "husband of the book's adorner" *(eornatricis libelli maritus)*.⁴⁹

Kello worked hard to secure payments for Inglis's scribal publications. In this occupation, he found himself in the unenviable position of pushing the powerful, such as Sir Anthony Bacon (Anne Cooke Bacon's son) and even Queen Elizabeth herself.⁵⁰ He exercised all the requisite tact but still emphasized his wife's authorship. In one of his letters to the queen, he even likened Inglis to Virgil or Ovid, observing that although Elizabeth had promised payment for his wife's work, there was unfortunately no "Maecenas in the kingdom of Augustus" *(Mecaenas in regia Augusti)*—no patron to remit the rewards due to writers favored by the reigning sovereign, as Maecenas had been for the greatest poets of Augustan Rome.⁵¹ This was a clever double compliment: the queen became Augustus and his wife became a literary celebrity. Apparently Elizabeth agreed that the manuscript was a treasure; she presented it to Christ Church, Oxford.⁵²

Further evidence of marital collaboration is the 1608 redaction of Yves Rouspeau's *Tratté de la préparation à la saincte Cène*. Aligned in their reformist piety and wider cultural ambitions, the Inglis-Kello "Treatise of Preparation to the Holy Supper" contains Kello's English translation of the French original and Inglis's calligraphy, as well as her dedication to Sir David Murray of Gorthy, a poet and gentleman of Prince Henry's Bedchamber.⁵³ Inglis emphasizes her husband's role as the translator and his intention to "benefit all those who truly love the Lord Jesus."⁵⁴ Her dedication, however, also showcases her own erudition.

Inglis's compliments to Murray constitute a Christian humanist sermon in miniature, studded with biblical and classical references. Her theme is the transitory nature of "temporal gifts," which may also become engines of divine wrath, as "the celerity of Asahel made him swiftly to run upon the spear of Abner," "Pompey's virtue caused the loss of his head," "Caesar's power was intolerable to Cassius," and "Cicero's eloquence was envied of Salustius and procured his death by the hand of Antonius." Only those "regenerate" and "sanctified" by their faith, who prioritize spiritual grace over everything else, can be considered truly happy. After citing Virgil and the book of Samuel, Inglis moves on to the canticles, averring, "I write this, Sir, to you, esteeming you in my heart most happy on whom God has multiplied many good gifts and graces not only of the body but likewise of the soul, so that truly it may be said to you which Our Savior says to the faithful soul, 'Behold, thou art fair, my love.'"[55] Inglis quickly shifts her language from affection to piety and patronage. Her experience of Murray's "godly disposition" and her obligation to him spurs her to "employ the travails of [her] pen upon this little Treatise." Like Isabella Andreini, Inglis secures the requisite propriety by reference to her husband. She reminds Murray that the treatise was "translated into English by my husband" and states that Kello intends to "dedicate it to [Murray] in sign of his thankfulness" as soon as he is able to have the text printed. In the meantime, Murray must accept this scribal version, which she is certain that he will do "in good part, as [he has] ever done anything proceeding from [her]."[56] The "Treatise" depended both upon Kello's translation and Inglis's connections, as well as her facility with the fulsome dedication.

A striking visual image of the Inglis-Kello partnership appears in the humanist George Craig's "Album of Friends" *(Album Amicorum)*, a yearbook of good wishes and *sententiae* that Craig collected from hundreds of European intellectuals during his travels in 1602–1605.[57] Esther Inglis is the only woman to be found within these 180 folios. While most of these learned "friends" jotted their name and a classical or scriptural passage with some formulaic regards, Inglis approached her page with characteristic bravura, using both French and English and displaying five different scribal hands with such precision that hers appears to be a lone printed contribution in a volume otherwise filled with scribbles.[58] Alongside his wife in this endeavor as in many others, Bartholomew Kello takes his place in Craig's collection. Kello's Latin greetings appear on the verso adjacent to his wife's work. These pages present an eloquent image of marital collaboration, but Inglis received pride of place: the recto.

Collaboration helped to establish Inglis's reputation, but as time went on she grew bolder in asserting her individual authorship. After about 1605, she approached her dedicatees directly.[59] By this time, her manuscripts were circulating in Scottish, English, and continental courts. She could now afford to experiment. Inglis's creativity appears with particular clarity in her prefatory material, which situated her as a confidant woman of letters. We have already witnessed the expanding range of personae that learned women of the later Renaissance employed, but Inglis represents a true master of self-presentation.

An image begins with a name. "Inglis" was a nom de plume: an anglicized version of her maiden name (Langlois), which signaled her paternal heritage.[60] Inglis underscored the point by including her father's Latin verses in her texts. Her role as a wife was equally important to her literary persona: she reproduced Kello's poems in her prefatory material and mentioned him in her dedications.[61] In short, for Inglis as for her predecessors and contemporaries, "domestic" positioning performed crucial cultural work.

Inglis's agility in shifting personae, however, reveals the new boundaries of the possible for learned women. Emblematic of this multidimensional approach are her transcriptions from the book of Ecclesiastes.[62] Like many of her creations, this work displays her calligraphic mastery and skilled embroidery on the velvet cover. But Inglis becomes a visible authorial presence on her ornate frontispiece, which asserts (as would all her others) that the volume was "written and illuminated by me, Esther Inglis." As Bianca Calabresi notes, Inglis's use of monumental epigraphy in her bylines—here and elsewhere—was a bold choice, given the contemporary association of Roman capitals with male royalty.[63]

Sixteen of Inglis's manuscripts go one step further in claiming authorship, by including a self-portrait holding a book and pen.[64] A familiar topos in women's writing and writing about women involved the connection between the needle and the pen—often mutually exclusive but sometimes mutually reinforcing.[65] Diana Robin has shown that Laura Cereta, for one, construed her "feminine" needlework and her "masculine" humanist writing as analogous.[66] Inglis performed a similar conceptual feat in her copybooks, some of which display her "feminine" needlework on the cover but show inside a self-portrait in which she wields a pen.[67]

Presenting herself as more than a mere copyist or needleworker, Inglis emphasizes her intellectual creativity. Her "Livre de l'Ecclesiaste" contains an elaborate frontispiece that mimics those found in printed volumes, upon which she inscribes a motto, "Spero, Vinco, Vivo" ("I hope, I triumph, I live").[68] Beyond situating herself as something like the work's publisher or printer, Inglis asserts her authorship through a self-portrait in which she stands at a desk, on the left side of which are a sheet of music and a lute. Her left hand rests on an open book, and her right hand is raised, having just dipped a pen into an inkwell. On the pages of the open book appears another of her authorial mottos: "The best be said of the Eternal One; of me, either criticism, or nothing" *(De l'Eternel le bien. De moi le mal, ou rien)*.[69] Scribal publication allowed Inglis to control every aspect of her image, and her use of the frontispiece portrait indicates her desire to mimic a common feature of the printed works of European intellectuals, male and female. The works of Christine de Pizan, Cassandra Fedele, and Isabella Andreini, to name only a few, displayed the author's portrait.

Inglis's sense of herself as a writer and intellectual becomes even more apparent in her decision to include in nearly all of her manuscripts lengthy dedications of the sort found in elite printed texts. These letters demonstrate her familiarity with high epistolary convention, including the gendered humility trope. Inglis acknowledged that sending her work to patrons might seem to confront notions of feminine propriety, but she nonetheless found ways to justify her authorship. One of her principal strategies was to claim that she desired only to immortalize her recipients' virtues and thereby put her pen to pious use. This technique appears in her dedicatory letters to male and female patrons alike.

In dedicating her "Livre de l'Ecclesiaste" to Anthony Bacon, Inglis termed him "most honorable, learned and virtuous."[70] As her epithets announced, the ensuing letter is a disquisition on erudition in the service of morality—a commonplace in humanist writing that I have termed "learned virtue." This letter to Bacon emblematizes Inglis's desire to associate herself with learned virtue as its scribe. A triumph of a lettered clientage, characteristic of the sophistication that Inglis displayed in soliciting patrons throughout Europe, the letter rewards close examination.

Inglis uses a gendered humility trope throughout, characterizing herself as a "simple lady" *(une simple Dame)* and her work as a "small little book" *(petit levret)*—a label that is both a grammatical privative and a literal reference the volume's miniature dimensions. Diana Robin has demonstrated that European women intellectuals, paradigmatically Cassandra Fedele, accommodated contemporary notions of feminine modesty by using a language of detraction when referring to themselves. As Robin cautions, however, this habitual "ef-facement" also contained a measure of irony.[71] Above all, the gendered humility trope, far from revealing "sincere" self-deprecation, signaled a mastery of the rhetorical game—a prerequisite for participation in literary exchange. Inglis accomplishes this by beginning her letter in standard humanist fashion, situating her dedicatee as the heir apparent of ancient excellence in learning and piety.

Since "the wise men of times past held it to be indisputably true that the virtue dwelling in the hearts of the honorable evokes an admiration that utterly ravishes the spirits of lesser folk, such that they believe the virtuous to rank with the gods," Anthony Bacon will not find it strange that Inglis, who has heard for so long about his manifold excellence, should desire to offer him a book, "having nothing more suitable to give him, who are so wise and learned." She claims, "[My work is] nothing other than a testament to the desire that I harbor for using my pen to make your famous virtues more manifest."[72] Inglis used the same approach in her dedicating a volume of moral verses to Lord Hayes in 1606.[73] So, too, Inglis took the same stance when approaching women patrons. Presenting a miniature copybook to Lady Erskine of Dirleton in 1606, Inglis disavowed any intention to overstep "the limits of shamefastness (wherewith [her] sex is commonly adorned)" by offering what she calls "this small work of my pen and pencil." And she was careful to note that she had offered Erskine's husband a volume the previous year.[74] Having dispensed with humility and propriety, however, she praised Erskine, as she did Bacon, as a pinnacle of "heroic" learned virtue.[75] In the same year, Inglis followed the pattern in dedicating another compendium of moral maxims to the Countess of Bedford. In this dedication, Inglis came closer to the celebratory feminism of Cassandra Fedele, expatiating on her recipient's complete mastery of music and literature.[76]

Inglis made good use of humility. Just as often, however, she minimized it. We might explain its relative absence in the letters to Lady Erskine and the Countess of Bedford as a result of her greater comfort in writing to women. Even when writing to Queen Elizabeth, she wore the modesty cloak lightly.[77] But Inglis could also present herself to male patrons in a triumphal manner, as, for instance, in her 1599 dedicatory epistle to the Protestant hero Maurice of Nassau. Perhaps she felt that their shared reformist commitment and the nature of her text (a collection of psalms) provided a sufficiently pious context for this approach. Yet Inglis far exceeded the syntax of piety by comparing her book to the *Iliad* and asserting that, "having almost immodestly chased away feminine fearfulness and taken on the spirit of a queen of the Amazons," she now "boldly turned to [her] Alexander."[78]

Inglis's Amazonian boldness intensified by 1624, when she dedicated her virtuoso reimagination of Georgette de Montenay's *Emblemes, ou devises Chrestiennes* to Prince Charles of England.[79] In this case, the trope of feminine timidity served as a pretext for deploying a barrage of classical references that linked Inglis analogically to a pantheon of ancient orators and poets. She compares her "timorousness" to that of "Demosthenes, being to speak before Philip, King of Macedon" and "Theophrastus before the Areopagites at Athens" and asks that Charles show her the same love and respect that Philip gave to Aristotle, Alexander to Pindar, Scipio Africanus to Ennius, and Artaxerxes to Hippocrates.[80] Even apart from its dramatic gender shift (feminine modesty is here reinscribed as a Greek orator's nerves), this oration on the support that royal figures owed to intellectuals borders on impudence. Retreating somewhat, Inglis disavows any intention to compare herself "with such famous men"—but she then proceeds to claim kinship instead with Biblical heroines such as Deborah and Judith.[81] What undergirded this audacity, which Inglis elsewhere termed her "more than feminine boldness"?[82] At the age of fifty-three, and as a longtime recipient of royal patronage, perhaps Inglis felt that she could afford to take some risks. What is certain, however, is that she could rely upon her reputation a cultural authority: scholarly celebrities validated her membership in their rarified circles.

The hallmark of an early modern intellectual was a society of mutual congratulation. As with her illustrious predecessors and contemporaries, Inglis used prefatory encomia to situate herself as an authority within her milieu. In contrast to many of her English predecessors, who partially veiled their identity through the use of initials, Inglis adopted an Italian mode of emphatic self-presentation. Following fifteenth-century humanists such as Fedele and Cereta, who published their letterbooks, and contemporary celebrities such as Isabella Andreini, who included laudatory poems from illustrious men in all of her published volumes, Inglis "owned" her works—perhaps even more so, since scribal publication allowed her to control every aspect of production. In Inglis's hands, the demotic form of the copybook became indistinguishable from an elite text, and she followed the continental pattern of self-authorization by weight of testimonials.

Dorothy Judd Jackson observed long ago that Inglis won the admiration of learned men such as Andrew Melville (1545–1622, principal of the University of Glasgow and St. Andrew's), John Johnston (ca. 1568–1611, professor at St. Andrew's), Robert Rollock (principal of St. Andrew's), and Bishop Joseph Hall (dean of Worchester), all of whom praised Inglis not just for her manual skills but for her status as an intellectual.[83] Recent studies of Inglis often cite these laudatory verses, but the importance of her admirers and the themes of their commendations require further analysis. For these learned men, Inglis was no mere copyist but rather a worthy Christian humanist of their own stamp.

Melville and Johnston were accomplished humanists. Melville played a leading role in the entrenchment of Presbyterianism in Scotland and was a central figure in the Scottish Renaissance, shifting the university curriculum toward a broad program of study in Greek, Latin, and Hebrew.[84] Johnston, Melville's younger colleague at St. Andrew's, wrote skillful Greek epigrams.[85] These two figures formed a miniature community of letters, which they instantiated in their collaborative publication, *Inscriptiones Historicae Regum Scotorum* (1602).[86]

Small wonder, then, that Inglis reproduced their congratulatory verses in thirteen of her manuscripts. In one instance, Melville praises Inglis's dual role as a thinker and artist, linking her intellect *(mens)* to her artistic skill *(manus)*. In intricate wordplay, he disavows the ability to "depict" *(pingere)* her excellence, either cognitively or manually.[87] In a second epigram, he emphasizes the inseparability of intellectual acuity and artistic invention in Inglis's work: "Your mind and that hand of yours have painted all of this: that which nature and art have portrayed, but also that which neither nature nor art have ever before depicted."[88] Melville ultimately points to Inglis's spiritual authority, her ability to manifest divine truth. Her texts become, in his formulation, "pious calligraphy" and "living emblems, redolent of heaven."[89] Echoing Melville, Johnston celebrates Inglis's remarkable ingenuity and invention, which (he claims) God had only bestowed on one other "author": Nature.[90] "Nature would grieve at being bested by a mortal's hand," he explains, "if she did not know that these are the rare gifts of the Great God."[91]

Melville and Johnston celebrate Inglis in the same terms that they use to praise each other. Johnston includes Latin encomia from Melville in his best-known work, the *Heroes ex omni historia Scotica lectissimi* (1602). Much as both men term Inglis an "intellectual artist" who fused *manus* and *mens*, Melville praises Johnston's poems for their reconciliation of apparent opposites, Mars and Pallas (war and wisdom): "Mars without Athena is death; Minerva without Mars is decay. / Mars lives well in the company of Athena; in the company of Mars, Minerva flourishes."[92] Melville also returns to the artistic metaphor that characterizes his compliments to Inglis, stating that as often as the learned and pious Scottish hero is "painted" *(pingitur)* by Johnston, so often does Johnston "depict" himself in those portraits ("te *pingis* in illis"). Johnston, Melville claims, is "in every picture" as "the first and best archetype" of the hero.[93] Praise of Esther Inglis by Melville and Johnston takes on a far deeper resonance, then, in light of the fact that they present her, like themselves, as an "intellectual artist."

Inglis used this recognition to support her larger project: the transmission of Christian humanist texts from her native France to cultural leaders in her adoptive Britain. In particular, she strove to disseminate the *Quatrains* (moral verses) of Guy du Faur de Pibrac, a syncretic work characteristic of the late humanist enterprise. At least thirteen of her manuscripts derive from this text.[94] Pibrac, a diplomat, magistrate, and linguist skilled in Latin, Greek, Hebrew, and law, embedded in these verses a philosophy of moderation both reminiscent of Erasmus and emblematic of his own commitments. Pibrac had been Charles IX's ambassador to the Council of Trent, where he urged the need for reformation within the church as a whole and called for the independence of the Gallican Church. Pibrac was also an ardent partisan of the Duc d'Anjou (Henri III) and used his posts as chancellor of the queen, Marguerite de Valois (Queen of Navarre), president of the Parlement of Paris (1577), and chancellor to Henri himself (1582–1584) as platforms for urging the reconciliation of Catholics and Protestants. A prominent member of the Académie du Palais as well, Pibrac shifted the focus of this musical society in the direction of philosophy and rhetoric.[95] Pibrac was, in short, a sterling example of the pious benefits of vast erudition. His *Quatrains*, 126 strophes of moral philosophy published continuously from 1574 through the end of the seventeenth century, posited (within the convention of a father's advice to his son) the urgent need for study, piety and moderation in all things. The *Quatrains* are often brushed aside as "moralizing," which is one reason that Inglis's participation in higher levels of intellectual endeavor has not been recognized.[96] At the least, these verses should be characterized as "classicizing," as they are filled with references to ancient philosophers; better still, they should be understood as a repository of "Christian Stoicism."[97]

Inglis used the *Quatrains* to bridge the French and British communities of knowledge. She dedicated her redactions of this text to men of account in England and Scotland. Inglis sped these verses to politicians such as Robert Cecil, Earl of Salisbury; Robert Kerr, Earl of Somerset (a favorite of James I at the time of her dedication); and Prince Charles (later Charles I), to whom she also dedicated her presentation copy of Georgette de Montenay's *Emblemes Chrestiennes,* another landmark text of learned French piety.[98] Inglis also bestowed the *Quatrains* upon divines, including Joseph Hall and Walter Balcanquall (later Dean of Rochester). And she gave them to literary men whom she termed her "particular friends," including Sir David Murray of Gorthy. At the time of this presentation to Murray (1614), Inglis termed him her "Maecenas," hinting that he had continued to offer the kind of support that she indicated in her 1608 dedication of the "Treatise of Preparation."[99] His assistance seems to have continued after 1614, as she placed Murray last in the roll call of British noblemen in her 1624 "Emblemes"—despite the fact that he was only a knight.[100] All of which suggests that Murray had been helpful in furthering her pious project.

By the end of her life, Esther Inglis held a place in the world of courtly literary culture analogous to Christine de Pizan's. Like Christine, moreover, Inglis was determined to secure her son's future, using her own celebrity as leverage. The goal that Inglis had in view for her son, Samuel, was a fellowship to Oxford or Cambridge, which would enable him to take a degree. In 1620 Inglis wrote to James I, who had already accepted her miniature version of the psalms of David in 1615.[101] In her letter, she explains "As Daedalus was not able to free himself of his imprisonment . . . but by the help of wings made of pens and wax, even so my son is not able to effectuate his affection but by the wings of your Majesty's letter composed by pen and wax through the which he may have his flight happily to some fellowship either in Cambridge or Oxford."[102] This appeal, like Christine de Pizan's, succeeded. Samuel Kello took his degree in theology at Oxford.

In sum, Esther Inglis deserves more capacious labels than "calligrapher" and "copyist." The better alternatives are "writer" and "intellectual," a point that the eighteenth-century biographer, George Ballard, suggested in the long section concerning Inglis in his *Memoirs of Several Ladies of Great Britain* (1752). Ballard's biography focuses upon her calligraphy, which he deemed "almost incredible" for its precision and variety. Inglis's talent and the breadth of her work justified his decision to place her alongside the dozens of British women "celebrated for their writings or skill in the learned languages, arts and sciences."[103] Modern scholars may go further than the anglophilic Ballard. Inglis belonged to a transnational elite of learned women, which other British women, working as artist-intellectuals, joined during the seventeenth century.

The Household Salon of Mary Beale

"I give and bequeath," attested the Cambridge-trained Puritan pastor and amateur painter John Cradock in the mid-1650s, "all my lands, as also all my money, books, household stuff, cattle and whatsoever other worldly goods God of his goodness has bestowed upon me unto my dear and sweet children John Cradocke my son, and Mary Cradocke my daughter to be equally divided betwixt them."[104] While the daughter, Mary, received half of her father's library, she would become the true "heir" of his intellectual and artistic patrimony.

Mary Beale was the most successful female artist in England, and among the most prolific. Her father's will had proudly asserted his own status as "Bachelor of Divinity"; painting was his hobby. The inverse was true of his daughter: her status derived from her successful career as a portraitist, while authorship was her avocation. Although Beale's principal composition, the treatise "On Friendship," remains in manuscript, she was nonetheless publicly heralded by learned divines as their friend and collaborator.

Little is known concerning Mary Beale's early education in art and letters. It is probable, however, that she benefited at least in part from her father's instruction. The Cradock family boasted two generations of university men and preachers by the time Mary was born.[105] Her grandfather, Richard, entered Clare Hall, Cambridge in 1580, and took his master of arts in 1588. He was ordained in 1593 and became curate at Newark-on-Trent. Favoring godly endogamy, Richard Cradock married two of his three daughters to Puritan divines and had his son, John (Mary Beale's father), raised by his brother Nathaniel, who conveniently lived in Cambridge.

John Cradock first attended Mr. Rodeknight's school in the town and later joined his cousins at Caius College in 1612, where he took a master of arts degree (1619). Proceeding to a bachelor's of divinity thereafter, he was ordained in 1628 and presented to the living of Rickinghall Superior, Suffolk. After the death of his father, he was transferred to Barrow, Suffolk. John Cradock's parliamentarian sympathies garnered him an appointment as elder of the Hundred of Thringoe (1645). However, his wife Dorothy died after giving birth to his son in 1643, leaving John in charge of not only an infant but his ten-year-old daughter, Mary.

By the mid-seventeenth century, girls' schools were available: contemporary accounts of women writers, as well as the writers themselves, sometimes note time spent at such institutions. The poet Katharine Philips, for instance, attended a school for girls run by a Mrs. Salmon in Hackney.[106] However, Mary Beale made no reference to her attending school, and neither did her family or friends. It seems most likely that her father served as her teacher in letters, because her treatise (to be discussed more particularly in the following chapter) demonstrates a thorough knowledge of classical moral philosophy (at least in translation), in addition to contemporary latitudinarian ("natural") religion and the debate on women.

John Cradock probably also provided his daughter's initial training in art. He himself had joined the Painter-Stainers' Company in 1648, after having submitted a still life of fruit. He also seems to have been a painter of miniatures (limner), as he makes a bequest of "all [his] empastered rounds" to his nephew in his will.[107] After her marriage, Mary may have received some instruction from Thomas Flatman, a poet, miniaturist, and member of the Royal Society, who was great friend of Mary and her husband. Flatman taught Mary's son Charles limning, and some of his letters refer to Mary Beale as his "scholar."[108]

At the very least, John Cradock helped to forge important connections for his daughter among his own intellectual and artistic colleagues in the thriving center of Bury St. Edmunds.[109] Mary was very well educated by 1651, when Charles Beale emerged as her suitor. He came from a Puritan family that had enjoyed several generations of reasonable success in the London courts and civil service. It was in a classicizing rather than moralizing mode, however, that Charles sent a love letter and poem to his nineteen-year-old sweetheart, "the Quintessence of all Goodness."[110] Worried that she might see only the infelicities in his composition, he begins by begging "pardon in the audacity of [his] now presumptuous attempt, hoping that [her] transcendent virtue will be pleased to overlook those many slips which [his] poor Muse (out of an ambitious honor to speak something concerning [Mary's] absolute perfections) has committed."[111] He assures her that the poem is "one of the first pieces of poetry which ever [he] composed." He continues, "Yet certainly your own unparalleled beauty is a theme able to infuse life into the dullest piece of earth and make it speak forth your praises in far and deep-fetched strains of Rhetoric."[112] Charles Beale's self-effacement, while certainly a trope for early modern authors, nonetheless suggests a real concern with his recipient's ability to recognize good (or bad) writing and to decode apt (or incongruous) metaphors.

The poem is a tribute to Mary's beauty, but it is also a compliment to her learning. His rhetorical figures consist entirely of literary and even scientific metaphor. He wishes that he could summon "some aromatic strain of pure / Emphatic Eloquence" to describe her excellence. But Mary is more perfect than his creative capacity could possibly summarize:

> Nature when she did first intend
> You to create, propos'd her end
> Which was that in one model she
> Might frame the just Epitome
> Of beauty, virtue and true wit
> For to adorn her Cabinet.

Here Charles not only reminds us of the tripartite mode of praise (for beauty, virtue, and learning) used by Isabella Andreini's encomiasts, but his reference to the "cabinet" (that is, cabinet of curiosities) also evokes the protomuseum culture that had begun to take a central place in the social and academic landscape during seventeenth century.[113] Charles was by this point already a student of chemistry, among his other pursuits, and he would become an active member of the Royal Society. Adding artistic metaphor, he goes on to write that Mary constitutes Nature's "best art's Master Piece."[114]

This elaborate poetic compliment had the desired effect. The couple married on 8 March 1652, a month before her father died. By 1655/56, the Beales had moved to London, where they and their two sons, Bartholomew and Charles, would spend the majority of their working lives.

The Beale household fits a pattern common to artistic families of the Italian Renaissance: it was a workshop where family members (including servants) contributed to the success of the master painter and breadwinner. In this case, however, it was the matriarch who played this dominant role. While Charles Beale's pigment sales, rents, and financial investments were an important source of revenue, they provided only about 30 percent of the Beales' budget; Mary's portrait commissions brought in the majority of their annual income.[115] As his notebooks indicate, Charles Beale directed much energy to putting his chemical expertise to use in mixing paints and canvas treatments. Both sons spent their childhoods learning draftsmanship and helping in the more pedestrian aspects of artistic production, including painting drapery and the stone cartouches for head-and-shoulder portraits. While Bartholomew would later take up a career in medicine, Charles continued to help his mother and eventually began an independent career as a miniaturist and draftsman.[116] Unlike the Italian model, however, this English workshop also included two female apprentices, Keaty Trioche and Sarah Curtis, who were unrelated to the Beales.[117]

There were few recognized women artist-intellectuals in Restoration England, but Mary Beale had many predecessors in Italy. Chief among them were the Cremonese portraitist Sofonisba Anguissola (1532–1625) and the Bolognese virtuosa Lavinia Fontana (1552–1614). Both were prolific in a variety of artistic genres and both presented themselves as women of intelligence. Anguissola, like her authorial counterparts, enjoyed a thorough classical education at the behest of her father, Amilcare, who had all six of his daughters, as well as his son, trained in the liberal arts, music, and painting.[118] Sofonisba, of all his children, exhibited the most talent in all fields and used her commissions to bolster her family's precarious finances. A student of Michelangelo through her father's auspices, Anguissola fashioned herself very much in Michelangelo's mold, as both an artist and an intellectual. In one of Anguissola's paintings, *The Chess Game*, or *Anguissola Sisters Playing Chess* (1555), she presented three of her sisters and their nurse not holding traditional "feminine" props, such as needlework, prayer books, or pets, but playing an intellectual game. Anguissola's self-portraits emphasized her own diverse talents. She depicted herself holding the painter's tools, playing the clavichord, and holding medallions and books with Latin inscriptions. Her earliest securely dated self-portrait (1554, Vienna, Kunsthistoriches Museum) depicts the artist holding a book open to a page that reads, in Latin, "Sophonisba Anguissola, a maiden, painted this image of herself" *(Sophonisba Anguissola virgo seipsam fecit)*. Through these devices, Anguissola underscored her mastery of both the visual and the liberal arts.

Contemporary observers collaborated in Anguissola's dual mode of self-presentation. Francesco Agostino della Chiesa praised Anguissola and her sister Laura as pinnacles of technical skill and inventiveness in the field of art, but he made this point as well: "Sofonisba has not only created the rarest and most beautiful images with her brush, but has also written several things with her pen—for she was also very learned—that have been much praised and admired by men of letters."[119]

A Spaniard by birth and an émigré to northern Italy, Pietro Paolo di Ribera was fascinated with Sofonisba as a northern Italian woman who had secured a well-paid post as court portraitist to the Spanish crown. Anguissola held for Ribera the hermeneutic centrality that Marinella possessed for Cristofano Bronzini. She received the longest treatment (four pages) in his collection of 845 illustrious women, and Ribera gave her pride of place at the end of his text, mentioning her as substantiation for his argument that contemporary women exhibit every form of excellence. While most of his biographies divide women into their field specialties, Ribera presents Anguissola as a virtuosa "musician, author and, above all, painter."[120]

Another important precursor for Beale was Lavinia Fontana, the daughter and apprentice of the painter Prospero Fontana (ca. 1508–1596).[121] Fontana's early training in drawing and painting was not geared toward a professional career but represented one aspect of a broad education intended to make her a "gentlewoman." As art historian Caroline Murphy has demonstrated, Prospero resented the humble status of the painter in Bologna—a city that, unlike Florence, still included painters in the same artisanal guild with saddlers and sword makers. An important component of Prospero's ambitious social strategy was raising his daughter as if she were a noblewoman. Until Lavinia reached her midteens, she learned drawing and painting as "accomplishments," with more emphasis being placed upon music and composing elegant letters. Once Prospero's illness and dwindling resources presented obstacles to his work that he could no longer surmount alone, however, he began to train his only child seriously in the painter's craft and to promote her artistic career. In 1577, however, prior to securing Lavinia's first serious commissions, he also assured his daughter's acceptability to patrons by arranging her marriage to Gian Paolo Zappi, a minor nobleman from Imola.

Like Anguissola, Fontana styled herself as an intellectual. Her first important commissions were portraits of leading male figures in the arts and sciences. Throughout her career, moreover, Lavinia often signed her paintings in Latin. Most importantly, her self-portraits emphasize accomplishments beyond artistic skill. She depicted herself as a scholar, writing in her study and surrounded by antiquities (*Self-Portrait in the Studiolo*, 1579). And she also portrayed herself at the keyboard—a setting in which women artists often represented themselves, because it evoked St. Cecilia (whose iconography included the "virginals," suggesting self-mastery with regard to the body and, by association, chastity) and because musical skill signified mental acuity.[122]

The Venetian painter Marietta Robusti, called "La Tintoretta" by her contemporaries for the way in which her works were indistinguishable from those of her father, Jacopo Tintoretto, underscores these same biographical and self-representational elements. Very little of her oeuvre has survived (or at least has been attributed to her), but she was another painter's daughter who benefited from her father's cultural ambitions. Like Prospero Fontana, Tintoretto nearly bankrupted himself in staging literary and musical evenings for the Venetian cultural elite at which his daughter performed on the keyboard and entertained the audience with her "lively wit." Only one securely attributed self-portrait remains, but it is telling that she depicted herself in this instance at the keyboard.

While we cannot with any certainty say that Robusti styled herself as an intellectual in the way that Anguissola, Fontana, and Beale did, Robusti's principal encomiast, Carlo Ridolfi (a Venetian humanist and biographer of her father), used her excellence in multiple fields as a point of departure for his argument about the nobility of the female sex. Ridolfi is often characterized as the "Venetian Vasari," for his *Lives of the Venetian Painters* (1648).[123] And his literary acumen appears, in the case of Marietta Robusti, in the way he positions her biography within the *querelle des femmes*. "Gossiping tongues shoot off arrows just as they wish," he begins. "They compose satires and invectives against the female sex, designating as [women's] highest achievements the use of the needle, spindle and distaff, as well as painting their faces." He points the reader instead to the many texts that tout the excellence of "Cornelia, Hortensia and of Lucrezia Marinella, who is still living." This list of accomplished women aptly introduces the life of "la Tintoretta," in which she appears as her father's heir not only in artistic talent but also in music and in liveliness of wit.[124] By the time Ridolfi was writing, true excellence in the Italian context was understood to be multidimensional, and any mastery on the part of a woman provided an entree into a larger argument for female capability.

Mary Beale's status as an interdisciplinary cultural contributor mirrored these Italian cases. So did her household salon. Like Tintoretto and Prospero Fontana, the Beales established a stellar salon, which convened in their Hampshire country house and fashionable Pall Mall home in London. The Beale circle included a wide range of professionals, lawyers, churchmen, civil servants, and writers. The Beales' more famous friends were leading Anglican ministers, such as Archbishop John Tillotson and Edward Stillingfleet. The membership of Charles Beale in the Royal Society served as one basis for his friendship with the mathematician and preacher John Wilkins (another friend of Tillotson), as well as Thomas Sprat, publisher of the Royal Society's first history (1667), who arranged the marriage (1661) between Charles's cousin Alice and the poet Samuel Woodford.

Charles Beale's notebooks reveal that he and his wife were connected to other members of London's educated elite. Watchful of their always precarious finances, Charles recorded each of the paintings that Mary completed and the fees she received. Indicative of true friendship, then, were those instances in which Mary Beale refused payment. Charles makes a note in his 1681 notebook, for instance, of the "pictures begun by [his] Dearest Heart which were done for friends and upon Account of Kindness and not profit."[125] These friends included Mr. Matthus, an apothecary; Dr. Edward Stillingfleet, dean of St. Paul's; the historian Gilbert Burnet; Dr. Patrick, dean of Peterborough College; and the poet and artist Thomas Flatman.

Of all the Beales' friends, Samuel Woodford seems to have been the closest. He often assisted them financially when their coffers ran dry. For their part, the Beales supported and housed him during his extended period of mourning after the death of his wife—support that Woodford amply records in his manuscript diary.[126] Woodford was also the most vocal admirer of Mary Beale's talent and erudition. One of her striking self-portraits represented Beale as the Greek goddess of warfare and wisdom, Pallas (Athena). Woodford duly underscored her excellence in both artistic and literary terms by commemorating this painting with a poem "to Belisa, the Excellent Mrs. Mary Beal." He begins triumphantly:

> Such would the learned Pallas choose to be,
> With all the Charms of Nature and of Art,
> Tho she had neither Shield nor Dart:
> For if the mighty Pallas were like Thee,
> Without those, she to Conquer, need but come, and see.[127]

Much as Puteanus found the medal of Isabella Andreini/Pallas-Athena a convenient pretext for reflecting upon the multiplicity of virtues that his friend exemplified, Woodford used Beale's self-portrait as the basis for praising her beauty, wisdom, and artistic skill.

In a marginal note of his *Paraphrase upon the Psalms of David*, Woodford also suggests the salon quality of Mary Beale's household. "We had frequently about this time at my Cousin Beale's," he observed, "the most agreeable conversation of the town, where & at Gresham College (the place where the Royal Society weekly met) I became acquainted with three persons who are now my best and most cordial friends."[128] Although Mary Beale's part in the conversations Woodford found so agreeable is only hinted, he goes on to credit her among other literary colleagues with prompting him to revise and expand the *Paraphrase*. He also praises her, alongside Lord Bacon, Sir Henry Wotton, and Bishop Hall, for having "done excellently particular Psalms" herself.[129]

Putting Beale above the other contributors to his volume, however, Woodford offers an extended comment on "that absolutely complete Gentlewoman": "I very hardly obtained [her leave] to honour this Volume of mine with two or three Versions, long since done by her, the truly Virtuous Mistress Mary Beale, amongst whose least accomplishments it is, that she has made Painting and Poesie, which in the Fancies of others had only before a kind of likeness, in her own to be really the same."[130] Writers since Horace had delighted in comparing the poetic and visual arts, but Woodford makes the striking claim here that his friend should be understood as a perfect fusion of both kinds of creative genius.

Aware that praising a woman by name might arouse suspicion, Woodford situates his compliments within his ties of friendship and kinship to Mary and her husband. Woodford hopes that his reader "will pardon this public acknowledgment which [he makes] to so deserving a person [Mary Beale], when I shall tell him that while as a Friend and one of the Family,

I had the convenience of a private and most delightful retirement in the company of her worthy Husband and herself, I both began and perfected this *Paraphrase*."[131] Domestic reference remained a useful means to indicate "proper" friendships between men and women.

Woodford's language of friendship and kinship reveals a certain continuity with humanist exchange. We have witnessed women humanists basing their literary exchange with men upon the mutual bonds of obligation inherent in both friendship and kinship. This rhetorical mode, however, was by no means peculiar to women. As Diana Robin has shown, the language of male friendship not only invoked the Ciceronian conception of an equal relationship between men but also served as a euphemism to occlude the hierarchical politics of patronage—a system that was itself closely based upon the structure of the ancient Roman family.[132]

By the mid-1600s, when Woodford was writing, however, "friendship" also encompassed a new brand of spirituality in England termed "latitudinarianism." A blend of science, ethics, and morality, latitudinarianism decried sectarian strife and attempted to encapsulate the teachings of Christianity, as well as classical moral philosophy, in a few uniting rubrics that would ensure a peaceable union within a reconceptualized universal church. Proponents of this protoenlightenment philosophy—such as Mary Beale's friends Archbishop John Tillotson, Edward Stillingfleet, and Jeremy Taylor (Beale's principal model for her own philosophical work)—often used "friendship" as a synecdoche for socioreligious union more broadly. A characteristic tactic of latitudinarian discourse was to interweave the Ciceronian notion that the principal obligation of friends is to encourage each other by example and by argument toward wisdom and "virtue," with the Christian notion that "virtue" specifically opened the heart to God's grace. This is precisely the strategy in Jeremy Taylor's *Discourse on the Nature, Offices and Measures of Friendship* (1657), which indeed emblematizes latitudinarian beliefs on the importance of friendship. As Tabitha Barber has noted, however, while Mary Beale followed latitudinarians like Taylor in a general way, her own treatise "On Friendship" was far from derivative. As we will see in the next chapter, Beale departs from her models in revising the possibilities and boundaries of "friendship" between men and women.[133]

Although Beale enjoyed the friendship of Archbishop John Tillotson, a prominent figure in the ecclesiastical and literary world, she nonetheless dedicated her treatise to his wife, Elizabeth. We should be wary of relegating this work, even though it is dedicated to another woman and remains in manuscript, to any "private" or lesser milieu than that of a published treatise dedicated to a man. Elizabeth Tillotson assumes the important role in Beale's world that the learned patronesses of the northern Italian courts had played for Cassandra Fedele, among others.

Daughter of Peter French (doctor of divinity at Christ Church, Oxford) and Robina Cromwell (Oliver Cromwell's sister), and later wife of the archbishop of Canterbury, Elizabeth Tillotson's natal and marital pedigree connected her to the most powerful political and intellectual figures in seventeenth-century England. It seems suggestive that her father's final will (1655) names her mother, Robina, sole executor and charges her with the upbringing all the children; should she die before their son, Robert, reaches his majority (at twenty-one), however, the education of Elizabeth, as well as her sister and brother, should be undertaken by three of his "very good friends," all of whom happened to be prebendaries of Christ Church.[134] French's choice of university men for the education not only of his son but also his daughters suggests that he (like many other seventeenth-century academics) expected his daughters to receive substantive training in addition to the hefty dowries that he also bequeathed to them.

Another tantalizing hint of Tillotson's participation in the world of "lettered piety," and especially her tendency to favor women in this world, appears in her own will (1702). After distributing her various expensive Bibles to her grandsons, George and John Chadwick, she bequeaths the bulk of her husband's literary estate, "all the volumes of [her] late husband's sermons bound in Red Turkey Leather and the Rule of Faith with the Volume in Folio," to her granddaughter.[135] In addition, Tillotson herself oversaw the publication of a few of her husband's sermons, which she sold to Dr. Ralph Barker (one of her executors) for the large sum of 2,500 guineas. The authority of this text, *Of Sincerity and Constancy in the Faith: In Several Sermons by the Most Reverend Dr. John Tillotson, Published from the Originals by Ralph Barker, D.D. Chaplain to His Grace* (London: Richard Chiswell, 1695), derived largely from Barker's preface to the reader. Yet Elizabeth Tillotson also played an important textual role as "the Author's Relict" in dedicating the sermons to King William. Barker stresses in his preface that he is publishing the "Genuine Works of that Great Man," and Elizabeth Tillotson's place on the frontispiece as transmitter of the material serves as evidence that the text is genuine.

Writing, then, to a woman who moved within the academic, religious, and literary elite, Mary Beale had in Elizabeth Tillotson an ideal recipient for her treatise. Beale's dedicatory epistle, dated 9 March 1666, combines learning, religion, and literary polish with a self-reflexive use of artistic metaphor. Much as Samuel Woodford praised Beale as a true embodiment of Poetry and Art, so Beale herself plays upon the connection between writing and painting in her letter to her "dear friend." Beale terms her treatise "[her] very imperfect draft after that immortal Beauty Friendship," which she might be ashamed to present if she did not realize that "we often esteem a Picture done by a very unskillful hand out of that great affection we may have for the person whom it was design'd to represent." Continuing the metaphor, she speculates that Tillotson may "call these [Beale's] conceptions rather the Portraiture of [Beale's] own inabilities," but she hopes that her recipient will nonetheless accept the gift as an "image" of a cherished subject.[136] Beale's intricate wordplay is at once a deft use of the humility trope and a subtle claim that the world of rhetorical "colors" is as much her province as the paints on her canvases.

For all the charm and even playfulness of her dedication, the treatise itself is a work of serious scholarship. Beale marshaled an impressive array of textual sources. Although she wrote in English, she possessed a thorough knowledge of ancient sources, such as Aristotle, Plutarch, and Cicero (at least in translation), as well as of the Bible and the patristic commentators, and a great facility with expository prose. Beale owed a debt to Jeremy Taylor, but she engaged with these sources herself, displaying her cultural literacy and authorial ambition.

Here is a learned woman from the least exalted background that we have yet surveyed: the daughter of an obscure country parson with little property and less status. John Cradock's bachelor's degree, parsonage, and journeyman rank at the Painter-Stainers' company constituted the sum total of his cultural assets. While Mary and Charles Beale did not come from complete obscurity to build a salon of "learned virtue" in quite the same way Isabella and Francesco Andreini had done, they nonetheless built much from very little.

Mary's portrait commissions and Charles's sale of his more successful chemical recipes provided a tenuous financial foundation for their own household salon. Money worries aside, however, Mary's patrons and Charles's connections to the Royal Society brought the couple a group of illustrious friends with whom to share ideas. Mary's elegant treatise demonstrates the stimulating effects of such associations. From the perspective of the modern scholar, it is a shame that she chose not to print this composition. Yet Beale herself probably viewed publication as a violation of friendship's sacred intimacy, just as she would not accept fees for portraits that she executed, in her husband's phrase, "on account of friendship."

Mary More

Around 1680 a woman named Mary More (d. ca. 1716) engaged an Oxford don named Robert Whitehall in a manuscript reprise of the debate on women that had been raging in European literary society for three centuries. More had already achieved some renown as a portraitist and would, by 1685, take on her own apprentices.[137] She introduced herself to Whitehall by sending him her copy of a portrait of Oliver Cromwell that she misidentified as a portrait of Sir Thomas More—or perhaps that she presented in that guise to suggest a family connection to England's greatest humanist. Thereafter, the two began what would appear to be a fraught and acrimonious exchange of poetry and treatises on the nature of womankind and especially women's "rights" in marriage. As Margaret Ezell has noted, however, More's treatise ("The Woman's Right, or Her Power in a Greater Equality to Her Husband Proved than is Allowed or Practised in England"), Whitehall's rebuttal ("The Woman's Right Proved False"), and their collected poems appear in a formal manuscript miscellany, intended for circulation, that was probably composed at the behest of Whitehall himself.[138] Their debates, then, resembled a game between friends—or at least friendly enemies.

Mary More's natal family and her education remain obscure. In terms of her adult family life, we know that she was married twice, first to a Mr. Waller (first name unknown) and second to a Mr. Francis More. She had a daughter, Elizabeth Waller, to whom she dedicated "The Woman's Right." Her son Richard Waller was the secretary for the Royal Society of London from 1687 to 1709.[139] His correspondence reveals some excellent connections that his mother had made among London's cultural elite, including Royal Society members Hans Sloane and Robert Hooke.[140]

Mary More, as a painter-author with substantial academic cachet, presents an analogous case to that of Mary Beale. More also points to a continuing tradition of learned women who put their classical learning in the service of reevaluating womankind as a category. More received an education akin to that which the More-Roper women enjoyed in the previous century and that which Anne Petty undertook in her own day. She does not specify the source of her education, nor have any other documents been found that provide substantive information. In her treatise, however, she contends that it is the responsibility of "parents" to "bring up their daughters learned."[141] This comment suggests that she had been educated at home and her use of the plural (parents) may indicate that both her father and mother supervised her studies. In any case, More was able to confound Whitehall with her exposition of what she considered to be intentional mistranslations by men who sought to prove women inferior. More aimed to set the record straight. Much as Isotta Nogarola deployed philology against Genesis, Mary More aimed her rather more creative than accurate Greek philology toward what she saw as a crucial distinction between "obedience" and "subjection" in 1 Corinthians.[142]

A persistent theme throughout this study has been the way in which women writers who had enjoyed the benefits of household academies and household salons often capitalized on their good fortune by offering critiques of the patriarchal order. Mary More's work similarly grew out of a household salon, but one in which the principal characters were a mother and daughter, and the background figures were two supportive husbands. In the first place, she dedicated this exercise in feminist philology to her daughter. Secondly, as Christine de Pizan had done long before her, More allows that she may seem an unlikely critic of marriage as an institution, given that she herself had enjoyed two happy and supportive marriages. She states, "[I] never had any reason as to myself to complain of the least ill carriage of my husbands to me, nor hath any occasion or action in my whole life ever offered anything, wherein the Power and Will of my husband hath been disputed on me, for we finding it [in] our Interests to be embarked in one bottom, and so must be guided and steered one way, have (I hope I may say it without Vanity) so ordered our affairs and actions to the utmost of our Power and Skill, to tend to the Comfort and good liking of both."[143] Her impetus to write was not unfortunate personal experience but rather "a trouble in [her] observing the sad consequences & events that have fallen on men and their Wives, through this mistake of men's pretending a Power over their Wives that neither God nor nature do allow."[144]

Mary More did not wish to deter her daughter from marrying but rather to inform her of the true nature of marriage based upon a careful reading of the Bible. She closed her dedication by wishing the young Elizabeth "a Religious, Wise, good tempered & loving husband."[145] It is noteworthy, however, that she did offer her daughter the choice of whether or not to marry. In the event, Elizabeth did marry. Margaret Ezell has located her marriage license, which indicates that she married an Alexander Pitfield, esquire, on 17 April 1680.[146] Hoping to find additional biographical information about Mary More, Ezell made a careful scrutiny both of this document and also the parish registers. These sources were silent.

One piece of the puzzle that can be added, however, is More's final will of 25 December 1714.[147] Not only does this establish the likely year of her death as 1716, when the will was proved, but also demonstrates that More's commitment to the advancement of women informed many of her decisions, in addition to her choice of subjects upon which to write. She had the freehold of numerous properties in the county of Essex and in London, which she left to be equally divided between her two granddaughters (daughters of Elizabeth), Anne and Winifred Pitfield, and thereafter to their legitimate heirs.[148] In addition, More made them joint executors of her will.[149] While she also left several generous cash bequests to her son-in-law and grandsons, the purpose of her testament was to provide her female descendants with financial independence.

Mary More represents a fitting end point for a study of Renaissance women intellectuals and Renaissance feminism. In her work, as we will see, pro-woman sentiment becomes an articulated discourse of rights that directly prefigures Mary Wollstonecraft. Beyond this textual change, however, More and the other seventeenth-century women writers demonstrate a transformation of the social paradigms surrounding women writers. While the cases of Inglis, Beale, and Petty suggest the continuing utility of the intellectual family, Mary More points toward a new era in the intellectual history of women, an era in which female authors are far more difficult to categorize.

"Woman as intellect" transcended geographic, socioeconomic, and disciplinary boundaries in seventeenth-century Britain. On the one hand, this expansion presents the historian with serious conceptual challenges. Italian women humanists all wrote in Latin and were celebrated for centuries in biographies of famous women. English women humanists translated religious texts from Latin and Greek into English and were praised as models of "learned virtue" for other women to follow. Italian and English women humanists anchored their credibility upon a domestic foundation. In contrast, seventeenth-century women writers seem to be doing many different things at once. Yet this very diffusion is perhaps the best testament to a shift in the range of possibilities for ambitious women. Inglis, Beale, Petty, and More demonstrate that women intellectuals could now be found in all sorts of places.

Learned women of previous generations frequently shared a determination to expose the disjuncture between women's capacities and their social roles. This commitment persisted within the diverse population of late-Renaissance women writers, but with a difference. The lines of feminist argument set down in the seventeenth century were bolder, more consistently explicit, and, in fact, political.

7

Discourses of Equality and Rights

FROM the beginning of the Renaissance era to the close of the seventeenth century, intellectual families produced generations of learned women who prompted literary society to think about the equality of the sexes in matters of the mind. Learned women, from Christine de Pizan to Mary More, used their status as "proper" women as a platform for intervening in and revitalizing the *querelle des femmes*. Not content with the praise that they received, women intellectuals used their pens to dismantle gender categories. Women writers of the seventeenth century, emboldened by an awareness that they participated in an unbroken succession of learned women from antiquity to their own times, brought a new level of intensity to the debate. Seventeenth-century feminism was explicit, arguing that women possess not only abstract "merits" but also equality and even "rights."

Women writers of the late sixteenth and seventeenth centuries, such as Moderata Fonte, Lucrezia Marinella, Mary Beale, Bathsua Makin, and Mary More, focused upon women's social roles. These latter-day Renaissance feminists updated Erasmian notions of the companionate marriage and suggested new institutional models for women's education. These descendants of the women humanists began to explore ways to create more women like themselves—women, that is, having a renaissance.

The keyword of seventeenth-century feminism is "equality." While Constance Jordan is right to note that programs of action for social change would not be advanced until the nineteenth century, critiques of sexual inequality and tentative proposals for rectifying women's inferior social roles emerged both in Italy and in England by the 1650s.[1] Egalitarian argument, nascent in the fifteenth and sixteenth centuries, predominated in seventeenth-century gender discourse. Writers maintained the intellectual equality of the sexes, the spiritual equality of the sexes, and even a provisional formulation of the equality of spouses within the institution of marriage. Rather than stopping with a general case for womankind's dignity, this latter-day *querelle des femmes* contended that women's "rights" had been usurped by men. The tone and terminology of explicit feminism transformed as the Renaissance drew to a close. Among the many contributions of later Renaissance feminists (both Italian and English), was their reconceptualization of "friendship" as a site for the expression of gender equality. Feminists such as Moderata Fonte and Mary Beale argued that women were as qualified as men to participate in egalitarian friendship.

Learned women of the seventeenth century also conducted themselves as professional academics and were recognized as such by male contemporaries. No longer prodigies to be praised, these women were scholars to be cited. Lucrezia Marinella, Anna Maria van Schurman, and Bathsua Makin referred to their colleagues by name; and Marinella brought a novel degree of immediacy to her arguments by citing the authors who supported her own view, as well as her antagonists. Concomitantly, male intellectuals worried less about situating women authors within their domestic milieu and more about providing bibliographies of their work and describing their arguments in detail. A representative of this shift whom we have already encountered is the seventeenth-century historian and editor Jacopo Filippo Tomasini, who published full-scale editions of the complete works of Cassandra Fedele and Laura Cereta in 1636 and 1640, respectively. Tomasini's instinct to treat women authors as literary authorities was widespread.

Seventeenth-century feminists pushed theoretical equality harder than their predecessors had done and began to formulate plans for rectifying social inequality. After 1600 women writers offered several different frameworks for secular communities of women. Moderata Fonte envisioned an informal society of friends. By citing other learned women, Lucrezia Marinella and Anna Maria van Schurman created an association of mutual reference, a textual community of women. Bathsua Makin founded a girls' school with a humanist curriculum. Whatever their particular plans, these women drafted the first blueprints for institutions to house what Laura Cereta had long before termed the "Republic of Women."

Italian Feminists on Education and Social Change

Moderata Fonte's dialogue, *The Worth of Women*, follows Baldassare Castiglione's *Courtier* and Pietro Bembo's *Gli Asolani* in genre, setting, and even tone, to a certain degree. Fonte diverged from her predecessors, however, in two respects. She recast the dialogic dramatis personae and shifted the focus from abstract ideals to social realities. Castiglione's speakers were almost always men; his female characters served as "judges" and plot movers more than as active participants. Even Bembo's dialogue, although interrupted at intervals by the women present, was nonetheless still driven by male speakers. Fonte, however, makes all of her seven characters women. Her group of "noble and valorous women, different in age and marital status, but similar in their gentle birth and habits, especially their refinement, virtue and lofty genius" comprises women at every stage in the female life cycle: we meet Adriana, an old widow; Adriana's daughter, Virginia, who is just now of marriageable age; Leonora, a young widow determined to remain single, at whose home the women convene for their discussion; Lucrezia, a woman who has been married for a number of years; Cornelia, a young wife; Corinna, a young woman who has decided to avoid both the convent and marriage; and Helena, a new bride.[2]

The second of Fonte's innovations was her transformation of the subject matter. While the title suggests that she wrote within the earlier tradition of proving women's "worth" and dignity, this dialogue is far from an abstracted or academic disquisition. On the contrary, while the tone remains light and humorous, the discussion constitutes an unflinching consideration of women's lived experience. Each of her characters comments on the financial, intellectual, and emotional difficulties that women confront.

The Worth of Women is a subtle didactic work. Above all, Fonte aims to educate her readers about the positive side of the debate on women—to expose sexual inequalities and to suggest new possibilities for women's intellectual and social self-realization. Her characters take up many of the arguments that date back to Henricus Cornelius Agrippa's *Declamation on the Preeminence of the Female Sex* (1529)—particularly the notion that it is women's virtue and talent that exerts a crucial civilizing influence on men, who are by nature rough and ungovernable. She also inverts the claim often advanced by male authors in their dialogues and satires that marriage is the doom of the learned man. Fonte's characters arrive at the conclusion that it is, conversely, women whose development is stunted by matrimony and that they might do well to avoid it.

Especially innovative in this regard is Fonte's central character, Corinna, a young woman who is single and determined to remain so. Fonte characterized her as a *dimessa,* a term that literally signified a member of the tertiary order founded by Antonio Pagani in the 1570s but that was beginning to be used to characterize any "respectable unmarried girl living at home, rather than in a convent."[3] As Virginia Cox contends, the figure of the "single (female) self" that emerges in the literary works of both Fonte and Lucrezia Marinella may well reflect the social realities of sixteenth-century dowry inflation and the often equally expensive alternative of claustration, both of which left many Venetian women without the resources to embark on either of their traditional "careers" as wife or nun.[4] Indeed, as Cox demonstrates, much of Fonte's dialogue laments the fact that women of even the best houses are forced to remain at home, battling their brothers for their share of the patrimony, or else to become their brothers' servants, helping their sisters-in-law with child rearing and housework.

The harsh realities of arranged marriages and women's domestic subjugation constitute important subjects in *Il merito,* but they are not the sum total of Fonte's contribution.[5] Her text also makes a linguistic shift, escalating the previous language of "merits" and "dignity" toward a discourse of "rights." Her characters contend that women's rights as equal beings have been consciously usurped by men from biblical times to the present day. And she posits that the principal means by which men have arrogated women's rights has been the systematic effort to keep them ignorant.

The first to assert this incipient discourse of rights is the learned Corinna. A latter-day woman humanist, Corinna is applauded early on in the dialogue by Lucrezia for her decision to avoid marriage and domestic responsibility and to devote herself to the life of the mind. "Directing your lofty thoughts to the precious study of secular and sacred letters," Lucrezia observes, "you have begun to live a celestial life while still in this world of travail and danger, which you abjure just as you spurn interaction with exceedingly duplicitous men, giving yourself wholly to those high endeavors that will make you immortal."[6] Wary of making Corinna seem exceptional, however, Leonora notes that her friend is not the only one "happy and blessed" in choosing the scholarly life, but also whoever follows her example.[7]

Corinna is the principal voice of the author. The dialogue, by definition, fractures the authorial voice, making it risky to assign any one character the sole persona of the author. Each of the voices may be "the author," or none of them. Or the author may test a range of his or her beliefs, doubts, and contradictory positions in the voices of different characters.[8] While it would be a mistake to assert that Corinna is the sole repository of Fonte's beliefs, this character contains the most imbedded references to the author herself. The character Lucrezia, for instance, urges Corinna to put her "divine intellect" to use in writing a volume on the subject of women leading a single life devoted to study, which would show "poor young women" the kind of life that "might be best for them."[9] Corinna replies that she is grateful for this suggestion and will consider writing such a book. Corinna thus represents the character of "author." She also represents the principal speaker and textual authority in the second day of the dialogue. Throughout the work, moreover, she recites poems that she has written for her friends' amusement and edification. Fonte herself was above all else a poet—in fact, *Il merito* is her only known prose composition. When asked (apropos of her disquisition on astrology) to name the most prominent contemporary astrologers, Corinna mentions "Signor Giovanni Niccolò Doglioni, a most genteel soul who, above and beyond his other singular accomplishments, is endowed with astonishing generosity and loyalty, which one rarely encounters in a man."[10] Doglioni was, as we have seen, Fonte's patron and promoter. Later, Corinna mentions that Venice's best lawyer is Filippo de' Zorzi, "whose devotion, faithfulness and ability are well known to Venice's most excellent Senate."[11] Zorzi was Fonte's husband. All of which positions Corinna as the dialogue's authoritative voice, if not the voice of the author.

Corinna's first major contribution is a discourse of rights. Virginia, the youngest of the group, inquires why it is that men are considered women's superiors if they are as faulty as Corinna suggests. Corinna explains to her that "men have arrogated this preeminence to themselves.

And although they say that we should remain their 'subjects,' the term should be understood in this way: we are 'subject' to them in the same sense that we are 'subject' to bad luck, illnesses and life's other misfortunes. This subjection, in short, is not an issue of obedience, but rather of forbearance." Because men wish to rule women, they have construed the term "subject" the other way around and, in so doing, "usurped the rulership [*signoria*] that they want to have over us, which really we should have over them." Corinna concludes that the masculine "prerogative" *(loro proprio)* "is just to leave the house each day and make a living for us."[12] Corinna's argument thus hinges on the distinction between "obedience" and "subjection"—between forbearance (tolerating an inconvenience) and legal subordination.

Leonora, a young widow determined to remain single, echoes Corinna's legalistic language. The new bride Helena, in love with her husband and enjoying the married woman's privilege of a more extensive social life, charges Corinna with showing women's inferiority by being so envious of men. Leonora counters by asking, "If they usurp our rights, should we not call them on it and announce that they have abused us?" Answering her own question, Leonora underscores Corinna's terminology: "If we are inferior to them in terms of legal authority, but not in terms of inherent worth, then this is a travesty—a travesty that has been established in the world through long-standing practice, which has made it seem licit and customary. Men wish that authority were theirs by virtue of reasoned argument, but it is really the result of strong-arming."[13]

The discourse of illegality that pervades the first day dissipates in the second day, as Corinna begins a series of lectures on every subject from natural science to rhetoric and poetry. We should not, however, understand this change in subject matter as a rejection of explicit feminism. Instead, Fonte shifts toward a practical feminism: she offers an educational primer for women. Virginia Cox observes in passing that this primer adds something new to the *querelle des femmes:* "Earlier contributors . . . had often denounced women's exclusion from education, and proclaimed their potential for mastering traditionally male fields of knowledge, but it is difficult to think of any precedent for this kind of activist response to the problem."[14] Fonte's didactic instinct, however, is best understood not merely as one component of her project but instead as its most important contribution. After providing her readers a textual attack upon the patriarchal order, on the second day she offers them a manual for becoming "women like us," that is, Renaissance women.

Some of her characters, especially Leonora and Cornelia, maintain their critical feminist stance: they attempt to redirect the second day's discussion back to deconstructing male hegemony. But Corinna, despite her former leadership in this project, keeps the discussion to academic matters. Corinna has not abandoned the fight. Rather, she has redirected her energy from complaint to practical solution. Leonora merely laments male control in the field of education, but Corinna takes it upon herself to provide her listeners (and, by extension, Fonte's female readers) with edifying material.

Corinna assumes the role of a tutor, offering synopses of the most important subjects of the era. She distills Aristotle, Pliny, and Galen on natural philosophy and medicine. She summarizes classical history (especially Suetonius), mythology (especially Ovid's *Metamorphoses*), and the central tenets of Greek and Roman moral philosophy. Corinna also glosses Horace and quotes Petrarch and Ariosto. Along the way, she recites many of Fonte's own poems, which are disingenuously attributed to "some gentleman author." Inspired by Corinna's erudite leadership, the other women bring their own knowledge (especially of poetry) into the discussion.

This all-female seminar may represent a feminization of the literary gatherings taking place in Venetian academies and salons. Like male academicians, these women engage in *paragone* (exercises in comparison and contrast), such as the relative merits of painting and poetry, music and poetry, painting and sculpture. Interwoven are numerous references to Venetian government and society; the most prominent contemporary male jurists, physicians, military heroes, poets, and artists; as well as illustrious Venetian noblewomen of their day who had been praised for their outstanding beauty and virtues.

One of the most revolutionary discussions that Corinna leads, however, is the one on friendship. After summarizing Cicero's *De amicitia* and Plutarch's *Moralia,* she presents an original argument. Friendship, for the ancients as for most of Fonte's contemporaries, was an exclusively male relationship. Fonte/Corinna overturns the paradigm, arguing that true friendship is a female phenomenon. This contention was already implicit in Fonte's choice of characters: a group of "virtuous and ingenious" women, who "had forged amongst themselves a close and well-founded friendship, and who often seized the opportunity to gather for informal conversation."[15] Corinna makes a feminist point of friendship, however, in contending that female friendships exhibit frankness and mutual encouragement toward virtue—qualities that, in fact, have defined friendship since antiquity but that (she claims) male friendships seldom have, as most men are duplicitous and immoral.

The feminization of friendship makes a case not merely for women's equality with men but indeed for their superiority. Corinna observes, "We, as women, are by nature more predisposed to piety and love. This can be seen also in our friendships, inasmuch as women make friends more quickly with other women and maintain their love better than men do in their friendships with each other."[16] As Cox argues, Fonte challenged the ancient and Renaissance idea of friendship as "an exclusively male phenomenon, whether it excludes women implicitly by simply ignoring them, or, as was the case in many Platonically inspired works, explicitly contrasts the spiritual friendship possible between males with the baser, because more sensual, attachments between men and women."[17]

Yet Fonte supersedes any male paradigm of friendship by focusing upon relationships between women. Her elimination of the male subject charts a new trajectory for the topic. Cornelia argues, "On account of men's innate malignity, even when they find someone with whom they are compatible, it is rare to find them forming special and inseparable friendships among themselves, or with women. As I've said, this is all because men are far less loving and for the most part far more inclined than we are to be overbearing and proud." Having placed women as the ideal subjects of friendship, Corinna instructs her companions on the nature and duties of this relationship as propounded by classical philosophers. Citing Diogenes, Aristotle, Seneca, and Cicero, Corinna underscores the point that friendship requires the honesty and affection that ideally obtain among blood kin. Fonte innovates, however, by asserting that women routinely possess this necessary love and honesty, whereas men seldom do.[18]

At the end of the second day, Cornelia (a married woman in her prime) becomes so enraptured by the discussion that she entertains the notion of abandoning the society of men. Her speech presents a vision of secular female community suggested by Fonte's setting but not to this point developed. Readers would not have failed to note that *The Worth of Women* was a feminist *Courtier*, in which a group of educated friends discuss a range of edifying topics in each other's company. None of the characters uses the terms "school" or "academy" for the setting in which they find themselves, and of course the "salon" as such had not yet coalesced as an institution. In Cornelia's speech, however, the salon emerges as an idea. Somewhere between a school and a literary society, or between an academy and a club, Fonte's female collectivity asserts a new idea in the intellectual history of women. Christine de Pizan's "Kingdom of Women" was a literary collection of women. Laura Cereta's "Republic of Women" was an inheritable lineage of female excellence. But Moderata Fonte's salon created a present-day society of learned women.

Fonte wrestles with the political ramifications of such a society. "Couldn't we live without men?" Cornelia asks near the end of the dialogue, "earning enough to support ourselves and conduct our own business without their help?" Answering her own questions, she exhorts her friends to "wake up and reclaim [their] freedom, honor and dignity, which have for so long been held hostage by men," and she exclaims, "When things reach a level of equality, we will finally be able to insult men in the way they insult us now."[19] Yet the final pages of the text do not pursue this assertion of women's potential to become autonomous political beings. Rather, Fonte opts for a partial, playful resolution: misandrist Leonora admits that she might be persuaded to marry again; and while the adolescent Virginia expresses a wish to follow Corinna's path as a single woman, her elders caution her against this hasty decision. The possibilities are laid out, in other words, but left unresolved. The queen disbands the group before nightfall, and the last line does not state that the participants have any immediate plan to reconvene; instead, the reader is left with the observation that "the women all bade each other farewell and then returned to their homes."[20]

One possible reading of the text, then, is that Fonte ultimately disowns this vision of female autonomy. I would suggest, however, that she intended to present her readers with the full range of options—from the single self that Corinna embodies, to the happily married wife and mother, to the contented widow. Whatever their decisions, *Il merito* evinces a determination to improve the education of all women and to encourage the formation of educated female communities outside the context of the convent.

One can only guess at how many of her female readers might have been inspired by Fonte's "textual salon" and created their own. It is clear, however, that woman-led salons were a prominent feature of the Italian literary world by the time Fonte wrote.[21] And, all formal (or semiformal) structures aside, any woman who could read Italian would have come away from *The Worth of Women* with a considerable amount of information on subjects ranging from botany to the current state of play in the debate on women. This was, I would argue, Fonte's ultimate purpose: to educate her female readers (or at least remind them of what they already knew) and to encourage them to think about ways to share their knowledge—if not in print, as she had done, at least with their friends.

Il merito was not a bestseller, but neither was it unsuccessful. Thanks to the efforts of her patron, Niccolò Doglioni, *Il merito* went through two printings (1600 and 1603). And Fonte's prominence in collections of female biography, defenses of women, and even Venetian guidebooks suggest that contemporaries appreciated her work.[22]

The quantitative aspect of *Il merito*'s history, however, pales in comparison to its qualitative reception. Male encomiasts cited all of her publications but gave *Il merito* pride of place. In 1609, for instance, Pietro Paolo di Ribera commemorated Fonte's achievements not only by glossing Doglioni's biography but also by citing all of Fonte's works and clearing up any confusion about her name. *Il merito*, however, elicited Ribera's most extensive commentary. He notes that she composed this work on the brilliance of her sex as a "refutation of some men who had failed to give women credit for wisdom, judgment, knowledge and courage" and trumpets her success in making her case, observing that the dialogue "turned out very well, both with respect to its subject matter and to the delightful complexity of its style." Ribera continues, "Indeed, on the judgment of knowledgeable people, it compares favorably with anything published these days. And if an untimely death had not prevented her, she certainly would have expanded and revised it."[23] Cristofano Bronzini copied Ribera almost word for word in his own defense of women, published in 1625.[24]

Male encomiasts had good reason to commemorate Fonte's feminism. By the early decades of the seventeenth century, the Italian reading public had demonstrated a keen interest in seeing women's views on the *questione della donna*. In Venice, publishers even began to commission women writers to compose responses to male-authored attacks on women, aware that customers would be eager to hear "her side" of the debate.[25] This interest guaranteed Fonte a continuing presence in Italian letters after her death and was one of the factors that contributed to the successful career of her younger contemporary Lucrezia Marinella.

Marinella published her own contribution to the debate on women, *The Nobility and Excellence of Women and the Defects and Vices of Men,* in 1601. A printer-publisher named Gian Battista Ciotti commissioned Marinella's scholarly treatise as a direct response to Giuseppe Passi's misogynistic tract *Concerning Womanly Defects (Dei donneschi difetti),* which was published in Venice the previous year. Marinella modeled her counterattack closely on the arguments raised in the 1530s by Agrippa and his imitators. She may have taken her basic structure directly from the 1529 Latin edition of Agrippa's *Declamation,* from an anonymous French treatise modeled on Agrippa, or from the Venetian editor Lodovico Domenichi's redaction, titled *Della nobiltà delle donne.*[26] Whatever her source, Marinella followed its precedent in arguing for female preeminence based upon a manipulation of the book of Genesis—for instance pointing to Eve's creation from Adam, rather than from mud, as evidence that she was made of more perfect material—and upon an inversion of Galen's medical theories concerning bodily humors. While antifeminists traditionally argued that women, cold and moist in composition, lacked the heat and air necessary for courage and higher cognitive function, Agrippa and his imitators contended that women's humors in fact made them both more charitable and more reflective than were hot and fiery men and that therefore women were more capable of philosophical subtlety. Marinella also follows Agrippa, as well as her many female predecessors, in focusing upon the issue of female erudition, which she substantiates with a customary list of women from history who proved the intellectual equality of the sexes.

Beyond presenting herself as a new Agrippa, Marinella revolutionized the debate through her method of explicit citation. She took aim at contemporary male authors who disparaged womankind, citing their names and works, then refuting their arguments. Whereas her predecessors often set themselves against a nebulous group of "women's enemies," Marinella states her intention to "dismantle" the claims of Boccaccio, Tasso, Passi, and even "the great Aristotle."[27]

Marinella begins with a clear statement of her scholarly aspirations. She claims membership in a category of authors who wish to make the truth apparent for everyone. "My aim," she announces, "is to bring this truth to everyone's attention: the female sex is more noble and excellent than the male sex. And I hope to substantiate this contention both with sound reasoning and examples, with the result that every man (however stubborn he might be) will be forced, with his own mouth, to affirm my argument."[28]

The most striking prefatory statement Marinella makes, however, is her assertion that she is proud to be a woman. She attests, "At no point have I ever wished, nor do I now have any desire, nor will I ever want to be a man." Yet Marinella was not so naive as to think that her treatise alone, however rigorous its exposition and however vast its array of classical citations, would make misogynists see reason. A second hope, expressed later in the work, is that women themselves (much as Fonte's Cornelia had urged) will wake up and assert themselves against men: "If women, as I hope, wake themselves from the lengthy slumber by which they are oppressed, then these ungrateful and overbearing men would learn humility."[29]

Marinella was a scholar bent on proving a point. Like Fonte, she directed her energy to exposing the injustice of women's economic deprivation in marriage and the frequency with which women found themselves in arranged marriages with drunken, dissolute, and violent men. And while her treatise posits no practical remedy for women's social situation—not even the potential remedy of the single life or the respite of learned conversations with other women—Marinella is perhaps even more revolutionary than Fonte in leaving the agency for social change not in the hands or minds of men but in those of women. She makes her female readers either the heroes of their own new narrative (teaching humility to "overbearing men") or else people complicit in their own subjugation if they fail to shake off their apathetic slumber.

Hoping to inspire this awakening by dint of examples, Marinella positions women's intellectual prowess as the most compelling evidence for the equality of the sexes more generally. After rehearsing the usual collection of ancient learned women, she points to the presence of contemporary cases across Europe, thereby making the tradition of learned women more visible than her predecessors had done. Whereas Laura Cereta, for instance, recognized that there was a lineage of learned women (a *generositas*) that she had inherited, her modern examples were limited to Isotta Nogarola and Cassandra Fedele. Marinella had many more women to cite, and she does so with relish.

Marinella's section on learned women reaches beyond the borders of Venice and even beyond the Italian peninsula. Alongside the "usual suspects," such as Hortensia, Cornelia, and Cassandra Fedele, she places Hildegard of Bingen and Catherine Parr, "wife of Henry VIII, King of England, [who] wrote a book of meditations on the Psalms." Marinella also points to Marguerite of Navarre, whom she characterizes as "most learned in sacred letters."[30]

Marinella emphasized the pan-European community of learned women but devoted the most space to the profusion of Italian exempla. *La nobiltà* predates Tomasini's 1640 edition of Laura Cereta's collected works, but Marinella had already become aware of Cereta as "a noble Brescian lady, called Laura," who wrote "very elegant epistles." From Giuseppe Betussi's revision of Boccaccio's *Famous Women*, Marinella culled the additional example of "Laura Veronese, daughter of Niccolò, who composed wonderful things, including Sapphic verse, epistles and orations in both Greek and Latin," and "Cassandra Fedele, who was extremely learned: she disputed publicly in Padua, wrote an elegant book that systematized various branches of knowledge and also penned very beautiful lyric poems." Marinella also gives a prominent place to Isotta Nogarola, emphasizing her learning and redirecting other authors' emphasis upon Nogarola's chastity. She notes that Nogarola "conserved her virginity always" but construes this as a manifestation of Nogarola's commitment to "a *philosophical* life, contenting herself with little," rather than a conformity to received notions of ideal Christian femininity. Nogarola's sister, Ginevra, also receives mention for being "famous for her epistles." And another fifteenth-century humanist, Costanza Sforza, appears here as a woman "devoted from her adolescence both to philosophy and to poetry," whom Poliziano had praised. Closer to her own era, Marinella brings out the examples of several erudite poets: Lucrezia d'Este, Duchess of Urbino; Veronica Gambara, Vittoria Colonna, and Laura Terracina.[31]

Emphasizing that even this impressive list is provisional, Marinella demonstrates that learned women are not merely a thing of the past but a contemporary proof of the good uses to which women commonly put their minds. "From these few examples that I have mentioned," she asserts, "and I say few in comparison to the many that I have passed over, anyone can recognize the profit women have taken in their studies and in all their other pursuits." Yet she is concerned as well with explaining the relative paucity of learned women in her own day, which she attributes to an increasing male hegemony over educational institutions—a gap between the ideal and the real that has deepened since the golden age of antiquity. "Few women devote themselves to study these days," she explains, "because men, fearing lest they lose their dominion and become the servants of women, often forbid women to learn even reading and writing."[32]

Overall, however, Marinella stresses continuity with ancient precedent more than disjuncture. She diffuses the belief that there are no longer women intellectuals, arguing that this belief is merely an effect of misinformation. She notes, "Some men, poorly read in history, think it impossible that there ever were and that there are not now women who are expertly learned in the sciences and arts. And so these men cannot appreciate the fact that they see and listen to such women every day."[33] In this sense, Marinella's treatise is an exercise in reshaping historical memory to allow a clear vision of "woman as intellect" in her present social world.

Marinella's strength is her use of citation. Unlike Laura Cereta, who conceived of herself as a singular voice, Marinella both situated her work against a continuing tradition of texts that criticized women and located her own contribution within a growing body of literature that praised women's abilities. Whereas Cereta had set herself against a fictional opponent—a "Bibolo Semproni" ("Always Drunk"), who stood as a representative for all antifeminists—Marinella strengthened her case by citing her opponents by name and refuting their arguments systematically. Her preface to section VI, "An Answer to the Spurious and Empty Arguments Adduced by Men to Bolster their Case" *(Risposta alle leggerissime e vani ragioni addotte da gli huomini in lor favore),* serves the roster of antifeminists a trial summons: "With a view toward resolving all doubts, I will now respond more particularly to several authors, including: Boccaccio, who penned the *Labyrinth of Love;* Ercole Tasso, who wrote an attack on marriage; Arrigo di Namur, who brought out his *Villainy of Women* in 1428; as well as Sperone Speroni and Torquato Tasso, both of whom censured women under the guise of praising them in their works titled *Dialogue on the Dignity or Nobility of Women* and *On*

Female Virtue, respectively. I will first describe their arguments and then I will refute them."[34] Unlike her predecessors, including Fonte, who somewhat diffused the strength of their critique by leaving misogyny in the abstract (writing, for example, "some men say"), Marinella cited her authors, chapter and verse. Making good on her prefatory promise, the second half of her treatise encapsulates and refutes each text, exposing the authors' logical inconsistencies and contradictions.

Marinella used citation as an effective weapon but also as a positive fortification. She bolstered her case with a supporting cast of male authors who upheld her own view. She begins with revered ancient authors, such as Plutarch and Plato, then proceeds to cite contemporary men writing in the defense of women, who prove that "there are and have always been (albeit they are few) writers who, lacking the vice of envy, have celebrated womankind with all their might. They have even discredited those men as deficient both in intelligence and in humanity, who have abused women either physically or verbally." The "modern" male defenders of women whom she cites include Petrarch, who praised Laura; the fifteenth-century humanist Angelo Poliziano, who praised Costanza Sforza and Cassandra Fedele for their erudition; the poet Ariosto (especially for his *Orlando Furioso,* in which he praises women in general and the Roman poet Vittoria Colonna in particular); the historian Marco Filippi, who praised the learning of St. Catherine; and the contemporary Venetian senator Orsato Giustiniano, who wrote poems in praise of his wife.[35]

Marinella also recognized her illustrious female predecessors in the world of print, most notably Moderata Fonte. She cites Fonte's earlier chivalric romance, *Tredici canti del Il Floridoro* (1581), probably because she had not yet seen Fonte's recently published *Il merito.* The first reference occurs in Marinella's argument concerning the equality of men's and women's souls. "If we should wish to speak as philosophers," Marinella writes, "we would say that women's souls are just as noble as men's, seeing as the one and the other are of the same type, and consequently of the same substance and nature—Moderata Fonte, knowing this, and in order to demonstrate that women are just as noble as men, says [so] in her *Floridoro.*" Marinella also cites the *Floridoro* as an authoritative text when demonstrating that women in the past have been known to achieve remarkable feats of learning and military valor but that this tradition has become weaker (though not extinct) in her own time by virtue of men's increasing control over women's education. She remarks, "Moderata Fonte, who is in some respects cognizant of the excellence of our sex, has left us these words, 'but few are those who give themselves over to their studies, or to military arts in these our own days, since men, fearing lest they lose their dominion [*signoria*], and become women's servants, often forbid them even to learn reading and writing.'" Similarly, Marinella quotes Fonte's warrior maiden in her own exhortation that fathers should train their daughters the same as they educate their sons, not only for the good of families, but for the preservation of the state itself. And she suggests the same pedagogical "experiment" that Fonte proposed: namely, that a boy and girl of equal age and abilities should be set to learning at the same time, to prove that the girl could easily equal the boy and even surpass him. The crucial point for Fonte and, following her, Marinella, was that women's lack of education (rather than "nature") produced their social subordination. Fonte's line, which Marinella quotes directly, is "because [a women] happens to be trained for different business, it is therefore on account of her education that she is so little esteemed."[36]

Marinella herself, however, was esteemed. Much as contemporary biographers began to cite Fonte's works and argument, so too did other intellectuals, male and female, cite Marinella's treatise as an authoritative text. Her patron, Lucio Scarano, mentioned her in his Latin dialogue *Scenophylax* (1601). As Letizia Panizza has pointed out, Scarano incorporated into his text (which concerned the classical meters used in ancient Greek tragedy and comedy) prominent mention of Marinella as an intellectual "with whom he [had] discussed literary matters requiring acquaintance with classical philosophy."[37] In his dedicatory letter, Scarano cites Marinella's *Arcadia felice* on the relationship of tragedy to pastoral and *La nobiltà* for the general principle of names signifying the nature of things. "For if names follow the nature of the things to which they were given," he writes, "which Plato states many times in the Cratylus, and the radiant maid Lucrezia Marinella, glory of our age and another Corinna, showed with much learning and abundantly in her highly polished book *On the Nobility and Excellence of Women*, full of so much learning, which she has recently published."[38] Panizza is right to point to Scarano's praise as indicative of the degree to which Marinella was taken seriously by her contemporaries. But it should also be emphasized that Scarano elevates Marinella to the level of an authority: not merely a female object of praise, she was a scholar worthy of citation.

Cristofano Bronzini surpassed Scarano in representing Marinella as a scholar and colleague. Panizza has noted that Bronzini's 1625 dialogue *On the Dignity and Nobility of Women* records that he had sent Marinella a draft of his book, and he also reproduced her answer in the printed text.[39] However, Bronzini's respect for Marinella as a scholar warrants further explication. His prefatory explanation notes that the character "Onorio" stands for himself ("Onorio, Difensore delle Donne è il Bronzini d'Ancona").[40] Onorio frequently brings Marinella forward as incontrovertible evidence for intellectual brilliance in women, and for the honorable uses to which educated women will put their learning. Indeed, Marinella is the "star" of the entire discussion in the fourth day, which concerns women intellectuals.

Following Marinella's argument, Onorio begins by refuting the notion that learned women are a thing of the past. "If I wished now to depart a bit from the subject at hand," he explains, "I could easily prove that all those histories were authentic and credible: it will be enough for us, however, to keep this argument to our own times, which lack neither Penthesileas and Camillas valorous in arms, nor most learned Diotimas." Bronzini mentions Vittoria Colonna, Veronica Gambara, Laura Terracina, and Laura Battiferra in passing but gives Marinella pride of place in this illustrious company. Noting her erudition in sacred letters, Onorio terms her an "expert in both moral and natural philosophy" and even claims that she, "by virtue of her rare accomplishments and virtuosity, has more power in one of her fingers alone than those vicious misogynist poets have in their whole bodies."[41]

Bronzini's other principal character, Margherita, has heard that women are often gifted in epistolary writing and she asks Onorio to tell her more. He responds by quoting in full the letter that Marinella has just sent to him. "The virtuous and most courteous Lucrezia Marinella of Venice," he explains, "writing to a person who had privately solicited her to critique some of his compositions in praise of women (a subject to which she herself has also contributed, along with other great writers of our day), offered her generous appraisal and good advice, in accordance with her prudent judgment and, what redounds even more to her honor, she has answered so modestly in this fashion."[42]

The letter that Bronzini reproduces is, of course, his representation of Marinella. It is all the more significant, however, because he presents her as an expert in a field that we would term "women's studies." The letter as he quotes it reads,

> Your Lordship has done me a great favor in making me not only a partic-
> ipant in your most noble and learned Discourse, but in praising and hon-
> oring in this work my little expertise—so much more than it warrants.
> With the light of your most learned words, you have made resplendent
> and shining the obscurity of my name . . . I have read and reread your
> book avidly and with an attitude not so much to correct such a worthy
> and perfect work, but in a spirit of admiration for its lofty and pleasing
> style, as well as the order of its exposition. And since you have com-
> manded me to express my opinion freely and sincerely, in order to obey
> you I say that this is a work most perfect in every part, charming and yet
> also full of doctrine, wisdom and authority . . . I beg you to publish the
> remaining discourses.

Bronzini, in short, staked his own authorial credibility on a female expert's assessment. Much as Giovanni Battista Andreini had used his learned mother's life and works to justify his own literary and theatrical careers, Bronzini fashions himself as a reliable defender of women by reproducing a letter of recommendation from Marinella—not just a woman but a recognized scholar in the field. He set her up as "one of many great authors in [his] day" who had composed works in this genre, and thereafter he bolstered his own intervention by citing her as an "external reviewer."[43]

Underscoring Marinella's status as a literary authority, Bronzini provides a complete catalog of her publications. On the subject of hagiography, Onorio mentions "a most beautiful volume written by Lucrezia Marinella entitled *The Heroic Deeds and the Life of the Most Marvelous and Angelic Saint Catherine of Siena*." He also mentions Marinella's poems on the lives of St. Francis and the Virgin Mary, as well as her *Arcadia felice* and her pastoral poem *Amore impazzito ed innamorato*. Beyond praising her accomplishments, Bronzini argues that Marinella's poetry should be studied for its replication of ancient dramatic styles. In his view, her "epic themes and her gravity and nobility of style" *(maestà di concetti, e grandezza e nobiltà di Stile)* equal that of Sophocles and Euripides. Bronzini provides his most extensive review, however, for Marinella's feminist treatise. He notes the persuasiveness of her argument and acuity of her attacks on Aristotle, Boccaccio, Ercole Tasso, and Passi, who (he informs his readers) "has now repented of his membership in the club of women's adversaries." At the conclusion of this lengthy review, Bronzini returns to Marinella's scholarly bravura, her "solid contentions and examples taken from innumerable historians," which make *La nobiltà* a tour de force "not merely to be read, but to be held in the greatest esteem."[44]

Although other seventeenth-century encomiasts were less effusive than Bronzini, Marinella nonetheless took an honored place in works of collective female biography akin to the place of Cassandra Fedele. Pietro Paolo di Ribera gave Marinella a substantial entry among his 845 biographies of notable women, praising her mastery of the humanities and her philosophical acuity. He also cited her works by title, including *La nobiltà*.[45] Francesco Agostino della Chiesa termed Marinella "a singular phoenix of our age" *(unica fenice dell'eta nostra)* and provided the titles of all her religious poetry. His most extensive commentary, however, concerned her feminist treatise, which he considered an authoritative work. "I believe," Chiesa opines, "that by virtue of the many works that have emerged from her divine genius, no other writer could be found who equals her, let alone surpasses her. She has written and published a discourse divided into two parts, the first part of which proves the nobility and excellence of women with sound arguments, authority and examples; the second part demonstrates with as many arguments and authorities that the defects of men by far surpass those of women. This work was published in Venice in 1601."[46]

Nor was Marinella's fame limited to male observers. The Dutch humanist Anna Maria van Schurman also knew and admired her treatise. In the mid-1630s, Schurman corresponded with André Rivet, a Leiden theologian, on the issue of women's education in the humanities. While Schurman proposed that women should receive the same training in ancient languages that she had received, she expressed reservations about the arguments for women's equality and even supremacy that were appearing in Italy and France. "I truly find this line of reasoning so inconsistent with virginal modesty," Schurman writes, "or at any rate with my inherent bashfulness, that it irks me to read Lucrezia Marinella's treatise, entitled *The Nobility and Excellence of Women, with the Defects and Vices of Men,* despite the fact that most of it is splendid. The same is true of the little dissertation by [Marie de] Gournay, *The Equality of Men and Women.* Where her fine style and cleverness are concerned, I find no fault, but I would not dare, nor would I wish, to sanction the work as a whole."[47]

Schurman was not prepared to speak in terms of complete equality between the sexes, but she was still a feminist inasmuch as she argued for women's intellectual equality and the need to educate women seriously. Drawing strength, like many before her, from the litany of ancient learned women, Schurman also pointed to modern women intellectuals in the course of her argument. Echoing Vives and Erasmus, one of Schurman's central arguments is that study constitutes the best means for women to keep their minds (and hearts) occupied. In this regard, she cites the daughters of Thomas More, as described by Erasmus in his letter to Guillaume Budé.[48] As evidence for advanced instruction as a tool for instilling reformist values, she points to Lady Jane Grey.[49]

Not only did Schurman cite other women to bolster her own case, but (like Marinella) she was also a scholar to whom male intellectuals offered deference. Gisbertius Voetius, a professor of theology at Utrecht and one of her mentors, also tried his hand at a defense of women. His essay "Concerning Women" appeared as part of his collected works (Amsterdam, 1663–1676). In his section championing women's education, Voetius urges his readers to consult Schurman's treatise for a definitive treatment on the subject.[50] Voetius's readers would have had access to several different editions: the 1641 Latin edition, published in the Dutch Republic; a French redaction published in Paris in 1646; and an English translation, printed in London (1649).

Siep Stuurman has recently shown, moreover, that Schurman's example proved a crucial piece of evidence for the feminist contingent in a series of academic debates on gender and education taking place during the 1660s at the Parisian Académie des Orateurs. While antifeminists argued that women should not be made learned, lest they seize masculine authority, the feminist party won by producing a roster of learned women, both ancient and modern, especially "that illustrious maiden, the Dutchwoman Marie Anne de Schurman." The feminist victory became a matter of public record: the academy's debates were published, including the final verdict on the intellectual equality of the sexes.[51]

Unlike Voetius or the Parisian academy, Schurman's principal mentor, Rivet, upheld the notion that most women would have little use for Latin, Greek, or Hebrew. He did not maintain that educating women was dangerous, however, or that women were somehow unequal to the task. By citing Vives and Erasmus, Schurman had even begun to persuade him that a positive effect of education was that it kept women's minds occupied. Rivet conceded this much, but the sticking point for him was the lack of pedagogical institutions suitable for women. "Before you persuade me," he remarked, "I would want to see you found colleges of erudite women, academies in which those maidens whom you would consecrate to such studies might be trained. For even you would not readily concede that all these women could be autodidacts, or have parents at home who could teach them (which happily occurred in your case). Nor would it be proper for them to attend public schools run by men and be mixed together with boys."[52] Rivet was not necessarily being sarcastic: indeed, he may have wished to see Schurman act on her feminism by setting up a girls' school with a serious curriculum. In any event, Schurman demurred. And, after her turn to Pietism late in life, she even renounced her earlier argument.

Scholars have argued that Lucrezia Marinella also contradicted her feminism late in life, but the evidence here is especially tricky.[53] What we have in support of this notion is her 1645 treatise, *Essortationi alle donne (Exhortations to Women)*, in which she ostensibly exhorts women to revel in domestic seclusion *(retiratezza)*, construed here as more appropriate for them than engagement with the world. She argues that women, like jewels, monarchs, and divine beings, risk debasement when made available for public consumption. Marinella even dissuades her female readers from study and writing, warning them about the emotional and physical tolls that the life of the mind exacts, as well as the slights that learned women receive from men and other women.[54]

A glance at the frontispiece should in itself make us suspicious of "sincerity": the publisher was Francesco Valvasenso, the favored printer for the Accademia degli Incogniti, an infamous sodality that delighted (at the least) in layered discourses.[55] As Paola Malpezzi Price and Christine Ristaino have demonstrated, moreover, Marinella's application of irony, paradox, and contradiction militate against reading the *Essortationi* as a recantation.[56] They classify the work as a *paignion*, an exercise in which propositions are meant to be understood as both serious and ironic, a claim substantiated by the text's ludic tone, the frequent appearance of the Greek orator Gorgias (a master of paradox), the contradictions between the meanings of the Italian prose and the marginal

Latin quotations, and Marinella's frequent self-citations—especially to *The Nobility and Excellence of Women*.

Even an uninformed reader would not have missed the greatest contradiction of the text: its author modeled the very activities that she urged women to avoid. She exhorted women to pick up the needle, but she wielded the pen. She told women never to seek fame, yet she continued to publish. Perhaps, as Price and Ristaino suggest, Marinella intended to highlight the tension between conservative prescriptions of feminine behavior and her own intellectual bravura. Marinella did alert readers to seek out hidden meanings, warning them in her prefatory letter to bypass the text's "bark" *(corteccia)* and head straight for its "pulp" *(midollo)*.[57] This circuitous rhetorical program may well have reflected her desire to evade counter-reformation censorship and to suit the tastes of her dedicatee, Gaspar de Teves y Gusman, a Spanish ambassador.[58]

Whatever her motivations for adopting a conservative mask, Marinella's satiric voice belies her injunctions. For instance, in urging women to avoid study, she provides an exaggerated catalog of its deleterious effects, chief among them exhaustion, illness, melancholy, and the destruction of feminine beauty. "Attend, my friends," she cautions, "and particularly you who spend the whole day [*tutto il giorno*] preening."[59] The exaggeration suggests satire, particularly when one recalls the traditional accusation that vanity was a "natural" female vice. It would be risible to suggest that spending "all day" in front of a mirror was in any sense a good thing for women, let alone preferable to philosophical rumination. Indeed, Marinella's tone, as well as her list of philosophy's physical and emotional tolls, echoes Erasmus's *Praise of Folly*.[60]

Marinella's hidden argument was that women should pursue the type of philosophical inquiry conducted in the treatise. Indeed, philosophy is the engine of the *Essortationi*. Marinella links the "seclusion" she ostensibly advocates to moral philosophy, the genre within which she situates the work as a whole. "Although my *Exhortations* concern economic and domestic matters," she explains to Teves, "Your Excellency will find them ornamented with many philosophical sententiae drawn from Aristotle, Plato and others, such as Hesiod and Homer, which are full of moral wisdom—a necessary thing for living well [*ben vivere*] and the foundation of civic happiness [*la felicità civile*]." She urges women to delight in solitude, which is the precondition for serious contemplation: "In quiet one becomes perfect, and it is for this very reason that so many men, the wisest philosophers and inventors of noble pursuits, loved seclusion." The marginal Latin tag (in this case) underscores the point: "Aristotle became a wise and knowledgeable man from sitting still and being quiet."[61] The secluded contemplative life ultimately signals women's superiority to men, who must labor in the corrupt world. By this circuitous logic, Marinella reprises the essential argument of *La nobiltà:* women's nobility, excellence, and even superiority to men.

The *Essortationi* performed a rhetorical trick. Marinella warned readers to engage in close reading, as Price and Ristaino note. But she also warned them to expect a clever deception. In her programmatic statement, Marinella cited two of her own works: the life of St. Francis (which established her theological credentials) and her epic poem about the 1204 sack of Constantinople that the Venetian doge, Enrico Dandolo, directed *(L'Enrico overo Bisantio Acquistato; Henry, or Constantinople Conquered)*. *L'Enrico*, she pointed out, proved her skill in describing military "strategies for deceiving the enemy" *(strategemi per ingannare lo inimico)*.[62] That she emphasizes the ability to deceive *(ingannare)* as she concludes her "Letter to the Readers" urges us to read the *Essortationi* themselves as a strategy for tricking a different sort of enemy: detractors of women.

While the later works of Marinella and Schurman certainly harbor tensions, the reception of both writers nonetheless points to a new phase in the intellectual history of women. By the seventeenth century, learned women were no longer just prodigies to praise, but scholars to cite. Simultaneously, the idea of a secular female community was beginning to take shape as a potential site for social change. Fonte offered one model: a conversation club of women. But even the conservative Rivet, in the context of his correspondence with Schurman, considered the possibility of establishing a girl's school with a rigorous academic program, which suggests that by 1640 an academy of women was imaginable.

Mary Ward (1585–1645), a learned English recusant, did more than imagine such an institution. Ward's Institute of the Blessed Virgin Mary, modeled on the English Jesuit college at St. Omer, established schools across Europe in which young girls learned everything from needlework to Latin and Greek. Expanding from 1609 to 1631, these institutions drew pupils by the hundreds, which suggests a widespread commitment to female learning. But Ward and her nearly three hundred colleagues were ultimately thwarted: the institute was suppressed at the order of

Pope Urban VIII in 1631.[63] Ward's determination that the institute should receive official recognition as an order of nuns but that the nuns should not be subject to enclosure doomed the enterprise. The decrees of the Council of Trent (1545–1563) were unequivocal about strict enclosure for all women's orders, a point that Urban emphasized in his condemnation *(Pastoralis Romani Pontificis)*. If Ward or her followers wished to continue in the religious life, then they were required to "take on themselves the yoke of the Lord," abjure the world, and "enter as soon as possible some order of nuns which [had] been approved by the . . . Holy See."[64] It is important to stress that while Urban repudiated the idea of female Jesuits, he did not censure women's education as such. And we should bear in mind, too, that Ward's schools had been popular among laypeople.

Fortunately, Ward was not the only English woman of the seventeenth century making new plans to implement sexual equality. Anna Maria van Schurman's achievements inspired Bathsua Makin to contend that women were men's scholarly equals, in her *Essay to Revive the Antient Education of Gentlewomen*, and to do what Rivet had suggested: establish a humanist school for girls. Mary More also cited Schurman as proof of women's intellectual equality, which was More's point of departure for arguing that women possessed a "right" to greater equality in marriage.

This intensification of feminist argument, the call for equality, and the attempt to reshape women's social lives at school and in marriage went furthest in England. While sixteenth-century English women humanists had seemed more reticent than their continental colleagues, their intellectual descendants surpassed all previous models of feminist argument. Learned English women of the seventeenth century introduced the powerful term "rights" into the lexicon of the *querelle des femmes*.

English Feminists on Rights and Equality

"Friendship is the nearest union which distinct Souls are capable of," wrote Mary Beale in her treatise on friendship of 1666.[65] Friendship offered Beale a point of departure for exploring social egalitarianism. She was concerned with women's equality in marriage, an institution that she redefined as a form of "friendship." Her boldest claim, however, is that women best perform the offices of what both ancient and contemporary theorists defined as a male political relationship. A century before, Moderata Fonte had idealized female friendship, but she did not emphasize women's ability to serve better than men as men's friends. Beale, hewing even closer to the bone of social reality than her predecessors, initiates this argument.

Moral philosophers, from Aristotle and Cicero onward, had defined friendship as a relationship between free men, between equals. Beale's innovation was to reconceptualize marriage as political friendship. While Erasmus had argued that marriage should be companionate, he did not posit the kind of equality between spouses that Beale envisions. And while Jeremy Taylor, Beale's contemporary and principal model, admitted that women could in many respects be considered "friends," he claimed that women lacked both the legal equality and the depth of knowledge necessary for providing wise counsel—a friend's principal duty.

The byword for Beale, as for her Italian and English contemporaries, is equality. Proceeding from Aristotle, Beale writes that "next to glorifying our Creator, man seems to be made for nothing more [than friendship]. For when God first created him, it is not fit (said He), that Man should be alone, & then he gave him Eve to be a meet help. And what can that imply but that God gave her for a Friend, as well as for a wife? A wife and Friend, but not a slave. For we find her not in the beginning made subject to Adam, but always of equal dignity and honor with him." Humanists writing long before Beale, such as Isotta Nogarola and Henricus Cornelius Agrippa, had made the same point about "original equality" but had been unable to extend this to "contemporary equality" because of Eve's punishments for her transgression, chiefly subjection to her husband. Beale contends that this paradigm has begun to shift in her own time. She points to "a small number, who by Friendship's interposition, have restored the marriage bond to its first institution."[66] Friendship, for Beale, is not only the precondition for doctrinal unity that other latitudinarians believed it to be but also the foundation of a new dispensation for women: marriage as a union of equals.

In English law, the principle of coverture deprived married women of individual political identity. Wives were subsumed into the "person" of the husband. Beale envisioned friendship as a loophole for unraveling coverture or mitigating its worst effects. She posits that marriage can and should be a foundation for the female self, insofar as the love upon which friendship (and marriage as a form of friendship) is based impels each party to desire only the happiness of the other. However different the "conditions and estates" of friends may be, Beale explains, their friendship "supposes its professors equal, laying aside all distance, and so leveling the ground that neither has the advantage of the other."[67]

Unlike her ancient predecessors, Beale can envision friendship existing between apparent unequals (such as husband and wife), provided that "their minds bear a like proportion to each other," allowing them to converse freely. Addressing the likelihood that the party with a more elevated "condition or outward estate" will attempt to dominate the lesser, Beale proposes that friendship blurs the distinctions that facilitate domination. Friendship, in her formulation, neither does nor should "take away that respect which inferiors, though Friends, owe to those whom providence has placed in a higher rank," but it removes "that awe which any such inequality may be apt and is not seldom want to produce." In other words, Beale maintains that the bond of friendship does not obliterate inequalities, but it minimizes them. A husband, for instance, possesses authority that his wife does not; yet, according to Beale's definition, friendship will compel him to avoid "exercising that authority which the advantage of Birth and Condition have given [him]." For her part, the wife will respect her husband's authority but not be so in "awe" of it that she cannot perform the offices of friendship. Beale emphasizes that "friends give their hearts mutually in hostage for the truth of their affections," a statement that affirms friendship's reciprocal obligations and its potential to catalyze social leveling.[68]

Beale admits that it is only a "small number" of modern marriages that become unions of true equals by "the intercession of friendship." Yet her argument hinges not on quantitative evidence but rather on the qualitative ability to conceptualize women participating as the equals of men in Ciceronian *amicitia*. Her formulation of women's social and political equality, however provisional, had been unthinkable for the women intellectuals of previous generations. Whereas earlier women humanists formed friendships with men on terms that were hierarchical, analogous to the relationship between daughters and fathers or between students and teachers, Beale shifts the domestic metaphor toward the more potentially egalitarian relationship of wife and husband.

Beale's treatise made an even more striking statement of the female self as friend. She did not, as Moderata Fonte had done, create a fictional community of learned women friends. Instead, this treatise immortalized

Beale's friendship with Elizabeth Tillotson, wife of the archbishop of Canterbury and Beale's dedicatee. In her dedication, Beale makes it clear that her model for ideal friendship is theirs, and the ideal friend in the singular is Tillotson. Beale asks her to view the infelicities in the composition with the indulgence that arises from a high esteem for the subject and exemplary friendship. Beale's errors, she explains, will give Tillotson chance to display "all those allowances which I have hinted must be indulged in a Friend." The treatise constitutes Beale's attempt to, in her words, "lay before you my heart, if not what it is, yet what I desire it should be," and she believes that her dedicatee's friendship will make that desired perfection a reality, since Tillotson has already deigned to admit Beale "to the honor" of being Tillotson's "truly affectionate and faithful friend and servant."[69]

The significance of this gender shift in the discourse of friendship cannot be overstated. Even the otherwise fearless Isabella Andreini adopted a male persona in her letters on friendship. After all, the foremost authority on friendship was Cicero—a writer very difficult for a female author to ventriloquize, unless she adopted a male voice, as Andreini did. In this sense, Beale mirrors Moderata Fonte's reconceptualization of friendship as potentially an all-female phenomenon. Yet Beale departed from Fonte in making female friendship a present issue rather than diffusing its power by setting it at a distance, within the imaginary community of a literary dialogue.

If ever there was a clear example of a woman redeploying classical models for her own ends, it is Mary Beale's appropriation of a Ciceronian voice to reimagine friendship as an expression of female equality. Beale was doubtless emboldened, in part, by the centrality of friendship in contemporary latitudinarian discourse. Friendship as a subject was no longer the province of Cicero and his modern academic imitators but had been "modernized" within that part of contemporary Lockean culture with which Beale associated herself. But this adaptation does not explain the way in which she presents herself as an authority on the subject.

Beale establishes her authority in several ways. In the first place, she works within the genre of the formal treatise, proceeding from major premises (the nature and causes of friendship) to minor premises (friendship's effects), and substantiates her argument with relevant passages from the venerable ancient canon. The most striking aspect of Beale's authorial self-presentation, however, is her assertion of female subjectivity. While Tillotson represents the ideal friend, Beale is the treatise's subject, an aspirant to "friendship" who must be examined.

Beale's discussion of the preconditions for friendship is a first-person deliberation. "It is necessary that myself," she explains, "or any who are industrious to enter into this alliance, consider both my own temper and theirs in whom I choose to repose this trust. And first I ought to make a serious enquiry and pass an impartial censure on myself so that I may the better understand how far I am qualified for so sacred a bond; & learning thence my own imperfections, may be able to strive against and restrain them, both by Religion and Reason."[70] Beale's use of the first person voices an authorial "I." The assertion of the scholarly female self was striking enough in the case of Mary Bassett, though Basset could hide (to a certain extent) behind her connection to Thomas More, England's greatest humanist. In contrast, Beale had no scholarly progenitors to "authorize" her, only her own skill in expository prose.

Beale's treatise exemplifies a growing confidence on the part of nonelite Englishwomen. Moving beyond the issue of feminism on the page, however, Beale's case also suggests the existence of feminist sensibility at the intersection of literature and the visual arts. Women writers were the most obvious category of female intellectuals in Renaissance Italy and England, but Beale's case directs attention to the cross-pollination of ideas in different fields of endeavor. Indeed, Beale's dedicatory letter invites us to associate her writing with her painting, as she terms her treatise "a Picture done by a very unskillful hand" and her arguments "the Portraiture of my own inabilities."[71] Of Beale's eighty securely attributed paintings, an impressive oeuvre for any artist, her self-portraits lend themselves well to a feminist reading.

Among the best examples of Beale's visual feminism is her self-portrait as Athena. This image was legible to her contemporaries, especially the poet Samuel Woodford, for whom the portrait served as a pretext for celebrating Beale's learning, artistic skill, and beauty. Beale made related statements about female power in other works, including her self-portrait of 1665/66, in which she represented herself holding smaller images of her two sons, which were executed on canvases prepared by her husband.[72] These images linked her artistic and biological fertility but also articulated her dominant position in this household salon. Like Sofonisba Anguissola, Lavinia Fontana, and Marietta Robusti before her, Mary Beale used her own image to emblematize female confidence and achievement.

Another painting that manifested Beale's feminism was her portrait (ca. 1682) of Aphra Behn, a Restoration playwright remarkable for her own vast oeuvre of sixty-some works, for the fact that she (like Beale) was a commoner who supported herself by taking up a professional career, and, above all, for the way in which her plays voiced current feminist concerns. Behn's eighteen best-known plays include large and heroic female roles, many of which decried the negative effects of marriage on women.[73] Maureen Mulvihill situates Beale's portrait at the heart of feminist historiography in our own time. "Little wonder today's feminists often select the Beale Behn as a pictorial complement to their scholarship," Mulvihill observes. "The image articulates much of the sitter's character and frank sexual dualism. Beale's canvas does not depict a genteel, fashionable lady, but rather a bare-knuckled careerist, up from the mean streets of London, burning to make her mark. It is all there—the strength, the ambition—in the eyes and in the attitude of the chin and the mouth, a mouth that all but smirks and the eyes that lock the viewer in a bold, ironic gaze."[74] Mulvihill has also suggested Beale's identification with Behn, pointing to the "draughtsmanship of the sitter's mouth, hair and bosom [which] resemble that in some of Beale's self-portraits, suggesting perhaps the painter's special identification with her subject, something not uncommon in the intimate dynamics of the portraiture medium."[75] While we cannot do more than speculate on Beale's intentions, it seems more than plausible that Behn served Beale as a model for her own cultural aspirations.

Fifteen years after Beale wrote her treatise exploring friendship as a potential catalyst for social equality, another portraitist and satellite of the Royal Society revitalized the woman question in yet another way. Mary More moved beyond the proposition of equality to an explicit consideration of women's "rights." In so doing, she broadened even Beale's discursive parameters.

More's treatise, "The Woman's Right" (1680s), demonstrates that it had become possible to conceive of women as political beings in late seventeenth-century Britain. Rights discourse was still in its infancy, and More was very much aware of her argument's novelty. Her thesis is that men's supposed "right" to dominance over their wives is like a lie that frequent repetition has given the semblance of truth. "So it is grown between husbands and their wives in our time," More argues, "by a long practicing of Power toward Wives (empowered to it by laws of their own making), I say they are by practice grown into a belief of their Right to that which I do not find allowed either by the Laws of God, nor nature." Her project is to dismantle traditional male dominance and inspire the implementation of "a greater equality between Husbands and Wives than is allowed and practiced in England."[76]

The crux of More's argument is that, even after the Fall, God intended for men and women to collaborate as mates and "yokefellows." She compares true marriage to a pair of oxen pulling a cart, her image for shared responsibility. And while she admits that Eve's sin disrupted the original and "perfect" equality of man and wife, she contends that a husband's authority is nothing more than "one of Eldership." More's principal complaint is that men have constructed theories about absolute male superiority and female inferiority in order to bolster false claims upon their wives' bodies, minds, and property.[77]

More's pivotal distinction, then, is between authority and tyranny. She does not contend that women should hold all of their property or dominate their husbands. Instead, she maintains, men must recognize that their domestic hegemony is built upon false grounds and that they should therefore concede to their wives what is "rightfully" theirs. Wives have a right, if not to autonomy, to fair treatment, respect, and support.

In the manner of the Italian women humanists, More constructs her argument upon a philological foundation. She characterizes women's obligation to men as obedience rather than subjection—analogous to the difference between authority and tyranny that she posited for men. More's case hinges upon her reading of Paul's letters to the Corinthians, in which (she argues) Paul spoke of women's "obedience" to their husbands but not of their "subjection."[78]

Mary More did not expect her male contemporaries to revise their prejudices, let alone common law, in accordance with her treatise. Analytical subtlety aside, she presented no clear suggestions for enacting the "greater equality of wives" for which she argued; indeed, it is unclear what exactly she means by women's "rights." As I suggested above, the text overall suggests that More did not mean political autonomy or complete independence but only fairer treatment and greater latitude for self-determination.

Problematic as her terminology is, however, More's treatise reveals an incipient language of rights.[79] The mature rights discourse of the eighteenth century would give feminists, paradigmatically Mary Wollstonecraft, a rich new language in which to call for the legal and political equality of women—albeit feminist terminology was far from stable even in Wollstonecraft's formulations.[80] This language was not available to Mary More, but she and her contemporaries were beginning to articulate this type of argument in their own words. Moderata Fonte and Lucrezia Marinella pointed to women's "nobility," even spiritual or intellectual "equality" with men, to support their claim that male hegemony was a myth, which customary practice afforded a sense of authority. Mary Beale went a step further toward political discourse by reinventing "friendship" in marriage as a venue for sexual equality. However unclear Mary More is about what she means by women's "rights," it is through this nebulous term that she announces the next phase in the history of women. After More, men and women began to think systematically about social change.

While Mary More wrestles with how to express women's social equality, she harbors no doubt that a recognition of sexual equality in intellectual terms is the first step toward something better, fairer, more egalitarian—the necessary precondition, in short, for improving women's lived experience. And she points to one program for initiating this transformation: women's education. The route out of masculine tyranny for her, as for Fonte, Marinella, and their myriad of male and female predecessors in Italy and in England, was women's substantive training in letters, which would provide women with the means to forge what might best be termed cognitive independence.

Women's intellectual equality informs More's treatise as a whole. In the first place, her own skill in Greek is the precondition for her central argument. Female intelligence, however, is also the central proof that women are beings equal to men and therefore have a right to better treatment. Running concomitantly with her biblical exegesis on "original equality" is a parallel argument about womankind's cognitive equality. Common experience alone proves that "whenever women give themselves to study, they prove as learned and good proficients with as much (or more) ease than men—there having nothing of value ever been done by men, but the same has been done by Women. What has been done may be done: this is a rule in Philosophy." As particular evidence, More cites Anna Maria van Schurman and Lady Jane Grey, "both great Scholars," as well as "Queen Elizabeth of England, who was also so expert in Tongues and Languages that she heard and gave answer to all Ambassadors herself and had the Greek and Latin so fluent that she frequently spoke verses in those languages extempore."[81]

More's conclusion returns to the theme of women's intellectual equality, but with a difference. Departing from the time-honored tradition of claiming women's inherent capability in matters of learning, or even Fonte's and Marinella's direct critique of men's arrogation of power through male control over pedagogical institutions, More makes the discussion of education explicitly political. She concludes that it is "the want of learning and the same education in women that men have, which makes them lose their right. Men always held the [P]arliament and have enacted their own wills, without hearing them speak—so then how easy it is to conclude [women] guilty. Were this Error in Parents amended in their not bringing up their Daughters learned, then I doubt not but they would as much excel men in that as they do now in Virtue."[82] More does not seem to have known the work of Fonte or Marinella, but her argument accords with a central strand in the latter-day *querelle des femmes:* education, not biology, determined women's inferior social roles; thus, if educational practice should change, then women's social and political marginalization would become things of the past.

Seventeenth-century theorists on both sides of the debate recognized the radical potential of women's advanced education. We have already examined many cases in which feminists, male and female, pointed to education as a way forward for women. Education was also the issue that most troubled antifeminists, or at least those who styled themselves as such to score rhetorical points.

Mary More's literary opponent, an Oxford don named Robert Whitehall, offered a rejoinder to her treatise, titled "The Woman's Right Proved False." Whitehall took her case seriously enough to offer a thorough counterargument to her work, which he termed an "ingenious discourse." He presented his rebuttal more as a rhetorical exercise than an expression of conviction, stating that his aim was to help More strengthen her case. "Because your Treatise boasts of demonstrating a Truth new and not commonly known," he explains, "and Novelty is commonly pregnant with Error, none can be reputed blameworthy for bringing it to the Test, weighing it in the Balance of Discretion, and propounding his objections, that these, vanishing by an Additional Light, it may shine with such Meridian Splendor that everyone that runs may read it and acknowledge it most Legitimate."[83] In other words, Whitehall engages More in a debate, challenging her argument in the hope that she will perfect the composition by responding to his objections.

Whitehall's rejoinder is full of gamesmanship, however. His letter to the reader, which precedes the letter to More, offers a humorous list of the potential accusations that "courteous" men and women will hurl at him as motivations for his rebuttal. Chief among these imagined motivations is sexual frustration. He admits that he "lives on Batchelor's Row" but situates his dwelling "at the Sign of Hope in the Land of Love." Despite Whitehall's jokes, his dedicatory letter to More lays out an academic and indeed legal framework that mirrors her style and terminology. He ends this letter with a statement that he has been provoked to "resist [More's] Charge, in order that so famous a Conquest may not be gained by one single stroke of a woman's hand; and to play the Defendant that the Plaintiff may not carry so momentous a Cause . . . *nemine contradicente* [with none objecting]."[84]

Whitehall's objections focus most upon More's notion of education as the engine of social change. In particular, whereas More made a strong case for women's natural intellectual capability (irrespective of male tuition), Whitehall emphasizes instead the need for masculine oversight. "If women arrive to any admirable degree in excellencies above the needle," he argues, "it must be with the conjunction, tuition or conduct of a man."[85] His emphasis on male supervision provides further evidence that the family model had succeeded so well because it satisfied notions of propriety in the minds even of those who adopted a misogynistic stance on female capability.

Although Whitehall aimed to refute "The Woman's Right," nonetheless he represents himself as being "seduced" by More's claim. By the time he reaches his conclusion, Whitehall concedes that, indeed, there ought to be a greater equality between spouses. He urges women to use their traditional powers of persuasion—affective, not rhetorical—to gain parity. "Plead[ing] for equal Authority" is not necessarily illegitimate, he reasons, but neither is it "the most plausible means to obtain it." He urges wives to use love and kindness as a means to become "Empresses of their Husbands' hearts." After this emotional conquest, a wife will have whatever she might desire, even command over her husband and "free dominion over all that is his." By pleasing their husbands (rather than adducing reasoned arguments), he counsels, wives will have access to whatever they want and "both husband and wife, Man and Woman, will have their due right, which is infinitely better than for one only to have theirs."[86] Whitehall's exhortations constitute, in part, a playful "performance" of the antifeminist position. Yet he also signals an attraction to More's argument.

Even if Whitehall and More were both learned people, the significance of their exchange is not its scholarly rigor. Instead, these texts reveal the pervasiveness of a now politically charged *querelle des femmes*. Unlike the similar but much earlier debate in Latin between Isotta Nogarola and Ludovico Foscarini, in which the terms were clear and the discussants addressed each other's arguments forensically, these English treatises are sophistical. Both authors often contradict themselves. And Whitehall, in particular, talks past Mary More in an exaggerated fashion— more committed to wit than debate. If there is one thing that More did not contend, it was that women should exercise "dominion." She did not even posit a full equality between spouses, but only a "greater equality." However, it is striking that a woman painter and an Oxford don should have conversed at all, let alone engaged in such an elaborate discussion.

Overall, Whitehall and More exchanged ideas as equals. Both treatises are contained in a presentation-copy manuscript, which was most likely compiled by Whitehall and intended for circulation. Along with the treatises we have discussed, the volume also included poems by Whitehall and More on the nature of womankind that probably predated their more academic debate. Once again, Whitehall adopts a misogynist stance—indeed, his crude sexual slurs take this performance further than "The Woman's Right Proved False." Taken as a whole, the poetic exchange seems at first glance sharply antagonistic—"antifeminist" versus "feminist." But both parties continued to share compositions in different genres, which suggests that they enjoyed the competition.

The context for the poetic exchange was that More had sent Whitehall what he took to be a copy of Holbein's portrait of Thomas More but that was in fact a portrait of Oliver Cromwell. Whitehall responded with a poem that praised More as "no less Virtuous than Ingenious" but then asserted in his sixth line that "every Lady knows [how] to draw Man In." Here Whitehall invoked a trope of women as cunning manipulators and at the same time made a joke about the female genitalia. Not to be outdone, More lambasted him in her poetic rejoinder as a "squint-eyed Muse," with a lamentable penchant for imitating the Roman poet Martial's bawdy doggerel. Where the sexual act was concerned, she urged him not to write about matters of which he had no experience: "Fellow and Batchelor, it must be so / Hide your sixth line—sure't speaks more than you know!" She ends her poem, which in turn ends the manuscript, with the assertion that she has taught Oxford to "take jeer for jeer from Mary More."[87] A note on the left margin of this folio indicates that the author of the volume (again, probably Whitehall) placed More's poem last. Literally, she got the last word.

The quality of the manuscript as a whole, then, is that of a joking exchange between colleagues. Distasteful as it is, Whitehall's poetry suggests that he treated her as a peer. Indeed, he treated male colleagues and even potential patrons in the same manner. Margaret Ezell has found several male contemporaries who were offended by Whitehall's poems, including the Earl of Rochester (John Wilmot, who was himself a notorious libertine), whom Whitehall certainly intended to impress; so perhaps his poems to More demonstrate his general lack of tact.[88] The fact that he continued his textual conversation with the feminist More and even preserved their exchanges makes Ezell's hypothesis seem all the more plausible.

Whatever the case, More was an explicit feminist both on the page and in practice. She did not, so far as we know, establish a girls' school in the way that her contemporary, Bathsua Makin, did. Yet More took steps along these practical lines when the women closest to her were concerned. As noted earlier, More provided for her granddaughters' financial independence in her final will. What requires emphasis here is that More also offered her daughter intellectual independence. Although her treatise emerged from an exchange with Whitehall, it is dedicated to her daughter, Elizabeth, which suggests that its author had "amended the Error of Parents in not bringing up their Daughters learned." Her dedication also expresses the hope that this composition will make Elizabeth cherish her self-respect and be careful in choosing a husband—should she decide to marry.

More's dedicatory letter to her daughter begins by addressing the apparent disjuncture between lived experience and literary expression: given that the author herself had enjoyed two happy marriages, why should she wish to criticize men or marriage as an institution? "That which has made me more than ordinary to consider this subject," More explains, "has been from a trouble in me observing the sad consequences and events that have fallen on men and their Wives, through this mistake of men's pretending to a Power over their wives that neither God nor nature do allow. And I dare be confident that any unbiased person observe it, they must conclude this to be the first and great cause of most breaches between men and their Wives."[89] More hopes to prevent her daughter from suffering such a misfortune, and the treatise as a whole informs her that male hegemony is a falsehood.

At a more practical level, More's preface offers four pieces of advice on choosing a husband. Provided that Elizabeth lives to her marriageable age and wishes to marry, her mother suggests first that she ask for God's direction in the matter. Thereafter, she must ensure that her potential suitor fears God, as "it is usually the want of grace and not knowing the Scriptures that is the principal cause of the ill-carriage of men to their wives." Next, her daughter should choose a "wise and understanding man," lest her dowry be wasted, with the caveat that Elizabeth should do everything in her power to keep her estate separate from her husband's. The next consideration is that Elizabeth ought to find, "so far as [she can] discover it," a good-tempered man, free from the "harshness and morosity that is sometimes natural in men." Finally, More's daughter must marry a man whom she loves and who loves her in return.[90]

Mary More's treatise is an odd, hybrid text—at once an advice manual for her daughter and a debate with her sparring partner, Robert Whitehall. While More's arguments seem to have remained within the limited circumference of manuscript circulation, "The Woman's Right" nonetheless serves as a gauge for measuring the conceivable in seventeenth-century England. In particular, More's understanding of education as a means to begin equalizing women's social roles reflected an idea that was gaining currency in her era.

Education was the fulcrum around which Italian feminist argument pivoted, as we have seen. Within the English context, we recall that Bathsua Makin even put this idea to the test. Makin's imitators, most notably Mary Astell, would continue to assert themselves as ambassadors for women's intellectual independence. This collective argument for women's education is the aspect of the latter-day *querelle des femmes* that directly prefigures modern feminist argument, paradigmatically Mary Wollstonecraft's *A Vindication of the Rights of Women* (1792). While Wollstonecraft's terminology reflects the evolving discourse of natural and political rights characteristic of the eighteenth century, she nonetheless echoed her predecessors in arguing that the precondition for women to seize control of their lives and become men's equals in marriage and in civic participation was that they receive precisely the same education as men.

Conclusion

OVER the last four decades, scholars have offered various rebuttals to Joan Kelly's contention that women did not have a renaissance, at least during "the Renaissance."[1] This collective reassessment divides into two strands: the historical recovery of women's writing, art, and music that demonstrates women's participation in Renaissance culture; and a systematic examination of a sustained argument in Renaissance literature (especially, but not exclusively, within the genre of the debate on women) that Constance Jordan a decade ago termed "Renaissance feminism."[2]

Emblematic of historical recovery, the series of edited texts titled the Other Voice in Early Modern Europe, edited by Margaret King and Albert Rabil, continues to remind us of the vast quantity of women's writing and writing about women that appeared during the Renaissance era.[3] For the English context, Ostovich and Sauer's recent anthology, *Reading Early Modern Women,* as well as The Early Modern Englishwoman: A Facsimile Library of Essential Works series (edited by Betty Travitsky and Patrick Cullen) have similarly brought an ever-expanding range of English women writers to our attention. However, edited texts and anthologies have the unintended consequence of making women writers appear isolated. How did these women relate to each other and to their male contemporaries? What made this clustering of women writers possible in the first place? Did they make any kind of collective contribution, beyond individually representing (as King and Rabil's series suggests) a counterargument to the negative assessment of womankind inherited from antiquity?

My own study provides a model for understanding these women in the aggregate: they all participated in the emergence of the more general category "woman as intellect," originally made possible by the biographical and rhetorical utility of what I have termed "the intellectual family." The historical significance of Renaissance women writers lies in their collective argument (by word and by example) for the intellectual equality of the sexes, which was the precondition for thinking about the political equality of the sexes.

Indebted to the early work of Patricia Labalme on the feminism of Venetian writers (especially Fonte and Marinella) and to Constance Jordan for providing Europeanists with "Renaissance feminism" as a concept, I have also aimed to provide scholars with a more nuanced model of early modern feminism. Labalme and, following her, Virginia Cox have elucidated the sustained critique of misogyny and patriarchy which emerged in Venetian women's writing of the late sixteenth century. The comparative approach that I have adopted will, I hope, eliminate any notion that Venice was unique in this regard.

Furthermore, by offering a tripartite model of feminist argument, my study aims to prompt a more complex examination of the different ways that early modern women and men articulated a pro-woman stance, beyond explicit critique. There were also "celebratory" feminists, who did not criticize misogyny or patriarchy directly but urged the need to rethink female capability and activity by praising women who had succeeded in male-dominated fields, especially letters. And I have offered the idea of "participatory" feminism as a category of action, especially useful for understanding the contribution that the first wave of English women intellectuals made to Renaissance feminism. While sixteenth-century women humanists neither explicitly criticized the social order nor celebrated the accomplishments of their predecessors, their participation alongside men as scholars and translators proved the equality of the sexes in matters of the mind.

In addition to these categories, this study makes a more critical point about the collaboration of women and men in Renaissance feminism. Scholarship on women writers still tends to situate them as marginal figures, at odds with their social worlds because they went, in Labalme's influential phrase, "beyond their sex."[4] But in fact contemporaries did not always (or even often) view learned women as aberrations or as transgressive "Amazons," in the terms that Margaret King has more recently suggested.[5] Instead, women intellectuals presented themselves and were often received as exemplary daughters, wives, and mothers. From the initial father-daughter paradigm of the fifteenth and sixteenth centuries to the more expansive marital household salon of the late sixteenth and seventeenth centuries, women writers and their male relatives, patrons, supporters, and encomiasts worked together to create a legitimate space for the female voice in literary society.

I situate "Renaissance feminism" at the nexus of text and practice. The best work on theoretical arguments for the dignity of womankind, paradigmatically Pamela Benson's *Invention of the Renaissance Woman*, offers a useful counterpoint to particular studies of women's writings inasmuch as it shows the figure of the "independent woman" emerging in male-authored literary works both in Italy and in England.[6] In so doing, Benson demonstrates the presence of what she terms a "profeminist" hermeneutic among Renaissance men that cries out for comparison and contrast with women's writings. However, the exclusively literary focus of such treatments excludes any attempt to merge rhetoric with lived experience. The present study has linked commonalities in women's biographies to their self-representational strategies to reveal the social foundation in which their feminist texts were grounded.

In short, women indeed had a renaissance during the Renaissance, and its significance was to lay the groundwork for the cognitive emancipation of womankind in Western society. In this sense, I follow an assertion made recently by Margaret King summing up her own response to Joan Kelly-Gadol. "Something changed during the Renaissance in women's sense of themselves," King has claimed, "even if very little changed or changed for the better in their social condition. That change . . . culminates in the consciousness put into words by the first feminists of the Renaissance. Not monsters, not defects in nature, but the intelligent seekers of a new way, these women wielded the picks of their understanding to build a better city for ladies."[7] Yet we can push the idea further. During the Renaissance, it became possible for women to live as recognized intellectuals in society. In addition to a shift in women's self-perception, important changes occurred in contemporary definitions of what it meant to be a woman and in the boundaries of "proper" female activity.

From Christine de Pizan and the early women humanists of the Venetian Republic to the English painter-feminists Mary Beale and Mary More, this study has charted the entrenchment of women intellectuals across geographic, socioeconomic, and disciplinary boundaries. It would be testament enough to women's increased options for self-expression that these women were recognized or indeed wrote anything. What makes them more historically significant, however, is that they so often put their pens in the service of womankind. Supported by their intellectual families, both literal and rhetorical, these women argued for the merit, equality, and finally the rights of women. Literary society did not always agree, but it listened.

Participating in both the project of historical recovery of early modern women writers and the theoretical evaluation of their texts as contributions to "Renaissance feminism," this study offers a fresh model for understanding the emergence and significance of educated women as a recognized figures in the world of European letters. As Pamela Benson and Victoria Kirkham have recently observed, the challenge for scholars is to produce analytical and interpretive models for understanding the profusion of women's writing that is now accessible to us.[8] Collectively, the essays in Benson and Kirkham's *Strong Voices, Weak History* assert the utility of reassessing the relationship of women writers to the broader issue of canon formation in a pan-European context. Diana Robin's latest contribution, *Publishing Women,* provides a different but equally fruitful model for understanding the importance of women writers, especially during the Catholic Reformation, and for understanding women's centrality in early modern culture more broadly. Through a rigorous analysis of dialogues and poetry written by women (many of which appear for the first time in English translation), Robin demonstrates the prominence of Italian women writers committed to religious reform, whose compositions were admired by contemporary men and women and published by leading printer-editors in solo-authored volumes and in poetic anthologies. Robin's work reveals, above all, the dominant role that women took in intellectual life as salonières, gathering intellectuals of both sexes together for discussion and forging communities of mutual support.

Robin's "salon" model marks a watershed in our current understanding of the sodalities from which women writers emerged. Indeed, her analysis has exerted a formative influence on my own conception of "the household salon." Whereas her study shows that widows, for instance, Vittoria Colonna, possessed a degree of freedom that facilitated their relationships with other women and with male colleagues, I have found that a similar latitude existed in households with a patriarch (either father or husband) present. Despite these different approaches, however, both of our studies are committed to understanding the rise of learned women in the aggregate and as a process of collaboration between women and men.

Indeed, this is an exciting moment for historians of women and gender in the early modern period. Scholars from a variety of different perspectives are beginning to write stronger histories for the many voices with which we are becoming familiar. In closing, I would like to highlight some promising avenues for further research that my own study has suggested.

From a theoretical standpoint, women's self-presentation demands further analysis. Stephen Greenblatt famously argued that the historical "self" is a cultural artifact, a site upon which meanings were (and are) inscribed.[9] In other words, our dramatis personae are always and ever constrained by social forces: they are constellations of representations that tell us a great deal about the values of contemporary culture but little or nothing about individual subjectivity. John Martin has redefined "self-fashioning" as a complex dialectic between constraint and invention.[10] However, while Martin punctiliously uses the phrase "men and women," women are not a real category in his work.[11] In contrast, I have argued that women fashioned themselves in the active terms that Martin has suggested. Constrained to a certain extent by social forces, chiefly the notion that women's proper place was in the family, women satisfied convention through use of domestic rhetoric. Moreover, I have contended that women's deference to social scripts was less evidence of constraint than a considered strategy for making their way into literary society.

But of course none of us can fight on all fronts. I have focused upon women intellectuals. The cases of Mary Beale, Mary More, and their Italian predecessors suggest, however, that much more work needs to be done on the strategies of women artists, as well as the cross-pollination of representational techniques between women artists and writers. The case study of Isabella Andreini, moreover, urges us to pay closer attention to actresses. In short, historians and literary critics have much to learn from art historians about "self-fashioning" as a visual practice and from scholars of early modern theater about the self as performative.

Beyond the issue of women's self-presentation, I have focused upon a new line of inquiry concerning the identity of early modern men as promoters, colleagues, and even protégés of learned women. Scholars of early modern masculinity have traditionally construed women (or the abstract concept of woman) as representative of the "other" in men's writing.[12] Women are presented as cosmic antagonists, idealized objects of desire, or the currency to be exchanged in male kinship and friendship economies. It is only within the last few years that scholars have begun to overturn this model. Diana Robin and Julie Campbell have led the way, by turning our attention to collaboration between women writers and their male colleagues and publishers. My own contribution in this regard is to point out that learned men not only worked with and supported their female peers but in fact conceived of women intellectuals as crucial extensions of themselves. Rather than forming their literary and social identities against women in a process of *altérité*, men from Thomas More to Charles Beale (and possibly even the rumbustious Robert Whitehall) understood their female relatives, protégées, and colleagues as representatives of their own most cherished ideals and as active contributors to their intellectual honor. Both Giovanni Battista Andreini and Cristofano Bronzini made learned women into authoritative figures upon whose approbation they staked their own authorial credibility. More generally, we have witnessed time and again early modern biographers presenting learned women, not as abstractions to be reviled or desired, but instead as ambassadors for the excellence of their age—embodiments, in other words, of their own aspirations.

As gender history progresses from its origin as a branch of women's history toward a nuanced understanding of how both "femininity" and "masculinity" were constructed in different times and places, there will doubtless be more systematic explorations of the ways in which relationships to women and "woman" shaped masculine identity than my own study could accommodate.[13] These observations suggest one direction that this exploration might take: that is, analysis of different categories of men and their particular relationships to the women with whom they were related by blood or choice and to the women whom they admired.[14]

Another pivotal issue that has haunted these many pages is religion, specifically the effects of the Reformations (Lutheran, Calvinist, and Catholic) on the emergence of learned women. An old chestnut in the historiography is that the Protestant Reformation exerted a positive influence upon women's education, because reformers stressed the necessity of reading the Bible (and some, including Luther, explicitly included women in this discussion). The trend in recent years has been to temper this claim, if not overturn it, by emphasizing the enhanced power of men as something like "priests" within reformist households. The dissolution of convents in Protestant territories, moreover, eliminated the one female community available to women before the proliferation of girls' schools in the modern era, albeit most women in convents had little choice in the matter. This is a vastly complex issue, in short, and this book must leave it unresolved. These pages are populated with learned women on both sides of the central confessional divide, whom observers heralded as exemplary for their erudite piety. Many of the writers examined here emerged when there could not have been more at stake in the act of putting pen to paper, but the dangers of stepping beyond the various "orthodoxies" seem to have been outweighed—or at least balanced—by the opportunities for contribution. Here we might think of the spiritual poetry of Moderata Fonte and Lucrezia Marinella, as well as the reformist projects of the Cooke sisters and Esther Inglis. What I mean to suggest is that, as we continue interrogating the effects of reform on the woman question, we would do well to think (perhaps paradoxically) of both constraint and opportunity.

Finally, I return to the problem of historical memory with which I began. On the one hand, Karen Offen has cautioned against amnesia—that is, against neglecting to bring the lines of feminist argument that developed before the modern era into our understanding of feminism as a form of social critique with a long history. On the other hand, scholars have cast a censorious eye upon the attempt to write a diachronic history of feminism and in particular to trace arguments about sexual equality from Renaissance Italy to Enlightenment Britain.[15] Amnesia seems the greater evil, however, inasmuch as Renaissance feminists themselves crafted collective, diachronic, and, in many cases, transnational histories of women. Disconnecting the ligatures effaces their project. The idea of a connected narrative of female achievement inspired Christine de Pizan's "Kingdom of Women" and Laura Cereta's "Republic of Women." It inspired Bathsua Makin's humanist curriculum and the biographical encyclopedias, from Betussi to Ballard, that immortalized learned women by the hundreds. Early modern women intellectuals and their male supporters did not always align precisely in their strategies and arguments, but they shared one quality essential to the genesis of feminism: a passionate desire to improve the lot of womankind.

Abbreviations

ADD MSS	Additional MSS
ASV	Archivio di Stato (Venice)
ASVe	Archivio di Stato (Verona)
BNM	Biblioteca Nazionale Marciana (Venice)
BL	The British Library (London)
Cl. It.	Classe Italiana
CWE	*The Collected Works of Erasmus*
EUL	Edinburgh University Library (Edinburgh)
NL	Newberry Library (Chicago)
NLS	National Library of Scotland (Edinburgh)
Test. Not.	Notarile Testamenti
TNA	The National Archives (London)

Notes

Introduction

1. Constance Jordan, *Renaissance Feminism: Literary Texts and Political Models* (Ithaca, N.Y.: Cornell University Press, 1991). Jordan's study prompted a wide scholarly audience to think about the "feminism" of Renaissance literature. Until that point, this line of inquiry had been restricted to a comparatively small group of Italianists, readers of Patricia Labalme's pathbreaking study "Venetian Women on Women: Three Early Modern Feminists," *Archivio Veneto*, 5th ser. vol. 117 (1981): 81–109.

2. A rich collection of essays addressing this question appear in Siep Stuurman and Tjitske Akkerman, eds., *Perspectives on Feminist Political Thought in European History from the Middle Ages to the Present* (London: Routledge, 1998).

3. For an early articulation of this model, see Patricia Labalme, ed., *Beyond Their Sex: Learned Women of the European Past* (New York: New York University Press, 1980); for a more recent approach, see Natalie Zemon Davis, *Women on the Margins: Three Seventeenth-Century Lives* (Cambridge, Mass.: Harvard University Press, 1995).

4. See Diana Robin, *Publishing Women: Salons, the Presses and the Counter-Reformation in Sixteenth-Century Italy* (Chicago: University of Chicago Press, 2007), and Julie Campbell, *Literary Circles and Gender in Early Modern Europe: A Cross-Cultural Approach* (Aldershot: Ashgate, 2006). See also Victoria Kirkham, ed. and trans., *Laura Battiferra and Her Literary Circle: An Anthology* (Chicago: University of Chicago Press, 2006).

5. Jane Stevenson's magisterial *Women Latin Poets: Language, Gender and Authority from Antiquity to the Middle Ages* (Oxford: Oxford University Press, 2005) brings to our attention an impressive collection of ancient and medieval women Latinists, but the origins of the former are scantly documented and the latter were principally learned nuns.

6. Leonardo Bruni, *De studiis et litteris liber ad Baptistam de Malatestis,* in Craig W. Kallendorf, ed. and trans., *Humanist Educational Treatises,* I Tatti Renaissance Library (Cambridge, Mass.: Harvard University Press, 2002), 92–125. For a broader discussion, see Charles Nauert, *Humanism and the Culture of Renaissance Europe* (Cambridge: Cambridge University Press, 1995), 45–46.

7. See Pamela Joseph Benson, *The Invention of the Renaissance Woman: The Challenge of Female Independence in the Literature and Thought of Italy and England* (University Park: Pennsylvania State University Press, 1992), and Constance Jordan, *Renaissance Feminism.*

8. Joan Kelly-Gadol, "Did Women Have a Renaissance?" in Renate Bridenthal and Claudia Koonz, eds., *Becoming Visible: Women in European History* (Boston: Houghton Mifflin, 1977), 139. Kelly-Gadol frames her argument as a challenge to "the Renaissance" as a term of periodization; see especially 152–161.

9. See especially Margaret L. King, "Book-Lined Cells: Women and Humanism in the Early Italian Renaissance," in Labalme, *Beyond Their Sex,* 66–90; King, "Thwarted Ambitions: Six Learned Women of the Italian Renaissance," *Soundings* 59 (1976): 280–304; King, "The Religious Retreat of Isotta Nogarola: Sexism and Its Consequences in the 15th Century," *Signs* 3 (Summer 1978): 807–822; Lisa Jardine, "Isotta Nogarola: Women Humanists—Education for What?" *History of Education* 12 (1983): 231–244 ; Margaret L. King and Albert Rabil, eds., *Her Immaculate Hand: Selected Works by and about the Women Humanists of Quattrocento Italy* (New York: Pegasus Press, 1992); Lisa Jardine, "'O Decus Italiae Virgo: The Myth of the Learned Lady in the Renaissance," *Historical Journal* 28, no. 4 (1985): 799–819.

10. The most comprehensive treatments of Italian women's writing are Virginia Cox, *Women's Writing in Italy, 1400–1650* (Baltimore: Johns Hopkins University Press, 2008); Letizia Panizza, ed., *Women in Italian Renaissance Culture and Society* (Oxford: European Humanities Research Centre of the University of Oxford, 2000), part 4; Letizia Panizza and Sharon Wood, eds., *A History of Women's Writing in Italy* (Cambridge: Cambridge University Press, 2000); Laura Anne Stortoni and Mary Prentice Lillie, eds. and trans., *Women Poets of the Italian Renaissance: Courtly Ladies and Courtesans* (New York: Italica Press, 1997). For women as letter writers, see Gabriella Zarri, ed., *Per lettera: La scrittura epistolare femminile tra archivio e tipografia secoli XV–XVII* (Rome, Viella: 1999). For the idea of woman in sixteenth-century writing, see Marina Zancan, ed., *Nel cerchio della luna: figure di donna in alcuni testi del XVI secolo* (Venice: Marsilio, 1983).

11. For the early model, see Suzanne Hull, *Chaste, Silent and Obedient: English Books for Women, 1475–1640* (San Marino, Calif.: Huntington Library, 1982); Margaret P. Hannay, *Silent but for the Word: Tudor Women as Patrons, Translators and Writers of Religious Works* (Kent, Ohio: Kent State University Press, 1985); and Axel Erdman, *My Gracious Silence: Women in the Mirror of Sixteenth-Century Printing*

in Western Europe (Lucerne: Gilhofer & Ranschburg, 1999). In contrast to this model, Margaret Ezell emphasizes women's literary agency and influence, in *The Patriarch's Wife: Literary Evidence and the History of the Family* (Chapel Hill: University of North Carolina Press, 1987). On the hermeneutics of women's manuscripts, see Elizabeth Clarke, "Women's Manuscript Miscellanies in Early Modern England," in Susanne Woods and Margaret P. Hannay, eds., *Teaching Tudor and Stuart Women Writers* (New York: Modern Language Association, 2000), 52–61. To appreciate the "Italianate" range and scope of Englishwomen's writing, see Helen Ostovich and Elizabeth Sauer, eds., *Reading Early Modern Women: An Anthology of Texts in Manuscript and Print, 1550–1700* (New York: Routledge, 2004).

12. See the rapidly expanding collection of edited texts published in the Other Voice in Early Modern Europe series.

13. Margaret L. King, *Women of the Renaissance* (Chicago: University of Chicago Press, 1991), 184.

14. Margaret Rosenthal, *The Honest Courtesan: Veronica Franco, Citizen and Writer in Sixteenth-Century Venice* (Chicago: University of Chicago Press, 1992), 61.

15. See Clarke, "Women's Manuscript Miscellanies in Early Modern England," 58; Susan Felch, "Anne Vaughan Lock," in Woods and Hannay, *Teaching Tudor and Stuart Women Writers*, 30–31.

16. Margaret Ezell, "To Be Your Daughter in Your Pen: The Social Functions of Literature in the Writings of Lady Elizabeth Brackley and Lady Jane Cavendish," *Huntington Library Quarterly* 51 (1988): 281–296.

17. Ingrid A. R. de Smet, "'In the Name of the Father': Feminist Voices in the Republic of Letters," in Michel Bastiaensen, ed., *Lettered Women in the Renaissance: Proceedings of the International Conference, Brussels, 27–29 March 1996* (Brussels: Peeters, 1997), 196.

18. Elizabeth Kowaleski-Wallace presents a negative assessment of eighteenth-century women writers as "daddy's girls." See her article "Milton's Daughters: The Education of Eighteenth-Century Women Writers," *Feminist Studies* 12 (1986): 275–294, and her more recent monograph, *Their Fathers' Daughters: Hannah More, Maria Edgeworth and Patriarchal Complicity* (New York: Oxford University Press, 1991), vii and 96, for her pejorative use of the term "daddy's girls." In the latter study, Kowaleski-Wallace considers Hannah More and Maria Edgeworth "complicit" with the patriarch in glorifying domestic harmony under male rule in biography and political allegory; both, in her view, were duped by their quasi-sexual attraction to a new species of "enlightened" father: a patriarch who built his authority upon subtle manipulation of psychological dependency.

19. Here I invert Kowaleski-Wallace's formula: while she posits that women writers were "complicit" in serving male interests by toeing the patriarchal line, I consider the possibility that patriarchs were "complicit" in serving

women's interests by encouraging their daughters and protégées to express their own ideas.

20. For a treatment of humanist orations on marriage, a new and thriving genre of literary discourse, see Anthony D'Elia, *The Renaissance of Marriage in Fifteenth-Century Italy* (Cambridge, Mass.: Harvard University Press, 2004). For the connection between rhetoric and personal experience, see especially 2, 83, and 134–137.

21. Joan Wallach Scott, *Only Paradoxes to Offer: French Feminists and the Rights of Man* (Cambridge, Mass.: Harvard University Press, 1996).

22. In *Renaissance Feminism*, Jordan argues that early modern "pro-woman" texts may be considered "feminist" to the degree that they contravened patriarchal assumptions about women's inferior nature and claimed female equality (6, 249), questioned the cultural influences that determine the meaning of gender (135, 157, 264), demonstrated that women have had a role in history (200–213), and "provided the substance of political debate [even without positing] an actionable program" (309).

23. For Benson's discussion of the dialectic between invention and containment of the independent woman as a literary character, see *The Invention of the Renaissance Woman*, 2, 47–51, 181 and 306.

24. In locating "Renaissance feminism" in the works of women writers themselves, I follow especially Diana Robin's studies on the quattrocento humanist Laura Cereta. See Robin, ed., *Laura Cereta: Collected Letters of a Renaissance Feminist* (Chicago: University of Chicago Press, 1997), chap. 2, and her essay "Humanism and Feminism in Laura Cereta's Public Letters," in Panizza, *Women in Italian Renaissance Culture and Society*, 368–384. My emphasis upon the collaboration of women authors with their male colleagues contributes to a new wave of scholarship, especially Robin's *Publishing Women* and Campbell's *Literary Circles*.

25. Siep Stuurman, *François-Poulain de la Barre and the Invention of Modern Equality* (Cambridge, Mass.: Harvard University Press, 2004), 21.

26. For the practice of the English gentry and aristocracy of sending daughters to other households for their basic education and "refinement," see Sharon Michalove, "Equal in Opportunity? The Education of Aristocratic Women, 1450–1540," in Barbara Whitehead, ed., *Women's Education in Early Modern Europe* (New York: Garland Publishing, 1999), 53–59. For the "home school" in the Italian context, see Christiane Klapich-Zuber, "Le chiavi Fiorentine del barbablu: L'apprendimento della lettura nel XV secolo," *Quaderni Storici* 57 (1984): 765–792.

27. Walter Haddon, *Sive exhortatio ad literas* (London: Ex Officina Richardi Graftoni, Regij Impressoris, 1552), sig. C4v.

28. See Stephen Greenblatt, *Renaissance Self-Fashioning: From More to Shakespeare* (Chicago: University of Chicago Press, 1980), and John Martin, "Inventing Sincerity, Refashioning Prudence: The Discovery of the Individual in Renaissance Europe," *American Historical Review* 102 (Winter 1997): 1309–1342. Greenblatt

demonstrates that conceptions of women contributed to male "self-fashioning," but he does not pursue the reverse. Martin finds Greenblatt's treatment (and New Historicism) useful as an interrogation of the ways in which political, social, and cultural institutions influence notions of "self" in the historical context. He criticizes this approach, however, arguing that the Renaissance "self" was a field upon which meaning was contested and created as much as it was constrained and "inscribed."

29. Judith Newton offers a useful discussion of the disjuncture between feminist "New History" and the aims of "New Historicism" in her review of Leonore Davidoff and Catherine Hall's *Family Fortunes: Men and Women of the English Middle Class, 1780–1850* (Chicago: University of Chicago Press, 1987). She sees New History (the analysis of the cultural construction of female identity) as effectively ignored by New Historicism (the reading of written texts as constructions of experience or the material world), despite their similar methodological perspectives. And her claim that "feminist theorists, if they are mentioned at all, are often assumed to be the dependent heirs of male intellectual capital" holds true for Renaissance "self-fashioning." See Newton, "Family Fortunes: 'New History' and 'New Historicism,'" *Radical History Review* 43 (1989): 6.

30. See Mario Biagioli, *Galileo, Courtier: The Practice of Science in the Culture of Absolutism* (Chicago: University of Chicago Press, 1993), 16–18, for a streamlined treatment of male patronage-seeking. For a detailed examination of this process, see Diana Robin, *Filelfo in Milan: Writings, 1451–1477* (Princeton. N.J.: Princeton University Press, 1991), chap. 1.

31. Judith Hallett, *Fathers and Daughters in Roman Society: Women and the Elite Family* (Princeton, N.J.: Princeton University Press, 1984): for affectivity, 31 and 134–135; for social standing, 34–60 and 207; for definition of filiafocality, 64.

32. Judith Hallett, "Woman as 'Same' and 'Other' in Classical Roman Elite," *Helios* 16 (Spring 1989), 62. See also her *Fathers and Daughters in Roman Society.*

33. Lucien Febvre and Henri-Jean Martin have noted eighty-four editions of his letters printed in the fifteenth century alone, of which many were the *Epistolae ad familiares* in particular. See Febvre and Martin, *The Coming of the Book,* trans. David Gerard (London: Verso, 1997), 255.

34. Rosenthal, *The Honest Courtesan,* 27, 73, 153–154, and 165.

35. Elissa Weaver, *Convent Theater in Early Modern Italy: Spiritual Fun and Learning for Women* (Cambridge: Cambridge University Press, 2002); quotation at 239.

36. K. J. P. Lowe, *Nuns' Chronicles and Convent Culture in Renaissance and Counter-Reformation Italy* (Cambridge: Cambridge University Press, 2003), 299–317, for canonesses' Latin orations at the Venetian Convent of Santa Maria delle Vergini. For other treatments of convent culture, see Jutta Sperling, *Convents and the Body Politic in Late Renaissance Venice* (Baltimore: Johns Hopkins University Press, 1999), and Craig Monson, ed., *The Crannied Wall: Women, Religion and the Arts in Early Modern Europe* (Ann Arbor: University of Michigan Press, 1992).

37. Arcangela Tarabotti, *Paternal Tyranny,* ed. and trans. Letizia Panizza (Chicago: University of Chicago Press, 2004). See also Tarabotti's *Lettere familiari e di complimento,* ed. Meredith Kennedy Ray and Lynn Lara Westwater (Turin: Rosenberg and Sellier, 2005), and Elissa Weaver, ed., *Satira e antisatira* (Rome: Salerno Editrice, 1998).

1. Her Father's Daughter

1. Quoted in Charity Cannon Willard, ed., *The Writings of Christine de Pizan* (New York: Persea Books, 1994), 196.

2. Sister Marie Louis Towner, ed., *Lavision-Christine* (Washington, D.C.: Catholic University of America, 1932), 2 (hereafter Towner, ed.) Willard makes the point that not only were Christine's father and maternal grandfather university-trained men, but they were also medical doctors. Her grandfather, Tomaso da Mondino, was also a counselor in Venice, a "conseiller salarié de la République." See also Marie-Josèph Pinet, *Christine de Pisan, 1364–1430, étude biographique et littéraire* (Paris: Librairie Ancienne Honoré Champion, 1927), 2.

3. Pinet, *Christine de Pisan,* 7.

4. See comment by Renate Blumenfeld-Kosinski, "Christine de Pizan and the Political Life in Late Medieval France," in Barbara Altman and Deborah McGrady, eds., *Christine de Pizan: A Casebook* (New York: Routledge, 2003), 9.

5. Margaret L. King and Diana Robin, eds. and trans., *Isotta Nogarola: Complete Writings: Letterbook, Dialogue on Adam and Eve, Orations* (Chicago: University of Chicago Press, 2004), 1 (hereafter, King and Robin).

6. Christine's manuscript tradition in France and her print tradition in England were strong. Her manuscript tradition in Italy is more difficult to assess. There are manuscript presentation copies of her biography of Charles V (1404), now in the Biblioteca d'Este in Modena and the Biblioteca Apostolica Vaticana. For the idea that her work was known to the northern Italian courts through manuscripts sent there from her French noble patrons, see Pinet, *Christine de Pisan,* 454. Christine herself mentions that her French patrons had sent some of her works to the Duke of Milan, Giangaleazzo Visconti, who then offered her a place at his own court. She presents this as a tempting prospect made all the more appealing because she was a widow in serious financial difficulty and Visconti had promised that his literary patronage would involve financial remuneration. She considers it further evidence of fortune's animosity that the duke died before she could accept his offer and rebuild her estate. The relevant passage appears in Towner, ed., 166–167.

7. Lady Philosophy is a literary interlocutor taken from Boethius's *Consolation of Philosophy.*

8. Willard, *The Writings of Christine de Pizan,* 196.

9. Ibid., 195–196.

10. Ibid., 196.

11. Christine probably had direct knowledge of Giovanni Andrea, who was a colleague of her father's at the University of Bologna. And Christine used John of Legnano's *Tractatus de Bello* at several points in her *Deeds of Arms and Chivalry*— Legnano had married into the Andrea family. See Willard, *The Writings of Christine de Pizan*, 211n35.

12. For a recent treatment of this text, see Anne Marie de Gendt, *L'art d'éduquer les nobles damoiselles: Le livre du Chevalier de la Tour Landry* (Paris: Honoré Champion, 2003). This text was popular not only in France but also in Germany and in England. William Caxton, who made great profit from printing French courtly literature that suited the tastes of his largely aristocratic clientele, printed his own translation of this text in 1484. For a thorough treatment of Caxton's biography and printing strategies, see N. F. Blake, *Caxton and His World* (London: Deutch, 1969). Caxton also printed two of Christine's texts and even credited her as their author (a practice not always followed by her early modern editors): the *Enseignements moraux* (*The Morale Proverbes of Christyene*, 1478) and *Le Livre des faits d'armes et de chevalerie* (*The Book of the Fayttes of Armes and of Chyvalrye*, 1489). There was also an English version of her *Livre de la Cité des Dames* (*Boke of the City of Ladies*, 1521).

13. In the Caxton edition of the *Book of the Knight*, the Knight's prologue adduces the highly limited rationale for women's instruction that I summarize in the text. Caxton's translation is printed in the *Book of the Knight of the Tower*, ed. M. Y. Offord (London: Oxford University Press, 1971), 12. The Knight states explicitly that women should be able to read but not necessarily to write (121–122).

14. Astrik L. Gabriel, "The Educational Ideas of Christine de Pisan," *Journal of the History of Ideas* 16, no. 1 (January 1955): 3–21; quotations at 11 and 13.

15. French text in Towner, ed., 161.

16. Ibid., 163.

17. Ibid.

18. G. L. Masetti Zannini, *Motivi storici dell'educazione femminile (1500–1650)*, vol. 1: *Morale, religione, lettere, arte, musica* (Bari: Editorialebari, 1980) and vol. 2: *Scienza, lavoro, giuochi* (Naples: M. D'Auria Editore, 1981).

19. As Willard observes, Christine's reference in *The Hours of Contemplation on the Passion of Our Lord* to having translated passages of sacred history from the Latin to the French (for the benefit of women who would not otherwise have been able to read them) serves as evidence that her Latin was far from rudimentary. See Willard, *The Writings of Christine de Pizan*, 347. Scholars have not been able to assign a specific date to this composition but only note that it was written between 1418 and 1429, and Maureen Boulton favors the latter end of the date range, speculating that Christine may well have written this reflective piece after the death of her son in 1425. See Maureen Boulton's chapter "'Nous deffens de feu, . . . de pestilence, de guerres': Christine de Pizan's Religious Works," in Altman and McGrady, *Christine de Pizan: A Casebook*, 223.

20. Willard, *The Writings of Christine de Pizan*, 6.

21. Ibid., x.

22. Towner, ed., 169.

23. Willard, *The Writings of Christine de Pizan*, x, 21, and 26n34.

24. Ibid., x.

25. Towner, ed., 174.

26. Willard, *The Writings of Christine de Pizan*, 197. The distracting effect of her mother's presence also appears symbolically in the opening section of her *City of Ladies*. While the author is lucubrating in her study, surrounded by her books, her mother calls her away to a meal—a needed break and refreshment but also a diversion from philosophical contemplation (in her masculine study) to the kitchen and dining room, parts of the household that are coded feminine. Christine makes a point that she returned to her study the following day; in the same way, she later emphasizes that her quest for philosophical understanding conquered her mother's urgent wish that she devote herself only to "feminine pursuits." See Willard, *The Writings of Christine de Pizan*, 171.

27. Towner, ed., 174.

28. Ibid., 165.

29. Her poem is printed in Maurice Roy, ed., *Oeuvres Poétiques de Christine de Pisan*, vol. 1: *Autres Ballades* (Paris: Librairie de Firmin, 1885), no. 22, 232–233; quotation at 233.

30. Towner, ed., 165–166.

31. Ibid., 166.

32. Roy, *Oeuvres Poétiques de Christine de Pisan*, 232–233.

33. Willard, *The Writings of Christine de Pizan*, 141.

34. Towner, ed., 168. Lori Walters suggests that Christine's writings reveal a tripartite framework of paternal heritage. In Walters's view, Christine represented herself as her biological father's daughter, the literary daughter of the king, her patron, and the intellectual heir of Thomas Aquinas. See Walters's "Constructing Reputations: Fama and Memory in Christine de Pizan's *Charles V* and *L'Advision Cristine*," in Thelma Fenster and Daniel Lord Smail, eds., *Fama: The Politics of Talk and Reputation in Medieval Europe* (Ithaca, N.Y.: Cornell University Press, 2003), 118–144.

35. This is a compliment that belongs to the Boccaccian mode of praising exemplary women for having exceeded the weakness commonly attributed to their sex and should not be taken to indicate that Gerson considered her a "virago" in the negative sense. See King's third chapter in *Women of the Renaissance*, "Virgo et Virago," for a good discussion of the problem.

36. This sketch of Christine's reception appears in Towner, ed., 12–13.

37. For the initial formulation of this argument, see Margaret L. King, "Book-Lined Cells: Women and Humanism in the Early Italian Renaissance," in *Beyond*

Their Sex: Learned Women of the European Past, ed. Patricia Labalme (New York: New York University Press, 1984), 66–90; for a reassertion of this claim, see King's *Women of the Renaissance* (Chicago: University of Chicago Press, 1991), 192–194.

38. Towner, ed., 164–165.

39. See especially Paula Findlen, "A Forgotten Newtonian," in William Clark et al., eds., *The Sciences in Enlightened Europe* (Chicago: University of Chicago Press, 1999), 215–224.

40. See King, *Women of the Renaissance*, 193, and "Book-Lined Cells," 78–79.

41. King, "Book-Lined Cells," 70. Text of the oration appears in G. B. Mittarelli, *Bibliotheca codicum manuscriptorum monasterii S. Michaelis Venetiarum prope Murianum* (Venice, 1779), cols. 701–702.

42. A slightly larger collection of work from Varano remains extant; texts are available in the appendix of B. Feliciangeli, "Notizie sulla vita e sugli scritti di Costanza Varano-Sforza," *Giornale storico della letteratura italiana* 23 (1894): 50–75. King outlines these family connections to Battista in "Book-Lined Cells," 67 and 83n3, noting also that Battista's great-granddaughter, Vittoria Colonna, would became the grande dame of sixteenth-century Italian poetry.

43. See Diana Robin, ed. and trans., *Cassandra Fedele: Letters and Orations* (Chicago: University of Chicago Press, 2000), 7, and Robin, ed., *Laura Cereta: Collected Letters of a Renaissance Feminist* (Chicago: University of Chicago Press, 1997), 7.

44. A recent approach to the interpenetration of the lagoon city with its mainland territories is Elisabeth Crouzet-Pavanne, "The Lion and the Land," chap. 3 in *Venice Triumphant: The Horizons of a Myth*, trans. Lydia G. Cochrane (Baltimore: Johns Hopkins University Press, 1999). A useful older essay by Eugenio Musatti appears as "La conquista della Terraferma," in Gianni Guadalupi, ed., *Repubblica di Venezia*, vol. 3: *Stati di Terraferma* (1400–1530): 23–37.

45. See Robin, *Laura Cereta*, 3.

46. King and Robin, 15.

47. Bianca dictated her final testament to a priest at the Chiesa di Santo Stefano in Verona; he attests that he wrote the will "because Madonna Biancha does not know how to write." Quoted from Isotta Nogarola, *Isottae Nogarolae Veronensis: Opera quae supersunt omnia*, ed. Eugenius Abel (Vienna: Gerold et Socios, 1886), 1: cxlix (hereafter, Abel). As King and Robin point out, Bianca was unconventional not only in educating her daughters but also in dividing much of her estate between her son Lodovico and daughter Isotta, whom she also names as her executors. See King and Robin, 29. Smaller financial bequests to her other daughters may hint at a desire to ensure the tradition for female learning initiated by Bianca's sister-in-law and continued by her daughters. She leaves to her daughters Isabella, Bartolomea, Laura, and Ginevra "ten libre apiece for purposes of instruction and for all other legitimate uses" (Abel, 1: cxlvii).

48. Abel, 1: 110.

49. King and Robin, 33.

50. The noble Barbaro family of Venice produced several noted intellectuals: Francesco; the Ermolao discussed here (who would become bishop of Verona in 1453); and a younger Ermolao (b. 1453/54), grandson of Francesco and an expert in the Aristotelian corpus. The connections between these men are found in their respective entries in the *Dizionario biografico degli Italiani* (Rome: Societa Grafica Romana, 1964–), 6: 95–97.

51. Abel, 1: 6–12.

52. Ibid., 1: 3–6.

53. Ibid., 1: 12–18.

54. Ibid., 1: 25–35. Another early correspondent was Antonio Borromeo, a Paduan nobleman and the sisters' maternal uncle. Isotta and Borromeo corresponded from 1436 to 1440, and she stayed at his residence in Venice during at least one extended visit to the city. See Abel, 1: 42–46.

55. King and Robin, 44.

56. Abel, 1: 7–8.

57. Ibid., 1: 44–45.

58. Ibid., 1: 61–64 and 72.

59. Ibid., 1: 77–78.

60. Ibid., 2: 164.

61. Ibid., 2: 72.

62. Ibid., 2: 81–82.

63. King and Robin, 42.

64. Ibid., 43.

65. Abel, 1: 86–87.

66. Ibid., 1: 89.

67. King and Robin, 43.

68. Abel, 1: 93–102.

69. Ibid., 1: 103–107.

70. King and Robin, 64 and n4.

71. Abel, 1: 156–157.

72. Ibid., 1: 157.

73. Archivio di Stato (Verona) (hereafter, ASVe), Archivietti Privati (Nogarola): B.41bis., f. 64., "Sacrae Theologae Magister Dominus Leonardus de Nogarolis q. alterius Domini Leonardi de Nogarolis de Sancta Cecilia Veronensis procurator."

74. See King and Robin, 3n4.

75. King and Robin, 6.

76. Cecil H. Clough, "The Cult of Antiquity: Letters and Letter Collections," in Clough, ed., *Cultural Aspects of the Italian Renaissance: Essays in Honour of Paul Oskar Kristeller* (New York: Manchester University Press, 1976), 46; Elizabeth McCahill, "Humanism in the Theater of Lies: Classical Scholarship in the Early

Quattrocento Curia" (PhD diss., Princeton University, 2005), especially 105–112 and 158–192; and Ingrid Rowland, "Revenge of the Regensburg Humanists, 1493," *Sixteenth Century Journal* 25, no. 2 (Summer 1994): 307–322.

77. Lauro Martines, *Strong Words: Writing and Social Strain in the Italian Renaissance* (Baltimore: The Johns Hopkins University Press, 2001), 24–25.

78. Ibid., 26.

79. Sharon Strocchia, "Gender and the Rights of Honor in Italian Renaissance Cities," in Judith Brown and Robert C. Davis, eds., *Gender and Society in Renaissance Italy* (London: A. W. Longman, 1998), 56–57.

80. For further details of the invective controversy, see Arnaldo Segarizzi, "Niccolò Barbo patrizio veneziano del secolo XV e le accuse contro Isotta Nogarola," *Giornale storico della letteratura italiana* 43 (1904): 39–54; King and Robin, 6–7.

81. King and Robin, 12.

82. There are several sources for these letters. In addition to Abel's edition of Nogarola's complete works (1886), which includes all of Foscarini's epistles, are the transcriptions made by the collector Emmanuele Cigogna in 1884 from a codex owned by Marco Foscarini: "De laudibus Isottae Nogarolae," Museo Correr (Venice), Cod. Cicogna MSS 3659/IV.

83. Gabriella Zarri, "Profeti di corte nell'Italia del Rinascimento," in Daniel Bornstein and Roberto Rusconi, eds., *Mistiche e devote nell'Italia tardomedievale* (Naples: Luguori Editore, 1998), 209–236.

84. Foscarini, "De laudibus," fols. 6v–8v.

85. These women are listed in Tommaso Nappo, ed., *Indice biografico Italiano*, 2nd ed. (K. G. Saur: Munich, 1997), culled from Maria Bandini Buti's "Poetesse e scrittrici," in the *Enciclopedia bio-bibliografica italiana* (Rome: Tosi, 1941–1942).

86. ASVe, Archivio Pindemonte-Rezzonico, B.380, item 1 (family tree). See also Lodovico's testament of 1483, AsVe, Test. B.75, n90.

87. Robin, *Cassandra Fedele*, 4.

88. Ibid., and Margaret L. King, "Thwarted Ambitions: Six Learned Women of the Italian Renaissance," *Soundings* 59 (1976): 280–304.

89. Diana Robin does not frame the issue in terms of influence, but makes the crucial point that learned women, prior to Cassandra Fedele and Laura Cereta, almost exclusively derived from the ruling elite. See Robin, "Editor's Introduction," in *Cassandra Fedele*, 7, and "Translator's Introduction" in *Laura Cereta*, 7.

90. For Robin's discussion of Nogarola's public speaking, see her comments in King and Robin, 12–14, and her chap. "The Black Swan," 160ff. Nogarola may have delivered her celebrated oration to Pope Pius II at the Congress of Mantua (1459) but may also have delegated this task to another intellectual (Robin, "The Black Swan," 175). It seems that Ippolita Sforza (at the age of fourteen) delivered a Latin oration at this congress. See Anthony D'Elia, *The Renaissance of Marriage in Fifteenth-Century Italy* (Cambridge, Mass.: Harvard University Press, 2004), 112.

91. Jacopo Filippo Tomasini, ed., *Clarissimae Feminae Cassandrae Fidelis, venetae Epistolae et orationes* (Padua: Franciscus Bolzetta, 1636), 94.

92. Tomasini, ed., *Clarissimae Feminae Cassandrae Fidelis*, 200–201.

93. As Letizia Panizza has noted, this is the only work of Fedele's to have been printed in her lifetime. See Panizza and Sharon Wood, eds., *A History of Women's Writing in Italy* (Cambridge: Cambridge University Press, 2000), 27.

94. See Diana Robin, *Filelfo in Milan: Writings, 1451–1477* (Princeton, N.J.: Princeton University Press, 1991), 6 and 43–44.

95. Tomasini, ed., *Clarissimae Feminae Cassandrae Fidelis*, 141–142.

96. Diana Robin, "Cassandra Fedele's Epistolae (1488–1521): Biography as Ef-facement," in Thomas F. Mayer and D. R. Woolf, eds. *The Rhetorics of Life-Writing in Early Modern Europe: Forms of Biography from Cassandra Fedele to Louis XIV* (Ann Arbor: University of Michigan Press, 1995), 193; see also Robin, *Cassandra Fedele*, 9.

97. Richard Saller, *Patriarchy, Property and Death in the Roman Family* (Cambridge: Cambridge University Press, 1994), 227.

98. Tomasini, ed., *Clarissimae Feminae Cassandrae Fidelis*, 52.

99. Ibid., 32.

100. Ibid., 167.

101. Ibid., 165.

102. Ibid., 166.

103. Ibid., 159.

104. Panfilo's oeuvre appears to be relatively small, consisting of four volumes of epigrams published in 1499 and his *Opera del preclarissimo poeta messer Panfilo Sasso* (1511). Both works postdate his correspondence with Cassandra Fedele, which suggests that she may have facilitated his connections with intellectuals of her acquaintance.

105. Tomasini, ed., *Clarissimae Feminae Cassandrae Fidelis*, 184.

106. Ibid., 185.

107. Robin, *Cassandra Fedele*, 6.

108. As to the lack of writing from her married years, this may not necessarily indicate that domestic duties interfered with her intellectual activity. She and Gian-Maria lost all of their possessions in a shipwreck on their return to Venice from Crete, where he had been practicing medicine. See Robin, *Cassandra Fedele*, 6.

109. By contrast, Fedele's most important seventeenth-century biographer, Tomasini, did note that "it pleased her father to give her, his dearest daughter, in marriage to Giovanni Maria Mapelli of Vicenza, noteworthy for his erudition and knowledge of medicine. While she herself seemed to prefer the love of letters and a life of solitude, nonetheless by virtue of her piety she did not disdain the counsel of her father" (*Clarissimae Feminae Cassandrae Fidelis*, 37).

110. Robin, *Cassandra Fedele*, 6.

111. Tomasini, ed., *Clarissimae Feminae Cassandrae Fidelis*, 190–191.

112. Ibid., 191.

113. Robin, *Cassandra Fedele*, 6.

114. See Stanley Chojnacki, *Women and Men in Renaissance Venice* (Baltimore: Johns Hopkins University Press, 2000), 98–130.

115. Archivio di Stato (Venice), Test. Not., Atti Baldigara, B.70, n50 (28 August 1556).

116. Ibid.

117. Venetian writers commensurate with Cassandra Fedele in terms of literary credentials, such as Modesta da Pozzo (Moderata Fonte) and Lucrezia Marinella, neither wrote autograph testaments nor signed the notarial copy. That even learned women do not always leave evidence of their literacy in this way cautions against using signatures on legal documents for determining literacy rates. This statistical approach has led one scholar to contend that women in high-medieval Venice (including nuns) were illiterate. See Irmgard Fees, *Eine Stadt lernt schreiben: Venedig vom 10. bis zum 12. Jahrhundert* (Tübingen: Max Niemeyer, 2002).

118. Albert Rabil, *Laura Cereta: Quattrocento Humanist* (Binghamton, N.Y.: Medieval and Renaissance Texts and Studies, 1981), 15–18 (hereafter, Rabil).

119. Robin, *Laura Cereta*, 25.

120. Ibid., 53.

121. Ibid., 27. For the Latin of her letter to Silvestro, and her long autobiographical letter describing her education, see Laura Cereta, *Laurae Ceretae Brixiensis Feminae Clarissimae Epistolae iam primum e MS in lucem productae*, ed. Jacopo Filippo Tomasini (Padua: Sebastiano Sardi, 1640), 40–42 and 145–154.

122. For her ironic but accurate use of legal terminology, see the letter to Bonifacio Bembo, a professor at Pavia and Rome who was one of her father's friends, see Cereta, *Laurae Ceretae*, 117–122; for the suit, see Cereta, *Laurae Ceretae*, letters 4, 7, and 9.

123. Rabil, 15–18.

124. Cereta, *Laurae Ceretae*, 42.

125. Robin summarizes the compositions of this era as Cereta's "fathering letters," when Cereta wrote to her father and acted as a father both to Silvestro and to her brothers. See Robin, *Laura Cereta*, 52–53.

126. To Bonifacio Bembo (professor of rhetoric), Cereta, *Laurae Ceretae*, letter 3 (17–18); to Alberto degli Alberti, attorney, Cereta, *Laurae Ceretae*, letter 22 (43–45); to Domenico Patussi, attorney, Cereta, *Laurae Ceretae*, letter 4 (18–19).

127. Letters to brothers Hippolito and Basilio, Cereta, *Laurae Ceretae*, letter 40 (87–88). To Olivieri, there are five letters, the most important of which are on her brothers' behalf; see Cereta, *Laurae Ceretae*, letter 39 (85–87). To further her own career, Cereta also sends Olivieri her compositions; see Cereta, *Laurae Ceretae*, letter 38 (83–85).

128. See Robin, "Translator's introduction" in *Laura Cereta*, 3–4.

129. See Cereta, *Laurae Ceretae:* for letters to her husband, pages 20–21, 23, 26–27, and 36–37; to her mother, 27–28; to her father, 40–41; to her sister Diana, 32–33; to her sister Deodata, a nun, 168–177; to her brothers Hippolito and Basilio, 86–87.

130. Robin, *Laura Cereta*, 34–35; Cereta, *Laurae Ceretae*, letter 11, 27–28.

131. Cereta, , *Laurae Ceretae*, 149.

132. Ibid., 149–150.

133. On "the heroic widow," see Liliane Dulac, "Un mythe didactique chez Christine de Pizan: Semiramus ou la veuve héroique," in *Mélanges de Philologie Romane offerts à Charles Campoux* (Montpellier, 1978), 315–343; and Louise Mirrer, ed., *Upon My Husband's Death: Widows in Literature and Histories of Medieval Europe* (Ann Arbor: University of Michigan Press, 1992).

134. Cereta, *Laurae Ceretae*, 7.

135. Rabil, 23.

136. Ibid., 7–9.

137. King, "Thwarted Ambitions"; Lisa Jardine, "Isotta Nogarola: Women Humanists—Education for What?" *History of Education* 12 (1983): 231–244.

138. Lisa Jardine, *Still Harping on Daughters: Women and Drama in the Age of Shakespeare* (Sussex: Harvester Press, 1983), chap. 3.

139. Pier Paolo Vergerio, *De Ingenibus Moribus et Liberalibus Adulescentiae Studiis Liber,* Craig Kallendorf, ed. and trans., Humanist Educational Treatises (Cambridge, Mass.: Harvard University Press, 2008), 2–91. See also Charles Nauert, *Humanism and the Culture of Renaissance Europe* (Cambridge: Cambridge University Press, 1995), 45.

2. Household Academies in Venice and London

1. Richard Mulcaster, *Positions,* ed. Richard de Molen (New York: Columbia Teacher's College Press, 1971), 127. (hereafter, Mulcaster).

2. Nicholas Harpsfield, *The Life and Death of Sir Thomas More,* ed. Elsie Vaughan Hitchcock (London: Oxford University Press, 1932), 92 (hereafter, Harpsfield). Nicholas Harpsfield (1519?–1575), archdeacon of Canterbury under Mary Tudor, was instrumental in dispatching Protestants during the her reign.

3. Walter Haddon, *Sive exhortatio ad literas* (London: Richard Grafton, 1552), sig. C4v.

4. I am grateful to Paula Findlen for pointing out Bembo's will and correspondence (published and unpublished) as a treasure trove of information about his academic ambitions for both children.

5. Testament in Biblioteca Nazionale Marciana (Venice), Cl. It. XI, 25 (=6671), fol. 1v (hereafter, BNM).

6. Italian text in Giuseppe Spezi, ed., *Lettere inedite del Card. Pietro Bembo e di Altri Scrittori del Secolo XVI,* Tratte da Codici Vaticani e Barberiniani (Rome: Tipografia delle Scienze Matematiche e Fisiche, 1862), 53 (hereafter Spezi, ed.).

7. BNM, Cl. It. XI, 25 (=6671), fol. 18r.

8. Ibid., fol. 16r and fol. 18r.

9. Spezi, ed., 49–51.

10. Ibid., 53.

11. Pietro Bembo, *Il quarto volume delle lettere di M. Pietro Bembo: a prencipesse, & signori & altre gentili donne scritte* (Venice: Girolamo Scotto, 1563), 63b–64a.

12. For Bembo's role in the "language wars," see Mario Sansone, "Il senso del Dibattito Cinquecentesco," in Francesco Tateo, ed., *Da Bembo a Galiani: Il dibattito sulla lingua in Italia* (Bari: Adriatica Editrice, 1999), 24–28.

13. Bembo, *Il quarto volume*, 70b–71a.

14. Ibid.

15. Spezi, ed., 56.

16. Ibid., 58–59.

17. One instance is Bembo's letter of 1544 from Rome (available in the published collection of Bembo's works vol. 3, Venice, 1729), quoted in BNM, Cl. It. XI, 25 (=6671), fol. 26r. Other instances of such letters are in BNM, Cl. It. XI, 25 (=6671), fol.28r–v and fol. 36r–v. In the latter case of "quanto padre," Bembo underscores his rhetorical intention by phrasing his signature "vostro come padre" (fol. 36r).

18. BNM, Cl. It. XI, 25 (=6671), fol. 26r.

19. Ibid.

20. In 1549 the Paduan lutist and composer Melchiore (de) Barberis dedicated to Torquato *Intabolatura di lauto* (Venice: Scotto), the ninth book of which was entitled "il Bembo." In 1550 Francesco Portinaro dedicated to Torquato a collection of *Madrigali* (Venice: Antonio Gardano).

21. Paula Findlen offers an excellent analysis of Torquato's dissipation of his father's famous *studio* (Bembo's collection of manuscripts, books, and antiquities) and, more broadly, the difficulties of sixteenth-century collectors in legally defining this kind of intellectual patrimony. See Findlen's "Ereditare un museo: Strategie familiari e pratiche culturali nell'Italia del XVI secolo," *Quaderni Storici* 115 (April 2004): 45–81.

22. Archivio di Stato (Venice), Misc. Test. Notai Diversi (Atti Giuseppe Volpini) B. 30, n3067.

23. Spezi, ed., 60–61.

24. Ibid., 61.

25. Bembo, *Il quarto volume*, 71b–72a.

26. BNM, Cl. It. XI, 25 (=6671), fol. 1r–v.

27. Pietro Bembo, *Il terzo volume delle lettere di M. Pietro Bembo, a Prencipi, Signori, & suoi famigliari amici scritte. Di nuovo riveduto & stampato* (Venice: Girolamo Scotto, 1563), 331a–b.

28. Ibid., 331b.

29. Bembo, *Il quarto volume*, 72a–b.

30. Ibid., 74a.

31. Ibid., 61b.

32. Letters praising Giulia's sagacity and expressing concern for her near-perpetual state of pregnancy and childbirth appear in Bembo's published letters to his nephew.

33. Francesco Sansovino, *Vita della illustre Signora Contessa Giulia Bemba della Torre* (Venice: Domenico and Gio. Battista Guerra, fratelli, 1565).

34. Sansovino, *Vita*, sig. A3v.

35. Ibid., sig. A3r.

36. Bembo, *Il terzo volume*, 221a–222a.

37. Ibid., 222b.

38. Bembo, *Il quarto volume*, 29a–30b.

39. Ibid., 31a.

40. Ibid., 31a, 35a, and 38b.

41. Ibid., 38b.

42. Ibid., 38b.

43. Ibid., 39a and 45a.

44. Thomas More, *Epigrammata Thomae Mori Angli* (London: Humphrey Mosley, 1638), sig. D8v–E1r.

45. Ibid., sig. E1r–v.

46. Ibid., E1v–E2r.

47. Ibid., E2r–E3r. I have not encountered anywhere else the representation of Eurydice as an educated woman nor other references to the daughter of Ovid as the heir of his poetic skill.

48. Kenneth Charlton, *Education in Renaissance England* (London: Routledge, 1965), 41.

49. Pathbreaking studies of humanism's connection to Christianity are Lewis W. Spitz, *The Religious Renaissance of the German Humanists* (Cambridge, Mass.: Harvard University Press, 1963), and Charles Trinkaus, *In Our Image and Likeness: Humanity and Divinity in Italian Humanist Thought* (Chicago: University of Chicago Press, 1970).

50. Elizabeth Rogers, ed., *The Correspondence of Sir Thomas More* (Princeton, N.J.: Princeton University Press, 1947), 96–97 (hereafter, Rogers, ed.).

51. Richard Hyrde (d. 1528) is best known for being the first English translator of Juan Luis Vives's *On the Education of a Christian Woman* (1529). More cultivated Vives during the 1520s, and Hyrde likely met him in More's household. For this connection, see Pamela Joseph Benson, *The Invention of the Renaissance Woman: The Challenge of Female Independence in the Literature and Thought of Italy and England* (University Park: Pennsylvania State University Press, 1992), 179–181 (hereafter, Benson).

52. For the Latin text, see Rogers, ed., 121–122.

53. Ibid., 122.

54. Ibid. As Benson also notes, More uses the subjunctive when discussing women's inherent wickedness, which attests that he feels the point far from certain—though some scholars have taken this passage literally and put More in the same camp as Vives and worse. See Benson, 223. See also Benson, 157–158, for contrasts between More and Vives.

55. Rogers, ed., 122.

56. Ibid., 123.

57. Ibid., 97. A similarly broad encouragement to secular studies, devoid of moral exhortation, appears in More's note to his whole school, "Toti Scholae Suae Salutem," Rogers, ed., 249–250.

58. Rogers, ed., 255.

59. Ibid., 256 (emphasis mine). John Guy has suggested that More never expected his son, John, to take up a profession. See John A. Guy, *Thomas More* (New York: Oxford University Press, 2000), 75. In any event, John never did make much of his training, but More did have high expectations for him in these early years.

60. Rogers, ed., 256–257.

61. Ibid., 135.

62. Ibid., 255.

63. Quoted from the translaton in Desiderius Erasmus, *Collected Works of Erasmus* (Toronto: University of Toronto Press, 1989), 29: 173 (hereafter, *CWE*).

64. Rogers, ed., 257.

65. Pole was the grandson of Richard III's brother, the Duke of Clarence, and would eventually become archbishop of Canterbury under Mary Tudor.

66. Rogers, ed., 301–302.

67. See Margaret L. King, *Women of the Reniassance* (Chicago: University of Chicago Press, 1991),142–143, for a discussion of the Colonna-Pole connection.

68. Lisa Jardine, "Isotta Nogarola: Women Humanists, Education for What?" *History of Education* 12 (1983): 40. See also Margaret L. King, "Book-Lined Cells: Women and Humanism in the Early Italian Renaissance," in Patricia Labalme, ed., *Beyond Their Sex: Learned Women of the European Past* (New York: New York University Press, 1980), 75–90; and Letizia Panizza and Sharon Wood, *A History of Women's Writing in Italy* (Cambridge: Cambridge University Press, 2000), 2–8 and 26.

69. Constance Jordan's review of the recent publications from the Other Voice in Early Modern Europe series revisits the notion that women's virtues included only chastity and silence. See Jordan, "More from 'The Other Voice' in Early Modern Europe," *Renaissance Quarterly* 55 (2002): 258–271.

70. John Jeffries Martin, "Inventing Sincerity, Refashioning Prudence: The Discovery of the Individual in Renaissance Europe," *American Historical Review* 102 (Winter 1997): 1333.

71. Rogers, ed., 302.

72. For a similar perspective on this passage, see Benson, 167–169.

73. Rogers, ed., 134 and 254.

74. Margaret L. King, *The Death of the Child Valerio Marcello* (Chicago: University of Chicago Press, 1994), 7–9.

75. Anthony Grafton and Lisa Jardine observe that a humanistic education was also a useless "ornament" for men—that the gap between accomplishment and employment for both sexes suggests that learning was effectively "for its own sake" in either case. See Grafton and Jardine, eds., *From Humanism to the Humanities: Education and the Liberal Arts in Fifteenth- and Sixteenth-Century Europe* (Cambridge, Mass.: Harvard University Press, 1986), 43–4 and 57. See also Lauro Martines's discussion of "philosophical" versus "civic" humanism in *The Social World of the Florentine Humanists, 1390–1460* (Princeton, N.J.: Princeton University Press, 1963), 5–6.

76. Rogers, ed., 501–506, 540–544, and 555–559.

77. Ibid., 511.

78. Ibid., 510.

79. Richard Trexler, *Public Life in Renaissance Florence* (New York: Academic Press, 1980), 131–158; quotation at 132.

80. John Najemy, *Between Friends: Discourses of Power and Desire in the Machiavelli-Vettori Letters of 1513–1515* (Princeton, N.J.: Princeton University Press, 1993), 23.

81. The fluidity between private and public in humanist correspondence speaks also to the recent rethinking of the "separate spheres" model within the fields of women's and gender history. Linda Kerber, for one, articulates the problem of coding the private realm "feminine" and the public "masculine" as an outdated model "imposing a static dynamic on relationships." See Kerber, "Separate Spheres, Female Worlds, Woman's Place: The Rhetoric of Women's History," *Journal of American History* 75 (1988): 38. See also Linda Kerber et al., "Beyond Roles, Beyond Spheres: Thinking about Gender in the Early Republic," *William and Mary Quarterly* 46 (1989): 565–585, and Mary Poovey, *Uneven Developments: The Ideological Work of Gender in Mid-Victorian England* (Chicago: University of Chicago Press, 1988), 10–11.

82. Alice Alington (wife of Giles Alington at the time of this letter) was the daughter of Thomas More's second wife, Alice, by her first husband, John Middleton.

83. R. W. Chambers,"The Continuity of the English Language," quoted in Rogers, ed., 514.

84. Richard Marius, *Thomas More* (London: Orion Publishing, 1999), 225.

85. Rogers, ed., 515.

86. For a debate concerning of the "tradition of misogyny," see especially Benson, *The Invention of the Renaissance Woman,* and Glenda McLeod, *Virtue and Venom: Catalogs of Women from Antiquity to the Renaissance* (Ann Arbor: University

of Michigan Press, 1991). Benson argues for a diminunition of misogynistic rhetoric, a diminution beginning with Boccaccio's *De mulieribus claris,* and thereby challenges McLeod's contentions for the perpetuation of classical misogyny in the Renaissance. See also Jerry C. Nash, "Renaissance Misogyny, Biblical Feminism and Helisenne de Crenne's *Épistres familieres et invectives,*" *Renaissance Quarterly* 50 (Summer 1997): 379–410.

87. Peter Iver Kaufman, "Absolute Margaret: Margaret Roper and 'Well-Learned Men,'" *Sixteenth Century Journal* 20 (1989): 451.

88. Rogers, ed., 515 (emphasis mine).

89. Ibid., 529.

90. Ibid. (emphasis mine)

91. Marius, *Thomas More,* 223. For an interesting comment on his effectiveness in this regard, see Erasmus's change of heart on the learned-woman question. Erasmus claimed that he once felt that educating women would contribute nothing either to their virtue or reputation but stated,"More has quite put it out of my head" (*CWE,* Ep. 1233: 112–115, quoted and translated in Erika Rummel, *Erasmus on Women* [Toronto: University of Toronto Press, 1996], 10).

92. More also characterized Margaret as one of his "friends." See, for instance, Rogers, ed., 559: "I pray you be *you and mine other friends* of good cheer" (emphasis mine).

93. Her two married names are Clarke and Basset. I will refer to her as Basset throughout, for clarity's sake.

94. James Basset made Rastell an executor of his will: 22 December 1558, National Archives (London), PROB 11/42A, fol. 144a (hereafter, TNA).

95. Nicholas Harpsfield, *The Life and Death of Sir Thomas More,* ed. Elsie Vaughan Hitchcock (London: Oxford University Press, 1932), 78.

96. Will of Mary Basset, 19 April 1572, TNA, PROB 11/54.

97. Roger Ascham, *Rogeri Aschami Epistolarum, Libri Quatuor* (Oxford: Oxford University Press, 1703), 270.

98. British Library (London), MS Harley 1860 (hereafter, BL).

99. TNA, PROB 11/54.

100. Will of William Roper, 21 June 1578, TNA, PROB 11/60.

101. Will of Mary Basset, TNA, PROB 11/54.

102. King, *Women of the Renaissance,* 207.

103. The writings of Anthony Cooke are scanty, including mainly letters to his son-in-law William Cecil (Lord Burghley) and a translation of Cyprian. See Marjorie McIntosh, "Sir Anthony Cooke: Tudor Humanist, Educator, and Religious Reformer," in *Proceedings of the American Philosophical Society* 119, no. 3 (June, 1975): 237–245.

104. McIntosh, "Sir Anthony Cooke," 238ff.

105. McIntosh posits that by 1541 Cooke was fluent in Latin and possibly had a reading knowledge of Greek. See "Sir Anthony Cooke," 238.

106. Will of Sir Anthony Cooke, 28 January 1577, TNA, PROB 11/59.

107. McIntosh, "Sir Anthony Cooke," 241.

108. Ibid., 235, especially n12.

109. Ibid., 239.

110. Ibid., n35.

111. McIntosh considers these suggestions undemonstrable, however. See "Sir Anthony Cooke," 239 n34.

112. McIntosh notes the timing of the friendships (ibid., 244) but not the connection to Anne's literary activity.

113. BL, MS Royal 12A II, fol. 2r.

114. BL, MS Royal 12A IV.

115. Ibid., fol. 126r. The English original for Mary Fitzalan's Latin translation was almost certainly Sir Thomas Elyot's *The Image of Governance, Compiled of the Acts and Sentences Notable, of the Emperor Alexander Severus* (itself derived from Eucolpius's Greek biography), which enjoyed its first printing in 1541.

116. BL, MS Add. 36659, "Transcript of Lumley MSS Catalog of Trinity College, Cambridge," fol. 291r.

117. Will of Henry, Earl of Arundel, 27 February 1580, TNA, PROB 11/62.

118. The exercises (largely collections of Latin and Greek maxims) of Jane and Mary show that most attention was devoted to their readings of Isocrates, Euripides, Cicero, Theognides, Demosthenes, Pythagoras, Xenophon, Sophocles, Plato, Aristotle, and Seneca.

119. BL, MS Royal 2B IX, and 14A I and VIII.

120. BL, MS Royal 15A IX, fol. 4r.

121. BL, MS Royal 12A IV, fol. 1r.

122. BL, MS Royal 7A XII, fol. 184r.

123. BL, MS Royal 15A IX, fols. 101v–102r. These transcriptions, like her translations, are in her own hand.

124. Letter of 23 May 1545 (autograph, from Rome), BNM, Cl. It. XI, 25 (=6671), fol. 32r.

125. TNA, PROB 11/54.

126. BL, MS Royal 12A I, fol. 1r. The same appears in MS Royal 12A II, fol. 2v; Royal 12A III, fol. 1v; Royal 12A IV, fol. 15v. This last she ends with a slight variation: "your daughter most solicitous of Your Lordship."

127. BL, MS Royal 15A IX, fol. 4v.

128. BL, MS Royal 7A XII, fol. 191v.

129. BL, MS Royal 17A IX, fol. 35r.

130. BNM, Cl. It. XI, 25 (=6671), fol. 1r.

131. William Roper, *The Lyfe of Sir Thomas More*, ed. Elsie Vaughan Hitchcock (New York: Oxford University Press, 1958), 6: "[More] resorted to the house of one master Colte, a gentleman of Essex, that had ofte invited him thither, hav-

ing three daughters, whose honest conversation and vertuous educacion provoked him there specially to sett his affection."

132. Desiderius Erasmus, *Opus Epistolarum Des. Erasmi Roterdami,* ed. P. S. and H. M. Allen (Oxford: Clarendon Press, 1922), 577.

133. Roper, *The Lyfe of Sir Thomas More,* 83.

134. Ibid. As Hitchcock notes in her glossary for this volume, "Tylle valle" is an "exclamation of impatience" (131).

135. Ibid., 75–76.

136. Will of Mary Basset.

137. Genealogy tracked by MacIntosh, "Sir Anthony Cooke," 235.

138. Printed in Styrpe, *Annals* 2.2, 605–606; as cited in McIntosh, "Sir Anthony," 248.

139. A further expression of this theme appears in a manuscript letter of Lucy St. John, William Cecil's daughter by his first marriage, to her father. Despite the fact that her stepmother, Mildred, was the more illustrious intellectual, Lucy seems to have learned her epistolary skills under her father's tutelage in much the same way as Margaret Roper had done. See BL, Lansdowne 104, fol. 175r.

140. BL, MS Add. 43827 A&B, fols. 3v–4r.

141. Ibid., fol. 2r and fols. 6v–7r.

142. Ibid., fols. 2v–3r and fols. 4v–5r.

143. For Locke's contributions to the evangelical cause, see Patrick Collinson, "The Role of Women in the English Reformation, Illustrated by the Life and Friendships of Anne Locke," *Studies in Church History* 2 (1965): 258–272.

144. BL, MS Add. 43827 A&B, fols. 13v–14r.

145. Anibale Guasco, *Discourse to Lady Lavinia, His Daughter,* ed. and trans. Peggy Osborn (Chicago: University of Chicago Press, 2003), 1.

146. Ibid., 1–2.

3. The Biographical Tradition

1. Margaret L. King, *Women of the Renaissance* (Chicago: University of Chicago Press, 1991), 186–188.

2. Stephanie Jed, "The Tenth Muse: Gender, Rationality and the Marketing of Knowledge," in Lorna Hutson, ed., *Feminism and Renaissance Studies* (Oxford: Oxford University Press, 1999), 107.

3. Giuseppe Betussi, *Libro di M. Gio. Boccaccio delle donne illustri, tradotto per Giuseppe Betussi* (Venice: Pietro de Nicolini da Sabbio, 1547), 151a–b (hereafter, Betussi).

4. Ibid., 153b–154a.

5. Ibid., 154b.

6. Ibid., 155a–b.

7. Ibid., 173a.

8. Ibid.

9. Ibid., 173a–b.

10. On exemplarity and exceptionality in the genre of the compendium, see Glenda McLeod, *Virtue and Venom: Catalogs of Women from Antiquity to the Renaissance* (Ann Arbor: University of Michigan Press, 1991). For analysis of Boccaccio's exceptionality tropes in *De mulieribus claris* and their deleterious effects for women intellectuals in subsequent eras (such as Cassandra Fedele), see Diana Robin, "Woman, Space and Renaissance Discourse," in Barbara Gold, et al., *Sex and Gender in Medieval and Renaissance Texts: The Latin Tradition* (New York: State University of New York Press, 1997), especially 168–169.

11. Betussi, 173b.

12. Ibid. (emphasis mine)

13. Ibid.

14. See Lisa Jardine, "'O Decus Italiae Virgo': The Myth of the Learned Lady in the Renaissance," *Historical Journal* 28, no. 4 (1985): 804–817, especially 804.

15. Betussi, 174b.

16. Beyond the volumes I discuss here, Diana Robin lists several other early modern biographical compendia in which biographies of Cassandra appear: Jacopo Filippo da Bergamo, *Liber de claris scelestisque mulieribus* (Ferrara: Laurentius de Rubeis, 1497); Giovanni Battista Egnazio, *De exemplis illustrium virorum venetae civitatis atque aliarum gentium* (Venice: Nicolaum Tridentinum, 1554); Battista Fregosa, *Factorum dictorumque memorabilium libri IX* (Venice, 1483); Jean Tixer de Ravisius, ed., *De memorabilibus et claris mulieribus aliquot diversorum scriptorum opera* (Paris, 1521); Antonio Riccoboni, *De gymnasio Patavino* (Padua, 1598). See Robin, ed. and trans., *Cassandra Fedele: Letters and Orations* (Chicago: University of Chicago Press, 2000), 169.

17. Castiglione's representation of women not only as figures present in the work but as "judges" of the dialogue, the lengthy rehearsal of arguments for women's comprehensive education in book III, as well as the degree to which the women shape the course of the debate with their occasional promptings, all constitute evidence for placing him in the "pro-woman" camp at a theoretical level. Yet Virginia Cox makes a good case against reading too much protofeminism into Castiglione in her article "Seen but Not Heard: The Role of Women Speakers in Cinquecento Literary Dialogue," in Letizia Panizza, ed., *Women in Italian Renaissance Culture and Society* (Oxford: Legenda, 2000), 385–400. See also Pamela Joseph Benson, *The Invention of the Renaissance Woman: The Challenge of Female Independence in the Literature and Thought of Italy and England* (University Park: Pennsylvania State University Press, 1992) 73–90, especially 75.

18. Ludovico Dolce, *Della istitutione delle donne* (Venice: Gabriel Giolito de Ferrara, 1547), sig. B7v.

19. Ibid.

20. Ibid.

21. Tomaso Garzoni, *Le vite delle donne illustri della scrittura sacra: Nuovamente Descritte . . . Con L'Aggionta Delle Vite Delle Donne oscure, & laide dell'uno, & l'altro Testamento; Et un discorso in fine sopra la Nobiltà delle Donne* (Venice: Domenico Imberti, 1586).

22. Tomaso Garzoni, "Discorso . . . sopra la noblita delle donne," in *Le vite delle donne illustri nella scrittura sacra,* 171.

23. Ibid.

24. On the idea that male admirers' "mythologized" women intellectuals, see Lisa Jardine, "'O Decus Italiae Virgo,'" and Virginia Cox, *Women's Writing in Italy, 1400–1650* (Baltimore: Johns Hopkins University Press, 2008), 28–34 and 142.

25. Garzoni, "Discorso," 171–172.

26. Pietro Paolo di Ribera, *Le glorie immortali de'trionfi, et heroiche imprese d'ottocento quarantacinque Donne Illustri antiche, e moderne* (Venice: Evangelista Deuchino, 1609). Ribera had evidently taken up residence in Venice by 1606, the year that he published his Italian translation of Don Alberto Vinitiano's Latin *Cronica istoriale Tremiti,* which appeared under the title *Cronica istoriale Tremiti: Composta in Latina dal Rev. P. Don Alberto Vinitiano; hora volgarizzata a commun beneficio da Don Pietro Paolo di Ribera Valentiano: Successo de Canonici regolari Lateranensi nelle loro isole Tremitane* (Venice: G. B. Colosino, 1606).

27. Ribera, *Le glorie immortali de'trionfi,* sig. A2v.

28. Ibid., sigs. A4r and Tt6r.

29. Ibid., sig. Qq2r.

30. Luigi Dardano, *La Bella e dotta difesa delle donne in verso, e prosa . . . contra gli accusatori del sesso loro: Con un breve trattato di ammaestrare li figliuoli* (Venice: Bartholomeo detto l'Imperatore, 1554), sig. B4v.

31. Ibid.

32. Francesco Agostino della Chiesa, *Theatro delle donne letterate, con un breve discorso della Preminenza, e perfettione del sesso donnesco* (Mondovi: Giovanni Gislandi e Gio. Tomaso Rossi, 1620).

33. Chiesa, *Theatro delle donne letterate,* sig. H1r.

34. Ibid., sig. N8v.

35. Cristofano Bronzini, *Della dignità e nobiltà delle donne: Dialogo di Cristofano Bronzini 'Ancona: Diviso in quattro settimane; E ciascheduna di esse in Sei Giornate: Alla Serenissima Arciduchessa d'Austria Maria Maddalena Gran Duchessa di Toscana. Settimana prima, e giornata quarta* (Florence: Zanobi Pignoni, 1625), sig. N4r. Both short biographies predate Jacopo Filippo Tomasini's published edition of Cereta's letterbook, Laura Cereta, *Laura Cereta Brixiensis,* ed. Tomasini (Padua: Sardi, 1640).

36. Chiesa, *Theatro delle donne letterate,* sig. F1r.

37. Ibid., sig. R1r.

38. Ibid., sigs. M8v–N1r.

39. Ibid., sig. O4r. The simile of the Trojan horse might seem to invoke negative connotations of trickery and in particular the destructive effect of cleverness upon an unsuspecting polity. Yet, given that the purpose of this text is to praise learned women, Chiesa probably utilized the image to suggest multitude and perhaps success as well: the Achaeans enclosed in the horse's belly were, after all, victorious. In any case, he qualifies the simile with "almost" *(quasi),* thereby cautioning the reader against a literal reading of the image.

40. Bronzini, *Della dignità e nobiltà delle Donne,* sig. P2r.

41. Ibid.

42. Four of Tomasini's other works specialize in Paduan literary history and archaeology: *Bibliothecae Patavinae manuscriptae publicae & privati* (Utini: Nicolai Schiratti, 1639); *Gymnasium patavinum* (Utini: Typis N. Schirattus, 1654); *Territorii Patavini inscriptiones sacrae et profanae* (Padua: Sebastiano Sardo, 1649; reprinted 1654); and his biography, *Titus Livius Patavinus* (Amstelodami: Sumptibus Andreae Frisii, 1670). He also offered an entry into the biographical compendium genre that includes both male and female subjects: *Elogia literis et sapientia illustrium ad vivum expressis imaginibus exornata* (Padua: Donatum Pasquardum & Socium, 1630; reprinted, Padua: Sebastiano Sardo, 1644). His other works include *Petrarcha rediviuus integram poetae celeberrimi vitam . . . accessit nobilissimae feminae Laurae brevis historia* (Padua: Paulo Frambotti, 1650); *De donariis ac tabellis votivis* (Utini: N. Schiratti, 1639; reprinted, Padua: Paolo Frambotti, in 1654); and a posthumous publication, *De tesseris hospitalitatis* (Amsterdam: Sumptibus A. Frisii, 1670).

43. Jacopo Filippo Tomasini, "Ad Lectorem," in Tomasini, ed., *Clarissimae Feminae Cassandrae Fidelis, venetae Epistolae et orationes* (Padua: Franciscus Bolzetta, 1636).

44. Tomasini, "Ad lectorem" in Cereta, *Laura Cereta Brixiensis.*

45. Tomasini, ed., *Clarissimae Feminae,* 12.

46. Ibid., 21.

47. Tomasini, in Cereta, *Laura Cereta Brixiensis,* sig. 3v–4r.

48. Ibid., sig. 4v–5r.

49. Ibid., sig. 5r.

50. Ibid., sig. 5v.

51. As he notes in the vita of Fedele, Tomasini remarks that marriage in accordance with a father's wishes was another aspect of Cereta's filial piety. See Tomasini, in Cereta, *Laura Cereta Brixiensis,* sig. 5v–6r.

52. Among the earliest works published in England concerning illustrious women are the translations of George de Scudéry's *Les Femmes Illustres,* titled in the English editions as *The Heroick Harangues of the Illustrious Women* (1681) and *The Female Orators* (1714); John Shirley's *The Illustrious History of Women* (1686); and Richard Burton's *Female Excellence* (1688 and 1728). Biographical encyclope-

dias of the Italian sort began to issue from the English presses in greater number during the late eighteenth and nineteenth centuries, including John Tillotson's *Lives of Illustrious Women of England, or a Biographical Treasury Containing Memories of Royal, Noble and Celebrated British Females of the Past and Present Day* (1855?); *Clever Girls of Our Time* (1863, 1875 and 1903); and *Fifty Famous Women* (1864 and 1879).

53. Quoted from the translation in Desiderius Erasmus, *Collected Works of Erasmus* (Toronto: University of Toronto Press, 1989), 29: 173 (hereafter, *CWE*).

54. Ibid.

55. Ibid.

56. For a holograph of one of Margaret's Latin letters to Erasmus, see Ernest Edwin Reynolds, *Margaret Roper, Eldest Daughter of St. Thomas More* (New York: P. J. Kenedy, 1960), 54–56. This is the only extant example of her own handwriting. For a discussion of Margaret as the "learned lady" see King, *Women of the Renaissance*, 181. As testament to the disjuncture between scholarship on the explicit literary contributions arguing for women's intellectual capacities and studies of historical women who actually received extensive training, Linda Woodbridge's persuasive analysis of the Tudor-Stewart prescriptive literature, it is worth noting, ignores the More household school entirely—even while commenting that Thomas's grandson Edward More published his own defense of women in 1560. See Linda Woodbridge, *Women and the English Renaissance: Literature and the Nature of Womankind, 1540–1620* (Urbana: University of Illinois Press, 1986), especially 14.

57. Letter to Guillaume Budé of 1521, printed in Desiderius Erasmus, *Opus Epistolarum Des. Erasmi Roterodami*, ed. P. S. and H. M. Allen (Oxford: Clarendon Press, 1922), 578.

58. Erasmus, *Opus Epistolarum Des. Erasmi Roterdami*, 576.

59. Ibid., 577.

60. Ibid., 577.

61. John Coke, *The Debate betwene the Heraldes of Englande and Fraunce* (London: Rycharde Wyer, 1550), sig. K1r. This point is discussed in Reynolds, *Margaret Roper*, 40.

62. Richard Marius, *Thomas More* (London: Orion Publishing, 1999), 226.

63. William Roper, *The Lyfe of Sir Thomas Moore*, ed. Elsie Vaughan Hitchcock (New York: Oxford University Press, 1958), 6 (emphasis mine; hereafter, Hitchcock).

64. Ibid., 7 (emphasis mine).

65. Elizabeth Rogers, ed., *The Correspondence of Sir Thomas More* (Princeton, N.J.: Princeton University Press, 1947), 123.

66. Elsie Vaughan Hitchcock reproduces the Latin text of the epitaph in her edition of Roper's *Lyfe of Sir Thomas Moore*, and she observes that her source is "Somner" but does not offer any further specifics (xliii).

67. Ibid. for Latin text.

68. Nicholas Harpsfield, *The Life and Death of Sir Thomas More, Knight*, ed. Elsie Vaughan Hitchcock (London: Oxford University Press, 1932), 78–79.

69. Ibid., 4 and 6; for Harpsfield's conversations with Roper, 6.

70. Ibid., 79.

71. Ibid., 79–80.

72. Ibid., 80.

73. Ibid., 80–81.

74. Ibid., 90–91.

75. Ibid.

76. Ibid., 5 and 83.

77. Thomas More, *English Workes*, ed. William Rastell (London: 1557), 1350. "Niece" was a term broadly used at the time to indicate a close female relative other than mother, wife, or daughter. Most frequently, it denoted "granddaughter."

78. Ibid.

79. *CWE*, 173.

80. Harpsfield, *The Life and Death of St. Thomas More*, 78.

81. Thomas Fuller, *History of The Worthies of England*, ed. P. Austin Nuttall (London: Thomas Tegg, 1840), 2: 363.

82. Ibid.

83. Harpsfield, *The Life and Death of Sir Thomas More*, 92.

84. Chiesa, *Theatro delle donne letterate*, sig. H7r.

85. Ibid., sig. Q2r–v.

86. Ibid., sig. Q2v. I have not encountered this story about Margaret Giggs anywhere else.

87. Marjorie McIntosh, "Sir Anthony Cooke: Tudor Humanist, Educator, and Religious Reformer," *Proceedings of the American Philosophical Society* 119, no. 3 (1975): 240–241.

88. Fuller, *History of The Worthies of England*, 509.

89. Ibid. Fuller explains that "The queen deigned Sir Henry Killigrew as ambassador for France, in troublesome times, when the employment, always difficult, was then apparently dangerous. Now Katherine his lady wrote the following verses to her sister Mildred Cecil, to improve her power with the lord treasurer her husband, that Sir Henry might be excused from that service."

90. Walter Haddon, *Sive exhortatio ad literas* (London: Ex Officina Richardi Graftoni, Regij Impressoris, 1552), sig. C4r.

91. Ibid., sig. C4v.

92. Richard Mulcaster, *Positions*, ed. Richard de Molen (New York: Columbia University Teacher's College Press, 1971), 127.

93. Ibid.

94. Ibid., 126.

95. Ibid., 143.

96. A. Bacon to [?], date unknown; British Library (London), Lansdowne 104, fol. 156r (hereafter, BL).

97. Ibid.

98. The signature reads "tua soror tui amantissima," but crossed out next to this is "G. hd." [i.e., "Gualterius Haddonus"]; so it is difficult to sort out the authorship.

99. Quoted in McIntosh, "Sir Anthony Cooke," 234.

100. Poems printed in Nicholas Bacon, *The Recreations of His Age*, ed. C. H. O. Daniel (Oxford: Clarendon Press, 1919), 14–15.

101. Ibid., 26.

102. Ibid., 27.

103. Dedicatory epistle printed in Théodore de Bèze, *Chrestiennes méditations*, ed. Mario Richter (Geneva: Librairie Droz, 1964), 39–40.

104. Bèze, *Chrestiennes Méditations*, 40.

105. Ibid.

106. BL, Add 35324.

107. Ibid., f. 18r.

108. Ibid.

109. George Ballard, *Memoirs of Several Ladies of Great Britain Who Have Been Celebrated for Their Writings or Skill in the Learned Languages, Arts and Sciences* (Oxford: W. Jackson, 1752), vi.

4. Models of Feminist Argument

1. Richard Mulcaster, *Positions*, ed. Richard de Molen (New York, 1971), 127.

2. See Constance Jordan, *Renaissance Feminism: Literary Texts and Political Models* (Ithaca, N.Y.: Cornell University Press, 1991), 6, 200–213, 249, and 309, for her definition of Renaissance feminism; for Pamela Joseph Benson's revision of this concept, see Benson, *The Invention of the Renaissance Woman: The Challenge of Female Independence in the Literature and Thought of Italy and England* (University Park: Pennsylvania State University Press, 1992), 2, 47–51, 181, and 306.

3. Siep Stuurman, *François Poulain de la Barre and The Invention of Modern Equality* (Cambridge, Mass.: Harvard University Press, 2004), 8; Karen Offen, *European Feminisms: A Political History, 1750–1950* (Stanford, Calif.: Stanford University Press, 2000), 19–26; Nancy Cott, *The Grounding of Modern Feminism* (New Haven, Conn.: Yale University Press, 1987), 4–5. See also Tjitske Akkerman and Siep Stuurman, "Introduction: Feminism in European History," in Akkerman and Stuurman, eds., *Perspectives on Feminist Political Thought in European History: From the Middle Ages to the Present* (London: Routledge, 1998), 1–33. While Stuurman has indeed located the elements of "feminist" thought that serve as common ground for Offen and Cott, it must be noted that his synthetic treatment

obscures a fundamental disjuncture in their perspectives. Offen sees feminism as a transhistorical phenomenon, albeit expressed in different ways at different times. Cott, however, holds that this multiplicity of vision, which she considers not only pluralist but even individualist in its expression, requires that scholars apply the term "feminist" only to the most politically charged discourse of early twentieth-century America. For an encapsulation of their respective stances, see Nancy Cott, "Comment on Karen Offen's 'Defining Feminism: A Comparative Historical Approach,'" *Signs* 15, no. 1 (Autumn 1989): 203–205, and Offen's "Reply to Cott," in the same issue, 206–209.

4. For "self-writing" as a category of analysis, see the essays in Thomas F. Mayer and D. R. Woolf, eds., *The Rhetorics of Life-Writing in Early Modern Europe: Forms of Biography from Cassandra Fedele to Louis XIV* (Ann Arbor: University of Michigan Press, 1995).

5. Charity Canon Willard, *The Writings of Christine de Pizan* (New York: Persea Books, 1994), xiii (hereafter, Willard). Willard also notes here that Christine's letters of the early *querelle des femmes,* taken together with her *Book of the City of Ladies* and its sequel, the *Treasure of the City of Ladies* (or *Book of Three Virtues*), "are also important for their influence on the first generation of women to play a visible role in public life: Louise of Savoy, Marguerite of Navarre, Diane of Poitiers, Anne of Beaujeu and, especially, Marguerite of Austria all owned and read these books."

6. On the invention of clerical celibacy, see Maureen Miller, *The Formation of a Medieval Church: Ecclesiastical Change in Verona, 950–1150* (Ithaca, N.Y.: Cornell University Press, 1993), especially 46 and 55–65.

7. This summary of medieval misogyny derives from "Les Normes de Contrôle," in Christiane Klapisch-Zuber, ed., *Histoire des Femmes en Occident,* vol. 2: *Le Moyen Age* (Paris, 1990): 31–168, and Glenda McLeod, *Virtue and Venom: Catalogues of Women from Antiquity to the Renaissance* (Ann Arbor: University of Michigan Press, 1991).

8. Willard, 43.

9. Judith L. Kellogg, "*Le Livre de la cité des dames:* Reconfiguring Knowledge and Reimagining Gendered Space," in Barbara Altman and Deborah McGrady, eds., *Christine de Pizan: A Casebook* (New York: Routledge, 2003), 129–146; quotation at 130.

10. My English translations are based on the modern French text in the Eric Hicks and Thérèse Moreau edition of Pizan, *Le livre de la cité des dames* (Paris: Editions Stock, 1986) (hereafter, *Cité*).

11. *Cité,* 42.

12. Ibid., 35–36.

13. Ibid., 36.

14. Ibid., 37–38.

15. Ibid., 39.

16. Ibid. As Willard notes, in Christine's era, the *Metaphysics* was available only in Latin translation. Willard, 174.

17. *Cité*, 39.

18. Ibid., 41–42.

19. Ibid., 49, 191, and 211.

20. Ibid., 144.

21. Ibid.

22. Ibid., 145.

23. Ibid., 146 and 147.

24. Ibid., 274 and 275.

25. Ibid., 91–92.

26. Ibid., 178–179.

27. Ibid., 275, 277, and 278.

28. James Laidlaw, "Christine and the Manuscript Tradition," in Altmann and McGrady, *Christine de Pizan: A Casebook*, 232.

29. See Marie-Josèph Pinet, *Christine de Pisan, 1364–1430, étude biographique et littéraire*. (Paris: Librairie Ancienne Honoré Champion, 1927), xiii, for the twelve manuscripts at the Bibliothèque Nationale, and Madame Étienne du Castel, *Ma grand-Mère, Christine de Pizan* (Librarie Hachette, 1936), 199–200, for the remaining citations.

30. Castel, *Ma grand-Mère Christine de Pizan*, 231.

31. Nadia Margolis, "Modern Editions: Makers of the Christinian Corpus," in Altmann and McGrady, *Christine de Pizan: A Casebook*, 252.

32. Willard, ix.

33. Ibid., 144.

34. For Christine's publishing history, from which the foregoing data is drawn, see Cynthia J. Brown, "The Reconstruction of an Author in Print: Christine de Pizan in the Fifteenth and Sixteenth Centuries," in Marilynn Desmond, ed., *Christine de Pizan and the Categories of Difference* (Minneapolis: University of Minnesota Press, 1998), especially 217.

35. See Isotta Nogarola, *Isottae Nogarolae Veronensis: Opera quae supersunt omnia*, ed. Eugenius Abel (Vienna: Gerold et Socios, 1886), 1: clvii–clxi (hereafter, Abel), and Margaret L. King and Diana Robin, eds., and trans., *Isotta Nogarola: Complete Writings: Letterbook, Dialogue on Adam and Eve, Orations* (Chicago: University of Chicago Press, 2004), 19 (hereafter, King and Robin).

36. King and Robin, 19.

37. Paul Oskar Kristeller, ed. *Iter Italicum: accedunt alia itinera: A Finding List of Uncatalogued or Incompletely Catalogued Humanistic Manuscripts of the Renaissance in Italian and Other Libraries* (Leiden: E. J. Brill, 1967–1997); index in vol. 7.

38. King and Robin, 1.

39. Jacopo (Giacomo) Filippo Tomasini, the seventeenth-century editor of the collected works of both Cassandra Fedele and Laura Cereta, mentioned, in

his note to the reader in Fedele, *Clarissimae Feminae Cassandra Fidelis, Venetae: Epistolae et Orationes,* ed. Tomasini (Padua: Franciscus Bolzetta, 1636), his plan to publish a similar volume for Isotta Nogarola. He does not seem to have followed through on this intention, but he did include a lengthy discussion of Isotta Nogarola and the other learned women in her family in his biographical collection of learned men and women, *Elogia literis et sapientia illustrium* (Padua: Sebastiano Sardo, 1630; reprinted 1644), 339–342. In addition to a thorough discussion of her life and writings, Tomasini also notes in the *Elogia* (342), "[I have] in my *museo* her unedited works, the Letter to Cardinal Julianus written at Verona 20 March 1439, two similar letters to Damiano Vigo and a third to the same man, this time given the family name Borgo; in addition to these I have one that she wrote to Eusebio Borgo when he was a teenager." Among the most influential modern treatments of her life and works are Margaret L. King, "Isotta Nogarola," in Rinaldina Russell, ed., *Italian Women Writers: A Bio-Bibliographical Sourcebook* (Westport, Conn.: Greenwood, 1994), 313–323; King, "The Religious Retreat of Isotta Nogarola (1418–66)," *Signs* 3 (1978), 807–822; Lisa Jardine, "Isotta Nogarola: Women Humanists—Education for What?" *History of Education* 12 (1983): 231–244. King and Robin's recent volume (2004) dispenses with the model of female "containment," emphasizing Nogarola's successful interaction with male humanist colleagues.

40. See Jane Stevenson, *Women Latin Poets: Language, Gender and Authority from Antiquity to the Eighteenth Century* (Oxford: Oxford University Press, 2005), 512.

41. Henricus Cornelius Agrippa, *Declamation on the Nobility and Preeminence of the Female Sex,* ed. and trans. Albert Rabil (Chicago: University of Chicago Press, 1996), 41–52. Albert Rabil notes that Agrippa's Latin *De nobilitate* was printed in French (1530), German (1540), English (1542), Italian (1544), and Polish (1575), and a translation was reissued at Lyon in 1537. A verse adaptation was published in Paris in 1541 (dedicated to the Duchess d'Étampes), and another translation was issued in Paris in 1578; further reissues were printed in 1686, 1713, and 1726. In addition, Rabil observes that "many if not most" of the texts on the same subject "counted [Agrippa] as their immediate source." See Agrippa, *Declamation,* 27–28.

42. The impact of Marguerite's mystical visions, however, was feared by the authorities. In the end, her work was denounced as heretical and she was burned at the stake (1310).

43. See Diana Robin, *Publishing Women: Salons, the Presses and the Counter-Reformation in Sixteenth-Century Italy* (Chicago: University of Chicago Press, 2007), xix and 61–78, for detailed discussion of salons, literal and "virtual"; for the related issue of collaboration between women and men, xxi, 18–26, 51–52, and 143. On collaboration, see also Julie D. Campbell, *Literary Circles and Gender in Early Modern Europe: A Cross-Cultural Approach* (Aldershot: Ashgate, 2006), 23, 30, 42, and 120–121.

44. Abel, 2: 187.

45. Ibid., 2: 189 and 190 (emphases mine).

46. Ibid., 2: 192, 193, 195, and 196–197.

47. Ibid., 2: 211 and 214–215.

48. Ibid., 2: 215.

49. See King and Robin, 187–190.

50. On the art of consolation, see George McClure, *Sorrow and Consolation in Italian Humanism* (Princeton, N.J.: Princeton University Press, 1991). For the Marcello volume, see Margaret L. King, *The Death of the Child Valerio Marcello* (Chicago: University of Chicago Press, 1994).

51. Abel, 2: 163–164.

52. Ibid., 2: 168.

53. King and Robin, 187–188.

54. Abel, 2: 169. This refers to Cicero's *Familiar Letters*, 4.5 and 4.6.

55. See Kristeller, *Iter Italicum*, 2: 122, 253, and 359; 5: 170b and 513b.

56. Diana Robin, ed. and trans., *Laura Cereta: Collected Letters of a Renaissance Feminist* (Chicago: University of Chicago Press, 1997), 63 and 65.

57. Ibid., 72–73.

58. Ibid., 74.

59. Laura Cereta, *Laura Cereta Brixiensis Feminae Clarissimae Epistolae iam primum e MS in lucem productae*, ed. Jacopo Filippo Tomasini (Padua: Sebastiano Sardi, 1640), 187.

60. Ibid., 188.

61. Ann Rosalind Jones, *The Currency of Eros: Women's Love Lyric in Europe, 1540–1620* (Bloomington: Indiana University Press, 1990).

62. Cereta, *Laura Cereta Brixiensis*, 188–189 (emphasis mine).

63. Diana Robin, ed and trans., *Laura Cereta: Collected Letters of a Renaissance Feminist.* (Chicago: University of Chicago Press, 1997), 76n40. The term Cereta employs in this passage is "largitrix," a feminized version of "largitror" (bestower), which does not possess a standard-use feminine correlative in the way that other nouns of this type do, for instance, "genitor" (m) and "genitrix" (f). The content of Cereta's letter is gynocentric, but so, too, is her technique of feminizing crucial terms.

64. Cereta, *Laura Cereta Brixiensis*, 188–189.

65. Ibid., 188–189, 191–192, and 193.

66. Ibid., 194–195.

67. Ibid., 123–124.

68. Ibid., 124–125.

69. Kristeller, *Iter Italicum*, 1: 22, 43, 44, 59, 212, 277, 327, 392; 2: 67, 249, 253, 260, 268, 359, 508; 3: 442a, 646b; 4: 492a, 646b; 4: 492a, 652a; 5: 111b, 185a, 472b; 6: 291b, 382b, 383a.

70. Modena, 1487; Venice, 1488; Nuremberg, 1489. See Robin, *Cassandra Fedele*, 13n3.

71. Fedele, *Clarissimae Feminae Cassandra Fidelis,* 163–164.

72. Ibid., 21.

73. Ibid., 19.

74. Ibid., 85.

75. Ibid., 33.

76. Ibid.

77. Robin notes (*Cassandra Fedele,* 29) that this document offers an "unusual instance of a eulogy honoring a prominent woman writer that was composed by an important woman patron of arts and letters."

78. Fedele, *Clarissimae Feminae Cassandra Fidelis,* 162.

79. Mary Ellen Lamb, "The Cooke Sisters: Attitudes toward Learned Women in the Renaissance," in Margaret Hannay, ed., *Silent but for the Word: Tudor Women as Patrons, Translators and Writers of Religious Works* (Kent, Ohio: Kent State University Press, 1985), discussed 115–116; quotation at 118.

80. Ibid., 116.

81. An excellent discussion of translation as a creative pursuit is Rita Verbrugge's essay "Margaret More Roper's Personal Expression in the Devout Treatise upon the Pater Noster," in Hannay, *Silent but for the Word.*

82. For a useful discussion of Margaret Roper in this context, see Peter Iver Kaufman, "Absolute Margaret: Margaret Roper and 'Well-Learned Men,'" *Sixteenth Century Journal* 20 (Autumn 1989): 443–486.

83. British Library (London), MS Harley 1860, fol. 1r (hereafter, BL).

84. Ibid., fol. 7v.

85. Ibid., fols. 7v–8r.

86. Ibid., fol. 8r. The translator to whom Basset refers is most likely Robert Estienne, whose edition of Eusebius was printed between 1544 and 1546.

87. Ibid., fol. 4v.

88. Ibid.

89. Ibid., fols. 3r–4r (emphasis mine).

90. Prologue to Caxton's translation of the *Book of the Knight of the Tower,* printed in W. J. B. Crotch, *Prologues and Epilogues of William Caxton* (London: Oxford University Press, 1928), 87.

91. BL, MS Harley 1860, fol. 4r.

92. Thomas More, *English Workes,* ed. William Rastell (London: 1557), 1350.

93. Ibid., 1399.

94. Ibid.

95. Ibid., 1363.

96. Ibid., 1375.

97. Ibid., 1350.

98. Scholars have revised the previous view of early modern manuscript circulation as "private" and therefore less prestigious than print publication. Sometimes termed "scribal publication," the circulation of manuscripts is now

seen as a public enterprise and one that contemporaries often understood as a more "noble" means of transmitting a text than printing. See especially Harold Love, *Scribal Publication in Seventeenth-Century England* (New York: Oxford University Press, 1993). For manuscript circulation as a useful medium for English women's writing, see Margaret Ezell, "Women Writers: Patterns of Manuscript Circulation and Publication," chap. 3 in *The Patriarch's Wife: Literary Evidence and the History of the Family* (Chapel Hill: University of North Carolina Press, 1987).

99. For more on the correspondence, see Patrick Collinson, *A Mirror of Elizabethan Puritanism: The Life and Letters of "Godly Master Dering"* (unknown binding, 1964).

100. Valerie Wayne, ed., *Anne Cooke Bacon.* The Early Modern Englishwoman: A Facsimile Library of Essential Works, part 2, vol. I (Aldershot: Ashgate, 2000), xiii.

101. Anne Cooke Bacon, trans., *Certayn Sermons of the Ryghte Famous and Excellente Clerk Barnardine Ochine* (London: John Day, 1551?), sig. A2v.

102. Ibid., sig. A3r–v.

103. Ibid., sig. A4r–v.

104. Ibid.

105. BL, MS Royal 17B XVIII.

106. Among the few printed translations of St. Basil the Great that appeared in England during the sixteenth century is *An Exhortation of Holye Basilius Magnus, to Hys Younge Kynsemen, Styrrynge Theym to the Studie of Humaine Lernynge, Tr. Oute of Greke by W. Berker* (J. Cawodde, 1557). Pole owned this, as well as translations by Sir T. Copley [?] of other works on the theme of justification by SS. Augustine, Cyprian, Chrysostom, and others, which were compiled and published by J. Foulerum (Louvain, 1569).

107. BL, MS Lansdowne 109, Item 78: Ld. Henry Seymour to Ld. Burghley stating the case of his dispute with his brother and the hardships met with; Lansdowne 115, Item 21, petition of the Lords of Council concerning the execution of Lord High Admiral Seymour, 1548; Add. 19398, fol. 52: Letters of (?) Edward Seymour, Duke of Somerset, Thomas Lord Seymour (brother of the Lord Protector), and others of the Privy Council; Cotton-Vespasian F. XIII, Item 137: "Edward Seymour, Earl of Hertford afterwards Protector Duke Somerset to the Lord Privy Seal (1539).

108. BL, MS Royal 17B XVIII, fol. 2r. This is probably autograph, and ca. 1550. She characterizes herself as Mildred Cecil, so it postdates her marriage.

109. Ibid., fol. 2r–v.

110. Ibid., fol. 2v.

111. Ibid., fols. 3r–4r.

112. See Hannay, *Silent but for the Word.* Hannay's framework of women's "silent" service to the propagation of religious texts appears in the recent volume by Axel Erdman, *My Gracious Silence: Women in the Mirror of Sixteenth-Century Printing in Western Europe* (Lucerne: Gilhofer & Ranschburg, 1999).

113. Ascham, Roger, *The Whole Works of Roger Ascham*, ed. John Allen Giles (London: J. R. Smith, 1864–1865) I: 228.

114. BL, MS Lansdowne 104, fols. 158r–159v.

115. For the thirty-pounds-a-year bequest, see BL, MS Lansdowne 104, fols. 148r–149v; for Wright's letter, MS Lansdowne 30, fol. 164r; for details concerning Wright's pension, MS Lansdowne 30, fol. 170r.

116. Alan Stewart, "The Voices of Anne Cooke, Lady Anne and Lady Bacon," in Danielle and Elizabeth Clarke, eds., *This Double Voice: Gendered Writing in Early Modern England* (St. Martin's Press, 2000), 98.

117. Ibid., 96–98.

118. Richard Hyrde, introduction to *A Devoute Treatise upon the Pater Noster, Made First in Latyn by the Moost Famous Doctour Mayster Erasmus Roterdamus, and Tourned in to Englisshe by a Yong Virtuous and Well Lerned Gentylwoman of XIX Yere of Age* (London, 1526), frontispiece and sig. A2r.

119. Hyrde, sig. A2r–v.

120. Ibid., sig. A3r–v.

121. Ibid., sig. A4r–v.

122. Ibid., sig. A4v.

123. Ibid., sigs. A4v–B1v.

124. Ibid., sig. B1v.

125. Ibid., sig. B2r–v.

126. Ibid., sig. B2v.

127. Ibid., sig. B3r.

128. Ibid., sig. B3v.

129. Matthew Parker, unpaginated prefatory letter in Anne Cooke Bacon, trans. *Apologie*.

130. Stewart, "The Voices of Anne Cooke," 93–94.

131. Ibid., 96.

132. Parker, unpaginated prefatory letter in Anne Cooke Bacon, trans. *Apologie*.

133. Ibid.

134. Benson, *The Invention of the Renaissance Woman*, 233–249.

135. Mulcaster, *Positions*, 133.

136. Ibid., 145 (emphasis mine).

137. Bradstreet's poem "In Honor of that High and Mighty Princess Queen Elizabeth" appears in a collection of her work titled *The Tenth Muse, Lately Sprung Up in America* (London, 1650; republished in America, 1678). The passage I have quoted appears in Anne Crawford et al., eds., *Europa Biographical Dictionary of British Women* (London: Europa, 1983), 60. Bradstreet's use of Elizabeth as an exemplary woman echoed the mainstream discourse concerning the queen during her reign and after her death. It is worth noting, however, that there was also an audible counterdiscourse that construed Elizabeth (as it did her father,

Henry VIII) as a sexual transgressor, tyrant, and indeed an epitome of everything that women should not be. See especially Julia M. Walker, ed., *Dissing Elizabeth: Negative Representations of Gloriana* (Durham, N.C.: Duke University Press, 1998).

138. BL, Harley MS 646, "The Life of Sir Simonds D'Ewes Written by Himselfe with His Owne Hande," fol. 19v.

139. Donald Cheney, introductory note to Betty Travitsky and Patrick Cullen, eds., *Elizabeth Jane Weston and Bathsua Reginald [Makin]*. The Early Modern Englishwoman: A Facsimile Library of Essential Works, Series I, Printed Writings 1500–1640, part 2, vol. 2 (Aldershot: Ashgate, 2000), xii.

140. Ibid., 42–43.

141. Ibid., 3–4.

142. Ibid., 9–10 and 20.

143. Ibid., 16 and 27.

144. Ibid., 20–21.

145. Ibid., 41 and 30–31.

146. Ibid., 28–29.

147. George Ballard, *Memoirs of Several Ladies of Great Britain Who Have Been Celebrated for Their Writings or Skill in the Learned Languages, Arts and Sciences* (Oxford: W. Jackson, 1752), vi.

148. Margaret L. King, *Women of the Renaissance* (Chicago: University of Chicago Press, 1991), 211.

149. Benson, *Invention of the Renaissance Woman*, 181.

5. Learned Wives and Mothers in Italy

1. Diana Robin, *Publishing Women: Salons, the Presses and the Counter-Reformation in Sixteenth-Century Italy* (Chicago: University of Chicago Press, 2007), xix.

2. See especially Patricia Labalme, "Venetian Women on Women: Three Early Modern Feminists," *Archivio Veneto*, 5th ser. (1981): 81–109, and Virginia Cox, "The Single Self: Feminist Thought and the Marriage Market in Early Modern Venice," *Renaissance Quarterly* 48, 3 (Autumn 1995): 513–581.

3. Niccolò Doglioni, "Vita della Signora Modesta Pozzo, d'i Zorzi, nominata Moderata Fonte" (written 1593), in Moderata Fonte, *Il merito delle donne* (Venice, 1600), sig. A2r (hereafter, Doglioni, "Vita").

4. Elissa Weaver, *Convent Theatre in Early Modern Italy: Spiritual Fun and Learning for Women* (Cambridge: Cambridge University Press, 2002). For another excellent analysis of education and creativity in convents, see K. J. P. Lowe, *Nuns' Chronicles and Convent Culture in Renaissance and Counter-Reformation Italy* (Cambridge: Cambridge University Press, 2003).

5. Doglioni, "Vita," sig. A1v–A2r.

6. Ibid., sig. A2r.

7. Virginia Cox, introduction to Moderata Fonte, *The Worth of Women*, ed. and trans. Cox (Chicago: University of Chicago Press, 1997), 5, and Valeria

Finucci, introduction to Fonte, *Tredici canti del Floridoro* (Bologna: Mucchi, 1995), 27–34.

8. Moderata Fonte, *Tredici canti del Floridoro* (Venice, 1581), 17.

9. Lucrezia Marinella, *La nobiltà et l'eccellenza delle donne et mancamenti de gli huomini* (Venice, 1601), 33–34 (hereafter, *La nobiltà*).

10. Letizia Panizza, trans., in her introduction to Lucrezia Marinella, *The Nobility and Excellence of Women and Vices of Men,* ed. Panizza, trans. Anne Dunhill (Chicago: University of Chicago Press, 1999), 3. Panizza demurs from arguing directly that Marinella was being self-referential here, but I would argue that we ought indeed to read Marinella's comment as autobiographical.

11. Giovanni Marinelli, *Gli ornamenti delle donne* (Venice, 1562), sigs. 2v–3r.

12. Panizza, introduction to Marinella, *The Nobility and Excellence of Women,* 3.

13. Dedication to *La nobiltà.*

14. Archivio di Stato (Venice), Test. Not., Atti Crivelli, B. 225 III, c. 8, fol. 9r (hereafter, ASV). Moderata Fonte's birth name was Modesta da Pozzo.

15. ASV, Test. Not., Atti Longin, B. 1200, fol. 59.

16. ASV, Test. Not., Atti Ziliol, B. 1262 III, fol. 99v.

17. I draw this observation from Virginia Cox, in Fonte, *The Worth of Women,* 37n19 and 63n30.

18. ASV, Test. Not., Atti Sacco, B. 1192, fol. 467.

19. Ibid.

20. ASV, Test. Not., Atti Bognolo B. 86, no. 101 (Doglioni's wife's will, the principal beneficiary of which is Modesta, their daughter); ASV, Test. Not., Atti Zuccato 1274, no. 276 is the will of Modesta Doglioni, the beneficiary of which is another Modesta, the daughter of her son Nicoletto. Another interesting link evident in the naming practices of the family is that Saracena Doglioni and her sister-in-law Moderata Fonte both named one of their daughters Cecilia.

21. Cecilia di Zorzi mentions in her final testament (1623) a considerable sum of money once given to her by Fausto Doglioni, who was Niccolò's grandson. See her will, ASV, Test. Not., Atti Caderta, B. 216, no. 15.

22. ASV, Test. Not., Atti Crivelli, B. 225 III, c. 8, fol. 8v.

23. Ibid.

24. Ibid., fol. 9r.

25. ASV, Avogadoria di Comun, Cittadinanze Originaire, Suppliche e scritture inespedite, B. 433, nos. 4 and 6.

26. Fonte, *Il Merito delle donne,* ed. Adriana Chemello, 84.

27. Ibid., 6. "Arpicordo" means "harpsichord," but in this context must refer to some sort of grammer aid. See Virginia Cox, ed. and trans. *The Worth of Women,* 35n12.

28. Panizza, introduction to Marinella, *The Nobility and Excellence of Women,* 3.

29. Moderata Fonte, *La Resurrettione di Giesu Christo* (Venice: Gio. Domenico Imberti, 1592), sig. +4v.

30. Will of Lucrezia Vacca, 1 May 1645, ASV, Test. Not., Atti Acerbi, B. 1147 III, fol. 22v et seq. Marinella was, by this point, a widow and her children were fully mature. She leaves Antonio as her universal heir, with small sums of money "in sign of love" going to her married daughter and to her granddaughter (Paulina's daughter).

31. *Il merito*, sig. A3r.

32. Pietro Paolo di Ribera, *Le glorie immortali de'trionfi, et heroiche imprese d'ottocento quarantacinque Donne Illustri antiche, e moderne* (Venice: Evangelista Deuchino, 1609), sig. Pp3r–v.

33. Cristofano Bronzini, *Della dignità e nobiltà delle donne: Dialogo di Cristofano Bronzini 'Ancona: Diviso in quattro settimane; E ciascheduna di esse in Sei Giornate: Alla Serenissima Arciduchessa d'Austria Maria Maddalena Gran Duchessa di Toscana. Settimana prima, e giornata quarta* (Florence: Zanobi Pignoni, 1625), sig. P3r.

34. Ribera, sig. Tt2v.

35. Ibid., sig. Tt3r.

36. Bronzini, *Della dignità*, sig. O4v.

37. Ibid., sig. P1v.

38. Lisa Jardine, *Erasmus, Man of Letters: The Construction of Charisma in Print* (Princeton, N.J.: Princeton University Press, 1993).

39. Fonte, *Tredici canti del Floridoro*, frontispiece.

40. Moderata Fonte, *La Passione di Christo* (Venice: Domenico & Gio. Battista Guerra, 1582), sig. A2r–v. On the significance of water images, see David Quint, *Origin and Originality in Renaissance Literature: Versions of the Source* (New Haven, Conn.: Yale University Press, 1983), especially chap. 2 on the "Virgilian source" and chap. 5 on Bruni, Spencer, and the Thames River.

41. Fonte, *La Passione di Christo*, sig. A3r.

42. Ibid., sig. A3v.

43. Fonte, *La Resurrettione di Giesu Christo*, sig. +2r.

44. Ibid., sig. +2v.

45. Ibid., sigs. +3v and +4r.

46. For Scarano's connection to one of Venice's principal literary "clubs," see Stephen Kolsky, "Moderata Fonte, Lucrezia Marinella, Giuseppe Passi: An Early Seventeenth-Century Feminist Controversy," *Modern Language Review* 96, no. 4 (October, 2001): 973–989.

47. *La nobiltà*, sig. A2 (emphasis mine).

48. André Rivet, letter in Anna Maria van Schurman, *Nobiliss: Virginis Annae Mariae à Schurman, opuscula Hebraea, Graeca, Latina, Gallica: prosaica et metrica* (Elzevir: 1648), 60–62 (hereafter, Schurman).

49. For the particulars of this fraught exchange, see Schurman, 64–80 (Schurman's position); Schurman, 80–90 (Rivet's response); Schurman, 94–95 (Schurman's capitulation).

50. See Joyce Irwin, introduction to Anna Maria van Schurman, *On Whether*

a Christian Woman Should Be Educated, ed. and trans. Joyce Irwin (Chicago: University of Chicago Press, 1998), 12–13.

51. Rivet, letter in Schurman, 61.

52. Schurman, 63.

53. Rivet, letter in Schurman, 80 and 90.

54. Schurman, 79–80.

55. Ibid., 68–69. Schurman cites de Gournay's *The Equality of Men and Women* in demonstrating that women's submission cannot be rationalized on textual grounds.

56. Marie le Jars de Gournay, *Preface to the Essays of Michel de Montaigne,* ed. and trans. Richard Hillman and Colette Quesnel (Tempe, Ariz.: Medieval and Renaissance Texts and Studies, 1998), 21.

57. Ibid., 27.

58. Translated in Tilde Sankovitch, *French Women Writers and the Book: Myths of Access and Desire* (New York: Syracuse University Press, 1988), 76.

59. Catherine Martin, "Le Premier Testament de Marie de Gournay," *Bibliothèque d'Humanisme et Renaissance* 67 (2005): 653–657; quotation at 654.

60. Francesca de' Angelis, *La divina Isabella: Vita straordinaria di una donna del Cinquecento* (Florence: Sansoni, 1991), 31 (hereafter, De' Angelis).

61. Torello Sensi, "Illustri Figli di Padova, Isabella Andreini," in *Estratto della Rivista Padova* (Padua: Società Cooperativa Tipografica, 1938), vol. 6, especially 3 and 12. Sensi's delightfully overblown rhetoric, rooted in the nationalist and feminist Italian discourse of the nineteenth and early twentieth centuries, mimics the kind of praise that Andreini received in her own day.

62. De' Angelis, 10.

63. Latin quoted in De' Angelis, 58 (translation mine).

64. Isabella Andreini, *Lettere della Signora Isabella Andreini Padovana* (Venice: Gio. Battista Combi, 1617), sig. A3r.

65. Justus Lipsius (1547–1606) is credited with establishing Neo-Stoicism as a dominant intellectual trend. While he was not quite the pan-European celebrity that Erasmus had been, Lipsius was a prominent figure in the world of late sixteenth-century humanism.

66. Epistolary of Puteanus, in Charles Ruelens, *Erycius Puteanus et Isabelle Andreini: Lecture faite à l'Académie d'Archéologie le 3 Février 1889* (Antwerp: Van Merlen 1889), Italian text quoted in De' Angelis, 51.

67. Anne MacNeil, *Music and Women of the Commedia dell'Arte in the Late Sixteenth Century* (Oxford: Oxford University Press, 2003), 91, 250–257, 288–292; for Borgogni, see also 321–322; for Andreini as a feminist, see 122 and 125; and for alternative translations of Andreini's poetry and letters, see "Documents," 305–323. MacNeil makes a salutary departure from the standard modern treatments of Andreini as an "extraordinary" woman and actress, such as Richard Andrews, "Isabella Andreini and Others: Women on the Stage in the

Late Cinquecento," in Letizia Panizza, ed., *Women in Renaissance Culture and Society* (University of Oxford: Legenda, 2000), 316–334, and Conor Fahy (in this same volume), "Women and Italian Cinquecento Literary Academies," 444. For treatment of Andreini that gives rightful credit to MacNeil's scholarship, see Julie Campbell's introduction to her translation of Isabella Andreini, *Mirtilla* (Tempe, Ariz.: Arizona Center for Medieval and Renaissance Studies, 2002), xi–xxvii.

68. Erycius Puteanus, *Epistolarum Promulsis* (Louvain: Officina Flaviana, 1612–1613), sigs. D1b–D2a. I have added quotation marks here to capture more clearly the way in which Puteanus plays with words.

69. Ibid., sig. D2a.

70. Ibid.

71. Italian text printed in Ruelens, *Erycius Puteanus et Isabelle Andreini*, 24 (hereafter, Ruelens).

72. Ruelens, 24.

73. Ibid.

74. Sulpicia was a Roman matron who famously abandoned a comfortable existence to join her husband, Lentulus Truscellio, in exile after he had been proscribed by the triumvirs. For ancient commentators and their Renaissance imitators, Sulpicia represented women's ability to exhibit virtues such as courage and loyalty to their full "masculine" extent. Puteanus uses the reference not only to praise Andreini's heroic wifely virtue in general terms but may also be making specific reference to her forsaking the comforts of home to accompany her husband on so many (potentially dangerous) theatrical tours in Italy and France.

75. Puteanus, *Epistolarum*, sig. A3b.

76. Ibid.

77. Ibid., sigs. A3b–A4a.

78. Ruelens, 26.

79. Puteanus, *Epistolarum* ("Bellaria" Epist. XI), sig. B4b.

80. Ruelens, 26 and 27.

81. De' Angelis, 51.

82. For instance, Andreini's first extant letter to Puteanus (14 November 1601) ends with this assurance: "I, along with my husband, kiss your hands, praying to God for your happiness." See Ruelens, 25.

83. Puteanus, *Epistolarum* (Ferc. Sec.), sig. P3v.

84. Ruelens, 26.

85. Ibid., 27.

86. Ibid., 27–28.

87. Isabella Andreini, *Lettere della Signora Isabella Andreini Padovana . . . aggiuntovi di nuovo li raggionamenti piacevoli dell'istessa* (Venice: Gio. Battista Combi, 1617), sig. A2v.

88. Ibid., sig. A2r.

89. Ibid., sig. A2r–v.

90. Ibid., sig. A2v.

91. Ibid.

92. Ibid., sigs. A2v–A3r.

93. Ibid., sig. A3r.

94. Diana Robin, ed. and trans., *Laura Cereta: Collected Letters of a Renaissance Feminist* (Chicago: University of Chicago Press, 1997), 17–18 and 30–31.

95. Andreini, *Lettere*, sig. A3r.

96. Ann Rosalind Jones, *The Currency of Eros: Women's Love Lyric in Europe, 1540–1620* (Bloomington: Indiana University Press, 1990).

97. Andreini, *Lettere*, sig. A3r–v.

98. Ibid., sigs. A3v–A4r.

99. Ibid., sig. A4r.

100. Julie Campbell observes that Andreini's "public relations campaign focused unceasingly on her marital chastity." See Campbell, *Literary Circles and Gender in Early Modern Europe: A Cross-Cultural Approach* (Aldershot: Ashgate, 2006), 57. Yet Andreini and her supporters used more themes in crafting her public image than "chastity" alone.

101. Isabella Andreini, *Rime* (Milan: 1607), sigs. A3v–A4r.

102. Jardine, *Erasmus, Man of Letters,* 18.

103. Andreini, *Lettere*, sig. A4v.

104. Ibid.

105. Ibid., sigs. A4v–A5r.

106. Ibid., sig. A5r.

107. Encomia, Andreini, *Lettere,* sig. A7v.

108. Ibid., sig. A8r.

109. See Andrews, "Isabella Andreini and Others," 317.

110. Italian text quoted in Nicola Mangini, *I Teatri di Venezia* (Milan: U. Mursia Editore, 1974), 23.

111. Francesco Andreini, *Le bravure del Capitano Spavento: Divise in molte ragionamenti in forma di dialogo, di Francesco Andreini da Pistoia Comico Geloso* (Venice: Giacomo Antonio Somasco, 1609).

112. Ibid., sig. +3v.

113. Ibid., sig. +4r.

114. Ibid., sig. ++1v.

115. Ibid., sig. ++2v.

116. Ibid.

117. Isabella Andreini, *Fragmenti di alcune scritture della Signora Isabella Andreini Comica Gelosa et Accademica Intenta, raccolti da Francesco Andreini Comico Geloso, detto il Capitano Spavento* (Venice: Gio. Battista Combi, 1617).

118. On the coauthorship of women and men see Campbell, *Literary Circles,* 30 and 120–121, and Robin, *Publishing Women,* 18–26.

119. Isabella Andreini, *Fragmenti,* sig. A5r.

120. Giovanni Battista Andreini, *La ferza: Ragionamento secondo contra l'accuse date alla Commedia* (Paris: Nicolao Callemont, 1625).

121. Nevia Buommino, "Lo specchio nel teatro di Giovan Battista Andreini," *Atti della Accademia Nazionale dei Lincei: Classe di Scienze Morali, Storiche e Filologiche,* 9th ser., 12 (1999), fasc. 1, 85–88.

122. Giovanni Battista Andreini, *La ferza,* sigs. A1v–A2r.

123. Ibid., sig. A3v.

124. Ibid., sig. B1v.

125. Ibid., sigs. B4v and D1v.

126. Ibid., sigs. D2r–D4v.

127. Ibid., sig. E1r.

128. Ibid., sigs. E1v–E2r.

129. Ibid., sigs. E3v–E4r.

130. Ibid., sig. F1r.

6. Collaborative Marriages in Britain

1. Margaret L. King, *Women of the Renaissance* (Chicago: University of Chicago Press), 213.

2. Ibid., 214. See also Patricia Crawford, "Women's Published Writings, 1600–1700," in Mary Prior, ed., *Women in English Society, 1500–1800* (London: Methuen, 1985), 266; and Betty Travitsky, "The New Mother of the English Renaissance: Her Writings on Motherhood," in Cathy N. Davidson and E. M. Broner, eds., *The Lost Tradition: Mothers and Daughters in Literature* (New York: Frederick Ungar, 1980), 33.

3. Harold Love, *Scribal Publication in Seventeenth-Century England* (Oxford: Clarendon Press, 1993). See also Margaret Ezell on "coterie publishing" in her article "To Be Your Daughter in Your Pen: The Social Functions of Literature in the Writings of Lady Elizabeth Brackley and Lady Jane Cavendish," *Huntington Library Quarterly* 51 (1988): 281–296, and the vast array of female-authored manuscripts in her monograph *The Patriarch's Wife: Literary Evidence and the History of the Family* (Chapel Hill: University of North Carolina Press, 1987).

4. Helen Ostovich and Elizabeth Sauer, eds., *Reading Early Modern Women: An Anthology of Texts in Manuscript and Print, 1550–1700* (New York: Routledge, 2004).

5. Charles Nauert, *Humanism and the Culture of Renaissance Europe* (Cambridge: Cambridge University Press, 1995), 215.

6. It might be objected that the dignification of the vernacular as a medium for "learned" writing was an established argument in Italy by the early sixteenth

century. For an excellent treatment of the early debates on the "questione della lingua" among Italian humanists, see Armand L. De Gaetano, "G. B. Gelli and the Rebellion Against Latin," *Studies in the Renaissance* 14 (1967): 131–158, and "G. B. Gelli and the Questione della Lingua," *Italica* 44, no. 3 (1967): 263–281. Gaetano has shown that the Florentine Academy aimed to disseminate knowledge in the vernacular to a broad audience.

7. Quoted in Anne Leslie Saunders, "Bathsua Reginald Makin (1600–1675?)," in Laurie Churchill et al., eds., *Women Writing Latin From Roman Antiquity to Early Modern Europe*, vol. 3: *Early Modern Europe* (New York: Routledge, 2002), 249.

8. Ibid., 248–249.

9. Ibid., 255.

10. Ibid., 247.

11. Lisa Jardine, "Isotta Nogarola: Women Humanists—Education for What?" *History of Education* 12 (1983): 231–244.

12. Moira Ferguson, *First Feminists: British Women Writers, 1578–1799* (Bloomington: Indiana University Press, 1985), 420.

13. The Petty papers contain very few letters from Anne, and these are early efforts that only communicate her good wishes for her parents' health. And we know very little about her pursuits after the death of her father and the concomitant end to the Petty papers in 1687. By virtue of her brothers' deaths, she did become the sole heir of her parents' considerable estates. She also married into the Fitzmaurice family of Kerry (Ireland), one descendant of which (Lord Edmond Fitzmaurice) published a biography of William Petty in 1895.

14. The fullest biographical accounts of Petty are Peter Alexander, "William Petty," in the *Dictionary of Seventeenth-Century British Philosophers* (Bristol: Thoemmes Press, 2000), and the much older biography, Lord Edmond Fitzmaurice, *The Life of Sir William Petty* (London: John Murray, 1895).

15. Will of Sir William Petty, 3 February 1688; The National Archives (London), PROB 11/390, fol. 166v (hereafter, TNA).

16. Ibid., fol. 168v.

17. John Aubrey, "A Brief Life of William Petty, 1623–87," in his "Lives of Eminent Men," or (as it was printed) *Brief Lives*, ed. Richard Barber (Woodbridge, Suffolk: Boydell Press, 1982), 243. Aubrey (1626–1697), an Oxford graduate as Petty had been, is best characterized as an antiquary and miscellaneous writer.

18. Ibid., 244.

19. British Library (London), ADD MS 72856, fol. 97r (hereafter, BL).

20. Ibid., fol. 131v.

21. BL, ADD MS 72899, fol. 110.

22. BL, ADD MS 72856, fol. 208r.

23. Ibid., fols. 194–254.

24. Ibid., fol. 194.

25. Ibid., fols. 177r, 225v, 230r, and 236r.

26. BL, ADD MS 72857, Petty Papers, vol. 8, fol. 142r–v.

27. Ibid., fol. 142v. This is Flavius Josephus (born 37 c.e., died ca. 101), a fascinating author for Petty to have Anne study. It is possible that Petty used Josephus for her instruction in Greek language, as Josephus's principal writings, *Peri tou Ioudaikou polemou (On the Jewish War), Ioudaike Archaiologica (Jewish Antiquities)* and his autobiography, *Phlaouiou Iosepou bios,* represent prime examples of elegant Greek composition. Conversely, she may have read these works in translation. Josephus's works had been available in Latin translation since late antiquity (Augustine and Ambrose read them in Latin) and, with the advent of print, were also broadly disseminated in German, French, and English.

28. BL, ADD MS 72856, fols. 139r and 215v.

29. Ibid., fol. 179r.

30. Ibid., fol. 181r.

31. Ibid., fols. 183r and 185r.

32. A further testament to Petty's liberality is that he left all three children "free to marry as God [should] direct them." Ibid., fol. 115r.

33. TNA, PROB 11/390, fol.168r

34. BL, ADD MS 72857, Petty Papers, vol. 8, fol. 3r–v.

35. Ibid., fols. 21r–v and 45v.

36. Ibid., fols. 7r–8r and 12v.

37. Ibid., fol. 15r–v.

38. Ibid., fols. 15v–16r.

39. Ibid., fol. 27v.

40. Ibid., fol. 40r.

41. The most exhaustive study of Inglis's life and works remains Dorothy Judd Jackson, *Esther Inglis: Calligrapher, 1571–1624* (New York: Spiral Press, 1937). Inglis recently appears under the subheading of "Applied Arts and Music" in Robert C. Evans, "Esther Inglis, Calligraphy of 'Octonaries' (c. 1600)," in Helen Ostovich and Elizabeth Sauer, eds., *Reading Early Modern Women: An Anthology of Texts in Manuscript and Print, 1550–1700* (New York: Routledge, 2004), 476–478. For Inglis's interaction with Tudor-Stuart politics, see Tricia Bracher, "Esther Inglis and the English Succession Crisis of 1599," in James Daybell, ed., *Women and Politics in Early Modern England, 1450–1700* (Aldershot: Ashgate, 2004). For Inglis's interactions with Guy du Faur de Pibrac, see Sarah Gwyneth Ross, "Esther Inglis: Linguist, Calligrapher, Miniaturist and Christian Humanist," in Julie Campbell and Anne Larsen, eds., *Early Modern Women and Transnational Communities of Letters* (Aldershot: Ashgate, 2009). The most crucial resource for all those interested in Inglis, however, remains A. H. Scott-Elliot and Elspeth Yeo, "Calligraphic Manuscripts of Esther Inglis (1571–1624): A Catalogue," *Papers of the Bibliographical Society of America* 84 (1990): 11–86 (hereafter "Catalogue").

42. The following overview derives from Jackson, *Esther Inglis,* 5–10.

43. Georgianna Ziegler, "'More Than Feminine Boldness': The Gift Books of Esther Inglis," In *Women, Writing and the Reproduction of Culture in Tudor-Stuart Britain,* ed. Mary E. Burke et al. (New York: Syracuse University Press, 2000), 21, and "Catalogue," 12.

44. "Catalogue," 12.

45. Anneke Tjan-Bakker, "Dame Flora's Blossoms: Esther Inglis' Flower-Illustrated Manuscripts," in *English Manuscript Studies, 1100–1700,* vol. 9: *Writings by Early Modern Women,* ed. Peter Beal and Margaret Ezell (London: British Library, 2000), 49.

46. BL, Sloane 987, fol. 32, "Livret contenant diverses sortes de lettres."

47. "Catalogue," 29.

48. See "Catalogue," 12; for a paradigmatic case of Kello's dual praise for author and dedicatee, see Inglis, "Les C.L. Pseaumes de David Escrites en Diverses sortes de lettres" (1599), Folger Shakespeare Library, V.a.93, cited in "Catalogue," 36.

49. "Catalogue," 50.

50. BL ADD MS 4125, fol. 354 for one of Kello's letters to Bacon, but also intended for Queen Elizabeth's eyes.

51. Ibid.

52. Jackson, *Esther Inglis,* 5.

53. Edinburgh University Library, MS Laing III.75, "Treatise of Preparation to the Holy Supper" (hereafter "Treatise of Preparation"). Murray would later publish at least one volume of his own, *The Tragicall Death of Sophonisba* (London: John Smethwick, 1611), which was printed together with his verses and dedicated to Prince Henry.

54. "Treatise of Preparation," fol. 1r.

55. Ibid., fol. 2r–v.

56. Ibid., fol. 3r.

57. Edinburgh University Library, MS Laing III.525, "Album Amicorum G. Craigii."

58. Ibid., fol. 8r.

59. Tjan-Bakker, "Dame Flora's Blossoms," 51.

60. Married women often signed legal documents with their maiden name; see "Catalogue," 12n15. However, as Inglis's manuscripts were not legal documents it is more likely that she used her maiden name as a nom de plume that linked her to her learned father.

61. BL ADD MS 27927, "Le livre de l'Ecclesiaste," fol. 3r (hereafter, "Le livre de l'Ecclesiaste").

62. Ibid.

63. Bianca F.-C. Calabresi, "'Alphabetical Positions': Engendering Letters in Early Modern Europe," *Critical Survey* 14, no. 1 (2002): 12–14.

64. Jackson, *Esther Inglis*, 4.

65. King, *Women of the Renaissance*, 180–181; Ann Rosalind Jones and Peter Stallybrass, "The Needle and the Pen: Needlework and the Appropriation of Printed Texts," in *Renaissance Clothing and the Materials of Memory* (Cambridge: Cambridge University Press, 2000), 145–171.

66. Diana Robin, ed. and trans. *Laura Cereta: Collected Letters of a Renaissance Feminist* (Chicago: University of Chicago Press, 1997), 21 and 30–31.

67. For "the needle as a pen" in the English context, see Jones and Stallybrass, "The Needle and the Pen," 148–171.

68. "Le livre de l'Ecclesiaste," fol. 1. For the dialectic between print and manuscript in Inglis, see Tjan-Bakker, "Dame Flora's Blossoms," 50; see also Georgianna Ziegler, "Hand-Ma[i]de Books: The Manuscripts of Esther Inglis, Early-Modern Precursor of the Artist's Book" in *English Manuscript Studies 1100–1700* Vol. 9: *Writings by Early Modern Women*, ed. Peter Beal and Margaret Ezell (London: British Library, 2000) 77–84.

69. "Le livre de L'Ecclesiaste," BL, Add mss 27927 fol. 2r.

70. "Le livre de l'Ecclesiaste," fol. 3r.

71. Diana Robin, "Cassandra Fedele's Epistolae (1488–1521): Biography as Ef-facement," in *The Rhetorics of Life-Writing in Early Modern Europe: Forms of Biography from Cassandra Fedele to Louis XIV,* ed. Thomas F. Mayer and D. R. Woolf (Ann Arbor: University of Michigan Press, 1995), 193.

72. "Le livre de l'Ecclesiaste," fol. 3r–v.

73. Newberry Library, Wing MS, "Les quatrains du Sr. de Pybrac," fol. 2.

74. Newberry Library, Wing MS miniature, "A New Yeeres Guift," fol. 2.

75. Ibid.

76. National Library of Scotland (Edinburgh), MS ACC 11624, "Une Estreine Pour Tresillustre et Vertueuse Dame La Contesse De Bedford," fol. 2r (hereafter, NLS).

77. Ziegler, "'More Than Feminine Boldness,'" 19–21.

78. Quoted and translated by Jones and Stallybrass, "The Needle and the Pen," 146.

79. British Library (London), Royal MS 17.D.XVI, "Emblemes Chrestiens." (Inglis's title)

80. Ibid., fol. 4.

81. Ibid.

82. See Georgianna Ziegler, "'More Than Feminine Boldness.'"

83. Jackson, *Esther Inglis*, 3.

84. See D. F. S. Thomson, "The Latin Epigram in Scotland: The Sixteenth Century," *Phoenix* 11, no. 2 (Summer 1957): 63–78, and Robert S. Rait, "Andrew Melville and the Revolt against Aristotle in Scotland," *English Historical Review* 14, no. 54 (April, 1899): 250–260.

85. Thomson, "The Latin Epigram," 70.

86. John Johnston and Andrew Melville, *Inscriptiones Historicae Regum Scotorum: Continuata annorum serie a Fergusio primo regni conditore ad nostra tempora* (Amsterdam: Cornelius Claessonius, 1602).

87. "Le livre de l'Ecclesiaste," fol. 2r.

88. Ibid.

89. Ibid.

90. Ibid., fol. 4v.

91. Ibid.

92. Andrew Melville, encomium in John Johnston, *Heroes ex omni historia Scotica lectissimi* (Edinburgh: Christopher Guyot, 1602), sig. B1r.

93. Ibid., sig. B1r–v. (emphasis mine)

94. "Catalogue," 41, and Tjan-Bakker, "Dame Flora's Blossoms," 68n1.

95. Howard Mayer Brown, "Ut musica poesis: Music and Poetry in France in the Late Sixteenth Century," *Early Music History* 13 (1994): 44–45.

96. See for instance, Ziegler, "Hand-Ma[i]de Books," 75.

97. See Arnaldo Momigliano, "The First Political Commentary on Tacitus," *Journal of Roman Studies* 37, parts 1 and 2 (1947): 91–101, especially 98; for Pibrac's role in the development of the "Senecan style," 100; for recognition of Pibrac's importance to the late-humanist enterprise, 98n38.

98. BL, Royal MS 17.D.XVI. For these presentation copies, see EUL, MS.La.III.439 ("Quatrains" for Robert Cecil); the private collection of Julian I. Edison, St. Louis ("Quatrains" for Robert Kerr); BL, Add. MS 19633 and Royal ms 17.D. XVI ("Quatrains" and "Emblemes Chrestiens" for Prince Charles.) For a complete list of Inglis' redactions of the "Quatrains," see "Catalogue," 25–84.

99. "Catalogue," 70.

100. BL, Royal MS 17.D.XVI, fol. 61.

101. NLS, MS 8874, "Les Pseaumes de David."

102. Letter on behalf of her son, to King James (20 June 1620) NLS, MS ADV 33.1.6, fol. 35r.

103. George Ballard, *Memoirs of Several Ladies of Great Britain Who Have Been Celebrated for their Writings or Skill in the Learned Languages, Arts and Sciences* (Oxford: W. Jackson, 1752), quotation at 267.

104. Will of John "Cradocke," TNA, PROB 11/242, fol. 294r.

105. The following discussion of the Cradock family's intellectual history derives from the introductory comments by Oliver Millar in Elizabeth Walsh and Richard Jeffree's museum catalog, *The Excellent Mrs. Mary Beale* (London: Inner London Education Authority, 1975), 9–10.

106. Noted in Anne Crawford et al., eds., *Europa Biographical Dictionary of British Women* (London: Europa Publishing, 1983), 326. For a broader treatment of English girls' schools, see Kenneth Charlton, *Women, Religion and Education in Early Modern England* (New York: Routledge, 1999).

107. Noted by Tabitha Barber in *Mary Beale: Portrait of a Seventeenth-Century Painter, Her Family and Her Studio* (London: Geffrye Museum Trust, 1999), 17.

108. Ibid., 18. For Flatman's use of the term "scholar" (or "scholer"), see especially his letter to Charles Beale of 1666, Bodleian Library (Oxford), MS Rawlinson, Lett. 104, fol. 108 (hereafter, Bodleian), which ends, "My humble service to your self & fair Lady my ever-honour'd Scholar."

109. See Mary Edmond, "Bury St Edmunds: A Seventeenth-Century Art Centre," *Walpole Society* 53 (1987), 108ff.

110. Letter and poem of Charles Beale, Bodleian, MS Rawlinson, Lett. 104, fol. 133r (hereafter, Letter and poem of Charles Beale).

111. Ibid.

112. Ibid.

113. See Paula Findlen, "Ereditare un museo: Strategie familiari e pratiche culturali nell'Italia del XVI secolo," *Quaderni Storici* 115 (2004): 45–81, and Findlen, *Possessing Nature: Museums, Collecting and Scientific Culture in Early Modern Italy* (Berkeley: University of California Press, 1994), for the importance of collections and "curiosity cabinets" among the culturally ambitious. For a similar phenomenon in London, see Deborah Harkness, *The Jewel House: Elizabethan London and the Scientific Revolution* (New Haven, Conn.: Yale University Press, 2007).

114. Letter and poem of Charles Beale.

115. Barber, *Mary Beale*, 19–20.

116. Ibid.

117. Ibid., 20.

118. My treatment of Anguissola follows Mary Garrard, "'Here's Looking at Me': Sofonisba Anguissola and the Problem of the Woman Artist," *Renaissance Quarterly* 47, no. 3 (1994): 556–622. Other useful studies of Anguissola and her work are Fredrika Jacobs, "Woman's Capacity to Create: The Unusual Case of Sofonisba Anguissola," *Renaissance Quarterly* 47, no. 1 (1994): 74–101; Caroline P. Murphy, *Lavinia Fontana: A Painter and Her Patrons in Sixteenth-Century Bologna* (New Haven, Conn.: Yale University Press, 2003), especially 20–24 and 72–79, for comparison of Fontana and Anguissola; Ilya Sandra Perlingieri, *Sofonisba Anguissola: The First Great Woman Artist of the Renaissance* (New York: Rizzoli, 1992); and Orietta Pinessi, *Sofonisba Anguissola: Un "pittore" alla corte di Filippo II* (Milan: Selene, 1998).

119. Francesco Agostino della Chiesa, *Theatro delle donne letterate, con un breve discorso della Preminenza, e perfettione del sesso donnesco* (Mondovi: Giovanni Gislandi e Gio. Tomaso Rossi, 1620), sig. U7r.

120. Pietro Paolo di Ribera, *Le glorie immortali de'trionfi, et heroiche imprese d'ottocento quarantacinque donne illustri antiche e moderne* (Venice: Evangelista Deuchino, 1609), sig. Rr2r.

121. The most extensive study of Fontana, from which the following discussion derives, is Caroline P. Murphy, *Lavinia Fontana: A Painter and Her Patrons in Sixteenth-Century Bologna* (New Haven, Conn.: Yale University Press, 2003).

122. See Garrard, "'Here's Looking at Me,'" 590–597, for women artists' use of musical imagery as a means to assert their self-mastery and intellectual capabilities.

123. Marietta's vita is appended to her father's in Ridolfi's *Lives*. The text I have consulted is from Carlo Ridolfi, *Vite dei Tintoretto: Da le maraviglie dell'arte overo le vite degl'illustri pittori veneti e dello stato, descritte dal cavalier Carlo Ridolfi*, ed. Giovanni Keller (Venice: Filippi Editore, 1994).

124. Ibid., 111–113.

125. Charles Beale, diary and notebook, Heinz Archive and Library, National Portrait Gallery (London), MS 18, fol. 144r.

126. Samuel Woodford, diary, Bodleian Library (Oxford), MS English Misc., fol. 381ff.

127. Quoted in Walsh and Jeffree, *The Excellent Mrs. Mary Beale*, 2.

128. Ibid., 3.

129. Samuel Woodford, *A Paraphrase upon the Psalms of David*, 2nd ed. (London: John Martyn, 1678), sig. B8v.

130. Ibid.

131. Ibid.

132. Diana Robin, *Filelfo in Milan: Writings, 1451–1477* (Princeton, N.J.: Princeton University Press, 1991), 13–30.

133. Barber, *Mary Beale*, 30.

134. Will of Peter French, TNA, PROB 11/244, fol. 301.

135. Will of Elizabeth Tillotson, TNA, PROB 11/465, fol. 133.

136. Mary Beale, "On Friendship," BL, MS Harley 6828, fol. 510r.

137. More's apprentices are noted in the records of the Painter-Stainers' guild. See Brian Stewart and Mervyn Cutten, eds., *The Dictionary of Portrait Painters in Britain up to 1920* (Suffolk: Antique Collectors' Club, 1997), 333.

138. Margaret Ezell, *The Patriarch's Wife*, 148–151 and 160, for the difficult issue of the friendship, animosity, or "academic one-upmanship" between More and Whitehall.

139. See Ezell's commentary in Ostovich and Sauer, *Reading Early Modern Women*, 87.

140. Ibid.

141. Mary More, "The Woman's Right, or Her Power in a Greater Equality to Her Husband Proved than is Allowed or Practised in England," BL, MS Harley 3918, fol. 58r.

142. Quoted in Ezell, *The Patriarch's Wife*, 201.

143. Ibid., 191.

144. Ibid., 191–192.

145. Ibid., 193.

146. Ibid., 144.

147. Will of Mary More, TNA, PROB 11/554, fols. 61v–63r. To the best of my knowledge, scholars have not yet taken note of this document.

148. Ibid., fol. 62r.

149. Ibid.

7. Discourses of Equality and Rights

1. Constance Jordan, *Renaissance Feminism: Literary Texts and Political Models* (Ithaca, N.Y.: Cornell University Press, 1990). Jordan argues that "pro-woman" texts refuted notions of women's inferior nature (6, 249), questioned the cultural influences that determine the meaning of gender (135, 157, 264), and "provided the substance of political debate" but stopped short of suggesting "an actionable program" (309).

2. Moderata Fonte, *Il merito delle donne, ove chiaramente si scuopre quanto siano elle degne e più perfette de gli uomini,* ed. Adrinana Chemello (Venice: Editrice Eidos, 1988), 14 (hereafter, *Il merito*).

3. Virginia Cox, in Moderata Fonte, *The Worth of Women,* ed. and trans. Cox (Chicago: University of Chicago Press, 1997), 45n5.

4. Virginia Cox, "The Single Self: Feminist Thought and the Marriage Market in Early Modern Venice." *Renaissance Quarterly* 48, no. 3 (Autumn 1995): 513–581.

5. Scholars are now familiar with the transition toward thinking about women's social roles that appears in the works of Moderata Fonte, Lucrezia Marinella, and their fellow Venetian feminist Arcangela Tarabotti (1604–1652). While the flashpoint for Fonte and Marinella is women's subjugation to their husbands in marriage, Tarabotti's *Tyrannia paterna* (published 1654 as *La semplicità ingannata di Galerana Baratotti*) lambasted greedy fathers for avoiding the expense of dowering their daughters by forcing them into convents and moved at the end to a general condemnation of the patriarchal order in Venice. The definitive analysis of Fonte, Marinella, and Tarabotti as social critics remains Patricia Labalme, "Venetian Women on Women: Three Early Modern Feminists," *Archivio Veneto,* 5th ser. (1981): 81–109.

6. *Il merito,* 18.

7. Ibid.

8. See especially Virginia Cox, *The Renaissance Dialogue: Literary Dialogue in its Social and Political Contexts, from Castiglione to Galileo* (Cambridge: Cambridge University Press, 1993).

9. *Il merito,* 18.

10. Ibid., 84.

11. Ibid., 138.

12. Ibid., 26.

13. Ibid., 27.

14. Virginia Cox, introduction to Fonte, *The Worth of Women,* 10.

15. *Il merito,* 14.

16. Ibid., 76.

17. Cox, in Fonte, *The Worth of Women,* 123n4.

18. *Il merito,* 77–80, quotation at 77.

19. Ibid., 169.

20. Ibid., 183. This may be nothing more than Fonte imitating a common ending in dialogic works, for instance, Boccaccio's *Decameron*, which ends with the same line.

21. See Diana Robin, *Publishing Women: Salons, the Presses and the Counter-Reformation in Sixteenth-Century Italy* (Chicago: University of Chicago Press, 2007).

22. Cox, in Fonte, *The Worth of Women*, 20–21.

23. Pietro Paolo di Ribera, *Le glorie immortali de'trionfi, et heroiche imprese d'ottocento quarantacinque donne illustri antiche, e moderne* (Venice: Evangelista Deuchino, 1609), sig. Pp3v.

24. Cristofano Bronzini. *Della dignità e nobiltà delle donne: Dialogo di Cristofano Bronzini 'Ancona: Diviso in Quattro Settimane; E ciascheduna di esse in Sei Giornate: Alla Serenissima Arciduchessa d'Austria Maria Maddalena Gran Duchessa di Toscana: Settimana Prima, e Giornata Quarta* (Florence: Zanobi Pignoni, 1625), sigs. P2v–P3r.

25. For this shift in literary culture, see Cox, in Fonte, *The Worth of Women*, 20.

26. See Letizia Panizza's introduction to Anne Dunhill's translation of Marinella, *The Nobility and Excellence of Women and the Defects and Vices of Men* (Chicago: University of Chicago Press, 1999), 2.

27. Lucrezia Marinella, *La nobiltà, et l'eccellenza delle donne, et mancamenti de gli huomini* (Venice, 1601), frontispiece (hereafter, *La nobiltà*).

28. *La nobiltà*, sig. A1v.

29. Ibid., sigs. A1v and H4v.

30. Ibid., sigs. C3v–C4v.

31. Ibid., sigs. C3v–C5v. (emphasis mine)

32. Ibid., sigs. C5v and B8v.

33. Ibid., sig. C3r.

34. Ibid., sigs. H4v–H5r.

35. Ibid., sigs. C2r–v.

36. Ibid., sigs. A6r–v, B8v, and C1r–v. See also Moderata Fonte, *Tredici canti del Floridoro* (Venice, 1581), 17.

37. Letizia Panizza, introduction to Marinella, *The Nobility and Excellence of Women*, 5.

38. Quoted and translated by Panizza, ibid., 5n10.

39. Ibid., 30.

40. Cristofano Bronzini, *Della dignita e nobilta delle donne*, sig. A3v.

41. Ibid., sig. L1v.

42. Ibid., sig. M1r.

43. Ibid., sig. M1r–v.

44. Ibid., sigs. M3v, P1r, and O4v.

45. Ribera, *Le glorie immortali de'trionfi*, sigs. Tt2v–3r.

46. Francesco Agostino della Chiesa, *Theatro delle donne letterate, con un breve*

discorso della Preminenza, e perfettione del sesso donnesco (Mondovi: Giovanni Gislandi e Gio. Tomaso Rossi, 1620), sig. O3v.

47. Anna Maria van Schurman, *Nobiliss: Virginis Annae Mariae a Schurman, opuscula Hebraea, Graeca, Latina, Gallica* (Elzevir, 1648), sigs. F6v–F7r.

48. Ibid., sig. C2v.

49. Ibid., sig. E7v.

50. Anna Maria van Schurman, *On Whether A Christian Woman Should Be Educated, and Other Writings From Her Intellectual Circle*, ed. and trans. Joyce Irwin (Chicago: University of Chicago Press, 1998), 39.

51. Siep Stuurman, *François Poulain de la Barre and the Invention of Modern Equality* (Cambridge, Mass.: Harvard University Press, 2004), 69.

52. Schurman, *Nobiliss: Virginis*, sig. F4v.

53. Panizza, introduction to Marinella, *The Nobility and Excellence of Women*, 15. Virgina Cox does not read the *Essortationi* as evidence of disillusionment, but she does characterize Marinella's dramatic shift in approach as "effectively tolling the death-knell of the Renaissance tradition of women's writing." See Cox, *Women's Writing in Italy, 1400–1650* (Baltimore: Johns Hopkins University Press, 2008), 204.

54. For women and learning, see Lucrezia Marinella, *Essortationi alle donne et agli altri, se a loro saranno a grado* (Venice: Francesco Valvasenso, 1645), 23–72 (hereafter, *Essortationi*).

55. Cox, *Women's Writing in Italy*, 223.

56. Paola Malpezzi Price and Christine Ristaino, *Lucrezia Marinella and the "Querelle des Femmes" in Seventeenth-Century Italy* (Madison, N.J.: Fairleigh Dickinson University Press, 2008), 120–155; quotation at 127.

57. *Essortationi*, 9; I render these terms in a slightly different way than Price and Ristaino do in *Lucrezia Marinella*, 121.

58. Price and Ristaino, *Lucrezia Marinella*, 125.

59. *Essortationi*, 47.

60. See Desiderius Erasmus, *Praise of Folly*, trans. Betty Radice (London: Penguin Books, 1993), 82. Here Folly remarks on learned people eager to publish (also a central category for Marinella): "[Their] health deteriorates, their looks are destroyed, they suffer partial or total blindness, poverty, ill will, denial of pleasure, premature old age, and early death, and any other such disasters there may be."

61. *Essortationi*, 5 and 9–10.

62. Ibid., 11.

63. Margaret Mary Littlehales, I.B.V.M., *Mary Ward: Pilgrim and Mystic* (London: Burns and Oates, 1998). See also Margaret L. King, *Women of the Renaissance* (Chicago: University of Chicago Press, 1991), 111–113.

64. Quoted and translated by Littlehales, *Mary Ward*, 255.

65. Mary Beale, "On Friendship," British Library (London), MS Harley 6828, fol. 510v (hereafter, BL).

66. Ibid.

67. Ibid., fol. 514v.

68. Ibid., fols. 514v–515r.

69. Ibid., fol. 510r.

70. Ibid., fol. 511r.

71. Ibid., fol. 510.

72. See discussion by Tabitha Barber, *Mary Beale: Portrait of a Seventeenth-Century Painter, Her Family and Her Studio* (London: Geffrye Museum Trust, 1999), 33 and 64–65.

73. See Merry Wiesner-Hanks, *Women and Gender in Early Modern Europe* (Cambridge: Cambridge University Press), 194–195.

74. Maureen E. Mulvihill, "Mary Beale, Portrait of Aphra Behn," in Helen Ostovich and Elizabeth Sauer, eds. *Reading Early Modern Women: An Anthology of Texts in Manuscript and Print, 1550–1700* (New York: Routledge, 2004), 493. Mulvihill treats the portrait in question carefully; there is a possibility that Beale was not actually the portraitist, but tradition has consistently attributed it to her.

75. Ibid.

76. Mary More, "The Woman's Right," BL, MS Harley 3918, fol. 49r.

77. Ibid., fols. 52r and 53v.

78. Ibid., fols. 55v–57v.

79. Scholars have pointed out that conceptions of rights obtained in intellectual discourse from late antiquity onward, but the standard narrative of a fully articulated rights discourse appearing in the eighteenth century has by no means been overturned. See Virpi Mäkinen and Petter Korkman, eds., *Transformations in Medieval and Early-Modern Rights Discourse* (Dordrecht: Springer, 2006).

80. For a splendid analysis of the "terms of feminism" in Wollstonecraft and their relationship to contemporary rights discourse, see Virginia Sapiro, "A Woman's Struggle for a Language of Enlightenment and Virtue: Mary Wollstonecraft and Enlightenment 'Feminism,'" in Tjitske Akkerman and Siep Stuurman, eds., *Perspectives on Feminist Thought in European History: From the Middle Ages to the Present* (London: Routledge, 1998); see also Sapiro's *A Vindication of Political Virtue: The Political Theory of Mary Wollstonecraft* (Chicago: University of Chicago Press, 1992).

81. More, "The Woman's Right," fol. 50r–v.

82. Ibid., fol. 58r.

83. Robert Whitehall, "The Woman's Right Proved False," BL, MS Harley 3918, fols. 2r and 3v.

84. Ibid., fol. 1v.

85. Ibid., fol. 6v.

86. Ibid., fols. 24v and 25r.

87. Ibid., fols. 59r and 60r.

88. Margaret Ezell, *The Patriarch's Wife: Literary Evidence and the History of the Family* (Chapel Hill: University of North Carolina Press, 1987), 150–151.

89. More, "The Woman's Right," fol. 47r.

90. Ibid., fol. 47v.

Conclusion

1. Joan Kelly-Gadol, "Did Women Have a Renaissance?" in Renate Bridenthal and Claudia Koonz, eds., *Becoming Visible: Women in European History* (Boston: Houghton Mifflin Company, 1977).

2. Constance Jordan, *Renaissance Feminism: Literary Texts and Political Models* (Ithaca, N.Y.: Cornell University Press, 1990).

3. Of the several series of edited texts that have appeared in recent years, the Other Voice in Early Modern Europe has attracted the most scholarly attention. See the review essays by Constance Jordan, "Listening to 'The Other Voice' in Early Modern Europe," *Renaissance Quarterly* 51 (1998): 184–192, and "More from 'The Other Voice' in Early Modern Europe," *Renaissance Quarterly* 55 (2002): 258–271.

4. Patricia Labalme, ed., *Beyond Their Sex: Learned Women of the European Past* (New York: New York University Press, 1980).

5. King posits the Amazon as a principal signifier for her chapter on learned women, "Virgo et Virago: Women and High Culture," *Women of the Renaissance* (Chicago: University of Chicago Press, 1991), 157–239.

6. Pamela Joseph Benson, *The Invention of the Renaissance Woman: The Challenge of Female Independence in the Literature and Thought of Italy and England* (University Park: Pennsylvania State University Press, 1992).

7. King, *Women of the Renaissance*, 238–239.

8. Pamela Joseph Benson and Victoria Kirkham, eds., *Strong Voices, Weak History: Early Women Writers and Canons in England, France and Italy* (Ann Arbor: University of Michigan Press, 2005), 1–11.

9. Stephen Greenblatt, *Renaissance Self-Fashioning: From More to Shakespeare* (Chicago: University of Chicago Press, 1980).

10. John Jeffries Martin, *The Myths of Renaissance Individualism* (New York: Palgrave Macmillan, 2004), especially 30–38, for summaries of his categories.

11. This is true in Martin's seminal article "Inventing Sincerity, Refashioning Prudence: The Discovery of the Individual in Renaissance Europe," *American Historical Review* 102 (Winter 1997): 1309–1342, and his recent monograph, *The Myths of Renaissance Individualism*.

12. See Hanna Fenichel Pitkin, *Fortune is a Woman: Gender and Politics in the Thought of Niccolò Machiavelli* (Berkeley: University of California Press, 1984); Charles Tarlton, "Fortuna and the Landscape of Action in Machiavelli's *Prince*," *New Literary History* 30, no. 4 (1999): 737–55; Frances Dolan, *Dangerous Familiars:*

Representations of Domestic Crime in England, 1550–1700 (Ithaca, N.Y.: Cornell University Press, 1994); and Mark Breitenberg, *Anxious Masculinity in Early Modern England* (Cambridge: Cambridge University Press, 1996).

13. See Joan Wallach Scott, "Gender: A Useful Category of Historical Analysis," *American Historical Review* 91 (1986): 1053–1075, and Scott, *Gender and the Politics of History* (New York: Columbia University Press, 1998).

14. Stephen Shapin demonstrates this approach in his analysis of Robert Boyle's collaboration with his sister, Lady Katherine Ranelagh. See Shapin, *A Social History of Truth: Civility and Science in Seventeenth-Century England* (Chicago: University of Chicago Press, 1994), 370–372.

15. Virginia Cox, *Women's Writing in Italy, 1400–1650* (Baltimore: Johns Hopkins University Press, 2008), xix.

Bibliography

Archival and Manuscript Sources

Archivio di Stato, Venice

Avogadoria di Comun, Cittadinanze Originarie, busta 433
Notarile Testamenti, Atti Baldigara, busta 70
Notarile Testamenti, Atti Bognolo, busta 86
Notarile Testamenti, Atti Caderta, busta 216
Notarile Testamenti, Atti Crivelli, busta 225 III
Notarile Testamenti, Atti Longin, busta 1200
Notarile Testamenti, Atti Sacco, buste 86, 1192, and 1274
Notarile Testamenti, Atti Giuseppe Volpini, busta 30
Notarile Testamenti, Atti Ziliol, busta 1262 III
Notarile Testamenti, Atti Zuccato, busta 1274
Notarile Testamenti, Atti Acerbi, busta 1147 III

Archivio di Stato, Verona

Archivetti Privati (Nogarola), busta 41

Biblioteca Nazionale Marciana, Venice

Classe It. XI, 25

Bodleian Library, Oxford

English Miscellaneous MSS
Rawlinson MSS

British Library, London

Additional MSS
Harley MSS
Lansdowne MSS

Royal MSS
Sloane MSS

Edinburgh University Library

Laing MSS

Heinz Archive and Library, National Portrait Gallery, London

MS 18, Charles Beale, Diary and Notebook

Museo Correr, Venice

Cicogna MSS

National Archives, London

PROB 11, Prerogative Court of Canterbury and Related Probate Jurisdictions:
Will Registers

National Library of Scotland, Edinburgh

ACC 11624, 11821
ADV 33.1.6
MS 8874, 25240, 2197, 20498

Newberry Library, Chicago

Wing MSS

Printed and Secondary Sources

Agrippa, Henricus Cornelius. *Declamation on the Nobility and Preeminence of the Female Sex.* Ed. and trans. Albert Rabil. Chicago: University of Chicago Press, 1996.

Alexander, Peter. "William Petty." In *Dictionary of Seventeenth-Century British Philosophers.* Bristol: Thoemmes Press, 2000.

Andreini, Francesco. *Le bravure del Capitan Spavento: Divise in molte ragionamenti in forma di dialogo, di Francesco Andreini da Pistoia Comico Geloso.* Venice: Giacomo Antonio Somasco, 1609.

Andreini, Giovanni Battista. *La ferza: Ragionamento secondo contra l'accuse date alla commedia.* Paris: Nicolao Callemont, 1625.

Andreini, Isabella. *Rime.* Milan, 1607.

_____. *Fragmenti di alcune scritture della Signora Isabella Andreini Comica Gelosa et Accademica Intenta, raccolti da Francesco Andreini Comico Geloso, detto il Capitano Spavento.* Ed. Francesco Andreini. Venice: Gio. Battista Combi, 1617.

_____. *Lettere della Signora Isabella Andreini Padovana . . . aggiuntovi di nuovo li raggionamenti piacevoli dell'istessa* Venice: Gio. Battista Combi, 1617.

_____. Letters to Henry de Put [Erycius Puteanus]. Printed in Charles Rue-
lens, *Erycius Puteanus et Isabelle Andreini: Lecture faite à l'Académie d'Archéologie le 3 Février 1889.* Antwerp: Van Merlen 1889.

_____. *Mirtilla.* Ed. and trans. Julie Campbell. Tempe: Arizona Center for
Medieval and Renaissance Studies, 2002.

Andrews, Richard. "Isabella Andreini and Others: Women on the Stage in the
Late Cinquecento." In *Women in Renaissance Culture and Society.* Ed. Letizia
Panizza. Oxford: Legenda, 2000.

Angelis, Francesca de'. *La divina Isabella: Vita straordinaria di una donna del
Cinquecento.* Florence: Sansoni, 1991.

Ascham, Roger. *Rogeri Aschami Epistolarum Libri Quatuor.* 4 vols. Oxford: Oxford University Press, 1703.

_____. *The Whole Works of Roger Ascham.* 3 vols. Ed. John Allen Giles. London:
J. R. Smith, 1864–1865.

Aubrey, John. "A Brief Life of William Petty. In *Brief Lives,* ed. Richard Barber.
Woodbridge, Suffolk: Boydell Press, 1982.

Bacon, Anne Cooke, trans. *Apologie or Answer in Defence of the Churche of Englande.* London: Reginald Wolfe, 1564.

_____, trans. *Certayn Sermons of the Ryghte Famous and Excellente Clerk Barnar-
dine Ochine.* London: John Day [1551?].

Bacon, Sir Nicholas. *The Recreations of His Age.* Ed. C. H. O. Daniel. Oxford:
Clarendon Press, 1919.

Ballard, George. *Memoirs of Several Ladies of Great Britain Who Have Been Celebrated for Their Writings or Skill in the Learned Languages, Arts and Sciences.* Oxford: W. Jackson, 1752.

Barber, Tabitha. *Mary Beale: Portrait of a Seventeenth-Century Painter, Her Family
and Her Studio.* London: Geffrye Museum Trust, 1999.

Basil, St. *An Exhortation of Holye Basilius Magnus, to Hys Younge Kynsemen, Styrrynge Theym to the Studie of Humaine Lernynge, Tr. Oute of Greke by W. Berker.*
J. Cawodde, 1557.

Bembo, Pietro. *Il quarto volume delle lettere di M. Pietro Bembo: A prencipesse & signore & altre gentili donne scritte.* Venice: Girolamo Scotto, 1562.

_____. *Il terzo volume delle lettere di M. Pietro Bembo: A prencipi, signori, & suoi
famigliari amici scritte.* Venice: Girolamo Scotto, 1563.

Benson, Pamela Joseph. *The Invention of the Renaissance Woman: The Challenge of
Female Independence in the Literature and Thought of Italy and England.* University Park: Pennsylvania State University Press, 1992.

Benson, Pamela Joseph, and Victoria Kirkham, eds. *Strong Voices, Weak History:
Early Women Writers and Canons in England, France and Italy.* Ann Arbor: University of Michigan Press, 2005.

Bergamo, Jacopo Filippo da. *Liber de claris scelestisque mulieribus.* Ferrara: Laurentius de Rubeis, 1497.

Betussi, Giuseppe. *Libro di M. Gio. Boccaccio delle donne illustri, tradotto per Giuseppe Betussi.* Venice: Pietro de Nicolini da Sabbio, 1547.

Bèze, Théodore de. *Chrestiennes méditations.* Ed. Mario Richter. Geneva: Librairie Droz, 1964.

Biagioli, Mario. *Galileo, Courtier: The Practice of Science in the Culture of Absolutism.* Chicago: University of Chicago Press, 1993.

Blake, N. F. *Caxton and His World,* London: Deutch, 1969.

Blumenfeld-Kosinski, Renate. "Christine de Pizan and the Political Life in Late Medieval France." In *Christine de Pizan: A Casebook,* ed. Barbara Altman and Deborah McGrady. New York: Routledge, 2003.

Boulton, Maureen. "'Nous deffens de feu, . . . de pestilence, de guerres': Christine de Pizan's Religious Works." In *Christine de Pizan: A Casebook,* ed. Barbara Altman and Deborah McGrady. New York: Routledge, 2003.

Bracher, Tricia. "Esther Inglis and the English Succession Crisis of 1599." In *Women and Politics in Early Modern England, 1450–1700,* ed. James Daybell. Aldershot: Ashgate, 2004.

Breitenberg, Mark. *Anxious Masculinity in Early Modern England.* Cambridge: Cambridge University Press, 1996.

Bronzini, Cristofano. *Della dignità e nobiltà delle donne: Dialogo di Cristofano Bronzini 'Ancona: Diviso in quattro settimane; E ciascheduna di esse in Sei Giornate: Alla Serenissima Arciduchessa d'Austria Maria Maddalena Gran Duchessa di Toscana. Settimana prima, e giornata quarta.* Florence: Zanobi Pignoni, 1625.

Brown, Cynthia J. "The Reconstruction of an Author in Print: Christine de Pizan in the Fifteenth and Sixteenth Centuries." In *Christine de Pizan and the Categories of Difference,* ed. Marilynn Desmond. Minneapolis: University of Minnesota Press, 1998.

Brown, Howard Mayer. "Ut musica poesis: Music and Poetry in France in the Late Sixteenth Century." *Early Music History* 13 (1994): 1–63.

Bruni, Leonardo. *"De studiis et litteris liber ad Baptistam de Malatestis."* In *Humanist Educational Treatises,* ed and trans. Craig W. Kallendorf. I Tatti Renaissance Library. Cambridge, Mass.: Harvard University Press, 2002.

Buommino, Nevia. "Lo spechio nel teatro di Giovan Battista Andreini." *Atti della Accademia Nazionale dei Lincei,* 9th ser., 12 (1999): fasc. 1.

Buti, Maria Bandini. "Poetesse e scrittrici." In the *Enciclopedia bio-bibliografica italiana.* Rome: Tosi, 1941–1942.

Calabresi, Bianca F.-C. "'Alphabetical Positions': Engendering Letters in Early Modern Europe." *Critical Survey* 14, no. 1 (2002): 9–27.

Campbell, Julie D. *Literary Circles and Gender in Early Modern Europe: A Cross-Cultural Approach.* Aldershot: Ashgate, 2006.

Castel, Madame Étienne du. *Ma grand-mère, Christine de Pizan.* Paris: Librarie Hachette, 1936.

Cereta, Laura. *Laura Cereta Brixiensis Feminae Clarissimae Epistolae iam primum e*

MS in lucem productae. Ed. Jacopo Filippo Tomasini. Padua: Sebastiano Sardi, 1640.

Chambers, R. W. "The Continuity of the English Language." In *The Correspondence of Sir Thomas More,* ed. Elizabeth Rogers. Princeton, N.J.: Princeton University Press, 1947.

Charlton, Kenneth. *Women, Religion and Education in Early Modern England.* New York: Routledge, 1999.

_____. *Education in Renaissance England.* London: Routledge, 1965.

Cheney, Donald. Introductory note to *Elizabeth Jane Weston and Bathsua Reginald [Makin],* ed. Betty Travitsky and Patrick Cullen. The Early Modern Englishwoman: A Facsimile Library of Essential Works, series 1, part 2, vol. 2. (Aldershot: Ashgate, 2000).

Chiesa, Francesco Agostino della. *Theatro delle donne letterate, con un breve discorso della Preminenza, e perfettione del sesso donnesco.* Mondovi: Giovanni Gislandi e Gio. Tomaso Rossi, 1620.

Chojnacki, Stanley. "The Power of Love: Wives and Husbands in Late Medieval Venice." In *Women and Power in the Middle Ages,* ed. Mary Erler and Maryanne Kowaleski. Athens: University of Georgia Press, 1988.

_____. *Women and Men in Renaissance Venice.* Baltimore: Johns Hopkins University Press, 2000.

Clarke, Elizabeth. "Women's Manuscript Miscellanies in Early Modern England." In *Teaching Tudor and Stuart Women Writers,* ed. Susanne Woods and Margaret Hannay. New York: Modern Language Association, 2000.

Clough, Cecil H., ed. "The Cult of Antiquity: Letters and Letter Collections." In *Cultural Aspects of the Italian Renaissance: Essays in Honour of Paul Oskar Kristeller.* New York: Manchester University Press, 1976.

Coke, John. *The Debate betwene the Heraldes of Englande and Fraunce.* London: Rycharde Wyer, 1550.

Collinson, Patrick. *A Mirror of Elizabethan Puritanism: The Life and Letters of "Godly Master Dering."* Unknown binding, 1964.

_____. "The Role of Women in the English Reformation, Illustrated by the Life and Friendships of Anne Locke." In *Studies in Church History* 2 (1965): 258–272.

Cott, Nancy. "Comment on Karen Offen's 'Defining Feminism: A Comparative Historical Approach.'" *Signs* 15, no. 1 (Autumn 1989): 203–205.

_____. *The Grounding of Modern Feminism.* New Haven, Conn.: Yale University Press, 1987.

Cox, Virginia. *The Renaissance Dialogue: Literary Dialogue in Its Social and Political Contexts, from Castiglione to Galileo.* Cambridge: Cambridge University Press, 1993.

_____. "The Single Self: Feminist Thought and the Marriage Market in Early Modern Venice." *Renaissance Quarterly* 48, no. 3 (Autumn 1995): 513–581.

_____. Introduction to *The Worth of Women,* by Moderata Fonte. Chicago: University of Chicago Press, 1997.

———. "Seen but Not Heard: The Role of Women Speakers in Cinquecento Literary Dialogue." In *Women in Italian Renaissance Culture and Society,* ed. Letizia Panizza. Oxford: Legenda, 2000.

_____. *Women's Writing in Italy, 1400–1650.* Baltimore: Johns Hopkins University Press, 2008.

Crawford, Anne, et al., eds. *Europa Biographical Dictionary of British Women.* London: Europa, 1983.

Crawford, Patricia. "Women's Published Writings, 1600–1700." In *Women in English Society, 1500–1800,* ed. Mary Prior. London: Methuen, 1985.

Crotch, W. J. B. *Prologues and Epilogues of William Caxton.* London: Oxford University Press, 1928.

Crouzet-Pavanne, Elisabeth. "The Lion and the Land." In *Venice Triumphant: The Horizons of a Myth* trans. Lydia G. Cochrane. Baltimore: Johns Hopkins University Press, 1999.

Dardano, Luigi. *La bella e dotta difesa delel donne in verso e prosa . . . contra gli accusatori del sesso loro: Con un breve trattato di ammaestrare li figliuoli.* Venice: Bartholomeo detto l'Imperatore, 1554.

Davis, Natalie Zemon. *Women on the Margins: Three Seventeenth-Century Lives.* Cambridge, Mass.: Harvard University Press, 1995.

De Gaetano, Armand L. "G. B. Gelli and the Questione della Lingua." *Italica* 44, no. 3 (1967): 263–281.

_____. "G. B. Gelli and the Rebellion against Latin." *Studies in the Renaissance* 14 (1967): 131–158.

D'Elia, Anthony. *The Renaissance of Marriage in Fifteenth-Century Italy.* Cambridge, Mass.: Harvard University Press, 2004.

Doglioni, Niccolò. "Vita della Signora Modesta Pozzo, d'i Zorzi, nominata Moderata Fonte." In *Il merito delle donne,* by Moderata Fonte. Venice, 1600.

Dolan, Frances. *Dangerous Familiars: Representations of Domestic Crime in England, 1550–1700.* Ithaca, N.Y.: Cornell University Press, 1994.

Dolce, Ludovico. *Delle institutione delle donne.* Venice: Gabriel Giolito de Ferrara, 1547.

Dulac, Liliane. "Un mythe didactique chez Christine de Pizan: Semiramus ou la veuve héroique." In *Mélanges de Philologie Romane offerts à Charles Campoux.* Montpellier, 1978.

Edmond, Mary. "Bury St Edmunds: A Seventeenth-Century Art Centre." *Walpole Society* 53 (1987): 106–118.

Egnazio, Giovanni Battista. *De exemplis illustrium virorum venetae civitatis atque aliarum gentium.* Venice: Nicolaum Tridentinum, 1554.

Erasmus, Desiderius. *Collected Works of Erasmus.* 86 vols. Toronto: University of Toronto Press, 1974–1994.

_____. *Opus Epistolarum Des. Erasmi Roterdami.* Ed. P. S. and H. M. Allen. Oxford: Clarendon Press, 1922.

_____. *Praise of Folly.* Trans. Betty Radice. London: Penguin Books, 1993.

Erdman, Axel. *My Gracious Silence: Women in the Mirror of Sixteenth-Century Printing in Western Europe.* Lucerne: Gilhofer & Ranschburg, 1999.

Evans, Robert C. "Esther Inglis, Calligraphy of 'Octonaries' (c. 1600)." In *Reading Early Modern Women: An Anthology of Texts in Manuscript and Print, 1550–1700,* ed. Helen Ostovich and Elizabeth Sauer. New York: Routledge, 2004.

Ezell, Margaret. *The Patriarch's Wife: Literary Evidence and the History of the Family.* Chapel Hill: University of North Carolina Press, 1987.

_____. "To Be Your Daughter in Your Pen: The Social Functions of Literature in the Writings of Lady Elizabeth Brackley and Lady Jane Cavendish." *Huntington Library Quarterly* 51 (1988): 281–296.

Fahy, Conor. "Women and Italian Cinquecento Literary Academies." In *Women in Renaissance Culture and Society,* ed. Letizia Panizza. University of Oxford: Legenda, 2000.

Febvre, Lucien, and Henri-Jean Martin. *The Coming of the Book.* Translated by David Gerard. London: Verso, 1997.

Fedele, Cassandra. *Clarissimae Feminae Cassandra Fidelis, Venetae: Epistolae et Orationes.* Ed. Jacopo Filippo Tomasini. Padua: Franciscus Bolzetta, 1636. Reprint, 1644.

_____. *Pro Bertuccio Lamberto Oratio.* Venice: F. Niger, 1488.

Fees, Irmgard. *Eine Stadt lernt schreiben: Venedig vom 10. bis zum 12. Jahrhundert.* Tübingen: Max Niemeyer, 2002.

Felch, Susan. "Anne Vaughan Lock." In *Teaching Tudor and Stuart Women Writers,* ed. Susanne Woods and Margaret Hannay. New York: Modern Language Association, 2000.

Feliciangeli, B. "Notizie sulla vita e sugli scritti di Costanza Varano-Sforza," *Giornale storico della letteratura italiana* 23 (1894): 50–75.

Ferguson, Moira. *First Feminists: British Women Writers, 1578–1799.* Bloomington: Indiana University Press, 1985.

Findlen, Paula. *Possessing Nature: Museums, Collecting, and Scientific Culture in Early Modern Italy.* Berkeley: University of California Press, 1994.

_____. "A Forgotten Newtonian: Women and Science in the Italian Provinces." In *The Sciences in Enlightened Europe,* ed. William Clark et al. Chicago: University of Chicago Press, 1999.

_____. "Ereditare un museo: Stragegie familiari e pratiche culturali nell'Italia del XVI secolo." *Quaderni Storici* 115 (2004): 45–81.

Finucci, Valeria. Introduction to *Tredici canti del Floridoro,* by Moderata Fonte. Bologna: Mucchi, 1995.

Fitzmaurice, (Lord) Edmond. *The Life of Sir William Petty.* London: John Murray, 1895.

Fonte, Moderata [Modesta da Pozzo]. *Tredici canti del Floridoro*. Venice, 1581.

———. *La Passione di Christo*. Venice: Domenico & Gio. Battista Guerra, 1582.

———. *La Resurrettione di Giesu Christo*. Venice: Gio. Domenico Imberti, 1592.

———. *Il merito delle donne*. Venice: Domenico Imberti, 1600.

———. *Il merito delle donne, ove chiaramente si scuopre quanto siano elle degne e più perfette de gli uomini*. Ed. Adriana Chemello. Venice: Editrice Eidos, 1988.

———. *The Worth of Women*. Ed. and trans. Virginia Cox. Chicago: University of Chicago Press, 1997.

Fregosa, Battista. *Factorum dictorumque memorabilium libri IX*. Venice, 1483.

Fuller, Thomas. *History of the Worthies of England*. 3 vols. Ed. P. Austin Nuttall. London: Thomas Tegg, 1840.

Gabriel, Astrik L. "The Educational Ideas of Christine de Pisan," *Journal of the History of Ideas* 16, no. 1 (1955): 3–21.

Garrard, Mary. "'Here's Looking at Me': Sofonisba Anguissola and the Problem of the Woman Artist." *Renaissance Quarterly* 47, no. 3 (1994): 556–622.

Garzoni, Tommaso. *Le vite delle donne illustri della scrittura sacra: Nuovamente descritte . . . con l'aggionta delle vite delle donne oscure, & laide dell'uno, & l'altro Testamento; Et un discorso in fine sopra* la nobiltà delle donne. Venice: Domenico Imberti, 1586.

Gendt, Anne Marie de. *L'art d'éduquer les nobles damoiselles: Le livre du Chevalier de la Tour Landry*. Paris: Honoré Champion, 2003.

Godbeer, Richard. "The Sanctification of Male Love: Religious, Social and Political Identities in Early America." Conference paper delivered at the University of Miami, 23 February 2006.

Goldberg, Jonathan. *Writing Matter: From the Hands of the English Renaissance*. Stanford, Calif.: Stanford University Press, 1990.

Gournay, Marie le Jars de. *Preface to the Essays of Michel de Montaigne*. Ed. and trans. Richard Hillman and Colette Quesnel. Tempe, Ariz.: Medieval and Renaissance Texts and Studies, 1998.

Grafton, Anthony, and Lisa Jardine, eds. *From Humanism to the Humanities: Education and the Liberal Arts in Fifteenth- and Sixteenth-Century Europe*. Cambridge, Mass.: Harvard University Press, 1986.

Greenblatt, Stephen. *Renaissance Self-Fashioning: From More to Shakespeare*. Chicago: University of Chicago Press, 1980.

Guasco, Annibale. *Discourse to Lady Lavinia, His Daughter*. Ed. and trans. Peggy Osborn. Chicago: University of Chicago Press, 2003.

Guy, John. *Thomas More*. New York: Oxford University Press, 2000.

Haddon, Walter. *Sive exhortatio ad literas*. London: Ex Officina Richardi Graftoni, Regij Impressoris, 1552.

Hallett, Judith. *Fathers and Daughters in Roman Society: Women and the Elite Family*. Princeton, N.J.: Princeton University Press, 1984.

———. "Women as 'Same' and 'Other' in the Classical Roman Elite." *Helios* 16 (1989): 59–78.

Hannay, Margaret P. *Silent but for the Word: Tudor Women as Patrons, Translators and Writers of Religious Works.* Kent, Ohio: Kent State University Press, 1985.

Harkness, Deborah. *The Jewel House: Elizabethan London and the Scientific Revolution.* New Haven, Conn.: Yale University Press, 2007.

Harpsfield, Nicholas. *The Life and Death of Sir Thomas More.* Ed. Elsie Vaughan Hitchcock. London: Oxford University Press, 1932.

Hudson, Winthrop S. *The Cambridge Connection and the Elizabethan Settlement of 1559* Durham, N.C.: Duke University Press, 1980.

Hull, Suzanne. *Chaste, Silent and Obedient: English Books for Women, 1475–1640.* San Marino, Calif.: Huntington Library, 1982.

Hyrde, Richard. Introduction to *A Devoute Treatise upon the Pater Noster, Made First in Latyn by the Moost Famous Doctour Mayster Erasmus Roterdamus, and Tourned in to Englisshe by a Yong Virtuous and Well Lerned Gentylwoman of XIX Yere of Age.* London, 1526.

Irwin, Joyce. Introduction to *On Whether a Christian Woman Should Be Educated,* by Anna Maria van Schurman, ed. and trans. Joyce Irwin. Chicago: University of Chicago Press, 1998.

Jackson, Dorothy Judd. *Esther Inglis: Calligrapher, 1571–1624.* New York: Spiral Press, 1937.

Jacobs, Fredrika. "Woman's Capacity to Create: The Unusual Case of Sofonisba Anguissola." *Renaissance Quarterly* 41, no. 1 (1994): 74–101.

Jardine, Lisa. "Isotta Nogarola: Women Humanists—Education for What?" *History of Education* 12 (1983): 231–244.

———. *Still Harping on Daughters: Women and Drama in the Age of Shakespeare.* Sussex: Harvester Press, 1983.

———. "'O Decus Italiae Virgo': The Myth of the Learned Lady in the Renaissance." *Historical Journal* 28, no. 4 (1985): 799–819.

———. *Erasmus, Man of Letters: The Construction of Charisma in Print.* Princeton, N.J.: Princeton University Press, 1993.

Jed, Stephanie. "The Tenth Muse: Gender, Rationality and the Marketing of Knowledge." In *Feminism and Renaissance Studies,* ed. Lorna Hutston. Oxford: Oxford University Press, 1999.

Johnston, John. *Heroes ex omni historia Scotica lectissimi.* Edinburgh: Christopher Guyot, 1602.

Johnston, John, and Andrew Melville. *Inscriptiones historicae regum Scotorum: Continuata annorum serie a Fergusio primo regni conditore ad nostra tempora.* Amsterdam: Cornelius Claessonius, 1602.

Jones, Ann Rosalind. *The Currency of Eros: Women's Love Lyric in Europe, 1540–1620.* Bloomington: Indiana University Press, 1990.

Jones, Ann Rosalind, and Peter Stallybrass. "The Needle and the Pen: Needlework and the Appropriation of Printed Texts." In *Renaissance Clothing and the Materials of Memory.* Cambridge: Cambridge University Press, 2000.

Jordan, Constance. "Listening to 'The Other Voice' in Early Modern Europe." *Renaissance Quarterly* 51 (1988): 184–192.

_____. *Renaissance Feminism: Literary Texts and Political Models.* Ithaca, N.Y.: Cornell University Press, 1991.

_____. "More from 'The Other Voice' in Early Modern Europe." *Renaissance Quarterly* 55 (2002): 258–271.

Kallendorf, Craig W., ed. and trans. *Humanist Educational Treatises.* The I Tatti Renaissance Library. Cambridge, Mass.: Harvard University Press, 2002.

Kaufman, Peter Iver. "Absolute Margaret: Margaret Roper and 'Well-Learned Men.'" *Sixteenth Century Journal* 20 (Autumn 1989): 443–486.

Kellogg, Judith L. "*Le livre de la cité des dames:* Reconfiguring Knowledge and Reimagining Gendered Space." In *Christine de Pizan: A Casebook,* ed. Barbara Altman and Deborah McGrady. New York: Routledge, 2003.

Kelly-Gadol, Joan. "Did Women Have a Renaissance?" In *Becoming Visible: Women in European History,* ed. Renate Bridenthal and Claudia Koonz. Boston: Houghton Mifflin, 1977.

Kerber, Linda. "Separate Spheres, Female World, Woman's Place: The Rhetoric of Women's History." *Journal of American History* 75 (1988): 9–39.

Kerber, Linda, et al. "Beyond Roles, Beyond Spheres: Thinking about Gender in the Early Republic." *William and Mary Quarterly* 46 (1989): 565–585.

King, Margaret L. "Thwarted Ambitions: Six Learned Women of the Italian Renaissance." *Soundings* 59 (1976): 280–304.

_____. "The Religious Retreat of Isotta Nogarola (1418–1466)." *Signs* 3 (1978): 807–822.

_____. "Book-Lined Cells: Women and Humanism in the Early Italian Renaissance." In *Beyond Their Sex: Learned Women of the European Past,* ed. Patricia Labalme. New York: New York University Press, 1984.

_____. *Women of the Renaissance.* Chicago: University of Chicago Press, 1991.

_____. "Isotta Nogarola." In *Italian Women Writers: A Bio-Bibliographical Sourcebook,* ed. Rinaldina Russell. Westport, Conn.: Greenwood, 1994.

_____. *The Death of the Child Valerio Marcello.* Chicago: University of Chicago Press, 1994.

King, Margaret L., and Albert Rabil, eds. *Her Immaculate Hand: Selected Works by and about the Women Humanists of Quattrocento Italy.* New York: Pegasus Press, 1992.

King, Margaret L., and Diana Robin, eds. and trans. *Isotta Nogarola: Complete Writings: Letterbook, Dialogue on Adam and Eve, Orations.* Chicago: University of Chicago Press, 2004.

Kirkham, Victoria, ed. and trans. *Laura Battiferra and Her Literary Circle: An Anthology.* Chicago: University of Chicago Press, 2006.

Klapisch-Zuber, Christiane, ed. "Le chiavi Fiorentine del barbablu: L'apprendimento della lettura nel XV secolo." *Quaderni Storici* 57 (1984): 765–792.

_____. *Histoire des femmes en Occident.* Vol. 2: *Le Moyen Age.* Paris, 1990.

Klein, Lisa M. "Your Humble Handmaid: Elizabethan Gifts of Needlework." *Renaissance Quarterly* 50 (1997): 459–493.

Kolsky, Stephen, "Moderata Fonte, Lucrezia Marinella, Giuseppe Passi: An Early Seventeenth-Century Feminist Controversy." *Modern Language Review* 96, no. 4 (2001): 973–989.

Kowaleski-Wallace, Elizabeth. "Milton's Daughters: The Education of Eighteenth-Century Women Writers." *Feminist Studies* 12 (1986): 275–294.

_____. *Their Fathers' Daughters: Hannah More, Maria Edgeworth and Patriarchal Complicity.* New York: Oxford University Press, 1991.

Kristeller, Paul Oskar, ed. *Iter Italicum accedunt alia itinera: A Finding List of Uncatalogued or Incompletely Catalogued Humanistic Manuscripts of the Renaissance in Italian and Other Libraries.* 6 vols. Leiden: E. J. Brill, 1967–1997.

Labalme, Patricia, ed. *Beyond Their Sex: Learned Women of the European Past.* New York: New York University Press, 1980.

_____. "Venetian Women on Women: Three Early Modern Feminists." *Archivio Veneto,* 5th ser. vol. 117 (1981): 81–109.

Laidlaw, James. "Christine and the Manuscript Tradition." In *Christine de Pizan: A Casebook,* ed. Barbara Altmann and Deborah McGrady. New York: Routledge, 2003.

Lamb, Mary Ellen. "The Cooke Sisters: Attitudes toward Learned Women in the Renaissance." In *Silent but for the Word: Tudor Women as Patrons, Translators and Writers of Religious Works,* ed. Margaret Hannay. Kent, Ohio: Kent State University Press, 1985.

Larsen, Anne R., ed. and trans. *From Mother and Daughter: Poems, Dialogues and Letters of Les Dames Des Roches.* Chicago: University of Chicago Press, 2006.

La Tour Landry, Geoffroy de. *The Book of the Knight of the Tower.* Trans William Caxton. Ed. M. Y. Offord. London: Oxford University Press, 1971.

Littlehales, Margaret Mary, I.B.V.M. *Mary Ward: Pilgrim and Mystic, 1585–1645.* London: Burns and Oates, 1998.

Love, Harold. *Scribal Publication in Seventeenth-Century England.* New York: Oxford University Press, 1993.

Lowe, K. J. P. *Nuns' Chronicles and Convent Culture in Renaissance and Counter-Reformation Italy.* Cambridge: Cambridge University Press, 2003.

MacNeil, Anne. *Music and Women of the Commedia dell' Arte in the Late Sixteenth Century.* Oxford: Oxford University Press, 2003.

Makinen, Virpi, and Petter Korkman, eds. *Transformations in Medieval and Early-Modern Rights Discourse.* Dordrecht: Springer, 2006.

Mangini, Nicola. *I Teatri di Venezia.* Milan: U. Mursia Editore, 1974.

Margolis, Nadia. "Modern Editions: Makers of the Christinian Corpus." In *Christine de Pizan: A Casebook,* ed. Barbara Altman and Deborah McGrady. New York: Routledge, 2003.

Marinella, Lucrezia. *La nobiltà et l'eccellenza delle donne et mancamenti de gli huomini.* Venice: G. B. Ciotti, 1601.

_____. *Essortationi alle donne et agli altri, se a loro saranno a grado.* Venice: Francesco Valvasenso, 1645.

_____. *The Nobility and Excellence of Women and the Defects and Vices of Men.* Ed. Letizia Panizza. Trans. Anne Dunhill. Chicago: University of Chicago Press, 1999.

Marinelli, Giovanni. *Gli ornamenti delle donne.* Venice, 1562.

Marius, Richard. *Thomas More.* London: Orion Publishing, 1999.

Martin, Catherine. "Le Premier Testament de Marie de Gournay." *Bibliothèque d'Humanisme et Renaissance* 67 (2005): 653–657.

Martin, John Jeffries. "Inventing Sincerity, Refashioning Prudence: The Discovery of the Individual in Renaissance Europe." *American Historical Review* 102 (1997): 1309–1342.

_____. *Myths of Renaissance Individualism.* New York: Palgrave Macmillan, 2004.

Martines, Lauro. *The Social World of the Florentine Humanists, 1390–1460.* Princeton, N.J.: Princeton University Press, 1963.

_____. *Strong Words: Writing and Social Strain in the Italian Renaissance.* Baltimore: Johns Hopkins University Press, 2001.

Mayer, Thomas F. and D. R. Woolf, eds.. *The Rhetorics of Life-Writing in Early Modern Europe: Forms of Biography from Cassandra Fedele to Louis XIV.* Ann Arbor: University of Michigan Press, 1995.

McCahill, Elizabeth. "Humanism in the Theater of Lies: Classical Scholarship in the Early Quattrocento Curia." PhD dissertation, Princeton University, 2005.

McClure, George. *Sorrow and Consolation in Italian Humanism.* Princeton, N.J.: Princeton University Press, 1991.

McIntosh, Marjorie. "Sir Anthony Cooke: Tudor Humanist, Educator, and Religious Reformer." *Proceedings of the American Philosophical Society* 119, no. 3 (1975): 233–250.

McLeod, Glenda. *Virtue and Venom: Catalogs of Women from Antiquity to the Renaissance.* Ann Arbor: University of Michigan Press, 1991.

Michalove, Sharon. "Equal in Opportunity? The Education of Aristocratic Women, 1450–1540." In *Women's Education in Early Modern Europe,* ed. Barbara Whitehead. New York: Garland Publishing, 1999.

Miller, Maureen. *The Formation of a Medieval Church: Ecclesiastical Change in Verona, 950–1150.* Ithaca, N.Y.: Cornell University Press, 1993.

Mirrer, Louise, ed. *Upon My Husband's Death: Widows in Literature and Histories of Medieval Europe.* Ann Arbor: University of Michigan Press, 1992.

Mittarelli, G. B. *Bibliotheca codicum manuscriptorum monasterii S. Michaelis Venetiarum prope Murianum.* Venice, 1779.

Momigliano, Arnaldo. "The First Political Commentary on Tacitus." *Journal of Roman Studies* 37, parts 1 and 2 (1947): 91–101.

Monson, Craig, ed. *The Crannied Wall: Women, Religion and the Arts in Early Modern Europe.* Ann Arbor: University of Michigan Press, 1992.

More, Thomas. *The Works of Sir Thomas More, Knyght.* Ed. William Rastell. London: John Cawod, 1557.

———. *Epigrammata Thomae Mori Angli.* London: Humphrey Mosley, 1638.

Mulcaster, Richard. *Positions.* Ed. Richard de Molen. New York: Columbia University Teacher's College Press, 1971.

Mulvihill, Maureen E. "Mary Beale, Portrait of Aphra Behn." In *Reading Early Modern Women: An Anthology of Texts in Manuscript and Print, 1550–1700,* ed. Helen Ostovich and Elizabeth Sauer. New York: Routledge, 2004.

Murphy, Caroline P. *Lavinia Fontana: A Painter and Her Patrons in Sixteenth-Century Bologna.* New Haven, Conn.: Yale University Press, 2003.

Murray, (Sir) David. *The Tragicall Death of Sophonisba.* London: John Smethwick, 1611.

Musatti, Eugenio. "La conquista della Terraferma" In *Repubblica di Venezia.* Vol. 3: *Stati di Terraferma, 1400–1530.* ed. Gianni Guadalupi. Milan: F. M. Ricci, 2003.

Najemy, John. *Between Friends: Discourses of Power and Desire in the Machiavelli-Vettori Letters of 1513–1515.* Princeton, N.J.: Princeton University Press, 1993.

Nappo, Tommaso, ed. *Indice biografico Italiano.* 2nd ed. K. G. Saur: Munich, 1997.

Nash, Jerry C. "Renaissance Misogyny, Biblical Feminism and Helisenne de Crenne's *Epistres familieres et invectives.*" *Renaissance Quarterly* 50 (1997): 379–410.

Nauert, Charles. *Humanism and the Culture of Renaissance Europe.* Cambridge: Cambridge University Press, 1995.

Newton, Judith. "Family Fortunes: 'New History' and 'New Historicism.'" *Radical History Review* 43 (1989): 5–22.

Nogarola, Isotta. *Isottae Nogarolae Veronensis: Opera quae supersunt omnia.* 2 vols. Ed. Eugenius Abel. Vienna: Gerold et Socios, 1886.

Offen, Karen. *European Feminisms: A Political History, 1750–1950.* Stanford, Calif.: Stanford University Press, 2000.

———. "Reply to Cott." *Signs* 15, no. 1 (1989): 206–209.

Ostovich, Helen, and Elizabeth Sauer, eds. *Reading Early Modern Women: An Anthology of Texts in Manuscript and Print, 1550–1700.* New York: Routledge, 2004.

Panizza, Letizia. Introduction to *The Nobility and Excellence of Women and Vices of Men,* by Lucrezia Marinella, ed. Letizia Panizza, trans. Anne Dunhill. Chicago: University of Chicago Press, 1999.

———, ed. *Women in Italian Renaissance Culture and Society.* Oxford: Legenda, 2000.

Panizza, Letizia, and Sharon Wood, eds. *A History of Women's Writing in Italy.* Cambridge: Cambridge University Press, 2000.

Perlingieri, Ilya Sandra. *Sofonisba Anguissola: The First Great Woman Artist of the Renaissance.* New York: Rizzoli, 1992.

Pinessi, Orietta. *Sofonisba Anguissola: Un "pittore" alla corte di Filippo II.* Milan: Selene, 1998.

Pinet, Marie-Josèph. *Christine de Pisan, 1364–1430, étude biographique et littéraire.* Paris: Librairie Ancienne Honoré Champion, 1927.

Pitkin, Hanna Fenichel. *Fortune is a Woman: Gender and Politics in the Thought of Niccolò Machiavelli.* Berkeley: University of California Press, 1984.

Pizan, Christine de. *Lavision-Christine.* Ed. Sister Mary Louis Towner. Washington, D.C.: Catholic University of America, 1932.

_____. *Le livre de la cité des dames.* Ed. Eric Hicks and Thérèse Moreau. Paris: Editions Stock, 1986.

Poovey, Mary. *Uneven Developments: The Ideological Work of Gender in Mid-Victorian England.* Chicago: University of Chicago Press, 1988.

Price, Paola Malpezzi, and Christine Ristaino. *Lucrezia Marinella and the "Querelle des Femmes in Seventeenth-Century England.* Madison, N.J.: Fairleigh Dickinson University Press, 2008.

Puteanus, Erycius [Henry de Put]. *Epistolarum Promulsis.* 5 parts. Louvain: Officina Flaviana, 1612–1613.

Quint, David. *Origin and Originality in Renaissance Literature: Versions of the Source.* New Haven, Conn.: Yale University Press, 1983.

Rabil, Albert. *Laura Cereta: Quattrocento Humanist.* Binghamton, N.Y.: Medieval and Renaissance Texts and Studies, 1981.

Rait, Robert S. "Andrew Melville and the Revolt against Aristotle in Scotland." *English Historical Review* 14, no. 54 (April, 1899): 250–260.

Ravisius, Jean Tixer de, ed. *De memorabilibus et claris mulieribus aliquot diversorum scriptorum opera.* Paris: Simon Colinaeus, 1521.

Reynolds, Ernest Edwin. *Margaret Roper: Eldest Daughter of St. Thomas More.* New York: P. J. Kenedy, 1960.

Ribera, Pietro Paolo di. *Le glorie immortali de'trionfi, et heroiche imprese d'ottocento quarantacinque donne illustri antiche e moderne.* Venice: Evangelista Deuchino, 1609.

Riccoboni, Antonio. *De gymnasio Patavino.* Padua, 1598.

Ridolfi, Carlo. *Vite dei Tintoretto: Da le maraviglie dell'arte overo le vite degl'illustri pittori veneti e dello stato, descritte dal cavalier Carlo Ridolfi.* Ed. Giovanni Keller. Venice: Filippi Editore, 1994.

Robin, Diana., ed. and trans. *Filelfo in Milan: Writings, 1451–1477.* Princeton, N.J.: Princeton University Press, 1991.

_____. "Cassandra Fedele's Epistolae (1488–1521): Biography as Ef-facement." In *The Rhetorics of Life-Writing in Early Modern Europe: Forms of Biography from*

Cassandra Fedele to Louis XIV, ed. Thomas F. Mayer and D. R. Woolf. Ann Arbor: University of Michigan Press, 1995.

_____, ed. and trans. *Laura Cereta: Collected Letters of a Renaissance Feminist.* Chicago: University of Chicago Press, 1997.

_____. "Woman, Space and Renaissance Discourse." In *Sex and Gender in Medieval and Renaissance Texts: The Latin Tradition,* ed. Barbara Gold et al. New York: State University of New York Press, 1997.

_____. "Humanism and Feminism in Laura Cereta's Public Letters." In *Women in Italian Renaissance Culture and Society,* ed. Letizia Panizza. Oxford: Legenda, 2000.

_____. *Cassandra Fedele: Letters and Orations.* Chicago: University of Chicago Press, 2000.

_____. *Publishing Women: Salons, the Presses and the Counter-Reformation in Sixteenth-Century Italy.* Chicago: University of Chicago Press, 2007.

Rogers, Elizabeth, ed. *The Correspondence of Sir Thomas More.* Princeton, N.J.: Princeton University Press, 1947.

Roper, Margaret, trans. *A Devout Treatise upon the Pater Noster.* Ed. Richard Hyrde. London, 1526.

Roper, William. *The Lyfe of Sir Thomas More.* Ed. Elsie Vaughan Hitchcock. New York: Oxford University Press, 1958.

Rosenthal, Margaret. *The Honest Courtesan: Veronica Franco, Citizen and Writer in Sixteenth-Century Venice.* Chicago: University of Chicago Press, 1992.

Ross, Sarah Gwyneth. "Esther Inglis: Linguist, Calligrapher, Miniaturist and Christian Humanist." In *Early Modern Women and Transnational Communities of Letters,* ed. Julie Campbell and Anne Larsen. Aldershot: Ashgate, 2009.

Rowland, Ingrid. "Revenge of the Regensburg Humanists, 1493." *Sixteenth Century Journal* 25, no. 2 (Summer 1994): 307–322.

Roy, Maurice, ed. *Oeuvres Poétiques de Christine de Pisan.* 3 vols. Paris: Librairie de Firmin, 1885.

Ruelens, Charles. *Erycius Puteanus et Isabelle Andreini: Lecture faite à l'Académie d'Archéologie le 3 Février 1889* (Antwerp: Imp. Van Merlen, 1889).

Rummel, Erica, ed. *Erasmus On Women.* Toronto: University of Toronto Press, 1996.

Saller, Richard. *Patriarchy, Property and Death in the Roman Family.* Cambridge: Cambridge University Press, 1994.

Sankovitch, Tilde. *French Women Writers and the Book: Myths of Access and Desire.* New York: Syracuse University Press, 1988.

Sansone, Mario. "Il senso del Dibattito Cinquecentesco." In *Da Bembo a Galiani: Il dibattito sulla lingua in Italia,* ed. Francesco Tateo. Bari: Adriatica Editrice: 1999.

Sansovino, Francesco. *Vita della illustre Signora Contessa Giulia Bemba della Torre.* Venice: Domenico and Gio. Battista Guerra, 1565.

Sapiro, Virginia. *A Vindication of Political Virtue: The Political Theory of Mary Woll-stonecraft.* Chicago: University of Chicago Press, 1992.

_____. "A Woman's Struggle for a Language of Enlightenment and Virtue: Mary Wollstonecraft and Enlightenment 'Feminism.'" In *Perspectives on Feminist Thought in European History: From the Middle Ages to the Present,* ed. Tjitske Akkerman and Siep Stuurman. London: Routledge, 1998.

Saunders, Anne Leslie. "Bathsua Reginald Makin (1600–1675?)." In *Women Writing Latin From Roman Antiquity to Early Modern Europe,* ed. Laurie Churchill et al. Vol. 3: *Early Modern Europe.* New York: Routledge, 2002 247–270.

Schurman, Anna Maria van. *Nobiliss: Virginis Annae Mariae a Schurman, opuscula Hebraea, Graeca, Latina, Gallica:prosaica et metrica.* Elzevir, 1648.

_____. *On Whether a Christian Woman Should be Educated, and Other Writings From Her Intellectual Circle.* Ed. and trans. Joyce Irwin. Chicago: University of Chicago Press, 1998.

Scott, Joan Wallach. "Gender: A Useful Category of Historical Analysis." *American Historical Review* 91 (1986): 1053–1075.

_____. *Only Paradoxes to Offer: French Feminists and the Rights of Man.* Cambridge, Mass.: Harvard University Press, 1996.

_____. *Gender and the Politics of History.* New York: Columbia University Press, 1998.

Scott-Elliot, A. H., and Elspeth Yeo. "Calligraphic Manuscripts of Esther Inglis (1571–1624): A Catalogue." *Papers of the Bibliographical Society of America* 84 (1990): 11–86.

Segarizzi, Arnaldo. "Niccolò Barbo patrizio veneziano del secolo XV e le accuse contro Isotta Nogarola." *Giornale storico della letteratura italiana* 43 (1904): 39–54.

Sensi, Torello. "Illustri Figli di Padova, Isabella Andreini." in *Estratto della Rivista Padova* XVI. Padua: Società Cooperativa Tipografica, 1938.

Shapin, Steven. *A Social History of Truth: Civility and Science in Seventeenth-Century England.* Chicago: University of Chicago Press, 1994.

Smet, Ingrid A. R. de, "'In the Name of the Father': Feminist Voices in the Republic of Letters." In *Lettered Women in the Renaissance,* ed. Michel Bastiaensen. Brussels: Peeters, 1997.

Sperling, Jutta. *Convents and the Body Politic in Late Renaissance Venice.* Baltimore: Johns Hopkins University Press, 1999.

Spezi, Giuseppe, ed. *Lettere inedite di Card. Pietro Bembo e di Altri Scrittori del Secolo XVI.* Tratte da Codici Vaticani e Barberiniani. Rome: Tipografia delle Scienze Matematiche e Fisiche, 1862.

Spitz, Lewis W. *The Religious Renaissance of the German Humanists.* Cambridge, Mass.: Harvard University Press, 1963.

Stevenson, Jane. *Women Latin Poets: Language, Gender and Authority from Antiquity to the Eighteenth Century.* Oxford: Oxford University Press, 2005.

Stewart, Alan. "The Voices of Anne Cooke, Lady Anne and Lady Bacon." In *This Double Voice: Gendered Writing in Early Modern England*, ed. Danielle and Elizabeth Clarke. New York: St. Martin's Press, 2000.

Stewart, Brian, and Mervyn Cutten, eds. *The Dictionary of Portrait Painters in Britain up to 1920*. Suffolk: Antique Collectors' Club, 1997.

Stortoni, Laura Anne, and Mary Prentice Lillie, eds. *Women Poets of the Italian Renaissance: Courtly Ladies and Courtesans*. New York: Italica Press, 1997.

Strocchia, Sharon. "Gender and the Rights of Honor in Italian Renaissance Cities." In *Gender and Society in Renaissance Italy*, ed. Judith Brown and Robert C. Davis. London: A. W. Longman, 1998.

Stuurman, Siep. *François Poulain de la Barre and The Invention of Modern Equality*. Cambridge, Mass.: Harvard University Press, 2004.

Stuurman, Siep, and Tjitske Akkerman, eds. "Introduction: Feminism in European History" In *Perspectives on Feminist Political Thought in European History: From the Middle Ages to the Present*. London: Routledge, 1998.

_____, eds. *Perspectives on Feminist Political Thought in European History: From the Middle Ages to the Present*. London: Routledge, 1998.

Tarabotti, Arcangela. *Lettere familiari e di complimento*. Ed. Meredith Kennedy Ray and Lynn Lara Westwater. Turin: Rosenberg and Sellier, 2005.

_____. *Paternal Tyranny*. Ed. and trans. Letizia Panizza. Chicago: University of Chicago Press, 2004.

Tarabotti, Arcangela, and Francesco Buoninsegni. *Satira e antisatira*. Ed. Elissa Weaver. Rome: Salerno Editrice, 1998.

Tarlton, Charles. "Fortuna and the Landscape of Action in Machiavelli's *Prince*." *New Literary History* 30, no. 4 (1999): 737–755.

Thomson, D. F. S. "The Latin Epigram in Scotland: The Sixteenth Century." *Phoenix* 11, no. 2 (Summer 1997): 63–78.

Tjan-Bakker, Anneke. "Dame Flora's Blossoms: Esther Inglis' Flower-Illustrated Manuscripts." In *English Manuscript Studies, 1100–1700*. Vol. 9: *Writings by Early Modern Women*, ed. Peter Beal and Margaret Ezell. London: British Library, 2000.

Tomasini, Jacopo Filippo, ed., *Clarissimae Feminae Cassandrae Fidelis, venetae Epistolae et orationes*. Padua: Franciscus Bolzetta, 1636.

_____. *Elogia literis et sapientia illustrium ad vivum expressis imaginibus exornata*. Padua: Donatum Pasquardum & Socium, 1630. Reprint, Padua: Sebastiano Sardi, 1644.

Travitsky, Betty. "The New Mother of the English Renaissance: Her Writings on Motherhood." In *The Lost Tradition: Mothers and Daughters in Literature*, ed. Cathy N. Davidson and E. M. Broner. New York: Frederick Ungar, 1980.

Trexler, Richard. *Public Life in Renaissance Florence*. New York: Academic Press, 1980.

Trinkaus, Charles. *In Our Image and Likeness: Humanity and Divinity in Italian Humanist Thought.* Chicago: University of Chicago Press, 1970.

Verbrugge, Rita. "Margaret More Roper's Personal Expression in the Devout Treatise upon the Pater Noster." In *Silent but for the Word: Tudor Women as Patrons, Translators, and Writers of Religious Works,* ed. Margaret Hannay. Kent, Ohio: Kent State University Press, 1985.

Vergerio, Pier Paolo. *De Ingenibus Moribus et Liberalibus Adulescentiae Studiis Liber.* Ed. and trans. Craig Kallendorf. Humanist Educational Treatises. Cambridge, Mass.: Harvard University Press, 2008.

Walker, Julia, ed. *Dissing Elizabeth: Negative Representations of Gloriana.* Durham, N.C.: Duke University Press, 1998.

Walsh, Elizabeth, and Richard Jeffree. *The Excellent Mrs. Mary Beale.* London: Inner London Education Authority, 1975.

Walters, Lori. "Constructing Reputations: Fama and Memory in Christine de Pizan's *Charles V* and *L'Advision Cristine.*" In *Fama: The Politics of Talk and Reputation in Medieval Europe,* ed. Thelma Fenster and Daniel Lord Smail. Ithaca, N.Y.: Cornell University Press, 2003.

Wayne, Valerie, ed. *Anne Cooke Bacon.* The Early Modern Englishwoman: A Facsimile Library of Essential Works, part 2, vol. 1. Aldershot: Ashgate, 2000.

Weaver, Elissa. *Convent Theatre in Early Modern Italy: Spiritual Fun and Learning for Women* Cambridge: Cambridge University Press, 2002.

Wiesner-Hanks, Merry. *Women and Gender in Early Modern Europe.* Cambridge: Cambridge University Press, 2000.

Willard, Charity Cannon, ed. *The Writings of Christine de Pizan.* New York: Persea Books, 1994.

Woodbridge, Linda. *Women and the English Renaissance: Literature and the Nature of Womankind, 1540–1620.* Urbana: University of Illinois Press, 1986.

Woodford, Samuel. *A Paraphrase upon the Psalms of David.* 2nd ed. London: John Martyn, 1678.

Zancan, Marina, ed. *Nel cerchio della luna: Figure di donna in alcuni testi del XVI secolo.* Venice: Marsilio, 1983.

Zannini, G. L. Masetti. *Motivi storici dell'educazione femminile, 1500–1650.* Vol 1: *Morale, religione, arte, musica.* Bari: Editorialebari, 1980.

_____. *Motivi storici dell'educazione femminile, 1500–1650.* Vol. 2: *Scienza, lavoro, giuochi.* Napoli: M. D'Auria Editore, 1981.

Zarri, Gabriella, ed. *Per lettera: La scrittura epistolare femminile tra archivio e tipografia secoli XV–XVII.* Rome: Viella, 1999.

_____. "Profeti di corte nell'Italia del Rinascimento." In *Mistiche e devote nell'Italia tardomedievale,* ed. Daniel Bornstein and Roberto Rusconi. Naples: Luguori Editore, 1998.

Ziegler, Georgianna. "Hand-Ma[i]de Books: The Manuscripts of Esther Inglis, Early-Modern Precursor of the Artists' Book." In *English Manuscript Studies*

1100–1700. Vol. 9: *Writings by Early Modern Women,* ed. Peter Beal and Margaret Ezell. London: British Library, 2000.

_____. "'More Than Feminine Boldness': The Gift Books of Esther Inglis." In *Women, Writing and the Reproduction of Culture in Tudor-Stuart Britain,* ed. Mary E. Burke et al. New York: Syracuse University Press, 2000.

Acknowledgments

It is a great pleasure to acknowledge that in the case of this study "art" has imitated life. The intellectual families who are the protagonists of this book could not have been located or understood (to the degree that I have understood them) without the unfailing support and constructive criticism offered by my own families, academic and natal.

The greatest boon that can befall a scholar are mentors outstanding as intellectuals and as human beings. I am therefore delighted to express my gratitude first of all to Edward Muir. His expertise and generosity of spirit have sustained this project from start to finish. Fortune has been a liberal patroness, providing me with three other wonderful guides in this ambitious undertaking: Ethan Shagan has been an indispensable help in negotiating the paths of British history; Robert Lerner has tolerated the worst of my neo-Burckhardtianism and offered many salutary exhortations to scholarly precision; and Bill Monter has urged me by word and by example to think about history as a process of finding meaning in surprising juxtapositions. I thank them all most sincerely for their advice, encouragement, and tireless reading of my prose. Many thanks also to Tessie Liu, Sara Maza and Alex Owen, who guided this project in its initial stages through the cultural, linguistic and hermeneutic "turns" of women's and gender history.

Nor would this study of women intellectuals have been possible without the collaboration of Diana Robin, a true authority on women humanists. I am deeply grateful to her for befriending my project, which follows so closely upon her own work, for offering invariably perceptive comments and criticisms, and for engaging in at least a thousand invigorating conversations. For similarly exceptional performance of the offices of friendship, I offer an emphatic *grazie mille* to Kenneth Gouwens, whose fellowship, ideas, and suggestions for emendation have exerted a great and positive influence upon the author and her study.

The course of research in the United States, Italy and the United Kingdom has been surprisingly smooth, thanks to the generous support of the Jacob K.

Javits Fellowship Program, The Gladys Krieble Delmas Foundation, the Andrew W. Mellon Foundation, and the Princeton University Committee on Research in the Humanities and Social Sciences. I also extend my thanks to the helpful and knowledgeable staffs of the many libraries and archives in which I have had the pleasure to work. Here I wish especially to thank Francis Harris of the British Library, as well as Kenneth Dunn and Sheila Mackenzie of the National Library of Scotland, for offering their expert assistance at critical moments in my information gathering.

Comparative projects create certain logistical challenges, to put it mildly. I would like to recognize here a few of the institutions, scholars and friends on both sides of the Alps who helped in meeting those challenges. The Warburg Institute (University of London) generously offered me a "base camp" in their Ph.D. room for many months and, of all the wonderful denizens of the Warburg, I extend particular thanks to Anita Pollard and Jill Kraye. Huge thanks as well go to Kate Lowe, my "Mellon mentor," whose guidance proved indispensable. I am also deeply grateful to Sylvia Gascoigne for her boundless generosity, without which my time in London would not have been the same. In the Venetian world, particular thanks go to Venice International University's Summer Institute in the Humanities, which provided two summers of support and scholarly exchange. I would also like to offer my fellow archive rats, Jana Byars and John Visconti, many thanks for their help and their bonhomie. And I am most grateful to Anne Jacobson Schutte, who allowed me to join the long tradition of wandering Venetianists who have taken shelter in her Cannaregio apartment.

I also owe a tremendous debt of gratitude to the Society of Fellows in the Liberal Arts at Princeton University for providing a most congenial environment for rethinking concepts and engaging in productive research as a postdoctoral fellow. Among this scholarly family, special thanks go to Leonard Barkan, Bianca Calabresi, Anthony Grafton, Mary Harper, Graham Jones and Andrea Schatz. In the same breath, I thank my new colleagues in the History Department at Boston College, who graciously allowed me to spend two years in postdoctoral lucubration before I joined them.

And I am most beholden to the two readers who reviewed the manuscript for Harvard University Press. Their lynx-eyed scrutiny of the text has enabled me to correct many errors, and their larger questions still resonate, though I could not address all of them as I would have liked. I am also most grateful to Kate Lowe and Anu Korhonen, together with the University of Helsinki's COL-LeGIUM Studies across Disciplines in the Humanities and Social Sciences, for including an article of mine on Cassandra Fedele in their e-book *The Trouble With Ribs: Women, Men and Gender in Early Modern Europe* (2007) and to Ashgate Publishing for permitting me to reprint some of my material on Esther Inglis, which appeared as an article in *Early-Modern Women and Transnational Communities of Letters* (2009), edited by Julie Campbell and Anne Larsen.

My greatest debt, however, is to Robert Merlin and Sandra DeShaffon Ross (aka Dad and Mom). Although words are paltry recompense, nonetheless I want to express my profound gratitude for decades of emotional, intellectual, and, yes, financial sustenance. Here I gladly acknowledge the connection between scholarship and autobiography. Like many of the women I study, my learned father has played a pivotal role in supporting and encouraging my academic aspirations. I thank him heartily for giving me the courage to articulate my ideas, for serving as my constant interlocutor, and, above all, for being a role model at every level worthy of emulation.

Index

Harvard University Press is a member of Green Press Initiative (greenpressinitiative.org), a nonprofit organization working to help publishers and printers increase their use of recycled paper and decrease their use of fiber derived from endangered forests. This book was printed on recycled paper containing 30% post-consumer waste and processed chlorine free.